HOW TO MAKE YOUR MONEY MAKE MONEY

THE EXPERTS EXPLAIN YOUR ALTERNATIVES, THE RISKS, THE REWARDS

HOW TO MAKE YOUR MONEY MAKE MONEY
THE EXPERTS EXPLAIN YOUR ALTERNATIVES, THE RISKS, THE REWARDS

Edited by
Arthur Levitt, Jr.

Dow Jones-Irwin   Homewood, Illinois 60430

ISBN 0-87094-236-0
Library of Congress Catalog Card No. 80-70617
Printed in the United States of America

1 2 3 4 5 6 7 8 9 0 K 7 6 5 4 3 2 1 0

CONTENTS

v

Arthur Levitt, Jr.

As chairman of one of the world's major securities exchanges, I believe very strongly in investing in stocks and bonds. Why, then, would I edit a book that describes in detail other investments in addition to securities?

Several years ago, I was creating investment strategies for over two million customers of the firm then known as Shearson Hayden Stone. The nation's economy was behaving in irrational ways and people were looking for new methods of investing their money. Individual investors were asking their brokers for advice on a whole range of opportunities that were beyond the brokers' expertise. It was not clear where a person could turn for knowledgeable counsel, and I felt there was a need for an authoritative investment guidebook.

I reviewed the list of alternative opportunities for investing. After careful study, I selected those that met commonly accepted standards of value. I then searched for people who could write introductory articles about those alternative investments. The people I selected to write for this book not only are recognized authorities about the particular field, but also are active and dispassionate investors in it. After reading the articles in this book, you will have a firm foundation for further study about those investment alternatives that interest you.

My hope is that this book will help readers make their choices as knowledgeably as possible, make their judgments as carefully as possible, gain confidence in their own ability to make final decisions and get the most—both financially and personally—out of their investment programs.

ABOUT THE EDITOR

Arthur Levitt, Jr., serves as Chairman of the Board of Governors and Chief Executive Officer of the American Stock Exchange. He was elected a Governor of the Exchange in 1975 and served as Vice Chairman in 1977. Prior to his election as Amex Chairman, he was President and a Director since 1969 of Shearson Hayden Stone Inc. and a partner of a predecessor firm since 1962. The product of the consolidation of several companies, Shearson is a New York-based securities and investment banking concern with an extensive network of domestic and international branch offices.

In 1978, President Carter named Mr. Levitt as Chairman of the White House Small Business Conference Commission, enhancing his activities as a spokesman for small business and individual investors. Mr. Levitt is Chairman of the American Business Conference and also is a member of the American Council for Capital Formation, the Advisory Board of the Securities Regulation Institute, Downtown-Lower Manhattan Association, the Advisory Council of the New York University Finance Club, and serves as a Director of the East New York Savings Bank.

Mr. Levitt was a Phi Beta Kappa graduate of Williams College in 1952. An ardent conservationist and supporter of the arts, Mr. Levitt wrote and sponsored the Conservation Bill of Rights presently incorporated in the New York State Constitution and was Chairman of the Conservation Committee at the 1967 Constitutional Convention. He was appointed to the New York State Council on the Arts in 1970, 1973, and 1978 and is a Trustee and former President of the MacDowell Colony and Chairman of the Twyla Tharp Dance Foundation.

Morris D. Crawford, Jr., is chairman of the Executive Committee of The Bowery Savings Bank in New York City, the second largest savings bank in the United States.

He was graduated from Harvard College, magna cum laude, in 1937, and from Harvard Law School in 1940. He then became associated with the New York law firm of Cadwalader, Wickersham & Taft, where he practiced law until 1953, with a break during World War II when he enlisted in the army.

In 1953, he was elected vice-president and office counsel of The Bowery Savings Bank. He became executive vice-president on January 1, 1959; a member of the Board of Trustees on May 10, 1961; president and chief executive officer in August 1965; and chairman of the Board of Trustees on January 1, 1966.

Mr. Crawford has served as president of the National Association of Mutual Savings Banks (1964–65) and as chairman of the Consultative Committee, International Savings Banks Institute. He continues to serve on a host of industry, educational, philanthropic, city, state, and national panels.

George L. Ball is president of E. F. Hutton & Company Inc., the large investment banking and brokerage firm, and president of the E. F. Hutton Group, the parent organization of the securities firm. He is member of its Board of Directors and Executive Committee, and heads Hutton's sales organization of more than 3,500 account executives in over 250 offices in the United States and abroad.

Mr. Ball, a native of Evanston, Illinois, joined E. F. Hutton in 1962 as an account executive trainee, advancing to manager of the Newark, New Jersey, office in 1967. He became an assistant vice-president in 1968, vice-president in 1969, senior vice-president in 1971, and executive vice-president in 1972. He was elected president in 1977.

Mr. Ball received a B.A. degree from Brown University and served as an officer in the United States Naval Reserve. He is a former treasurer and member of the Board of Directors and Executive Committee of the Securities Industry Association, and was also a director of the Chicago Board Options Exchange. His current positions include membership on the Board of Governors of the American Stock Exchange, and on the Board of Governors of the Bond Club of America.

Sidney Homer was graduated magna cum laude from Harvard College in 1923, specializing in philosophy and immediately went to work on Wall Street.

He started as a credit investigator for Equitable Trust Company. Then, moving to Gilbert Elliott & Company, he became successively manager of the Statistical Department, Sales Department, and Bond Department.

From 1932–43, he was president of Homer & Co., dealers in high-grade institutional bonds. During World War II, he worked in Washington for the Foreign Economic Administration.

Returning to New York, he became manager of the Institutional Department of Schudder, Stevens & Clark.

In 1961, he joined Salomon Brothers, where he was general partner and in charge of the Bond Market Research Department. Now in retirement, he is a limited partner of the firm and continues as a consultant for Salomon and others.

He is the author of *A History of Interest Rates,* covering 40 countries over 40 centuries; *The Bond Buyer's Primer;* co-author of *The Price of Money* (with Richard I. Johannesen), and co-author of *Inside the Yield Book* (with Martin Leibowitz).

Howard Stein is chairman of the board, president, and chief executive officer of The Dreyfus Corporation. He also serves as chairman and president of The Dreyfus Fund, and is a director and officer of various other mutual funds managed by The Dreyfus Corporation.

Mr. Stein was born in New York City, where he attended the Juilliard School. He was associated with Bache & Company before joining the securities firm of Dreyfus & Company, where he organized the Investment Management Department. He became an officer of The Dreyfus Corporation and its chairman and chief executive officer when it went public in October 1965.

With assets under management of over $6.5 billion, for more than 500,000 investors, Dreyfus is one of the largest investment companies in the world.

Mr. Stein is also a member of the Board of Trustees of Corporate Property Investors, a leading real estate investment trust.

William Zeckendorf, Jr., has been in the real estate and hotel business for 28 years, working very closely with his father, a legendary figure in the industry, on such projects as Place Ville Marie in Montreal, Century City in Los Angeles, and shopping centers in the United States and Canada. These efforts also led to development of some of the largest urban renewal projects in the country, including L'Enfant Plaza in Washington, D.C., Society Hill in Philadelphia, and Kips Bay Plaza, Park West Village, and Lincoln Towers in New York.

During the past five years, Mr. Zeckendorf and his associates have completed such New York City projects as purchase of the Delmonico Hotel; negotiation and subsequent sale of the Mayfair House; negotiation and purchase of the Navarro Hotel; purchase and resale of the Airlines Terminal Building at Park Avenue to the Philip Morris Company for its corporate headquarters; advisor and participant in acquisition of the Biltmore and Roosevelt Hotels and the lease negotiations with overseas groups; and purchase of the New York Statler Hotel.

Mr. Zeckendorf was also active in the negotiation and acquisition of the Shoreham Hotel in Washington, D.C.

Brigadier General Harold L. Oppenheimer was born in Kansas City. He was graduated from Harvard in 1939 at the age of 19. While in charge of a Harvard anthropology expedition to Bolivia, he made the second ascent of Huani Potosi, a 23,000-foot peak in the Andes.

He enlisted in the Marines in 1941. He was cited two times for bravery in action on Okinawa, receiving the Bronze Star, a Letter of Commendation, and the Presidential Unit Citation. At age 25, he was the youngest battalion commander in the Marine Corps.

Returning to civilian business in Kansas City, he was activated with his Reserve battalion for the Korean War, and was subsequently assigned to the Combined Arms Staff at Quantico and put in charge of Arctic warfare.

After the war, he developed Oppenheimer Industries into the largest cattle management firm in the United States, with over 110,000 head running on 4 million acres over 14 states.

During the Vietnam fighting, he was assigned duty as special assistant to the commander of the Third Marine Amphibious Force, Vietnam, where he received the Legion of Merit, Navy Unit Commendation, the Vietnamese Service Medal with two Bronze Stars, and the Vietnamese Cross of Gallantry with Cluster. While serving in Vietnam, he was selected for promotion to brigadier general and his selection was confirmed by the Senate on January 31, 1968.

General Oppenheimer is chairman of the board of Oppenheimer Industries, the Armendaris Corporation, Atlas Small Business Investment Corporation, National Cattlemen's Cooperative, and a director of Kansas City Southern Industries. He is the author of *Cowboy Arithmetic, Cowboy Economics,* and *Land Speculation,* and co-author of *Cowboy Litigation* and *Cowboy Securities.* He has also authored a book about the Marine Corps, *March to the Sound of the Drums.*

Dr. Henry G. Jarecki is chairman of the board of Mocatta Metals Corporation which, with its affiliates, is the largest gold and silver bullion dealer in the world. The Mocatta companies have been involved in trading precious metals for over three centuries.

Dr. Jarecki is a member and director of Commodity Exchange (COMEX) of New York; is a member of the Chicago Board of Trade, the New York Mercantile Exchange, and the Winnipeg Commodity Exchange; and has served on the Commodity Futures Trading Commission's Advisory Committee on Market Instruments.

His recent writings include "Regulating Commodity Frauds" (with Thomas A. Russo), the *New York Times,* July 1979; "Development of U.S. Gold Market after its Weak Start," in *World Gold in the 1980s,* a Financial Times Conference, Montreux, Switzerland, June 1979; "The Bullion Market: Silver Threads Among the Gold," *Euromoney,* March 1979; "Commodity Options: The Birth of the Market," *Euromoney,* September 1978; "The Gold Market: Why U.S. Treasury Sales Are Not Bringing Down the Price," *Euromoney,* August 1978; "Will Gold Clauses Be Used?," *Euromoney,* February 1978; "Trading in Options—How the U.S. System May Operate," *Euromoney,* April 1977.

Benjamin Zucker is a gem merchant with Precious Stones Company in New York City and travels regularly to the gem capitals of the world (Hong Kong, Bangkok, Bombay, London, Paris), purchasing rubies, emeralds, and sapphires. His company has loaned what may be the world's most valuable sapphire to the Museum of Natural History in New York City. He is a certified gemologist and lectures on the history of jewelry and the evaluation of estate pieces at the Fashion Institute of Technology.

A graduate of Harvard Law School and Yale University, Mr. Zucker represents the third generation of his family in the gem business. His grandfather was a rabbi and gem merchant, and his uncles are among the largest diamond dealers in Antwerp.

He contributes articles on how to tell the value of rubies, emeralds, sapphires, colored diamonds, and white diamonds to *Connoisseur* magazine regularly. Mr. Zucker is the author of *How to Buy and Sell Gems* (Times Books, 1980).

Maxwell Leibler sold the successful electronics business he had built from scratch and, putting the proceeds to work in a field he had studied carefully, became president of Marsh, Block, Leibler & Co., a securities option firm.

Meanwhile, with his coin collecting hobby as background, he developed a growing interest in precious metals. When the U.S. Government legalized ownership of gold, he entered the field and has since directed gold investment programs for major securities firms.

He presently heads his own independent consulting firm, Maxwell Leibler Associates, dealing in precious metals.

A frequent panelist on television and radio talk shows, he is in demand as a speaker at seminars. He has written many magazines articles on precious metals and is on the Editorial Board of *Commodities* magazine ("The Magazine of Futures Trading").

Mr. Leibler's book, *Rare Coin Acquisition as an Investment Medium,* has received wide distribution. He is presently at work on another book, *Alternative Investment,* which will soon be issued by a major publisher.

Leo Melamed is special counsel to the Board of the Chicago Mercantile Exchange, is one of the pioneers of financial futures. As chairman of the International Monetary Market from its founding in 1972 until its merger with the CME in 1976, he was responsible for guiding the first financial futures exchange as it developed contracts in currencies, gold, and interest rates. Today, the IMM carries the most diversified range of financial contracts found at any futures exchange.

Mr. Melamed became a member of the Chicago Mercantile Exchange in 1954. He was first elected to the Board of Governors in 1967, and served three consecutive years as chairman in 1969, 1970, and 1971. After four years as head of the International Monetary Market, in 1976 he was again elected chairman of the CME when the IMM became a division of the CME. In January 1977, the Board of Governors appointed him to his present position as special counsel to the Board.

As founder and chairman of Dellsher Investment Company, a clearing member firm of the Chicago Mercantile Exchange, Mr. Melamed has been active in futures market trading as well as in managing the development of the CME and its IMM division.

In 1978, the University of Chicago Graduate School of Business established the Leo Melamed Prize for outstanding scholarship of teachers in business administration.

Mr. Melamed received his Doctor of Law degree from John Marshall Law School, Chicago, in 1955.

Barrie M. Damson is a lawyer by training, and became involved in the oil business as an attorney practicing oil and gas law.

In 1964, with a group of lawyers, accountants, and Wall Street bankers as investors, he started a company that participated in private drilling partnerships. In 1969, management of the Damson companies and the investing groups exchanged their interests in the various drilling funds for stock of a publicly held company which was renamed Damson Oil Corporation. Mr. Damson is chairman of the board and president of Damson Oil, as well as the largest stockholder of the company, which is now listed on the American Stock Exchange.

Mr. Damson has served as the president of the Oil Investment Institute and as a director of the Independent Petroleum Association of America. He is a founding member of the American Business Conference. He also serves on the Board of Directors of two publicly held European companies: Damson Royalty Investments S. A. and Viking Resources International N. V. Mr. Damson was graduated from Harvard University in 1956 and New York University School of Law in 1959.

Tennyson Schad was a practicing attorney with Cravath Swaine & Moore from 1958 to 1962. For the following eight years, he served as editorial counsel with Time, Inc.

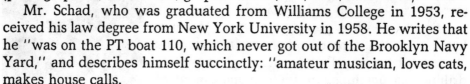

In 1970, he established his present private practice which specializes in art, literary, and publishing law. While developing this practice, in 1971 he opened LIGHT Gallery, a Fifth Avenue, New York gallery which has become one of the world's most prominent showcases of contemporary photography.

Six years later, he founded *American Showcase*, an annual reference book on commercial photography and art (photographers, illustrators, graphic artists, TV, film, and video).

Mr. Schad, who was graduated from Williams College in 1953, received his law degree from New York University in 1958. He writes that he "was on the PT boat 110, which never got out of the Brooklyn Navy Yard," and describes himself succinctly: "amateur musician, loves cats, makes house calls.

Robert D. Schonfeld is former director of Institutional Services and Market Research of Sotheby Park Bernet. He received an M.B.A. in Management and Portfolio Analysis from the New York University of Graduate School of Business Administration. His thesis, on the management and financial history of the Beatles, was published by Simon and Schuster in 1972 under the title *Apple to the Core*.

Mr. Schonfeld received his training in investments at H. Hentz & Company, which became part of Shearson Loeb Rhodes in 1973. He has been involved in the art market, particularly its financial aspects, since that time, working as a consultant to dealers and private collectors before joining Sotheby Parke Bernet in August of 1978.

Mr. Schonfeld's responsibilities involve the marketing of Sotheby's products and services to institutions such as investment banks, commercial banks, law firms, and corporations.

He also appears frequently as a public speaker for the firm. Mr. Schonfeld has appeared on television's MacNeil-Lehrer Report and has written about the art market for such publications as *The Wall Street Journal, Barron's,* and *Trusts and Estates* magazine.

Nancy Hoffman studied at Wellesley and Barnard and worked at the Asia House Gallery from 1964 to 1969. She then went on to become director of French & Co., a gallery of contemporary art.

In 1972, she opened her own gallery, Nancy Hoffman Gallery, in the heart of the artistic SoHo district of New York City. There, she exhibits works by both beginning and recognized artists from all over the country. The works on display cover a wide range, reflecting the variety of styles encountered in today's art world.

Ms. Hoffman serves as juror at art competitions and lectures on art throughout the country.

James J. Lally was appointed head of the Chinese Works of Art Department at Sotheby Parke Bernet in 1973.

Mr. Lally graduated from Harvard in 1967. He credits his interest in Chinese art to the many fine collections in the museums around greater Boston, particularly the Fogg Museum at Harvard. His undergraduate studies were followed by graduate work in economics at Columbia University (M.B.A. 1969) and a fellowship in the International Fellows Program while studying at the School of International Affairs at Columbia (M.I.A. 1970).

He joined Sotheby in 1970, starting in the financial division. After a stint in Los Angeles, where he made the decision to focus on Chinese art as a full-time profession, he joined Sotheby London, where he worked in the Chinese Department. He returned to the United States in 1973 and soon was put in charge of the Chinese Department in New York. He participated in the establishment of the firm's Hong Kong office in 1974 and continues to take an active part in the auctions held semi-annually there.

George Peppard, an actor in motion pictures, television, and on the stage, has expanded his career and now serves as director, producer, and star of his own company, Long Rifle Productions.

While majoring in civil engineering at Purdue University, he developed an interest in the theater and transferred to the Carnegie-Mellon University where he earned a Bachelor of Fine Arts degree. He took over the family contracting business, moonlighted as a disc jockey and engineer at a small Pennsylvania radio station, and earned extra money teaching fencing.

After coming to New York, he studied at the Actor's Studio and worked as a taxi driver, at a bank, and as a motorcycle mechanic. His first small television roles quickly led to more important parts, critical acclaim, and a long succession of major acting assignments.

Mr. Peppard lives in Beverly Hills, California.

Gerald Schoenfeld is chairman of the board of The Shubert Organization, the famous theatrical organization that owns and operates legitimate theaters in New York, Philadelphia, Boston, Chicago, and Los Angeles, and has produced such recent attractions as *The Sly Fox, Sherlock Holmes, Children of a Lesser God, Dancin', The Act, The Gin Game,* and *Ain't Misbehavin'.*

He is also a member of the Board of Governors of the League of New York Theaters and Producers, Inc., the New York City Visitors & Convention Bureau, the Broadway Association, and the Mayor's Task Force on Urban Theaters (Boston).

Mr. Schoenfeld received a B.S. degree from the University of Illinois and and LL.B. from New York University School of Law. He also studied at the Massachusetts Institute of Technology and Columbia University.

Frank Prial is a foreign correspondent currently assigned to the Paris bureau of the *New York Times*. Before this current overseas assignment, he created and, for almost eight years wrote, the "Wine Talk" column in the *Times*. His articles on wine also appeared on a twice-a-month basis in the *Sunday New York Times Magazine*. When the *Times* began its special Business Day section, Mr. Prial created and wrote the "People in Business" column.

He has written extensively on wines for many magazines. His book, *Wine Talk*, was published by Bantam in 1978.

Before joining the *Times*, Mr. Prial was a reporter with *The Wall Street Journal*.

Alan Joel Patricof received a B.S. degree in finance from Ohio State University in 1955 and a M.S. degree in finance from Columbia University Graduate School of Business in 1957.

After a position with the investment counseling firm of Schroder, Naess & Thomas, he joined Lambert & Co., forerunners of the venture capital industry.

In 1960, he became assistant vice-president and, subsequently, vice-president of Central National Corporation, a private family investment management organization with assets in excess of $100 million. There, he managed a diversified investment portfolio and initiated developments that lead to his becoming a founder of New York Magazine Company and subsequently the president and chairman of the board. He was responsible for the company's acquisition of the *Village Voice*, the beginning of *New West* magazine, and their eventual sale to City Post Publishing Company in 1976. It was also while he was at Central National that he participated in the founding of Datascope Corporation, a leading medical electronics manufacturer (of which he is still a board member), and was a founder and director of Lin Broadcasting Corporation.

In 1970 he formed Alan Patricof Associates, Inc., to manage the investments of a limited number of clients in the venture capital area. He subsequently formed Decahedron Partners, a pool of capital, and was responsible for the financing and developing of a number of companies, both public and private. He still serves as a member of the board of several of these firms, including Computer Identics, Adams Laboratories, RSR Corporation, Bustop Shelters, Periphonics, Network Analysis Corporation, and Mineral Energy, of which he is chairman.

Mr. Patricof also serves as treasurer and member of the Board of Governors of the New York Academy of Sciences and is a member of the board of the American Women's Economic Development Association.

Know Thyself

Arthur Levitt, Jr.

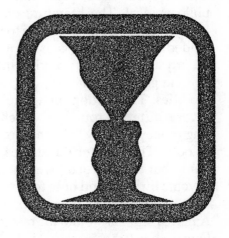

In whatever types of investments you make, your basic philosophy should be consistent. It is a mistake to think that you can safely take a higher risk in art than in stocks, in theater than in real estate. You should always begin by making a judgment as to how much of a chance you want to take, and the same rule should apply in all fields. A number of people I know are doing extraordinarily well with non-traditional investments, but many more are not for the very reasons they would probably do poorly in the market. They lack a clear definition of their own investment motives, so they make poor decisions and suffer the consequences. This book does not tell readers how to develop their own philosophies of investing; it tells them what their options are once their philosophies are well established.

Another common mistake is to invest in a field about which you have only the most primitive understanding. In such cases, judgment is based on hearsay rather than the kind of diligent research that must precede any financial commitment. It is all too easy to fall victim to false investment cults or to find yourself suddenly stranded in a dangerously unfamiliar landscape without a clue as to how to get out. I hope that the chapters in this book will help readers learn how to do their homework properly. This is especially important as the options proliferate. Some of the comparatively esoteric fields described here may provide the first investment experience for a new generation of investors who, in less tumultuous eras, might have thought only of stocks and bonds.

My intention in this book is to give readers a chance to listen to experts in a variety of areas and decide for themselves whether one or another field is worth exploring. I am grateful for the considerable time and effort each of the authors has contributed, and believe that, as a result of their collective efforts, one can get a truly comprehensive picture of the different kinds of investment opportunities that are available in today's marketplace.

I am also grateful to Lawrence Armour, our Dow Jones editor, who helped us pull it all together.

The chapters written by these experts vary as widely as the opportunities they discuss. Some of these pieces are "how-to-do" presentations. Others describe a particular area in depth. Still others are more philosophical. The literature on many of these subjects is sparse or so technical as to be inaccessible to the average investor. These essays are intended to fill in some gaps in public understanding and unravel some of the mysteries in areas of vital interest.

One group of chapters discusses different ways of investing in commodities. The section on agricultural investments for instance, explains several different routes by which an investor can enter this field—by putting money directly into basic production, in land, or into a combination of both. The chapter on futures gives a detailed introduction to this exciting but treacherous investment vehicle, in which the author finds "a psychic thrill second only to sex." The chapter on investing in oil includes many useful remarks and tips based on the optimistic assessment that America still has abundant reserves likely to be discovered in the future. One of the attractive aspects of investing in real estate, as explained in the chapter on that subject, is that it is an asset that usually keeps pace with inflation—a quality that makes it worth considering at a time when the economy is down. The chapter on gold and silver explores the mystique of the precious metals in terms of what the author calls "moneyness," and explains how to invest in non-physical gold through future contracts, options, and mining shares.

The book also explores a number of opportunities that offer psychic rewards above and beyond the economic benefits involved. Investing in art, whether in Old Masters or in contemporary works, or in precious porcelain or antique furniture, can bring to the investor greater—but perhaps less easily measured—returns than the hoped-for profits. Investing in films or theater can provide glamorous psychic rewards, too, but potential investors must realize the riskiness of these ventures and the high premium that you must pay for the glamour. The chapter on wine contains some shrewd advice for investors in this area with some provocative information about vineyards and vintages.

Other chapters cover the more traditional investment media such as stocks, bonds, savings bonds, and mutual funds. This latter chapter describes the relatively recent expansion of mutual funds into full-line financial service organizations, which provide investors with the sort of diversification, professional management, liquidity, and convenience that may make mutual funds preferable to many personal portfolios. The chapter on savings banks makes its case by emphasizing the financial security provided by having one's money insured and the extra benefits in investment-related services presently being offered by many institutions. The chapter on bonds stresses the value of income that offsets the rate of inflation with airtight, guaranteed payments.

My personal experience with investments has convinced me that there is no substitute for doing your homework thoroughly. The price you pay for taking shortcuts and betting on "sure-fire" tips can be enormous. I know a doctor who listened to such a tip from an acquaintance who happened to use a locker next to his at his golf club; he rushed off to buy a security that proved to be worthless. A homemaker joined an investment club for the companionship of the other club members; she lost virtually all of her money. A star-struck insurance salesman put his money into a Broadway show just to be invited to the opening night party; the show was a flop. A business executive invested in a piece of real estate because of the huge tax benefits, forgetting that the real estate had to be a viable property. A neophyte investor in cattle was more interested in playing cowboy than in gaining a good return on his investment. An interior designer who thought he was an expert in art discovered that he was simply following current fads instead of acquiring works by serious artists.

People often fall prey to temptations that blind them to economic motives and lure them into taking heavy investment risks. Discipline, therefore, is a very important measure of any investment judgment. Investors must realize that second-hand advice can never take the place of first-hand experience, and that the emotional rewards derived from an investment should be considered separately from the economic considerations. Whether you invest in stamps, antique bottles, or race horses, you must approach the economic aspects of the investments with the same disciplined, methodical attitude you would use in buying a security or in starting a new business. The chapters in this book are intended to set the ground rules and guidelines for knowledgeable investments and provide warning signals for the traps to be avoided.

At various times in my life I have invested in cattle, movies, theater, diamonds, oil, stamps, coins, gold, silver, real estate, and art, so I am a good subject for the lessons offered by this anthology. Fortunately, most of these investments worked out reasonably well. A number did not, however, and since books of this kind tend to dwell only on fabulous success stories, it might be useful to mention one of my early fiascoes as a way to illustrate a point.

Many people have come to realize that real estate provides an almost infallible investment opportunity to beat back inflation. My own first experience with real estate, however, was the one that I would like to forget. The project involved building a resort hotel in a Middle-Eastern country. Although I knew very little about real estate and even less about building hotels, I felt confident about this particular venture because a fellow investor was one of the world's most experienced and astute hotel owners. A man who could successfully commit large sums of money to build vast numbers of rooms certainly could not miss on a modest 120-room venture. I believed that my own homework was unnecessary in light of my partner's unquestioned wisdom and experience. I could not have been more mistaken. For, as I discovered too late, what was a meaningful investment for me was only a trifling philanthropy for my wealthy partner. I did not consider that his motive and mine might have been different. As it turned out, the area where we built our hotel barely could have sustained a falafel stand, let alone a resort. The project proved to be a resounding failure, and I lost every penny I put into it. I never visited the property. It was akin to buying highly promoted Arizona wasteland (fit only for Gila monsters), sight unseen. I never took that first obvious step: a personal inspection of the goods. I learned the hard way why it is crucial to do your own research and why it is foolish to put all your trust in the wisdom and experience of your partners. If I convey no other thought in this book, I hope the story of my misadventure in the desert will highlight the importance of calling your own shots when making investment decisions.

By way of contrast, I once made another real estate investment that had strong personal motivations, and so turned out quite differently. It was in 1959 when I lived in Kansas City and worked for a Missouri agricultural investment company. Less spectacular than the boom-and-bust cycles of residential land, the values represented by rural grazing acreage tended to appreciate regardless of the economic environment. As a matter of personal interest I attended a land auction in Gallatin, a country town with no paved streets. The auction took place at the county courthouse, where the local custom was for friendly neighbors to buy up distressed property. When I arrived—a complete stranger, and worse, a New Yorker—I created quite a stir. In the course of the auction I successfully bid for a small farm, astounding the people of Gallatin. Why, they asked, had an outsider chosen to invest in this little corner of Missouri? On the spur of the moment, I said that in about twenty years I hoped there would be an engagement announcement in *The New York Times* of my baby daughter and I would like her residence to be listed as being both in New York City and Gallatin, Missouri. Naturally, I had a twinkle in my eye when I said it, but they accepted my "explanation" in good humor and welcomed me as a new neighbor who planned to stay. I still own that farm and have even expanded my holdings over the years. Today my family shares my pleasure in knowing that we own some land in Missouri and I have the satisfaction of knowing that should I ever want to sell it, the property is worth far more than I paid for it. That was an investment that came from the heart as well as the head and depended on nobody's instinct or interests but my own.

An avid theater-goer, I have enjoyed being involved in the chaotic process of producing shows, a business Gerry Schoenfeld describes in his chapter on investing in plays. That essay makes it clear that one has to be a little bit crazy to be a theatrical "angel." There are, however, creative rewards from being part of an artistic project that warrant taking the kind of economic risk involved. The first play I invested in, *An Evening with Nichols and May*, produced by Alex Cohen, was a big hit. After that, I was hooked, and proceeded to invest in a series of flops, which shall be nameless. Success in the theater is even harder to predict than success in the stock market. I will probably continue to be a theatrical "angel" in the future because it is an involvement that fulfills my creative aspirations, and because my investment philosophy permits me to utilize a certain portion of my resources for high-risk artistic projects that may prove to be more satisfying from an esthetic, rather than an economic, point of view.

Because I have always had an interest in the fine arts as well as in the performing arts, I have been a collector of paintings, drawings, prints, and photographs. Having works of art in my home and office enriches my life, but I also take pleasure in knowing that the works I acquired have appreciated in value. A compelling desire to live with a particular work of art is, for me, the most reliable signal that it is worth buying. I first learned that lesson when my wife and I were living in Kansas City and our neighbor happened to be the well-known painter Thomas Hart Benton. After a while, we got to know the artist and his wife, and were invited to spaghetti dinners at their home. These were great occasions, not only because of the food and the company, but because I admired Mr. Benton's paintings so much and was excited to be in their presence. My wife and I were eager to buy some of his paintings but could not afford the prices. Mr. Benton, sensing the depth of our feelings for his work, volunteered to sell me paintings for 5 percent down, with 10 years to pay, and no interest charges. It was a superb opportunity and we have treasured our collection of his work ever since. Although we have no intention of ever selling our Bentons, I know that acquiring them was one of the better investments I have made.

I cannot overstress the importance of believing in your investments on the basis of personal experience. In committing a certain amount of your capital, you are investing something of yourself—just as you do in choosing a wife or husband, a business partner, a career, a house, a lifestyle. Judgments in all such instances are not made purely on a risk/reward basis although this factor may always be one of the considerations. More important is the nature of your personal makeup. This manifests itself in the subjects in which you did exceptionally well in school, the books and magazines you like to read, the television programs you watch, the sports you play, the kind of vacations you take, your relationships with your family, friends, colleagues. These are the elements that should come into play when one is choosing an investment medium. A person who regularly goes to galleries and museums, buys art books, and subscribes to art magazines obviously should investigate the opportunities for investment in one or another of the visual arts. An habitual theater goer should seriously consider trying his or her luck at putting up some money for the production of a new play. A horse lover or a race-track fan is an obvious candidate for an investment in syndicate horses. The point is that by becoming an investor you graduate from being an onlooker into being a participant. You enhance your own experience and capitalize on your instinctive judgment as the basis for making promising personal investments.

There is, to be sure, another rule to keep in mind. As I suggested earlier, investment should follow a process of disciplined analysis. The only people I have known who have a long and consistent record of investing successfuly are those who have developed the techniques of doing careful research about any prospect, exploring all the options available, and weighing the pros and cons of different courses of action. Whenever these people are attracted by an investment opportunity, whether it be real estate, movies, antiques, or any other area, they know that substantial preparation and analysis must precede any final decision. Thus, while I stress the importance of instinct, intuition, and personal interest as prerequisites for sound investment, I am convinced that these elements must be combined with systematic, thorough analysis if the investment is to have the best chance for success.

The most experienced investors keep in mind that all investments are alternatives and must be viewed in terms of other opportunities that may be available at a given point in time. In today's economy, investors are exposed to a broader variety of investments than ever before. Only when it seems reasonably clear that a certain investment is better than others available at the moment should funds be applied. Although I believe that the foundation of every individual's program—as well as the foundation of the American economy—should be investment in common stocks, there are periods when the best decision you can make about the stock market is not to invest at all. Market conditions may be such that there are no prospects to which a responsible investor should commit funds. The better investment would be to put those funds to work somewhere else. An oil investment may appear to be very attractive, but not as good as the 17 or 18 percent offered by corporate bonds. Investment decisions must always be made in the context of alternative possibilities.

The entrepreneurial spirit is, of course, inherent in the American economic system. Indeed, our very survival, I believe, depends on individual initiative and the willingness to take chances. The question is, How much of a chance should you, the investor, reasonably be expected to take? In terms of financial investments this means assessing the cost of entry. Is the proposed investment too much—or too little—for your bank account? Will the investment be liquid enough for your needs? How easy will it be for you to get out? Is the prospective reward of sufficient importance to you to warrant the degree of risk? How important are non-economic benefits? Is the potential liability a reasonable one for you? Is the investment consistent with your personal philosophy?

There are many specific guidelines you should keep in mind while appraising the value of a proposed investment. On a major investment, it is a good idea for you to ask the sponsor for a minimum of six references from other investors who have participated in the program for several years. You should consult these investors to make sure the sponsor has lived up to his or her commitment. You should also ascertain if the sponsor has been accessible to investors seeking current information on the investment and if financial data have been supplied on request. If there is an investment advisor involved, you should find out if the advisor is receiving a fee from the sponsor. If so, this could indicate a problem. Generally speaking, the advisor should receive a fee from no one but the investor. When there is any financial connection between the advisor and the sponsor, the investor has a right to be very wary of the proposition.

And when you finally decide to invest money in a particular project, you should consult with your attorney, accountant, banker, stockbroker, or perhaps a combination of all four to find out how best to get into the program. If an investment is being considered for tax reasons, the project must be reviewed with tax counsel to make sure your information on that tax law is up-to-date. For instance, if you are thinking of a cattle deal because you understand one is able to deduct from one's income twice the amount invested in the year of the investment, experienced tax counsel will make it clear that certain provisions of the tax shelter law were changed in 1974 making the desired tax deduction no longer possible.

Risk taking, especially in today's insecure economy, can be nerve-racking. No one wants to lose. But even the "smart" investment involves risk taking, and you must learn to accept some degree of risk taking as a positive, creative, enterprising course of action.

One of the most vivid lessons I learned about the value of taking risks occurred during an Outward Bound experience. Outward Bound is a Colorado-based organization that makes a business of putting groups of people into wilderness situations where survival depends on mutual trust and teamwork. The risks are substantial but the rewards are even greater.

My group included 20 businesspeople from the securities industry, four guides, and a physician from Denver whose presence lent a somewhat ominous note to the expedition. For a week this unlikely crew navigated down a plunging, white-water tributary of the Colorado River. We scaled cliffs, hiked treacherous trails, took chances. It was a strenuous experience, but for the hardships we experienced, we were rewarded with some valuable discoveries: the natural beauty around us, our own untapped resourcefulness, and the value of camaraderie. By the end of the trip not only had we survived, but we had also grown in our willingness to dare the elements—whether in nature or in the marketplace—as a necessary step toward reaching an agreed-upon goal.

Making an investment requires taking responsible risks—not playing it safe. Taking risks, whether we ultimately win or lose is, in itself, a function of being alive, using your imagination and creativity to achieve worthy ends.

After you have done all the necessary homework and assessed the degree of risk involved, a moment of truth arrives in which the decision whether to take the chance has to be made. This is the crucial moment—one that puts many people off. To go, or not to go? Will the investment succeed or not? What will happen if it fails?

Some people stand for hours at the edge of a swimming pool with one toe in the chilly water as they wait for the breeze to die down or the sun to come out, afraid to make the ultimate plunge. Others jump in once they have made the definite decision to take a swim. My advice is to take all the time you need to make your decision, but once it's made—jump! If you have followed your instincts and weighed all the odds, and you think the move is right for you, go ahead. It is a lonely experience but, after you have received all the advice you can get from available sources, it is best if you make the ultimate decision for yourself. After all, it is your money and it is your future that is at stake.

The Bedrock

Morris D. Crawford, Jr.

In *The Dowbeaters: How to Buy Stocks That Go Up* (Macmillan, 1979), Ira U. Cobleigh, an economist and financial columnist for over half a century, makes the following point:

> A penny saved is a penny earned. Therefore, the first and foremost investment every "investor" should make in structuring an East Pool [Cobleigh's term for a pool of capital consisting of ultraconservative investments], should be in a regular passbook savings account. A savings account provides the investor with instant availability to his money without market depreciation and a solid building block for financial success. A savings account should be the bedrock foundation of your financial pyramid.

Then Cobleigh adds this:

> A second vehicle for capital deployment in the East Pool is the certificate of deposit, taken on an annual basis. These notes provide the investor with a slightly better yield than a savings account, and they add to the diversification of the East Pool.

Another financial writer, Andrew Tobias, author of *The Only Investment Guide You'll Ever Need* (Harcourt Brace Jovanovich, 1978), comes to a similar conclusion:

11

The first several thousand dollars of anybody's money (aside from equity in a home) should be in a savings bank. And for many people, that's *all* their money.

The economic, cultural, and social environment has changed radically since the first savings banks were chartered in 1819, but they are still fulfilling a basic need: the need for financial security. It was this need during the Industrial Revolution that caused the spread of the savings bank idea in America.

Accompanying the Industrial Revolution was a mass immigration of Irish, Polish, German, Italians, and English who came to America to escape cholera epidemics, famines, and depressions. Although most found work, many became public charges when they lost their jobs or when tragedies such as fire or death struck. This emerging class of industrial workers had no way of safekeeping funds or saving for the future. Commercial banks existed, but they were interested in bigger customers. Thus, the founders established the first savings banks as a philanthropic cause to help the "little people" who had no other way to save.

Today, savings banks are obviously more than a place for the small saver. In fact, Ira Cobleigh declares in his book, they are a place where the rich get richer because they know, "It is not the killing which makes for market success, but rather the compounding effects that a consistent investment strategy provides over a period of years." Over a ten-year period even a small amount of money turns "into a plump nest egg." For example:

At 5 percent, $10,000 grows into $16,289 over a decade.
At 6 percent, into $17,908.
At 7 percent, into $19,672.
At 8 percent, into $21,589.
At 10 percent, into $25,937.
At 12 percent, into $31,058.

These rates, which are currently available at mutual savings banks in the 17 states in which they are chartered (rates vary with maturity and size of accounts), are backed by government insurance, high liquidity, convenience, and flexibility—hallmarks of the industry since the first "people's bank" opened its doors.

In competition with the stock, bond, and option markets, mutual savings banks are somewhat overshadowed as investment vehicles. But for over a century and a half, through regular compounding of interest, they have been quietly building medium and large fortunes for their depositors with a minimum of bookkeeping and anxiety and a maximum of safety.

Savings banks have survived wars, depressions, and recessions and maintained the solid trust and confidence of the American people. They have enjoyed a record of safety unmatched by any other type of financial institution. Because of the comparatively conservative investment policies mutual savings banks followed during the 1920s, they had sufficient cash and liquidity to cover almost all their withdrawal requests in the 1930s. While other financial institutions were failing, savings banks generated a confidence among savers to the extent that they enjoyed a net savings inflow almost every year of the Depression decade.

As a testament to the confidence of Americans, there are 37 million accounts totalling $152 billion in mutual savings banks today. Established solely to provide a safe haven for the average citizen, they now hold approximately 12 percent of all U.S. savings dollars—a significant share of the market considering there are some 463 savings banks compared to more than 14,500 commercial banks. Additionally, savings banks are located in only 17 states while commercial banks, savings and loans, and credit unions exist in all 50.

As mentioned, safety has always been one of their hallmarks. Deposits at mutual savings banks are backed by the reserves each has built up over decades. In addition, all mutuals except those in Massachusetts are insured by the Federal Deposit Insurance Corporation—a U.S. government agency. In Massachusetts, savings are insured by the state-sponsored Massachusetts Central Fund.

The FDIC insures an individual's accounts in a single institution up to $100,000 and to $100,000 in Individual Retirement Accounts or Keogh accounts. This includes all the individual's accounts—savings, certificates of deposit, checking, cash in trust funds—at a single bank.

However, insurance of funds can be multiplied far beyond $100,000 by structuring accounts in different ownership capacities. For example, an investor can have separate deposit insurance up to $100,000 on each of three accounts ($300,000) at the same bank: his or her own individual account; a joint account with another person; and an account held as a trustee for someone else.

The investor can increase coverage further by dividing ownership of funds in the same bank or by opening individual accounts in separate banks. A widow with $140,000 in funds from the sale of a home or from life insurance proceeds could, if she wished, deposit $100,000 in one institution and the balance in another. And the manager of a large foundation could invest $10 million by putting $100,000 into each of 100 insured savings banks—and sleep nights.

In recent years, higher yielding time accounts and increased savings bank services have made savings banks far more attractive for the small saver. Many people want to know, however, which type of investment makes most sense.

This question should be considered in the context of one's entire financial situation. Unfortunately, most people do a poor job of planning their financial future. A recent survey by the Social Security Administration reveals that 35 percent of married couples over the age of 65 receive total income that is considered below the poverty level; likewise, 77 percent of unmarried people over the age of 65 do not have income sufficient to maintain even a modest standard of living. Consequently, people must save to augment what they expect to receive from Social Security and pensions. The picture looks bleak when one considers that the U.S. rate of personal savings is currently the lowest of all the major industrial countries.

For vast numbers of Americans, financial planning is limited to depositing a check in a checking account on pay day, possibly putting something into savings, and then writing checks to cover expenses. Most people don't even consider retirement planning until they are in their forties, even though they should have begun planning in their twenties.

Part of the problem lies in the fact that the average consumer does not know where to go for sound financial advice. The dilemma is not a new one. An article that appeared in the July 11, 1934 issue of *The New York Times* tells the story of a woman who had her palm read by a fortune-teller who sold her on a scheme to double her money. The woman withdrew her $14,000 of savings in the form of twelve $1,000 bills and four $500 bills. She took them to the fortune-teller who rolled the bills in a handkerchief and waved it around her head while muttering incantations in a strange tongue. The fortune-teller then told her to wear the handkerchief around her waist for two months without opening it and she would find that her money had doubled. When the woman opened the handkerchief two months later she found 16 strips of newspaper cut to bank note size, plus $23. The fortune-teller was never to be found.

Needless to say, the woman in the article was in dire need of sound financial advice and perhaps other counsel as well. Unfortunately, much of the financial information the modern-day consumer receives is from people with something to sell. Insurance agents, tax shelter salespeople, stockbrokers—each is out to prove that his or her product is the answer to one's financial need. Although savings banks do not function as financial counselors, many strive to fill the gap by conducting consumer information programs aimed at helping the consumer plan for his or her financial future.

The various types of savings plans and services offered by savings banks have won them recognition as family financial service centers.

Individuals can benefit financially not only by depositing funds in savings banks but also by taking advantage of various loans and services. Virtually all offer mortgage loans for homes and home improvement and co-op loans. In New York and other states where savings banks exist, customers can obtain checking account services, interest bearing checking (NOW) accounts, low-cost life insurance, and student loans.

Savings bank life insurance, another major service offered in some states, has several distinct advantages: it is low cost, has liberal cash and loan values, and pays early dividends.

Student loans, another service offered by savings banks, are growing in popularity. They are guaranteed either by the federal government or by state governments. The proceeds of student loans programs go directly to the student while attending school. All interest charges on the loan are paid by the government, but the student must begin repaying the loans from nine months to one year after completion of studies.

Passbook savings accounts and time deposits

Savings banks offer a wide variety of accounts in terms of rate, term, and type of ownership. An investor should keep specific needs in mind in order to select the best form. With respect to rate and term, there are two basic forms of interest bearing accounts: passbook savings accounts and time deposits. Within these basic forms, there are further choices.

Passbook savings accounts pay a lower rate of interest than time accounts, but they offer the investor immediate access to his or her funds with little or no loss of earnings. In early 1981, New York savings banks offered two forms of passbook savings accounts: regular and day-of-deposit/day-of-withdrawal accounts (DOD/DOW). In 1981, a regular savings account paid interest at the rate of 5½ percent per annum, with interest compounded on a daily basis at most institutions. Interest is credited quarterly, but if a depositor withdraws funds before the last three business days of the quarter, then the interest on the funds withdrawn for that quarter is lost. On the other hand, the depositor benefits from certain grace days since funds can be withdrawn during the last three business days of the quarter and still receive interest for the entire quarter. Also, interest is earned from the first of the month on amounts deposited before the tenth business day of that month.

Day-of-deposit/day-of-withdrawal accounts permit the depositor to withdraw funds at any time during a quarter and receive interest to the day of withdrawal, provided a minimum amount such as $5 is left on deposit. As the name implies, the depositor earns interest for each day that the funds are on deposit with the savings bank.

In the case of time deposits, the depositor must select a period during which the funds will remain on deposit, and the rate paid on the account varies with the length of the term. Shorter-term deposits generally pay lower rates than longer-term deposits. For example, a 90-day account pays interest at the rate of 5¾ percent per annum; the longest term account (eight years or more) pays 8 percent per annum. As in the case of passbook savings accounts, interest is credited quarterly and compounded daily at most institutions.

Generally speaking, depositors are not permitted to withdraw principal from a time account before the account matures. However, a savings institution may consent to a premature withdrawal; if it does, the depositor will be charged a penalty at least as severe as that prescribed by federal law. The law requires that for the accounts opened after June 30, 1979, the depositor will lose at least six months' interest on an account of more than one year. A penalty equal to at least three months' interest is required on accounts of one year or less.

Table 2-1 shows an example of what's available in time accounts. The Bowery Savings Bank, New York's largest savings bank, offered this range of certificates (investment savings accounts, certificates of deposit or CDs) at the start of 1981.

Table 2-1. Investment savings accounts offered by the Bowery Savings Bank.

Minimum Term Required	Minimum Deposit	Guaranteed Annual Rate	Effective Annual Yield
1–2½ years	$500	6.50%	6.81%
2½–4 years	$500	6.75%	7.08%
4–6 years	$500	7.50%	7.90%
6–8 years	$500	7.75%	8.17%
8–10 years	$500	8.00%	8.45%

Rates on accounts of $100,000 or more are negotiated at each savings institution and vary according to money market conditions.

To stem the outflow of deposits during the periods of high short-term interest rates, federal regulatory agencies have permitted savings banks to offer two forms of time accounts with rates determined on the basis of money market conditions. One such account, the Six-Month Money Market Certificate, pays a rate equal to the average auction discount rate for six-month U.S. Treasury bills plus one-fourth of 1 percent. The Treasury bill rate is determined at an auction held at the beginning of each week and effective the following Thursday, so that the rate paid on a Six-Month Money Market Certificate changes accordingly for certificates sold during that week. When the average auction discount rate on six-month

Treasury bills drops below 8¾ percent, the rate paid by savings banks may be up to one-half of 1 percent greater than the average auction discount rate (but not to exceed 9 percent), but once the depositor purchases a Six-Month Money Market Certificate, the rate will be fixed for the six-month term of the account. A $10,000 minimum deposit is required by law for this account.

The other form of money market account offered by savings banks is a Variable Rate Account, with maturities of two and one-half years (30 months) or more, where the rate is determined every two weeks, based on the average yield on two-and-one-half-year Treasury obligations. Before the beginning of each biweekly period, the Treasury announces the rate, and savings banks can then offer 30-month (or more) accounts that pay a rate that is the lesser of 12 percent per year or an annual rate that is equal to the two-and-one-half-year Treasury yield. The rate in effect when the account is opened is the rate that remains in effect for the entire term of the account. Federal law prohibits compounding of interest in the case of Six-Month Money Market Certificates, but permits it in the case of 30-month (or more) Variable Rate Accounts.

A depositor must determine the rate and term of the account best suited to his or her needs, recognizing that generally a higher rate is obtainable by agreeing to tie up money for a longer term. But in periods of high short-term rates, the Six-Month Money Market Certificate or the Variable Rate Account may be an attractive short-term investment.

To get maximum leverage from one's savings, the investor must choose the right savings media, that is, the proper mix of passbook and time certificates. While it appears that savings banks do not offer a significant hedge against inflation, they have competed aggressively—and successfully—over the past ten years with such other investments as stocks, bonds, and mutual funds.

Indeed, the cream of corporate America—the Fortune 500—showed a total return (dividends plus price appreciation) of 2.85 percent over the decade 1969–1978. Thus, a $10,000 investment in the Fortune 500 that would have earned 2.85 percent during the decade, would have resulted in a net return of $285 and a final sum of $10,285 at the end of the decade.

An investment in the Fortune 500 would have entailed a high degree of risk and uncertainty. For example, many of the Fortune 500 Industrials showed negative rates of return over the ten-year period. By contrast, an investment of $10,000 in a mutual savings bank compounding daily at the rate of say 5 ⅛ percent (the average rate paid during 1969–78) would have resulted in dividends of $6,813 and total capital of $16,813 at the end of ten years.

Estate planning

Estate planning is simply a technique for minimizing taxes and legal costs while ensuring that assets will be handled the way the owner wants them to be. The vast array of accounts offered by savings banks can be useful in estate planning. As one New York bank detailed:

> Estate planning with trusts as the central feature can be valuable for people of relatively modest means, most particularly when there's a need for management of assets belonging to someone who is elderly or ill or who hasn't the financial sophistication to handle his or her own affairs.

> As a practical manner, of course, a trust becomes more worthwhile as an individual goes up the scale in terms of assets. But most people who haven't taken the time to add the value of their property probably would be astounded at how much they are worth. When you count life insurance proceeds, profit sharing, and pension benefits, a house, a car or two, and maybe a boat, along with securities, personal possessions, receivables, and so on, the total can mount surprisingly high.

While savings banks do not operate trust departments, they can be used effectively by individuals even of modest means with or without the assistance of an attorney.

In estate planning, money can be saved by giving it away. Hence, individuals with funds no longer needed during their lifetimes can make annual gifts to children or others by opening savings accounts in their names and depositing money into these accounts. The gifts must be irrevocable and become the property of the donee. There is no tax on gifts of up to $3,000 per year per donee, and taxes on future income of the accounts are paid by the donee. Giving money away during a person's lifetime can save on federal and state estate taxes and can also reduce the estate's size and administrative costs; the latter can run from 5 to 10 percent of the total estate.

Lifetime gifts of money can be made by establishing certain forms of savings accounts such as irrevocable trust accounts, deed of gift accounts, and custodial accounts under the Uniform Gifts to Minors Act. Parents and grandparents often find it convenient to open a so-called Totten Trust Account, a special form of revocable trust account by which an individual depositor, or joint depositors, name another party (often a child) to receive the balance of the account upon the death of the depositor or depositors. The Totten Trust Account has been referred to as the "poor man's will" since it designates the disposal of the account upon death, but the "poor man" designation may be incorrect since many banks place no limit on the size of the account. Although a Totten Trust Account is an effective means of passing property after death, the funds in the account at the time of the depositor's death are included in the depositor's estate, since a Totten Trust does not effect a transfer of property during the depositor's lifetime.

Investing for education

The principal of putting money away is particularly useful for building a nest egg for education. There is no need to tell parents that higher-education costs are skyrocketing. Tuition and board at private colleges now total around $8,000 a year, and other universities are not far behind.

Savings banks were pioneers in fostering programs to ease the financial strains of higher education and offer students or their parents several financial aid programs. The Bowery Savings Bank's special education account, which employs the principle of systematic savings, is a good example. Deposits are placed initially in a passbook account and when the required minimium ($500) is met, the funds are automatically transferred to a higher-rate time account for maximum return.

In addition, The Bowery discusses with depositors the use of Custodial Accounts established under the Uniform Gifts to Minors Act for the purpose of saving for education. Such accounts have been particularly useful since the depositor is able to accumulate funds in the account with the earnings taxed to a child who generally is in a far lower tax bracket. When the child reaches college age, the funds continue to earn interest without a severe tax impact, and the funds can be used for the child's educational benefit, as well as other purposes. In many states, the minor receives control of the account upon reaching the age of majority at 18.

Tax sheltered accounts

Savings banks have developed sophisticated accounts that give depositors the opportunity to control funds that they desire to give to others for reasons of old-fashioned generosity or for tax planning purposes. In this connection, savings banks offer Irrevocable Trust Accounts, Deed of Gift Accounts, and Custodial Accounts established under the Uniform Gifts to Minors Act.

There are important legal distinctions between the three accounts, but the one thing they have in common is that they pass ownership funds, and in most instances the earnings on the funds, to the beneficiary of the account. In this way, a parent can pass the incidents of income taxation on earnings of certain funds that he wishes to give to a child and, at the same time, retain some measure of control over those funds. Again, individuals must carefully select the form of account best suited to their needs, and seeking professional advice from a lawyer, accountant, or tax advisor is a good idea. Although savings banks are not in the business of giving investment advice to individuals, they do provide a wide variety of accounts that can help individuals plan for their own futures, as well as for the futures of those near to them.

Investing for retirement

Americans are an aging population. At the beginning of the twentieth century there were a mere 4.6 million Americans aged 60 or over. Today, approximately 35 million Americans are approaching, or are in, retirement. The Census Bureau estimates that there will be 71 million Americans past 60 by the year 2035.

Not only is there a bulge in the sheer number of retirees and near-retirees, but Americans are also living longer. In 1900, the average American man could expect to live to age 46.5, the average American woman to 48.3. Thanks to rising living standards and improved medical care, the average American male now lives to 69, the average American female to 76.

Although retirees can expect to live longer, they are beset by galloping inflation. Medical expenses are a major problem for many; while senior citizens currently account for 11 percent of the population, those 65 and over are charged with 29 percent of all medical expenses. Thus, planning for retirement is essential if one wishes to maintain a respectable standard of living. To this end, savings banks offer a variety of tax deferred retirement accounts.

Keogh Accounts

Savings banks have offered Keogh Plan accounts since their establishment under the Self-Employed Individual Tax Retirement Act of 1962. Keogh Accounts (also known as H.R. 10 Plans) cover the self-employed. That includes professionals and handymen, freelance writers and barbers, sole proprietors and business partnerships.

To establish a Keogh Retirement plan, an individual must have earned income from self-employment. Employed persons who do free-lance work can also qualify with respect to their free-lance income. Employees must also be covered by the Keogh Plan, including immediate family members of the Keogh Plan subscriber if they work with or for the subscriber.

Self-employed individuals may contribute annually up to $7,500, or 15 percent of earned income, whichever is less. They must also contribute for employees with three or more years of service (or who have worked in the enterprise as long as the employer if less than three years). However, to avoid the need to cover seasonal or part-time employees, an employee need not be given credit for any in which less than 1,000 hours are worked.

Above this, self-employed individuals and employees may voluntarily contribute to the plan up to 10 percent of their earned income, or $2,500, whichever is less, provided at least one employee is covered under the plan. The single most cogent aspect of the Keogh Plan is its tax advantages. Tax deductions are taken by the employer for the amount contributed each year to the plan. If the funds are placed in a bank, taxes are not paid on the interest earned. The voluntary contributions of up to 10 percent of earned income are not tax deductible, but interest accumulates on a tax-deferred basis until retirement.

Owner-employees (those who own more than 10 percent of the business) may not withdraw funds from their Keogh accounts prior to age 59½ (unless disabled) and must start withdrawals at age 70½. However, owner-employees still working after age 70½ can continue to make additional tax-deductible contributions—even after withdrawals have begun.

In the event of total disability, Keogh Plan participants are permitted to withdraw money at any age; in the event of death, beneficiaries can receive the entire amount on deposit.

Taxes are payable when money is withdrawn. However, the retiree usually has a choice at that time: (1) to receive monthly payments taxed as ordinary income (the retiree at this time is usually in a much lower tax bracket) or (2) to receive the accumulation in a lump sum. This lump sum will be taxed, in whole or part, as ordinary income. However, a special ten-year income averaging formula may reduce the tax burden. In addition, a portion of the lump sum may be eligible for capital gains treatment.

In the case of the owner-employee, withdrawals from the Keogh Plan before age 59½ involve severe penalties. Ordinary income taxes plus a penalty tax of 10 percent must be paid on the withdrawn sum; in addition, contribution to the plan cannot be made on the individual's behalf for the next five years.

Unlike some commercial banks, savings banks do not presently charge for administering Keogh accounts. Nor do savings banks have front-end commissions or loading charges as do insurance companies and mutual funds.

How much can a Keogh Plan depositor accumulate over the years? Table 2-2, based on an 8-year time deposit certificate on an 8 percent basis and earning 8.45 percent a year, tells the tale. In a little more than 30 years, annual contributions of $7,500 will make one a millionaire—to spare.

Table 2-2. Accumulations in Keogh Plan accounts.

Annual Contribution	Monthly Deposits	Amount Worth at End of		
		10 Years	20 Years	30 Years
$750	$ 62.50	$ 11,603.34	$ 37,716.32	$ 96,482.87
$1,500	$125.00	$ 23,206.68	$ 75,432.64	$192,965.74
$3,000	$250.00	$ 46,413.35	$150,865.28	$385,931.48
$7,500	$625.00	$116,003.94	$377,163.19	$964,828.69

Individual Retirement Accounts

Keogh Plans are for the self-employed. For the estimated 40 to 45 million American employees not covered by a corporate or governmental pension plan, profit sharing plan, thrift plan, or tax-sheltered annuity under section 403 (b) of the Internal Revenue code or by a Keogh Plan, the Individual Retirement Account (IRA) is the ideal tax-deferred retirement program.

Eligible workers may make a tax deductible contribution to an IRA of up to 15 percent of gross annual earnings, not to exceed $1,500 per year. (With a non-working spouse, the upper limit is $1,750, provided that separate IRAs are established for each and equal contributions of $875 are made to each.) Individuals already receiving benefits from a corporate retirement, Keogh, or military service plan (but not currently accruing any additional benefits) can also adopt an IRA.

All dividends and interest in the IRA grow tax free (exactly as under Keogh) until actual distribution. Again, contributions made to IRA plans may not be withdrawn (except under penalty) until the individual has attained age 59½. Withdrawals must start by age 70½. Unlike the Keogh Plan, however, no deductible contributions may be made to an IRA after age 70½.

An employed husband and an employed wife may each contribute to their own IRA up to a $3,000 total annually ($1,500 each).

The penalty for premature withdrawals from an IRA is 10 percent of the distribution in addition to the regular tax on the distribution. Withdrawals for death or disability are not subject to the penalty tax. IRA distributions are taxed as ordinary income and are eligible for five-year income averaging, but not for special ten-year income averaging.

The retiree may choose installment payments over the combined life expectancy of both him- or herself and spouse, or may use the payout to purchase an insurance annuity. Importantly, an individual age 65 or over receives a double tax exemption so that $7,400 (assuming husband and wife both are over 65) of all income is tax-free to the retiree.

A company may also establish IRA programs for any or all of its employees, contributing any part or all of the 15 percent/$1,500 year contribution. Company contributions to an IRA are deductible by the company as business expenses.

It is important that the right type of plan be adopted, for one IRA can be far more advantageous than another, depending, in part, upon the needs of the individual. But all add up: indeed, $1,500 contributed annually to a savings bank IRA program at 8 percent (compounded daily, yielding 8.45 percent annually) would bring the account to $24,074 in 10 years and to $78,251 in 20 years. The employee would have invested $15,000 in the first decade and $30,000 by the end of the second decade.

By contrast, one insurance company calculated a retirement insurance program for 20 years with an annual premium of $1,500. If the worker died at any time, the beneficiaries would collect a death benefit of $22,339. In addition, this life insurance company guaranteed the worker a specific yield as well as an estimated yield based on dividends expected to be earned. The worker was guaranteed $35,563 at the end of 20 years and, with estimated dividends, the total would add up to $54,023.

In short, the bank account at the end of 20 years would total $78,251, the insurance company account, $54,023. Moreover, by buying a retirement life insurance policy, the worker does not get the full tax advantage of his contribution. Under the Internal Revenue Code, the portion of the $1,500 that goes to buy life insurance (as opposed to retirement benefits) cannot be deducted as an IRA contribution. On the other hand, the insurance company plan includes life insurance (typically an endowment-type policy) which may well be of significant value to the individual who has no other life insurance protection.

IRA rollover

Since only a fraction of employees remain with one employer their entire working lives, the law now provies for a "portable pension." Thus, when a worker leaves a company or retires and receives benefits from a pension or profit-sharing plan in a lump sum distribution in one taxable year, all or part of the distribution can be deposited ("rolled over") into an IRA account within 60 days without his having to pay income tax on the amount rolled over. This also applies if the company discontinues or terminates its retirement plan and the employee receives a total distribution in one taxable year. The ordinary 15 percent/$1,500 annual limit on contributions does not apply to rollovers.

This, in effect, creates a portable pension which continues to grow, tax-deferred, until it is withdrawn from the IRA. And if the worker is rehired by a company with a pension plan, the IRA rollover may be able to be transferred from the savings bank into that pension plan. Further, if the worker is employed by another company without a pension plan, a second personal IRA program can be established at a savings bank, permitting a contribution of up to $1,500 per year or 15 percent of the employee's earnings, whichever is less.

If the worker becomes totally and permanently disabled, rollover funds may be taken out at any age without penalty for early withdrawal. To facilitate distribution upon the death of the owner, beneficiaries may be named; if no beneficiary is named, proceeds will be paid to the owner's estate.

Defined Benefit Pension Plan

In this type of plan, the business owner shelters a sizable portion of income for management and employee retirement. Employing an actuary, the company's management decides (subject to certain legal requirements) who will be covered, what benefits are to be paid at retirement, and how the benefits will be funded. In short, unlike the individual retirement programs, there is a predetermined dollar retirement goal.

The Defined Benefit Pension Plan is quite effective as a true investment-type retirement program. It provides definitely determinable benefits at retirement; it may give all plan members full credit for service before the plan is established; and it may offer adequate benefits for older employees who are nearing retirement.

A Defined Benefit Pension plan calls for a definite financial commitment, since contributions are made annually in order to reach the actuarially determined funding goal. However, the funds accumulated in a pension plan, undiminished by taxes, can be working to generate more funds. And, as time goes by, and given today's high interest rates, the funds may generate enough income to reduce future company contributions.

Profit Sharing Retirement Plan

The Profit Sharing Retirement Plan is funded, as its name implies, through the company's current or accumulated net profits, subject to certain legal limitations regarding amounts that may be contributed. Other methods are available to increase one's retirement income, notably accumulating cash through company dividends or increasing one's take-home pay. But these are more costly from an investment standpoint, since either would require larger current tax payments.

Increasing one's salary immediately means larger taxes. Accumulating cash through dividend payments would be even more onerous, since the dividends paid would not be deductible by the company and therefore would be taxed twice. On the other hand, profit sharing retirement plans are tax-sheltered—the full amount of the company's contribution can be deductible, and the contributions accumulate in a tax-exempt fund. Furthermore, any return on investment is also tax deferred, rather than taxable immediately as additional income.

In addition, the profit sharing retirement plan substantially decreases the company's taxable income, benefiting company, employees, and stockholders. For example, if Kathy Smith's company has taxable income of $100,000, it would be necessary for the company to set aside $13,652 in order to pay her a $10,000 dividend from after-tax earnings. If her personal tax bracket is 30 percent, the $10,000 would be taxed again, leaving her only $7,000 out of the original $13,652 earned by the company. This represents a shrinkage of $6,652, or nearly 49 percent.

The Keogh, Individual Retirement Account, and corporate plans all offer individuals certain important advantages. First, contributions (within defined limits and except in the case of rollover or voluntary contributions) are deductible for the year for which they are made. Second, earnings on the funds invested under such plans are not includable in the income of the participants in the plans while they continue to participate. Although amounts distributed from the tax qualified retirement plans are includable in income of the year of receipt, distributions from the Keogh and corporate plans may be taxed under advantageous formulas which include ten-year forward averaging and capital gains treatment.

Savings banks have become an important factor in the area of qualified retirement plans, even though this is a relatively new service for them. Recognizing a long history of safety and soundness, as well as the special advantages of deposit insurance, many individuals and small corporate employers are beginning to find savings banks a convenient and helpful place to invest their retirement funds, especially as form and quality of the service offered are broadened.

Summary

The savings bank system plays a central role in the investment programs of millions of Americans. As "people's banks," they have existed since their founding for the benefit of depositors. Over their long and successful history, the paramount purpose of benefiting depositors has led them to adapt and change to meet their goals and desires. During some periods, it has appeared as though savings banks have outlived their usefulness as a safe, sound, and convenient depository for small savers. However, the banks have weathered wars, panics, inflation, deflation, and other ills. The reason, of course, is that they supply services that millions of investors need.

The Cornerstone

George L. Ball

Bethlehem Steel soared from $10 a share to $200 between 1914 and 1915. Warner Bros. Pictures rose from $10 to $138 between 1927 and 1928. National Distillers climbed from $13 to $124 between 1932 and 1933. Northwest Airlines rocketed from $7 to $171 between 1961 and 1965. National Semiconductor catapulted from $23 to $109 during the 1973 bear market. And Charter Co. soared from $5 to $50 during 1979 alone.

I missed the boat on every one of these issues, although, to be fair, I wasn't even born when Bessie, Warner Bros., and National Distillers made their moves. I had lots of company, though, for it has been my experience that few investors ever make really big killings in the stock market. Of those who do, fewer still manage to hold on to their winnings.

Does this mean, then, that common stocks as a class are not attractive investments? To the contrary. For while it is true that very big scores are few and far between, millions of investors *have* realized substantial and consistent returns over the past five decades through intelligent selection of and investment in equities. The cornerstone of any well-crafted investment program is composed of common stocks.

Indeed, the gains available through stocks have been even more substantial and consistent, I might add, than those returns generated by the alternative investment vehicles we hear so much about today. In the post-Depression era, for instance, common shares have far outpaced inflation, and have been much more rewarding than long-term corporate bonds, long-term government bonds, and U.S. Treasury bills. While it cannot be denied that the stock market did lag behind such alternative investments as gold, stamps, rare books, and diamonds over the past decade, there are good reasons to believe that common stocks will be a more rewarding investment vehicle in the 1980s. What's required is perspicacity, patience, and a touch of perversity.

Six key questions

In solving the riddle of common stock investment today, six key questions demand answers:
 1. What are common stocks and what do they actually represent?
 2. In what types of economic climates can money be made in common stocks?
 3. How have stocks performed relative to inflation and other investment vehicles in recent years?
 4. What went wrong in the 1970s?
 5. How are stocks likely to perform in the 1980s?
 6. Which types of stocks might be most rewarding in the decade ahead?

None of these questions has an absolute answer. Judgment, interpretation, and an element of guesstimating are present in each. But if you have money, and want to keep it, or make it grow, there are no perfectly certain, perfectly safe harbors; one must venture opinions and take stands to succeed as an investor.

What are common stocks and what do they represent?

This should be the easiest of our six questions; certainly it is the most basic, and yet it is the one that is perhaps most subject to confusion. So maybe I should start by pointing out what common stocks are *not*.

They are *not* mere collectibles. This is a very important point, so let me repeat it: common stocks are *not* simply a form of collectible such as Chinese jade, French Impressionist paintings, Oriental rugs, or Latvian postage stamps, all of which derive *their* value from strictly esthetic (rather than truly economic) considerations. That is, such items as antiques, stamps, and paintings derive their worth from the fact that they are considered esthetically pleasing and therefore desirable to hold or look at or own; they do not generate a return on their own but only indirectly provide a return (positive or negative) when they are sold to another collector at a profit or loss. To that extent, the collector or "investor" in collectibles is subject to the whims, fads, and fancies of others: the coin, postage stamp, or painting does not change, but its value in others' eyes (and, therefore, in the marketplace) does over time, subjecting the collector to the consequences of price changes that may be totally unpredictable and solely psychologically (rather than economically) based.

For the most part, however, this is not true of common stock certificates. Their value generally does not come from their color, the quality of their printing, the signatures affixed thereon, their design, or any of the other factors which give value to rare books, postage stamps, and prints. No one I know ever bought shares of IBM, General Motors, or American Telephone because of the color or design on their stock certificates, and I doubt if anyone ever will.

Rather, common stocks are valued not for the esthetic characteristics of their certificates but for what they *represent:* proportionate interests in productive or potentially productive corporate enterprises. The investor in common stocks is not simply buying pieces of paper, no matter how pretty or ugly they might be. Rather, the investor is acquiring interests in the assets, earnings, cash flow, and dividends of the companies issuing those certificates.

What this means is that the common stock investor is not solely at the mercy of changing moods and fashions. By making an intelligent investment in the stock of a well-managed, profitable, growing company, the investor will realize a satisfactory return on the investment, at least through dividend payments, over time, even if other investors become disenchanted with the stock for non-economic reasons. But the "investor" in collectibles always remains dependent upon the attitudes of other collectors toward his or her holdings, since art, antiques, stamps, and the like, handsome and rare though they may be, have no intrinsic or productive value of their own, independent of their value in others' eyes.

Now, if the real value of common stocks is a function of the real value of the assets, earning power, and dividend-paying ability of the companies they represent, then it is the level and potential growth of those assets, earnings, and dividends that ultimately will determine the value of common stocks—no matter what fads and foolishness may prevail over short periods. And in a politically stable, basically capitalistic, growing country like the United States, that suggests that common stocks should prove to be solid investments—and inflation hedges—over time. As, indeed, they have been.

Incidentally, common stocks have other advantages over collectibles as investments which should not be overlooked. Among those are the much greater *liquidity* of equities than, say, ceramics, art, or real estate. For most major common stocks, one can almost always get a reasonable bid, generally within pennies a share of its last price, on one of the principal stock exchanges or in the over-the-counter market. Contrast that with the weeks or months which may transpire in attempting to negotiate the sale of a non-fungible piece of real estate or a one-of-a-kind antique, as well as the wide spreads between bid and asked prices in those markets.

Similarly, one always has a good idea of what his or her stocks are worth—an investor can call a broker or check a newspaper to determine the price at which they last sold, generally only minutes or hours before. Not so with other collectibles, whose most recent market valuation could be weeks, months, or even years old.

Finally, it is worth noting that shareowners spanning a broad range of risk classes can tailor their holdings to meet their specific investment needs. Common stocks run the gamut from highly conservative (such as A.T.&T.) to highly speculative (such as start-up, wildcat drillers). Those willing to accept a higher level of risk in return for a greater profit potential can leverage themselves, either through the use of margin accounts or through the purchase of common stock options on one of the five major options exchanges.

Common stocks in different times

Noted market pundit Eldon Grimm, writing in the *Financial Analysts Journal,* commented "If you want to make your pile, you have to be in style." He may not be a great poet but he does know investing well. Industries and individual stocks come into and go out of style continuously on Wall Street. During depressions, recessions, and economic recoveries, deflation and inflation, peace times and war times, there have always been ways to make money in the stock market. Successful investors have been those most able to identify promising investment opportunities before the crowd has, and before the big price movements have taken place. Conversely, successful investors have been willing to get out after a large move has taken place, often selling to less sophisticated investors who have latched on too late.

What represented the most fundamentally attractive investment opportunities on Wall Street in the past? During World War I, Bethlehem Steel was strongly favored, and it rose from $10 a share in 1914 to $200 one year later. During the 1920s, a decade of unrivaled prosperity, the introduction of talking pictures propelled Warner Bros. from $10 in 1927 to $138 in 1928, while the growing popularity of radio enabled RCA to soar from $19 in 1922 to $101 in 1929. Tragically, however, prosperity turned to speculative excess as the decade ended. Between March 1928 and

September 1929, Montgomery Ward rose from $133 to $467, for example, and General Electric from $129 to $396, and those excesses laid the foundation for the bust that followed. Investors, some of whom undoubtedly missed the tremendous advance that had been posted by the market earlier in the decade, became increasingly convinced that what goes up would continue to go up, and plunged into stocks right at their peaks. Within two months, G.E. tumbled to $168, RCA to $28. Within three years, G.E. was $9, RCA $3. From its 1929 high to its 1932 low, the Dow Jones Industrials declined by about 90 percent. What goes up, especially sharply, becomes increasingly vulnerable to a correction. But more on that later.

What about the Depression? After the market touched bottom in 1932, the handful of individuals who still had money to invest found plenty of opportunities to make it grow. The market as a whole did well following its post-1929 collapse, despite the woeful state of the economy. The Dow Industrials more than quadrupled during the five-year period from 1932 to 1937. Gold stocks were in special favor; Homestake Mining climbed from $81 to 1931 to $544 in 1936. The repeal of Prohibition propelled National Distillers from $13 in 1932 to $124 only a year later.

When World War II ended, the market entered its longest bull phase in recent memory. Between 1949 and 1966 the Dow Industrials rose from about 160 to just under 1,000. Like the 1920s, the 1960s witnessed periods of rampant speculation following on the heels of a long and, for the most part, fundamentally justifiable rise in stock prices. Increasingly dominated by institutional investors, Wall Street latched on to growth stocks early in the decade and bid the price of issues such as IBM, Texas Instruments, Microwave Associates, and Perkin-Elmer up to as many as 85 times earnings.

Corporate names implying that a company was a participant in the burgeoning electronics industry drew enormous investor attention: Astron, Dutron, Transitron, Vulcatron, Circuitronics, Supronics, Videotronics and Electrosonics were, to many investors, irresistible. New issues, particularly ones with faddish names like these, were offered in record numbers. Some doubled in price during their first day of public trading and quadrupled within a year. Not surprisingly, many of the investors who caught speculative fever in 1959–1961 paid the piper in 1962, during which Texas Instruments, for example, plunged from $207 to $49, Microwave Associates from $60 to $8, and Perkin-Elmer from $84 to $25. During this period, many new issues became nearly or totally worthless.

The 1960s was also the decade in which multi-industried "conglomerates" became market leaders. Through creative accounting, many conglomerators were able to convince Wall Street that their companies were growing rapidly when they were hardly growing at all. They gobbled up one company after another, issuing either common stock, which was often selling at outlandish ratios of market price to earnings (or P/E ratios), or convertible preferreds or bonds (which kept the outstanding share base small and boosted earnings per share). Such leading conglomerates as Automatic Sprinkler, Litton Industries, and Teledyne were bid up to as many as 50 times earnings at the 1967 peaks. Guess what happened then. Of course. Litton announced lower earnings, faith in the sustainability of the industry's earnings growth was shaken, and investors sold with a vengeance. By 1969 Litton had dropped from $120 to $35, Teledyne from $72 to $28, and Automatic Sprinkler from $74 to $11. The moral: what goes up, especially sharply, becomes increasingly vulnerable to a correction.

Finally, let's remember the 1970s, the decade in which so-called "one-decision" stocks as Disney, Hewlett-Packard, International Flavors, McDonald's, and Polaroid sold for 65–90 times earnings while everything else languished. The one-decision stocks were those for which earnings and share prices were expected to rise indefinitely so that the investor could hold them forever. The only decision necessary was when to buy.

The result was a "two-tier" market, the top tier being the high-priced one-decision stocks and the bottom tier everything else. Predictably, the one-decision concept was a bad decision, and things reverted fairly quickly—and extremely painfully—to a one-tier market by the end of the decade. Investors in one-decision growth stocks belatedly recognized that even those vaunted issues had limits to their growth and value potential. The moral? By now you could say it in your sleep.

What has this short tour of twentieth century stock market history taught us? That at the right time, and at the right price, it has been possible to make large sums of money in steel, movies, gold, distillers, electronics, growth stocks, new issues, and conglomerates. In recent years, office equipment, airline, recreational vehicle, gambling, and other issues have also been winners. We also should have learned, however, that by the time a given group has had a big run-up, the potential rewards have been greatly reduced and the potential risks substantially increased. More often than not, the best time to buy is when everyone else is selling, and vice versa. This is where a bit of perversity, coupled with patience, can produce profits.

Common stocks, bonds, and inflation

Perhaps the most ambitious and informative work comparing returns on common stocks with inflation was done by Roger G. Ibbotson at the Graduate School of Business of the University of Chicago and

Rex A. Sinquefield of the American National Bank & Trust Company of Chicago. Their recent study compared total rates of return for common stocks, long-term corporate bonds, long-term government bonds, and Treasury bills with the Consumer Price Index over the 53-year period from 1926 through 1978. Total returns comprised dividend and interest income and capital gains or losses. Common stock performance was measured utilizing the broad-based Standard & Poor's 500 Stock Index.

What Ibbotson and Sinquefield discovered was that, over the 53-year period, common stocks provided an average annual total return of about 9 percent compared with 4 percent for long-term corporates, just over 3 percent for long-term governments, and about 2.5 percent for U.S. Treasury bills. During the same period, inflation, as measured by the CPI, averaged 2.5 percent annually. Clearly, over the past half century, common stocks have kept well ahead of inflation, and have significantly outperformed alternative fixed-rate investments. Generally speaking, stocks fared least well during periods of deflation, such as from 1926 through 1932, and periods of very high inflation, such as from 1973 through 1978. During the period between 1948 and 1968 when the cost of living was rising at a moderate rate, the S&P 500 outstripped the CPI in 16 out of 21 years.

What went wrong in the 1970s?

Yet, after topping 995 in 1966, the Dow Jones Industrials retreated, hitting a low of 578 in 1974 and rising to only 839 at the end of 1979. Adjusted for inflation, the Dow Industrials lost 65 percent of their value from 1966 to 1979, hardly a record designed to stimulate confidence. After more than a decade of relatively miserable performance, the stock market had trouble convincing people that it would ever again outrun inflation.

How badly did stocks perform compared with other investment vehicles? The definitive answer comes courtesy of Robert S. Salomon, Jr., of Salomon Brothers, who compiled compound annual growth rates for 13 well-known investment vehicles spanning the 1968–1979 period. According to the study, gold, Chinese ceramics, and postage stamps each appreciated in value at a 19 percent compound annual rate during the period; rare books at 16 percent, silver at 14 percent, non-gold U.S. coins and old-master paintings each at 13 percent, diamonds at 12 percent, farmland at 11 percent, single-family homes at 10 percent, a basket of foreign currencies at 6 percent, high-grade corporate bonds at 6 percent, and common stocks at 3 percent. During the same period, the CPI rose at a 6½ percent annual rate.

In the 11 years through 1979, common stocks finished last, trailing far behind such non-traditional investments as ceramics, stamps, rare books, and fine paintings and lagged the CPI by more than 50 percent. Not surprisingly, many investors lost faith in common stocks and abandoned Wall Street altogether. Others balked at paying the kinds of P/E multiples that they would have considered bargains in the past, especially in light of the high competitive returns available from alternative short-term, less risky money market instruments. Uncertainty about the economy, especially about inflation, was high. The severe 1974–1975 recession, long periods of high inflation, high interest rates, and bouts of high unemployment soured many people on the stock market. Thus, even though corporate earnings and dividends continued to grow at a pace higher than the rate of inflation over the past decade, investors were willing to pay only about 8 times earnings for stocks overall, compared with 18 times earnings in 1973. Clearly, it was this dramatic downward revaluation in the "appraisal" of equities in the marketplace, and not an inability on the part of most corporations to grow at or in excess of the inflation rate, that accounted for the stock market's dismal performance in the 1970s.

Should the 1980s be better?

To my mind, there are five key reasons why stocks should shine in the 1980s.

1. By most statistical benchmarks—price-earnings multiples, dividend yields, ratios of market values to book values—common stocks are cheaper today than they have been in three decades. And the time to be a buyer, as we have seen, is when something is unpopular.

The market, as measured by the S&P 400 Industrial Stock Index, has recently been selling at a lower multiple of earnings (a lower price/earnings ratio) than at any time in the past 30 years and at about 50 percent of the multiple it commanded in the 1960s. In addition, many companies are selling at sizable discounts from stated book value and even larger discounts from replacement value. For example, E. F. Hutton's Equity Research Department follows more than 900 companies intensively. Our analysts expect those 900-plus companies to increase their earnings at an average annual rate of 12 percent during the first half of the 1980s, and their stocks are presently yielding more than 5 percent, based on the most recent quarterly dividends. Consequently, even if P/E ratios were to remain at their present depressed levels and dividends were not raised at all, the typical stock we follow could provide shareholders with an average annual pretax total return of about 17 percent over the next 5 years (assuming our analysts' growth expectations are achieved). That return would be almost twice the 53-year average return derived from the Ibbotson-Sinquefield study.

2. Considering the degree to which common stock prices have lagged

those of gold, stamps, rare books, and diamonds over the past decade, equities today are substantially undervalued vis-a-vis those tangible alternatives and, therefore, appear to offer greater appreciation potential.

Bear in mind the moral of our brief jog through the canyons of Wall Street. That's right. What goes up, especially sharply, becomes increasingly vulnerable to a correction. Between 1968 and 1979, according to the Salomon study, gold, Chinese ceramics, and postage stamps each increased almost sevenfold; rare books fivefold; silver, rare coins, and old-master paintings fourfold; and diamonds, farmland, and single-family homes threefold. In stark contrast, common stocks were up only 40 percent. Now you tell me who should be able to sleep at night and who should not!

3. A growing conviction on the part of more sophisticated investors that stocks represent excellent value could rub off on others in the decade ahead.

You probably have noticed a rather hectic level of merger and take-over activity in the stock market in recent years. The activity stems in no small part from a growing awareness on the part of large corporations that stock prices today do not adequately reflect the full value of their underlying assets. Because the gap between price and value is often quite large, many corporations have been willing to pay substantial premiums over market value (in some cases as much as 100 percent) for the stock of companies they are interested in acquiring. Also, numerous corporations are buying back their own shares at what they consider to be bargain basement prices. It shows that corporate chieftains think stocks are cheap. Both of these trends are likely to persist over the near term, and the value-awareness displayed by large corporations could well rub off on other types of investors in the years ahead.

4. Institutional demand for (a relatively stable supply of) stocks could increase dramatically, putting substantial upward pressure on stock prices.

Equities have faced stiff competition in recent years from sky-high interest rates that have been offered on a variety of alternative cash-equivalent investments. Institutional investors like banks, insurance companies, and pension funds have been reluctant to commit funds to the stock market. Pension funds alone (the largest single source of investment capital in the United States) now appear to have $250 billion of their more than $500 billion of assets tied up in non-equity investments. A gradual shift out of fixed-rate, income oriented investments and back into equities by these goliaths over the next few years, prompted in part by a return to more normal interest rate levels, would significantly increase the demand for a relatively fixed supply of common stocks.

Demand would also rise sharply, simply if a greater percentage of new funds were earmarked for stocks. In the late 1960s private pension funds were putting 100 percent of all new funds they received into stocks and also were liquidating bonds to buy stocks. In 1979, only 10–15 percent of their new funds were directed to new equity commitments. But the pendulum has a way of swinging. In a late 1979 poll of 60 institutions that manage more than $100 billion of pension fund assets, *Institutional Investor* discovered that fully two-thirds of the respondents planned to increase their equity holdings over the near term. Similarly, demand for common stocks could increase if foreign investors, lured by attractive values, favorable exchange rates, and high levels of political and economic security in the United States, become more aggressive buyers. This trend will be accentuated if foreigners feel that the erosion of the dollar vis-a-vis other currencies has been reversed.

5. Finally, the general economic environment of the 1980s should be more conducive to a rise in share prices than were conditions in recent years.

Americans appear to be increasingly vocal in their demands for less government regulation and spending, reduced taxes, a balanced budget, tight control over inflation, and greater incentives to save and invest. Congress is starting to listen and reflect this mood. Passage of Proposition #13 in California was quickly followed by enactment of similar spending/taxing restrictions in a dozen other states. The airline industry has been deregulated and the trucking industry may be next. Capital gains taxes have been reduced and the investment tax credit has been liberalized. All of these moves—and others designed to reduce inflation, strengthen the dollar, and generally provide a healthier economic climate in this country—should help to rebuild investors' confidence in the economy and the stock market in the 1980s and should have a favorable influence on stock prices.

Which types of stocks should one consider?

If it makes sense to build an investment portfolio for the 1980s around common stocks, we must try to determine which types of stocks could be the most rewarding in the decade ahead. As we saw earlier, at virtually any moment in time during the twentieth century, there has seemed to be an industry, a group, or a concept worth investing in. Many of the stocks that were especially strong market performers represented companies that were selling products or services that were strongly in demand (Bethlehem Steel during World War I, National Distillers following the lifting of Prohibition, and gambling stocks after casinos were legalized in Atlantic City, for example). Common stock selection tends to be a common-sense thing. You need to identify value, buy before a stock or industry is in the headlines, and have some patience. It is also a good idea to be ready to admit mistakes. Do not hesitate to sell when your premise for making a commitment has been wrong.

Looking to the 1980s, several industries appear well positioned:

1. Energy.
2. Capital goods.
3. Health care services.
4. Semiconductors.
5. Instrumentation.
6. Forest products.
7. Defense.

Energy

Although petroleum will continue to be the world's main energy source in the 1980s, it is highly unlikely that sufficient new reserves will be discovered to meet future requirements. Production cannot keep growing indefinitely and, as energy demand increases, oil is expected to supply a diminishing share of worldwide energy. In all probability, most of the large, easy-to-reach reserves have already been found. New discoveries will likely be made at greater depths, in more remote areas, and at higher costs. To counter those higher costs and the greater uncertainty relating to future oil discoveries, coal, nuclear, solar, and other alternative energy sources will have to be developed and will meet a steadily increasing share of the world's growing energy demand. While oil has been in the headlines constantly in recent years, many alternative energy sources have not. They are likely to receive greater attention from the media in the decade ahead, however, and many coal, nuclear, and solar energy stocks still seem reasonably priced.

The OPEC nations, which own about 50 percent of the world's oil production and 60 percent of the remaining reserves, control both the pricing and availability of oil supplies, and can be expected to limit production in order to keep prices rising at least in line with inflation. As a result, oil reserves almost anywhere in the world will become more valuable. From an investment viewpoint, those companies that own or are developing significant reserves, or have access to large production in the more politically stable areas of the world, are in favorable competitive positions and should enjoy increasing earnings and cash flows in the years ahead. Investment in these companies should also provide some hedge against inflation due to the increasing value of their oil and other assets.

Capital goods

Seldom has the outlook for the capital goods sector of the economy been as promising as it is today. Worldwide population is projected to reach 6 billion by the year 2000, a 50 percent increase in just 20 years. The world will need more food and housing and better transportation. It will need to construct more factories, schools, hospitals, and office buildings and to develop more of its natural resources including coal, timber, and minerals. Further, since energy and capital resources are finite, increasingly sophisticated fuel- and labor-efficient equipment will be needed to do the job. The technological strengths of the U.S. capital goods industry appear to ensure its full participation in this global boom. A heightened awareness in the United States of the need to increase productivity (as a means of reducing inflation), as well as to conserve fuel and develop alternative energy sources, should also be beneficial.

Health care services

The continuing well-above-average earnings gains of the leading hospital management companies are expected to continue in the 1980s. Increased spending for health care in the United States, the development of new medical services and technologies, and expansion of total capacity via aggressive construction and acquisition programs should favorably affect earnings for the group. Finally, many of the voluntary, charitable, and religious hospitals throughout the country, lacking the financial resources, management skills, and economies of scale needed to operate efficiently in the current economic environment, may turn to the professional hospital management companies for certain management services or may turn out to be acquisition candidates.

Semiconductors

To some observers, semiconductors appear ready to do for our nation in the 1980s what crude oil did for it in the 1950s and 1960s. They will fuel and lubricate the continuing advances in technology that are needed to increase productivity, minimize energy consumption, and improve our standard of living. Fast-paced advances in semiconductor technology are paving the way for a variety of new product introductions in the computer, telecommunications, instrumentation, and defense industries. The industry continues to offer more complex solid state devices incorporating more useful functions at a considerably reduced cost. A significant upgrading of the microprocesor (a computer on a chip first introduced during the 1970s) will make it the industry's major product area for the 1980s. By incorporating on a chip more and more of the routine programming needed by most users, manufacturers will be able to bring a wider variety of products to a broader array of customers. Millions of small computers, programmed to do a few specific jobs and a number of larger, complex chores, will be offered. Real growth for the industry as a whole is expected to average about 20 percent annually over the next decade.

Instrumentation

Analytic, test, and measuring instruments are a cornerstone of increased productivity. Measurement and analysis increases efficiency and reduces costs. Increasing government regulation in the areas of health, safety, and the environment should increase demand for these products. A steady flow of new and improved products, many utilizing chip technology, will be able to perform functions at reduced costs, thus enhancing prospects for instrumentation in the 1980s.

Forest products

The 1980s began on the wrong foot for the forest products companies. With new home construction accounting for about 40 percent of total lumber and plywood demand, the sharp decline in 1980 housing starts, to about 1.3 million units from 1.7 million in 1979, adversely affected profits. Beyond 1981, however, and for most of the remainder of the decade, the forest products industry is expected to do well. With the passing of the recession, housing starts should recover to the 2 million level by 1982–83, and remain in that vicinity over the balance of the decade in order to meet expected strong demand. Demographic trends in the prime home-buying age group will be highly favorable. While the near-term market outlook for forest products is less than robust, pent-up and growing demand for new homes should lead to higher earnings and rising stock prices in this group in the years ahead.

Defense

Spending will almost certainly increase steadily during the 1980s. The need to strengthen the U.S. defense posture relative to the Soviets is widely recognized. After years of neglect following the Vietnam War, concerted efforts are necessary to develop and procure the technology, weapons systems, manpower, and operating supplies needed to enlarge and improve our military forces. While no crash program is anticipated, healthy increases in "real" military outlays are scheduled well into the decade. Many aerospace, electronics, and other suppliers will benefit, and those defense contractors that also participate in the growing commercial jetliner market have special investment appeal. The countercyclicality of earnings, rising dividend payments, and a high degree of confidence in projected earnings gains should lead to improvement in relative P/E ratios.

Conclusion

Objectivity, a value orientation, and patience have been the cornerstones of investment success in the past. You will need all of them in the 1980s.

What you must avoid at all costs are big mistakes, the kinds that greedy, unthinking, and unsophisticated investors made in the late 1920s and during much of the 1960s in the stock market.

And you *can* avoid them. You have learned the moral of the "What goes up . . . " story. You understand that those who made money in gold, stamps, rare books, and fine paintings bought *before* prices tripled and quadrupled, *not after*. Finally, you realize that, even if P/E ratios do not widen at all and dividends are not raised one penny, stocks offer you the opportunity to move, and remain, well ahead of inflation in the 1980s.

While such alternative investments as precious metals and diamonds have a place in many portfolios, income-producing stocks and bonds in combination should represent the backbone of any investment program and should generally account for between 50 and 75 percent of total investable assets (exclusive of the value of one's home). We would opt for the higher end of that range when the market is relatively depressed and the lower end after a substantial increase in share prices has occurred.

Of course, it would be foolish to expect everything to turn out precisely as we have outlined it. There is no certainty in forecasting of any sort—least of all in the area of investments. Some of the industries we have singled out as especially attractive, for example, may fare poorly for reasons no one could predict today, while others we have not even mentioned might do very well. But in the absence of clairvoyance, which no one we know has, we think it most prudent to base an investment program on the kind of reasoned examination and analysis of facts that we have attempted in this chapter. Indeed, we know of no better way to start.

So what are you waiting for? Sharpen your pencil, turn on your calculator, and open your *Wall Street Journal*. The stock market awaits you.

A Question of Maturity

Sidney Homer

In December of 1928, Joe and Mary X sold their family business for $2 million and retired young. Each got half of the proceeds and both were determined to invest it for a safe income to last, they hoped, for the rest of their lives. They did not want to worry about quotations, Wall Street, interest rates, or anything.

Joe bought a block of prime New York State 4s due in 1958 (30-year bonds) at a price of 100 to yield him a safe 4 percent, or $40,000 a year. Mary wanted to do a little better so she bought a block of then good grade New York City 4s of 1958 at 98 to yield 4.12 percent. She loved that extra .12 percent. She was $1,200 a year ahead of her husband. And so they sailed away to a life of travel and fun, and the income came in regularly twice a year and they never looked at a paper or a quotation.

Let us look. Came the panic followed by the Great Depression. Seven years later, in 1935, Joe's New York State 4s were selling at a price of 130 to yield 2.30 percent. That was an era of low interest rates but only for prime credits like New York State. At the same time, Mary's New York Cities were under a credit cloud and were selling at a price of 65 to yield 7.10 percent. At these prices, Joe could sell his New York States and buy two city bonds for every State bond, a move that would double the maturity value of his bonds and greatly increase his income.

Of course he did no such thing. He didn't even know about the market price of these investments. He and Mary still had their bonds in 1958 and both were paid off at 100. Who won? Technically, Mary, of course; she collected the extra income. But she took an inordinate risk to get a small reward. Joe's investment policy was much the wiser. Also, if they had known about the market, would Joe have capitalized on the steep profit on his States in the 1930s and 1940s? Probably not; that would reduce his income and he would have to live on part of his capital gain (taxable). Worse still, if she had been aware of those quotations, Mary might well have panicked and sold out her Cities at a disastrous loss and taken a major cut in her income.

This little case history (based on actual market quotations) raises several important questions for the bond investor. It illustrates the dynamics of the market for bonds of all quality groups. For example, these New York States sold as high as a price of 159 in 1940, up 59 percent from 1928 cost. Such paper profits or losses mean nothing, however, unless they lead to action: sales at premiums or, if depressed, buying. And as all bonds approach within a few years of maturity, both premiums and discounts tend to vanish.

A dynamic market

The bond market is highly dynamic, full of opportunities for profit and loss. The tradition, however, up to a few years ago, was quite the opposite. It was widely assumed that high grade bonds were dull, stable investments paying a small return. I well remember the trouble I used to have persuading people that high grade bonds were dynamic. When I would meet a lovely lady at a party, often she would say, "Oh, Mr. Homer, you are in Wall Street. Come over here and tell me all about the market." But when I came over and explained that I was a bond man, she would drift politely away. Not today! Widows—and other investors—love 14 percent.

Today, private investors large and small are buying bonds in enormous quantities at 10 percent, 12 percent, and even 14 percent. Low-bracket investors (45 percent effective tax rate or more) are buying Treasury bills, notes and bonds, and corporate bonds. High-bracket investors are buying tax exempt notes and bonds. Some accept lower quality for maximum yield but most insist on high quality. Some prefer short maturities where the yields are about as high as long maturity yields or higher. Others who want assurance of high income over a long period buy long-term bonds for income. Still others buy long-term discount bonds, hoping for capital gains in addition to income. For example, if yields were to return to their 1965 levels, a discount long 5 percent bond bought at today's prices would appreciate 140 percent. More modestly, if yields returned to their 1976 level, the gain would be a worthwhile 33 percent. Corresponding losses would of course be a possibility, some would say a probability. In any event, small and large investors are buying all sorts of bonds. The income at today's rates does not quite offset the rate of inflation but it comes closer to doing so than any other marketable investment medium that enjoys airtight guaranteed payments.

Short maturities versus long maturities

Every department of the bond market is dynamic. This is so in prosperous times as well as in times of crisis or depression. Some long-term investors, hoping to avoid the dynamics of the long-term bond market, seek protection in a portfolio of short-term paper: Treasury bills, short bonds and notes, or short municipal paper. If income is important, they can be penalized because short interest rates are much more variable than long-term bond yields. The dynamics of long-term, high grade bonds is entirely in their wide price fluctuations. For shorts, the price scarcely changes, but the rate of return swings widely.

Thus, if Joe X in 1928 had bought short Treasury Bills or commercial paper, he would have obtained 4.5 percent, a satisfactory income. This rate or higher lasted for a year or so, but alas, in 1930, when he rolled over his shorts and bought new shorts, the rate was down to 2 percent. So his income was cut in half, a family tragedy. But worse was to come. In 1931, his rate of income from short bills was again cut in half in a single year. He now had to live on 1 percent. And soon even this rate declined and stayed at nominal levels for over a decade. No, Joe did not escape the dynamics of the market if he sought refuge in shorts. Short securities are valuable for many reasons and for many investors, but not as a means to avoid the dynamics of the market. Table 4-1 is a summary of U.S. Treasury three month bill rates during recent years. All high grade, short securities fluctuated about as much.

Looking now at long-term, high grade corporate bonds, Exhibit 4-1 shows the life history to date of Atchison, Topeka & Santa Fe General 4s of 1995, in terms of annual high and low prices, since they were issued in 1895 as 100-year non-callable first mortgage bonds. These bonds used to be market leaders in the market for prime credits. The chart also shows a market average of prime corporate bond yields, the dotted line, adjusted for 4 percent coupon due in 1995. It will be seen that the Atchison bonds followed closely the prime average with the exception of two periods: their first 10 years, when they were becoming seasoned and achieving their prime credit rating, and a few years in the late 1930s when all rails were under a credit cloud.

Exhibit 4-1. Life history of a bond.

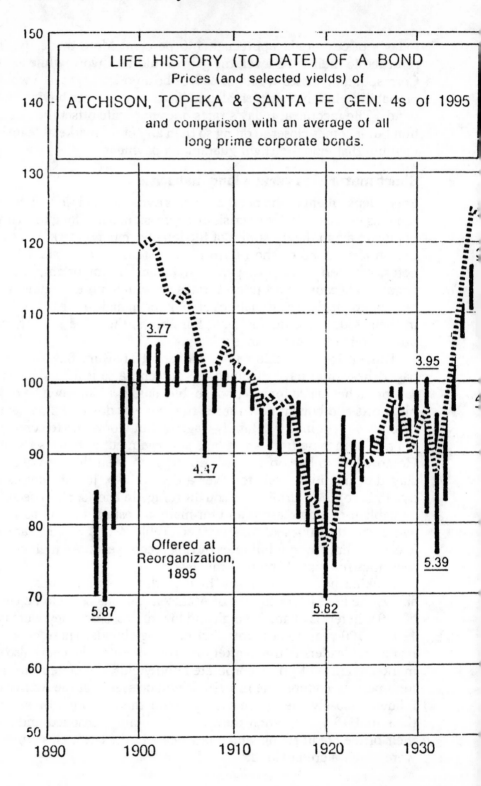

LIFE HISTORY (TO DATE) OF A BOND
Prices (and selected yields) of
ATCHISON, TOPEKA & SANTA FE GEN. 4s of 1995
and comparison with an average of all
long prime corporate bonds.

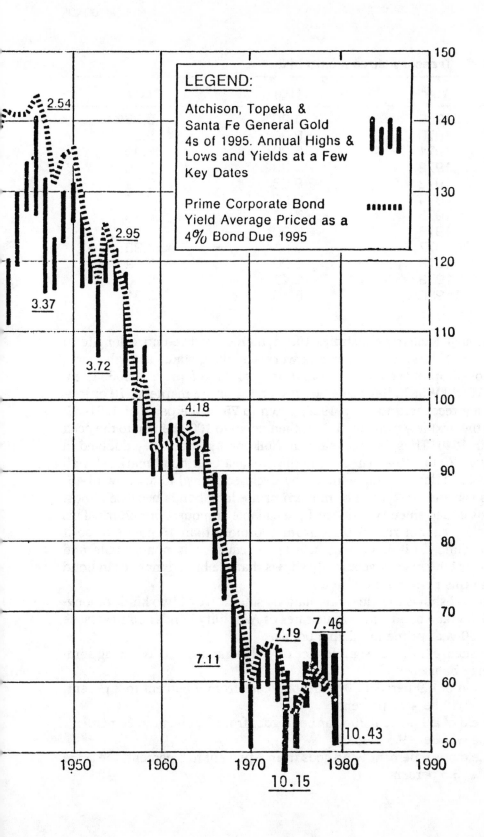

LEGEND:

Atchison, Topeka &
Santa Fe General Gold
4s of 1995. Annual Highs &
Lows and Yields at a Few
Key Dates

Prime Corporate Bond
Yield Average Priced as a
4% Bond Due 1995

2.54

2.95

3.37

3.72

4.18

7.46

7.19

7.11

10.43

10.15

150

140

130

120

110

100

90

80

70

60

50

1950   1960   1970   1980   1990

Table 4-1. Treasury three month bills.

Year	High	Low
1965	4.20%	3.86%
1970	8.00	5.25
1971	5.30	3.40
1972	4.88	3.35
1973	8.66	5.72
1974	9.00	7.26
1975	7.10	5.18
1976	6.20	4.50
1977	·6.21	4.33
1978	9.00	6.12
1979	12.47	9.60
1980	16.55	6.31

Exhibit 4-1 clearly illustrates the dynamics of the entire long-term bond market. First, as these bonds were achieving status as high grade, they moved up in the market from a price of 70 to a price of 105. Then, during World War I, they came down with the entire market to 70 or less. Then they recovered to 95 in 1928, down to 75 in the panic of 1931–32, then in the next few years up to 115, then down to 100, then up to the peak of 140 in 1946. Thus, in this, the great bull bond market, they doubled in price from 70 to 140+. Then came the greatest bear bond market for all time, 1946 to date, during which they declined from 140 to a low of 45.

This issue is not typical of modern prime long bonds because almost all bonds issued since World War I are callable at modest premiums. This means they cannot rise in price from 100 more than 15 points or so if yields decline. This issue was selected because it is non-callable and because its long history accurately shows that the high dynamics in bond prices in this period are not new.

Table 4-2 shows the yield fluctuations since 1970 of two kinds of long-term high grade bonds: new issue rates of AA utility bonds and new issue rates of 30-year prime municipal bonds.

To visualize the price significance of yield changes, the following summary may be useful:

If the yield of a 9 percent 30-year bond goes from 9 percent to 8 pecent, the price will be +11 percent.

If the yield of a 9 percent 30-year bond goes from 9 percent to 10 percent, the price will be −9.5 percent.

If the yield of a 6 percent bond goes from 6 percent to 5 percent, the price will be +15.5 percent.

If the yield of a 6 percent bond goes from 6 percent to 7 percent, the price will be −12.5 percent.

Table 4-2. Prime long-term bond yields.

Year	AA New Issue of Long-Term Utility Bonds		AAA Municipal 30 Year	
	High	Low	High	Low
1965	4.80%	4.40%	3.50%	3.15%
1970	9.20	8.25	6.95	5.25
1971	8.15	7.00	6.25	5.20
1972	7.60	7.25	5.30	5.00
1973	8.50	7.35	5.50	5.10
1974	10.40	8.05	6.50	5.15
1975	10.10	8.85	7.00	6.30
1976	9.20	8.13	6.40	5.50
1977	8.43	7.80	5.60	5.30
1978	9.55	8.65	6.15	5.40
1979	11.90	9.50	7.10	5.85
1980	14.75	10.88	9.30	6.75

Selection

The choice between long or short maturities is the investor's single most important decision. Often it is dictated by personal requirements. A person who will or may need the money in a few years will buy shorts. A person who is making a more or less permanent investment will have to choose among investment considerations. An investor who expects a long future period of rising interest rates will buy short maturities. A person who expects interest rates to be stable or lower in the years ahead will buy long-term bonds. Without a firm opinion on these points, an investor may buy some of each, the classical straddle. Interest rate trends will be discussed at the end of this chapter.

Selection of maturity is only a first step. The field of other choices is wide. This is a complex, many-faceted market. The first and most general choice is among these:

U.S. Government bills, notes, and bonds.

U.S. Agency notes (in a wide range of maturities).

Corporate notes and bonds (short, medium, and long maturities).

Municipal notes and bonds (short, medium, and long maturities).

An effective tax bracket over 45 percent may well limit an investor to municipals. If so, the first priority of all is maturity as discussed above. Almost as important is the choice of quality. This need not be a blind choice: good values are often found in medium grade or lower grade municipal and corporate bonds. The point is to be adequately paid for the risk. In both the corporate and municipal bond markets, the yield advantage from taking credit risk is highly dynamic. At times, there is very little yield spread in favor of medium grade (as when Mary X bought Cities). At other times, there is an excessive spread (as when Mary's Cities sold down to 65).

The investor in municipals should be careful about marketability; their marketability is usually very poor, but large issues are apt to enjoy good marketability. On no account should one buy odd lots (under $10,000 par), and really good marketability requires lots of $25,000 and up. There are, however, some no-load municipal mutual funds that provide professional management, diversification, and excellent marketability.

For the low-bracket investor or institution, one of the most important choices is between U.S. government and corporate bonds. At times, governments are by far the best buy when they yield almost the same as prime corporates. For example, at times in 1964 the new issues of corporate bonds provided only 12 basis points more yield than governments. Again, a few years later some prime corporates were offered to yield 200 basis points more than governments. As a consequence of this massive shift in yield spread, the subsequent price decline in the corporate bond market was twice as large as the price decline of long governments.

The corporate bond market has many subdivisions, some of which are: utility bonds; industrial bonds; finance bonds; railroad bonds and equipment trust certificates; convertible bonds. All are available in long, medium, and short maturities. All are available in various quality categories.

Convertible bonds are those that are convertible at various terms into the common stock of the issuing companies. At times, these are very popular, for they provide an opportunity to profit if the stock rises and some sort of floor if the stock declines. Alas, in many cases, this floor is not very reliable.

In the market for government agency notes, there are dynamic shifts in the yield spread of certain agencies compared with Treasuries of the same maturity. Sometimes this spread will be almost zero (if so, of course, Treasuries are to be preferred), sometimes very large (if so, agencies should be preferred). Again, there are dynamic shifts in the yield spreads between industrial and utility bonds of similar coupon and maturity. Finance bonds sometimes command excellent yields compared with other corporates and sometimes do not.

In the second and third grade bond market, there are hundreds of issues, often selling at high yields and carrying high risk. If purchased at the wrong time: disaster; if at the right time: handsome profit. For example, the first mortgage 3.5 percent bonds of Penn Central used to sell at 112 or higher and mistakenly were considered of prime quality. After bankruptcy, these bonds defaulted and sold down to a price of 13 with three years' interest unpaid. A good friend of mine bought a block of them at a price of 15. After the 1978 reorganization; they sold up to a price of 65. It is often said that the best time to buy second grade bonds is six months after they have defaulted. Such bonds do not fluctuate with any market; each issue is a thing unto itself.

Most of the time the various departments of the high grade bond market and also individual issues fluctuate at different rates, providing frequent opportunities for portfolio improvements. The active, sophisticated investor can sell overpriced issues from his or her portfolio and buy underpriced issues. A good rule is: every issue bought should be suitable to be held to maturity but none should be held to maturity. Today's best value is not apt to be a best value one year hence.

Another important choice is between new issues (or other issues selling around par) and discount issues of the same quality and maturity selling in the '70s or '80s. Discount issues are obviously much better protected from call and thus have much more profit potential. For this and other technical factors, discount issues fluctuate much more widely than issues selling around par and they usually yield less, in part because some of their yield will be capital gain. The rule is that in a bull bond market discount issues are to be preferred because they will rise more; in a bear bond market, par and especially premium issues are to be preferred because they will decline less. The differential in yield between discount and par issues is high variable and thus often presents attractive opportunities for switching back and forth.

The size of the great American bond market

The American capital market is one of the seven wonders of the world. There is nothing like it anywhere. Table 4-3 shows that in December 1979 the total of credit instruments then outstanding amounted to $3,730 billion, in other words almost $4 trillion, and the total was growing at a rate of nearly $400 billion a year. This should be considered a dangerous credit boom. It is the easy availability of credit at a high price and the willingness of borrowers to borrow huge amounts in spite of high yields that have financed inflation.

As the table shows, real estate mortgages are the largest credit instrument, growing at a rate of over $100 billion a year and reaching over $1 trillion. Next comes federal government debt, including the rapidly growing federal agency debt. Corporate bonded debt amounts to $476 billion;

if short-term corporate debt is added in, the total corporate debt is a huge $1,025 billion. Municipal debt is less. All of these figures are sensationally higher than they were ten years ago.

Table 4-3. The size of the credit market (estimated 12/31/79).

By Type of Credit Instrument		
Real estate mortages (publicly held)	$1,103	billion
Corporate (and foreign bonds)	476	
U.S. Government and Agency (publicly held) Debt	760	
Municipal bonds and notes	328	
Sub-total	2,667	
Short-term business borrowing	577	
Short-term consumer borrowing	489	
Total short	1,064	
Total credit	3,730	
By Type of Holder		
Institutions (non-bank)	$1,672	billion
Commercial banks	1,092	
Foreigners	299	
Miscellaneous	193	
Households	524	
Total credit	3,730	
Stocks outstanding at market	984	
Total	4,717	

Thus a large and receptive credit market is paradoxically both essential to American prosperity and a serious threat to our currency. Look around: almost everything you see is, or was, financed on credit: every factory, toll road, hospital, school, courthouse, hotel, office building, condominium, ship, bus, automobile, home. Much of this feverish building activity could not have occured 20 years ago. New credit forms have been invented; new leasing procedures, new types of credit and new forms of mortgages, many guaranteed by the federal government. And the basic money for all of this has been provided by the Federal Reserve Banks. Inflation requires ever larger doses of credit. Will it be financed in the years to come? Inflation is the chief cause of high interest rates. Interest rates in the future, as discussed below, will most probably rise or fall with the rate of inflation.

The lower part of Table 4.3 shows who has made all these loans or, more accurately, who owns these credit instruments. The largest creditors are non-bank institutions: savings and loan associations, savings banks, insurance companies, pension funds, and so forth. This group of investors, which tend to make long-term loans, are the principal bond buyers. Next come commercial banks; traditionally, they supply a large part of the short-term credit. Next in size of holdings come private investors (and some miscellaneous groups).

Private investors are the swingers. For 30 years until 1960 or so, they bought few bonds, except municipals, placing their savings largely in institutions. However, whenever market interest rates rose substantially above the rates the savings institutions paid, the public switched large amounts out of institutions into all sorts of credit instruments, some long-term, some short-term: governments, corporates, and municipals. In recent years, private investor holdings have grown to a very large $524 billion, but a glance at the public's remaining holdings of term bank deposits shows that there is a big future potential for more of the process, called by the ugly name of "disintermediation."

Finally, at the bottom of Table 4-3, is the total of American stocks outstanding at the market. While almost $1 trillion, this is less than one-quarter of the grand total.

Historic origins

The bond market as we know it today originated in the tiny Dutch Republic of the seventeenth century. Annuities had been a popular investment medium during earlier centuries: annuities on one life, or two lives, or perpetual. These annuities were not considered to be loans at interest, which were often illicit, but rather as guaranteed incomes which could be bought and sold. The principal of an annuity never had to be repaid but could be redeemed at the option of the debtor (usually a political body), which promised not to redeem for a stated number of years. Some are still outstanding. The danger was that the creditor would pay off the contract and the valuable income would stop. The wealthy Dutch burghers loved these perpetual annuities. They could retire rich from their East Indies or Baltic trade and live in style during old age, while the annuities assured the financial future of their families or their charitable endowments.

When, in the sixteenth century, the Reformation removed the ban on interest, an active money market developed in Amsterdam. Because the Dutch were fighting an 80-year war for liberation with the giant Spanish Empire, they needed money to hire German mercenaries. Therefore, the various provinces of tiny Holland issued a large quantity of perpetual annuities. A market for these annuities arose because they were very popular. The medieval rates on perpetual annuities had often been 8⅛ percent.In seventeenth century Holland, a series of dramatic refundings were carried out by a very capable government. The old 8⅛ percent annuities were retired; new 6s were issued, then refunded at 4 percent, and finally at 3½ percent. Investors rioted, protesting these low rates, but they bought nevertheless. In the meantime, the king of Spain was borrowing illicitly at 40 percent! Guess who won the war.

At this time, both stocks and bonds (annuities) were traded actively in Amsterdam, and most modern trading methods were invented: long positions, short positions, bulls and bears, hedges, options, manipulation, market letters, margins, syndicates, commercial paper, trade bills.

During the late seventeenth century, the Dutch William of Orange became William III of England, and promptly Dutch Finance (as it was called scornfully by the Tories) was imitated in the City of London. The Bank of England was established, a market for short-term Treasury bills was organized, the perpetual annuities were issued to pay for a war. Their rates started at 8⅛ percent, but in 25 years they came down to 3 percent. Near mid-century the whole English national debt was called in and refunded into the 3 percent Consols. These bonds, subsequently refunded as 2½ percent Consols, are still outstanding: no maturity date, refundable at 100 at the option of the State, recently selling around 15 to yield 16 percent.

The British made two improvements on the Dutch methods: they consolidated all annuities and thus achieved an active uniform market, and they made public all the finances of their government. This kind of market was only possible where the people had complete confidence in the financial integrity of their government.

During the eighteenth and nineteenth centuries, the British sold vast amounts of perpetual bonds. Usually the market rate rose in times of war to 6 percent or so (a price of 50 for the 3s) and declined in times of peace to 2½ percent or less. There was absolute worldwide confidence in sterling and in the Bank of England, which managed sterling (and was really managing the gold standard around the world). In a sense, during these centuries, Britain sold large amounts of bonds, and bought herself an empire with the proceeds.

These Consols were "the Funds" that we read about in Victorian novels. Many wealthy estates were in the Funds. When the market for these 3s declined sharply, old Soames Forsythe said, "The country's going to pot." There is a legend that the English Rothschild doubled his fortune by buying Consols during the Battle of Waterloo because his own private carrier pigeons brought him the news of victory a day before the market got it.

Of course, other industrial nations soon imitated Great Britain, and, on a smaller scale, each was successful according to the degree of confidence its people had in their government's integrity. An exception was one large European country which defaulted on its government debt four times in each of the last three centuries. It has no worthwhile capital market today. But most followed the British example.

Alexander Hamilton imported the British system to the United States. As soon as the new government was formed, he issued perpetual 6 percent bonds to refund the war debt of the Congress and the states. The act established the credit of the new country. Those bonds were redeemable at the pleasure of the government in an amount not exceeding 2 percent a year. In fact, due to a sinking fund, they were all paid off in the 1830s when the government had no debt. Perpetual bonds were issued from time to time. Fixed maturity dates did not appear until late in the Civil War and then they were usually 40 years or up to 100 years.

In the early days, such secondary market activity as there was for American government, municipal, and corporate securities took place mostly in Boston. After the Civil War, trading improved and much of the market went to the New York Stock Exchange. Railroad bonds appeared and dominated market activity. Some of these achieved prime status by 1880 or so. There were also many defaults by railroads and by states.

The last quarter of the nineteenth century saw a steep decline in bond yields from 6 percent or so to around 3 percent. During those years, many great historic fortunes were made by holding long-term non-callable bonds for capital gains, presumably on margins. For example, Morris & Essex 7s of 1915 rose in price from 97 in 1873 to 142 in 1899, while Chicago & Northwest 7s of 1915 rose from 83 in 1873 to 145 in 1899. By the turn of the century, Wall Street, the bond market, and the stock market were dominated by a group of great underwriting firms. Often they paid little attention to the secondary market for securities, and trading activity was therefore left to smaller firms. Anyone who wanted to was free to trade bonds over the counter.

Early in this century, wealthy investors made up almost the whole of the bond market; there were few large institutions. In the 1930s, for tax and other reasons, private investors of all sorts deserted the taxable bond market; at the same time institutions grew enormously and bought bonds. By the 1950s the bond market was almost entirely an institutional affair. Since 1967, however, high yields have attracted private investors, small and large, and at times they have cushioned the market when institutions were strapped.

The bond market today

In today's enormous American bond market, institutional investors are still predominant as they have been since the 1930s. This has had three consequences: (1) both underwriting and secondary bond market trading are predominantly over the counter, even though a good many issues are listed on the New York Stock Exchange; (2) the size of blocks of bonds traded is usually large, running from 100 bonds up to millions; (3) the market is intensely competitive and therefore dealer spreads (profit margins) are small.

All three of these facts make it more difficult for private investors to buy high grade bonds in modest-sized lots. Exceptions are convertible bonds and second grade bonds, which are more often traded on the New York Stock Exchange where the unit of trading is one bond ($1,000 par). However, now that private investors are back in the high grade market in a big way, some progress has been made toward servicing them efficiently, on or off the exchange. The problem is that a market structure suitable for institutions (big block trading) is unsuitable for most private investors. Odd lots are hard to buy and hard to sell in the secondary market.

Almost all bonds have a par value of $1,000. They are quoted as a percent of par; thus, one bond quoted at a price of 90 would cost $900. The unit of trading on the Stock Exchange is one bond, but almost all trading is in larger amounts. In recent years some securities have been offered in minimum size blocks of five or ten bonds or more.

There are three kinds of firms or functions in the bond business today: (1) the underwriters, who sometimes are purely wholesalers and often avoid all secondary market trading, even in their own issues; (2) the traders, who make markets in many or all issues and stand ready to buy for their own account if a customer or other dealer or broker wants to sell, or to sell from their positions if the customer (or dealer or broker) wants to buy. Some of these traders make very close markets, such as 99¾–100 or even 99⅞–100 bid and asked; (3) brokers, who take no positions, do no underwriting but execute customer orders for a commission, sometimes one-fourth point or one-half point.

A broker with a bond order will buy from or sell to a dealer (trader). This then involves two dealer profits, the broker's commission plus the trader's spread. Many firms carry on all three of these functions, underwriting, trading in the secondary market (sometimes only for their own issues, sometimes for the whole field), and brokerage for customers. There are also wholesale firms that do all three but only for large institutional customers and other dealers. Many of these firms also are active in the stock market, both for private investors and for institutions.

In the secondary market for bonds of all sorts, the difference between a good execution and a bad execution can be very large, especially for inactive bonds. Too much emphasis has been put in recent years on the size of brokerage commissions; the cost of doing business is often chiefly the spread between bid and asked, plus a brokerage commission. An experienced and diligent (on your behalf) broker can be worth much more than a cut-rate broker.

The typical private investor of small size will probably do best, in buying bonds, to buy a no-load bond fund which offers diversification, marketability, and management. The typical private investor of medium size (who buys in lots of $10,000 up) will have a stockbroker execute the bond order on a commission basis. Lacking a broker, the investor's bank will probably handle the transaction. The larger investor (lots of $50,000 up) can either give the business to a broker or go to a trading firm directly and perhaps save the commission. If the investor wants to buy bonds on margin, a broker or a bank can handle this. Some types of bonds, notably governments, can be carried on very narrow margins.

Now let us take another overview of today's bond market. We have discussed its size in terms of aggregates; let us look at the dramatis personae. There are quoted today 119 issues of federal government bonds and notes and 39 issues of Treasury bills. There are quoted 244 issues of federal agency notes. There are outstanding today over 5,000 issues of all sorts of corporate bonds. Thus, the institutions and lower-bracket investors have a vast choice of taxable issues to pick from. However, many of these corporate bond issues are so inactive that it is not worthwhile to try to buy them; dealers' bond quotation sheets will list most of the active issues each day. A recent dealer list quotes 277 issues of American corporate bonds and notes, mostly medium- and long-term.

No figures are available on the number of municipal bond issues outstanding, but most are tiny local loans. It is said that there are over 50,000 governmental units in the United States, all of which could issue bonds. For purposes of marketability, the investor should choose large issues. Also, unlike most corporate bonds, most municipal issues are in serial form, some due every year or six months, sometimes with a balloon on the long end. This subdividing of a bond issue reduces the marketability of all the bonds. Nevertheless, these tax-exempt bonds are very valuable to many investors and usually sell to yield much less than taxable bonds. The business is usually concentrated in new issues and for most general obligation municipal bonds the secondary market is often poor. Good secondary markets, however, often develop for large issues of tax-exempt revenue bonds.

The trend of bond yields, past and future

The most important decision for the bond investor is maturity: long maturity bonds, medium maturity bonds or short-term bills, or notes or bank deposits. The nature of the funds to be invested will often dictate the choice. If the funds are more or less permanent with no quick liquidity requirements for decades to come (like most pension funds, endowment funds, and Joe X), the investor will choose a maturity policy largely on the level of yields in a historic context and on the outlook for higher or lower yields.

Exhibit 4-2 traces high-grade new-issue bond yields monthly since 1959. The chart vividly portrays the second half of the greatest of all bear bond markets, which started in 1946 and is shown in full in the Atchison chart on a price basis. The chart shows that a long-term (secular) trend to high yields was from time to time interrupted by rallies which usually coincided with business recessions or mini-recessions as in 1959–60, 1966–67, 1968, 1970–71, and 1974–75. After these interruptions, yields continued to decline during the first years of business recovery, but then, as the recovery gathered steam, they rose again. During the last two recessions, yields continued to rise during the first half of the recession, due no doubt to inflation. The high yields pictured in this chart from 1969 on were far above any prime long yields that occurred in this country for the past century or more.

In judging the future of yields, the investor must assess two kinds of trends: (1) the medium-term (2–3 years) cyclical trends, which are closely tied in with the business cycle, and (2) the long-term secular trends, which often last many decades. This bear bond market is already over 30 years old and the preceeding bull bond market lasted 25 years. These long-term trends are caused by sociological and political worldwide trends. The rule seems to be that if both trends are moving in the same direction, we get a very large bull or bear bond market; if they are moving in opposite directions, we get a much smaller, briefer swing. The chart clearly shows the dominance of the great secular swing to higher yields up to the present.

The long-term investor should not pay much attention to the medium-term cyclical swings based on outguessing the business cycle. The soundest cyclical judgments have time and again been refuted by the great secular trend to higher yields.

Some students of the bond market believe its peak yields have been reached. Many more expect that the secular trend to higher yields has a way to go. The answer, of course, is intimately tied in with the future of inflation and this, in turn, is tied in with sociological trends and inter-

national tensions. America's devastating experience with double-digit inflation seems to be causing a swing towards a conservative political
philosophy on the part of a large body of voters. It is too early to say
whether this swing has gone far enough to permit politicians to take the
necessary painful steps to end the inflationary spiral. Each investor must
try to outguess this basic economic force.

Table 4-4 is a summary of available yields as of December 1980.

Table 4-4. Yield highlights on December 1980.

	Short Maturity [1 Year]	Medium Maturity [Around 10 Years]	Long Maturity [20-30 Years]
U.S. Treasury one-year bills	13.42%		
U.S. Treasury notes		12.50%	
U.S. Treasury bonds			12.20%
U.S. Agency notes		12.90%	
New issue AAA Utility Bonds		13.00%	13.75%
New issue AAA Industrial Bonds			12.75%
New issue A Utility Bonds		13.75%	14.50%
Seasoned Discount AAA Utility Bonds			13.00%
Seasoned Discount AAA Industrial Bonds			12.40%
New issue AAA G.O. Municipals	7.00%	7.60%	9.00%
New issue AA Electric Revenue			9.75%

Exhibit 4-2.

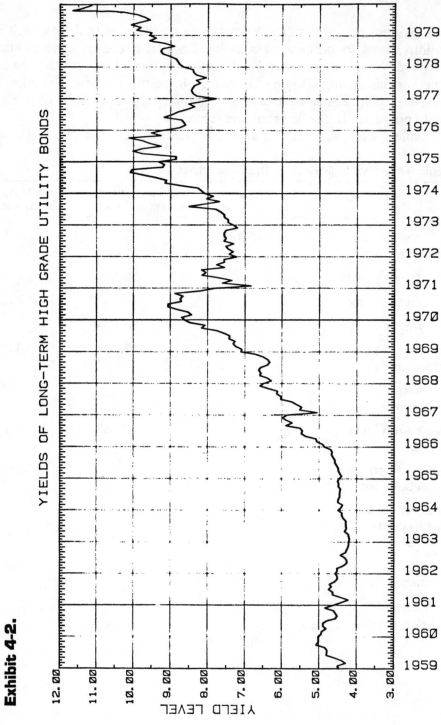

YIELDS OF LONG-TERM HIGH GRADE UTILITY BONDS

Safety in Numbers

Howard Stein

King William I of the Netherlands is not recorded in history books as a very successful king. Soon after the downfall of Napoleon, he was installed on the throne to rule over Belgium, as well as Holland. Within a few years he lost Belgium and later had to abdicate the throne of Holland. However, King William had at least one solid achievement to his credit: in 1822, he founded a company that was the forerunner of the modern investment company. Now called the Societe Generale de Belgique, the company has changed its structure, but is still in business. It has assets of more than $800 million and extensive investments in industry and finance in Belgium, Canada, and elsewhere.

The mutual fund industry in the United States, which can trace its roots to these regal beginnings, is now a prime example of economic democracy in America. Mutual funds, including money market funds, invest more than $130 billion for more than 10 million accounts. Approximately one dollar in every ten is entrusted to investment institutions. This is close to 2 percent of all the financial assets of Americans, including checking accounts, savings accounts, life insurance, and pension fund savings.

For years, mutual funds have offered the average investor a way to have a stake in stocks and bonds, without personally having to select the securities, and with the distinct advantage of pooling his or her money with the money of many other investors to hold shares in a portfolio that can include dozens, even hundreds, of different securities.

But anyone who was familiar with mutual funds in the 1950s and '60s would not recognize them today. Funds now offer financial services that were unheard of when the Dreyfus Lion first stalked out of the subways and onto full-page newspaper ads and television screens in 1958 to advertise The Dreyfus Fund. In addition to the traditional stock and bond vehicles, mutual funds now provide such services as cash management, check-writing privileges, income tax shelters, insurance plans, annuities—and, very importantly—higher *interest* on *savings* than is generally available from banks currently.

Sales methods also have changed drastically since the days when funds were sold primarily by armies of door-to-door salespeople, some of whom worked only part-time in the mutual fund industry. Today, many investors do business directly by mail or telephone with mutual fund main offices. Perhaps the greatest innovation of all is that mutual funds, once regarded chiefly as the "little person's" investment, now are being used by large institutions such as corporate pension funds, bank trustees, and other organizations that invest others' money. At the same time, the appeal of mutual funds to small investors continues to grow.

While the high interest rates paid by "money market" funds on spare cash have attracted the most attention, the funds that invest in stock have performed extremely well in recent years, in spite of very weak conditions in the stock market generally.

An independent service that reports on the performance of mutual funds, Lipper Analytical Distributors, found that over a period of five years ending September 1980, the average increase for all mutual funds was greater than for either of the two broadly based stock market averages: the Standard & Poor's 500 and the Dow Jones Industrial Average. The five-year gain for the mutual fund industry amounted to 127.21 percent, while the S&P 500 stocks rose only 90.75 percent and the Dow Jones Average only 54.07 percent. (All figures assume dividends were reinvested.) In fact, during the same period, the gain by the mutual funds was enough to keep ahead of the overall inflation rate. In other words, the average mutual fund investor who held shares during the 1975–80 period had good reason to be pleased with that decision. Very few investors who pick their own stocks could claim that their personal portfolio selections did as well.

One success story that already is a part of the folklore of the mutual fund industry is the spectacular performance of The Dreyfus Fund in the 1950s and 1960s when it "discovered" some of the great growth stocks of the period. This is a story I can tell without immodesty because, although I was involved with the Dreyfus organization at the time, the Fund was being run by its founder, Jack Dreyfus, Jr.

Polaroid first caught my attention before I joined the Dreyfus organization and before I knew that Jack Dreyfus also was interested in the stock. I began to follow Polaroid in the early 1950s when 3-D movies were introduced and became an instant vogue in movie theatres. I found that Polaroid manufactured the special lenses used for viewing the films, and thought the company might have investment possibilities. Later, I heard that the company also was working on an instant picture camera—a far more durable success than 3-D lenses—and, as it turned out, a far more significant basis for a rise in the value of the stock. When I joined Dreyfus and learned that the Dreyfus Fund had been acquiring Polaroid stock, we greatly expanded our holdings.

Purchase of Polaroid stock soon after its innovative camera became a gleam in the eye of its genius inventor, Edwin H. Land, was probably the Fund's single most successful coup. Dreyfus Fund started buying Polaroid stock in January 1953 when it was selling around 32¾. During the years that followed, the holdings were enlarged substantially and then reduced. After several splits, the cost basis of the original stock was $0.455 per share, a 60-fold increase in value when the position was finally closed.

The Polaroid story is now part of financial history, but there were other investment decisions during those years that also turned out extremely well for The Dreyfus Fund and its shareowners. For example: we invested early in American Motors because the company marketed a small car, well ahead of its time, and we sold the stock long before the company encountered its recent difficulties. We bought Lorillard Tobacco on the strength of the low-tar Kent cigarettes, also trend-setters in their field. We bought airline stocks in time for their boom market in the 1950s and 1960s and we were one of the first to recognize—and act on—the profit possibilities in Japanese stocks.

The late 1970s, a period of inflation and depressed equity prices, were much more difficult years for stock investments. As a result, the successes have not been as spectacular. Yet even during these years, there were a number of instances of financial "serendipity." One prime example was our organization of a fund to specialize in stocks of companies "committed to improving the American way of life." Specifically, we decided to seek out promising companies involved in advanced technology, companies supplying goods and services that helped to reduce pollution, companies that enhanced equal employment opportunity, occupational health and safety, or purity of consumer products. We called this the Third Century Fund, because we established it at the time that America was approaching its Bicentennial. During a recent span of five years, Third Century Fund increased in net asset value by an impressive 275 percent—not because of one or two spectacular stock selections, but because, as it turned out, well-managed companies that work at improving the quality of American life are very good investments.

A growth industry

The new products and services offered by the mutual funds and their records of performance are responsible for very vigorous growth in this form of investing. From 1940 to late 1980, according to statistics collected by the Investment Company Institute:

• The number of publicly offered mutual funds grew from approximately 70 to more than 700.

• Mutual fund assets grew from less than $.5 billion to about $130 billion.

• Shareholder accounts grew from 300,000 to more than 10 million, representing more than 8 million individual shareowners.

• Dividends and capital gains distributions to shareholders increased from $20 million in the year 1940 to more than $3.2 billion.

The impressive rise in mutual fund assets was due to two factors: recruitment of more investors holding more shares, plus a rise in the value of portfolio assets. There is a continual flow of investment money into and out of mutual funds, as investors, for a variety of reasons, cash in some or all of their shares. This capital is replaced by the sale of new shares to either existing investors or to new ones. Though redemptions have exceeded sale of new shares in some years, the past 30 years have shown an upward curve in the net assets of all mutual funds as a group.

For example, in 1979 investors bought $119.3 billion of new mutual fund shares, compared with $37.2 billion in 1978, $4.6 billion in 1970, $2.1 billion in 1960, and $50 million in 1940. Redemptions in 1979 totalled $86.6 billion, compared with $31.5 billion in 1978, $3 billion in 1970, $842 million in 1960, and $35 million in 1940. Exhibit 5-1, Net Assets: Open-End Investment Companies 1946–1979, illustrates this growth (*1980 Mutual Fund Fact Book*, Investment Company Institute, 1980).

Exhibit 5-1. Net assets of open-end investment companies, 1946–1979.

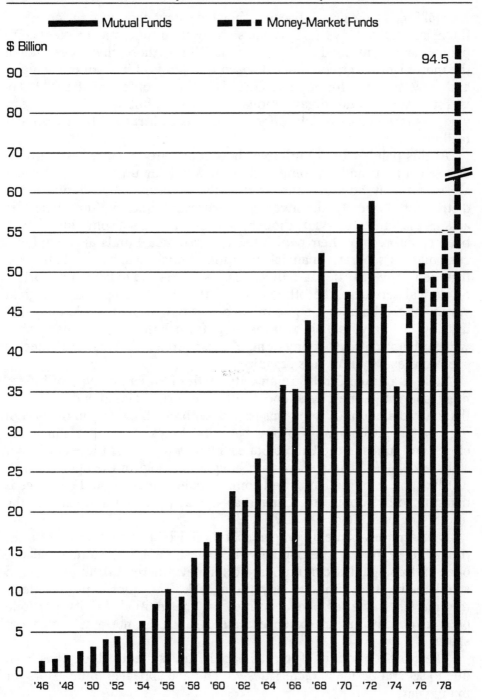

Why people buy funds

Mutual funds have grown because they have kept pace with the changing financial needs of investors. While some mutual fund management companies have continued along traditional lines, those that have shown the most vigorous growth have devised new kinds of investment vehicles and new services for their clients. In other words, the trend today is for mutual fund organizations to become full-line financial service organizations, which offer a very broad range of investment facilities.

At this point, a brief outline of how funds are organized is in order. The structure usually is composed of the following units: the fund itself; an investment advisor; and frequently, a principal underwriter or distributor. Typically, the investment advisor or underwriter/wholesaler acts as the fund's sponsor, though in a few rare cases some funds have been sponsored by their own internal personnel. Funds also employ a custodian—a separate financial institution which usually is a bank or a trust company—to safeguard the investors' assets and to perform a variety of clerical services. The other units of the structure appear in a great variety of combinations. Some funds perform their own wholesaling and distribution, provide their own research, furnish their own management, while others contract for any or all of these services. A fund's prospectus spells out exactly how it is organized.

Today's mutual funds are an outgrowth of an earlier type of investment company—the closed-end fund. The term "closed-end" signifies that a fixed amount of stock was issued, with no obligation on the part of the investment company to buy back its shares. There are still many closed-end funds in the United States, many with shares traded on major stock exchanges. These shares are bought and sold in the open market, just like shares of industrial and commercial companies, and the price is determined by supply and demand as well as by changes in value of the underlying portfolios.

Open-end investment companies, otherwise known as mutual funds, proved to be much more popular with investors. As the name indicates, open-end companies continuously offer new shares to the public and stand ready at all times to buy them back. The quoted price reflects the market value of the securities in the mutual fund's portfolio on a given day, minus expenses or fees—i.e., the net asset value per share.

The growth of mutual funds as popular investment vehicles has been due to several basic characteristics which have appealed to investors for many years.

Diversification

One of the strongest attractions has been the concept of spreading investment risk over many types of securities. A single share in a mutual fund
represents an interest in a portfolio that very often contains securities of
50, 75, 100, or even several hundred companies. In theory, of course, an
investor could diversify by buying one share or a few shares in each of
several dozen companies. Before doing this, however, the individual
would have to select a portfolio from the hundreds of securities on the
market. Then, too, acquiring the portfolio would be expensive. For instance, just one share in each of the 30 stocks in the Dow Jones Industrial
Average as of December 9, 1980, would have have cost an individual investor approximately $1,362. The brokerage commissions for buying
single shares are higher than for purchases of 100 shares at a time, which,
of course, reduces the actual amount of money left over for investment
after expenses.

Every mutual fund has its own investment policy clearly stated in the
prospectus that is required by law to be given to investors before they invest. The kinds of securities each fund holds, and the industries those
securities represent, will vary with the investment objectives of the fund
and, of course, with the judgment of the fund's managers.

For many years, public utilities were a favorite investment for portfolio managers. While utility stocks as a whole are still important in many
portfolios, the world shortage of energy has catapulted oil stocks,
especially, to the favorite position during the past few years. Financial
stocks, including banks and insurance companies, also have long been
very important groups, and in recent years electronic and electrical equipment has gained in popularity, with the chemical industry also maintaining a leading position in many portfolios.

Tables 5-1 and 5-2, compiled by the Investment Company Institute
(the trade organization of investment companies), show the diversification of portfolios by mutual funds in the latest available years, ranked by
market value and by percentages.

Professional management

Another reason investors turn to mutual funds is that, by buying fund
shares, they are in effect hiring professional investment managers to look
after their money.

The prospectus for The Dreyfus Fund, which is one of the largest equity funds, expresses it this way:

> Let's assume that you have $1,000 put away for use in later life. In fact, you
> hope that the money can grow for you. Suppose you took this money to a

Table 5-1. Shareholder accounts and total net assets, 1955–1978.

Calendar Year End	No. of Reporting Funds	No. of Accounts [in thousands]	Assets [in billions]
1955	125	$ 2,085.3	$ 7.8
1956	135	2,580.0	9.0
1957	143	3,110.4	8.7
1958	151	3,630.1	13.2
1959	155	4,276.1	15.8
1960	161	4,897.6	17.0
1961	170	5,319.2	22.8
1962	169	5,910.5	21.3
1963	165	6,151.9	25.2
1964	160	6,301.9	29.1
1965	170	6,709.3	35.2
1966	182	7,701.7	34.8
1967	204	7,904.1	44.7
1968	240	9,080.2	52.7
1969	269	10,391.5	48.3
1970	361	10,690.3	47.6
1971	392	10,901.0	55.0
1972	410	10,635.3	59.8
1973	421	10,330.9	46.5
1974			
Mutual Funds	416	9,970.4	34.1
Money Market Funds	15	103.8	1.7
1975			
Mutual Funds	390	9,712.5	42.2
Money Market Funds	36	208.8	3.7
1976			
Mutual Funds	404	8,879.4	47.6
Money Market Funds	48	180.7	3.7
1977			
Mutual Funds	427	8,515.1	45.0
Money Market Funds	50	177.5	3.9
1978			
Mutual Funds	444	8,190.6	45.0
Money Market Funds	61	467.8	10.9

NOTE: Figures for shareholder accounts represent combined totals for member companies. Duplications have not been eliminated.

Table 5-2. Distribution of mutual fund assets, calendar year end, 1964-1978.

Year	Total Net Assets	Net Cash & Equivalent	Corporate Bonds	Preferred Stocks	Common Stocks	Municipal Bonds	Long Term U.S. Gov't.	Other
				[in millions of dollars]				
1964	29,116	1,329	2,149	687	24,951	NA	NA	NA
1965	35,220	1,803	2,554	595	30,268	NA	NA	NA
1966	34,829	2,971	2,915	505	28,438	NA	NA	NA
1967	44,701	2,566	2,959	755	38,421	NA	NA	NA
1968	52,677	3,187	3,408	1,675	44,407	NA	NA	NA
1969	48,291	3,846	3,586	1,190	39,669	NA	NA	NA
1970	47,618	3,124R	4,286	1,143	38,540	NA	NA	525R
1971	55,045	2,601R	4,910	1,206	45,891	NA	NA	437R
1972	59,831	2,598	5,068	993	50,735	NA	NA	437
1973	46,519	3,426	4,196	623	37,698	NA	NA	576
1974	34,062	3,357	3,611R	426	26,103	NA	NA	565R
1975	42,179	3,209	4,766	506	33,158	NA	NA	540R
1976	47,582	2,352	6,977	655	37,158R	NA	NA	440R
1977	45,049	3,274	6,475	418	30,746	2,256	1,295	585
1978	44,980	4,507	5,545	405	30,678	2,550	1,093	202
				[percentages]				
1964	100.0	4.6	7.4	2.4	85.6	NA	NA	NA
1965	100.0	5.1	7.3	1.7	85.9	NA	NA	NA
1966	100.0	8.5	8.4	1.4	81.7	NA	NA	NA
1967	100.0	5.7	6.6	1.7	86.0	NA	NA	NA
1968	100.0	6.0	6.5	3.2	84.3	NA	NA	NA
1969	100.0	8.0	7.4	2.5	82.1	NA	NA	NA
1970	100.0	6.6	9.0	2.4	80.9	NA	NA	1.1
1971	100.0	4.7	8.9	2.2	83.4	NA	NA	0.8
1972	100.0	4.3	8.5	1.7	84.8	NA	NA	0.7
1973	100.0	7.4	9.0	1.3	81.0	NA	NA	1.3
1974	100.0	9.9	10.6R	1.2R	76.6	NA	NA	1.7R
1975	100.0	7.6	11.3	1.2	78.6	NA	NA	1.3
1976	100.0	4.9	14.7	1.4	78.1	NA	NA	0.9R
1977	100.0	7.3	14.4	0.9	68.2	5.0	2.9	1.3
1978	100.0	10.0	12.3	0.9	68.2	5.7	2.4	0.5

R—Revised

group of people whom you had studied and felt were quite capable in the field of security investments.

Suppose you said to that group: "Gentlemen, I have made something of a study of you. I think you are conscientious and work hard at the business of investing. I would like you to take my $1,000 and invest it for me for many years to come. I expect you to pay close attention to my money, changing the securities which you buy for me from time to time as markets change and your opinions change. And for this I am going to pay you $6.50 a year.

Well, after the investment group had recovered from the shock of the suggestion, they might say to you: "It is completely infeasible for us to do what you ask for $6.50 a year. But if you will get 20,000 people together and all of you put your money in one joint account with each of you paying $6.50, it might become worth our while to handle the account in the fashion you have suggested."

Obviously, this is not how a mutual fund gets started; no individual would be willing or could afford to get together 20,000 strangers in order to have his or her own $1,000 managed. This is why a mutual fund has to have a sponsor to assume the expense, effort, and risk necessary in trying to sell and manage the fund. The Dreyfus Fund, for example, is sponsored by The Dreyfus Corporation, which also sponsors eight other mutual funds, each with differing investment goals and objectives. The basic appeal, however, common to all the funds sponsored by Dreyfus, and to all funds in the investment company industry, is that they receive full-time investment management from professional investors. The professionals should be able to do consistently better than amateurs at stock selection and, from time to time, they should achieve a "spectacular" success.

Few individual investors have the time or the knowledge to evaluate all the economic, business, and financial factors that should be weighed in selecting investments. For example, there are approximately 25,000 securities issues available on the organized exchanges and in the over-the-counter markets of the nation. From this enormous pool of securities (worth well in excess of 1 trillion dollars at the end of 1979), mutual funds held an estimated 4,700 issues—bonds, preferred and common stocks—of more than 3,000 corporations.

In order to make their selections, mutual fund managers conduct constant research to appraise three general factors: the outlook for the economy; the outlook for specific industries; and the prospects of individual companies.

Specialists on the staff of mutual fund organizations not only carefully study the stock and bond tables, but they also keep in close touch with what is happening on Wall Street each day. To do their jobs properly, they must also go out into the field, personally visiting industrial plants or shopping centers and talking directly with management. In short, they must keep their hands directly on the pulse of the industries they are considering for investment. This is a kind of day-to-day detailed service no single investor can do alone; yet it is economical when it is performed by a mutual fund organization on behalf of thousands of shareholders.

Liquidity

With some kinds of investments—real estate, for example—a wait of many months often is required to find a buyer, once the investor has decided to sell. With other investments—such as bank certificates of deposit—there may be a penalty for cashing in before a stipulated date. By contrast, an investor in a mutual fund is assured that on any business day he or she may normally redeem—or cash in—all or part of the fund shares. The price will reflect the fund's net assets at that specific time, which may, of course, be higher or lower than the original price.

Convenience and efficiency

When you invest on your own in the stock or bond market, you have the responsibility of making your own security selections, in addition to being burdened with the chores of record-keeping, safekeeping, and other custodial duties. In a mutual fund, all this is done for you by fund management. They handle all paperwork involved in buying, selling, and holding securities. These professionals watch for notices of stock splits, tender offers, and other such developments that might affect your holdings. They receive and account for all dividends, distributions, and interest payments; offer advice on the tax status of dividends and capital gains; and send you regular reports of activity in your account and the general status of the portfolio as a whole.

In addition, there are cost savings to you as the investor. The wholesale buying power of a mutual fund enables the fund to buy and sell securities at lower transaction costs than are available to an individual. The savings are passed along to fund shareowners.

Government regulation

A number of federal securities laws apply to mutual funds. The Securities Act of 1933, which requires registration of securities with the Securities and Exchange Commission before they may be offered for public sale, also governs the sale of offerings made by mutual funds. One important requirement of this act is that a prospectus, setting forth all relevant information about the fund, must be given to the investor before a sale is consummated. Let me emphasize that this is no empty formality. Investors should carefully read the prospectus before investing. Because mutual funds continually offer shares for sale, the 1933 act is important in their operations—and in the protection it offers to investors.

The Securities Act of 1934, which created the quasi-public National Association of Securities Dealers—the self-regulating unit for the over-the-counter market and mutual funds—placed a federal regulatory umbrella over other parts of the mutual fund industry, such as the way proxies are solicited, as well as standards for sales practices and advertising.

The key legislation governing mutual funds was the Investment Company Act of 1940, with important amendments enacted in 1970. This law prescribes, among other things, standards for mutual fund boards of directors. It also regulates the management and underwriting contracts of companies that manage mutual funds, and deals as well with management fees, financial reports that are furnished to shareholders, contractual purchase plans, and many other areas of fund operations.

While government regulation in no way implies any government guarantees of an individual investment, investors are nonetheless assured that the government prescribes strict rules for conduct of the mutual fund business. Much of this legislation has been devised by Congress in close cooperation with the mutual fund industry, which recognizes that government ground rules are a strong attraction to investors. No other form of investment, outside of the banking system itself, is so closely regulated by the federal government, and this, of course, has been a distinct advantage to the industry.

How the new services work

The new services that funds provide build on the basic characteristics of a fund and adapt them to current investment needs. Two of the most popular kinds of funds today—money market funds and tax-exempt funds—did not even exist in the early 1970s.

Money-market funds

These have been, indeed, the "hot" investment vehicles of recent years. In a little over three years, the total amount of money in money-market funds has skyrocketed from less than $4 billion to $76 billion—an increase of more than 18 times. Surely, such a dramatic increase in so short a time deserves a place in the financial history books alongside Polaroid! The reason for the phenomenal growth of the money-market funds, of course, is the very sharp rise in interest rates, well above what savings banks have been allowed to pay. Money-market funds (also called liquid asset or cash funds) were in a position to satisfy the desire of investors to earn high yields, with relative safety of principal. And they have provided a product that does exactly that.

Funds of this kind invest in short-term money-market instruments such as U.S. Treasury bills, bank certificates of deposit, and commercial paper. The value of such portfolios is subject to some fluctuation because of changes in interest rates and credit risk, yet these price movements are relatively minor when compared to long-term debt instruments or equities. Indeed, for all practical purposes, some money-market funds virtually fix the net asset value of their shares to eliminate fluctuation.

The climb of interest rates in the late 1970s brought billions of dollars (and thousands of new investors) into these funds. In 1978, money-market funds sold a phenomenal $30,452,000,000 in shares, only partially offset by redemptions of $24,294,500,000. High interest could be earned without any waiting period or the early withdrawal penalties that prevail in time deposits and bank certificates of deposit. Many investors regarded money-market funds as a safe and rewarding alternative in those more traditional types of investments. Some who owned stock or bond funds switched temporarily into money-market funds, using an exchange privilege offered by many mutual funds.

The latest expansion in money-market funds dates from 1977, when portfolio yields began to exceed 5 percent. By December 1978, yields had surged to 9.25 percent, and assets of money-market funds rose by $1.2 billion in that single month. By late 1980, with yields nearing 15 percent, total assets of money-market funds exceeded $76 billion.

No doubt one of the attractions also was that investors may use their money-market fund accounts almost like a checking account—writing checks for payment of large bills against the funds in their money-market accounts.

The boom in money-market mutual funds touched off a sub-boom in another kind of fund that gave a new look to an old type of investment company—the unit trust, a form of closed-end company. Several investment firms, including The Dreyfus Corporation, found they could offer investors access to the very high interest rates available in the Eurodollar market by selling units in closed-end investment trusts formed specifically to invest in six-month certificates of deposit issued in London by branches of U.S. banks. Those selected had at least $3 billion in assets. The certificates were repayable in dollars and were thus immune from foreign exchange fluctuation. The unit trust shares were snapped up by eager investors; by the end of 1979, an estimated $10 billion had been invested in these money-market unit trusts.

Tax-exempt bond funds

It is a familiar truism that income taxes take a very large share of investment income. During the last few years, two developments have accentu-
ated this problem for many Americans. One is the effect of inflation,
which results in frequent increases in the dollar level of wage and salary
incomes, despite the fact that real purchasing power (in terms of prices)
may merely stay even or actually decline. With our income tax laws based
on a progressive tax structure—the higher the income, the higher the tax
rate—this has the effect of putting most employed people into a higher tax
bracket every year or so, even though their actual purchasing power may
not improve. The other factor at work to increase the tax load is the makeup of the progressive tax tables—it doesn't take much of a salary increase
to propel a family into what seems like a very high tax bracket.

In 1976, the U.S. Congress authorized a solution to this dilemma for
many investors. Mutual funds, organized as corporations, were authorized to pass on to their shareowners the tax-exemption features of income
from municipal bonds. The mutual fund industry vigorously championed
the idea in the halls of Congress.

How significant the resulting tax break has been is clear in the Table
5-3, which shows how much an investor must earn from a taxable investment to equal a tax-exempt yield of 6 percent to 6.50 percent.

Starting from "ground zero" in 1976, two years later the tax-exempt
bond funds were accounting for more than one-fourth of all new sales of
shares in stock of bond funds.

Stock and bond funds

Money-market funds and tax-exempt funds are two glamorous new products. However, traditional kinds of investment vehicles continue to have
a strong appeal.

Common stock funds. These invest primarily in equities, though their
objectives may vary widely.

For example, one category of equity funds concentrates on seeking
long-term growth of capital. Funds of this kind look for companies which,
due to the nature of their business or financing, offer opportunities for
substantially increased income and profits in the future as the companies
develop.

In contrast to this kind of equity fund, other funds concentrate on
"blue chip" investments, the stocks of older, well-established companies
which are leaders in their respective fields and which have long records
of dividend payments and earnings.

Table 5-3. Comparing tax exempt versus taxable yields.

To determine the rate of return from a taxable investment to equal a 6–6½ percent tax exempt yield, find your taxable income and read across that line. Separate taxable income ranges are shown for individual and joint tax returns.

| Taxable Income | | Tax Bracket | In order to equal a tax-exempt yield of | | |
Joint Return	Single Return		6%	6¼%	6½%
			a taxable investment would have to earn a yield of:		
$24,600–29,900		32%	8.82%	9.19%	9.56%
	$18,200–23,500	34%	9.09%	9.47%	9.85%
$29,900–35,200		37%	9.52%	9.92%	10.32%
	$23,500–28,800	39%	9.84%	10.25%	10.66%
$35,200–45,800		43%	10.53%	10.96%	11.40%
	$28,800–34,100	44%	10.71%	11.16%	11.61%
$45,800–60,000	$34,100–41,500	49%	11.76%	12.25%	12.75%
$60,000–85,600		54%	13.04%	13.59%	14.13%
	$41,500–55,300	55%	13.33%	13.89%	14.44%
$85,600–109,400		59%	14.63%	15.24%	15.85%
	$55,300–81,800	63%	16.22%	16.89%	17.57%
$109,400–162,400		64%	16.67%	17.36%	18.06%
$162,400–215,400	$81,800–108,300	68%	18.75%	19.53%	20.31%
$215,400 & over	$108,300 & over	70%	20.00%	20.83%	21.67%

Example: Based on 1979 federal tax rates, a married couple filing a joint return with taxable income of $30–35,000 would have to earn a taxable return of 9.92 percent (an increase of more than one-half) in order to equal a tax exempt return of 6¼ percent.

There can, of course, be no guarantee that the fund will achieve any particular tax exempt yield.

While a substantial portion of the income will be exempt from federal income tax, investors may be subject to some state or local tax.

There also are common stock mutual funds that specialize in a specific industry, or group of industries, such as chemicals or electronics. Other funds invest mainly in stocks from a selected geographical area, or even a single state. Still another approach is followed by some funds which select stocks in companies that have a commitment to new technology or to social objectives such as equal employment, cleanup of pollution, or consumer protection. Dreyfus Third Century is a leading example of this approach.

While all common stock funds hope to see growth in the value of their holdings, some have policies that can be described as "aggressive" in seeking growth—in other words, they accept a greater proportion of risk to obtain their objectives. Other funds invest in stocks primarily to generate high income, and usually these funds also hold bonds in order to attain their objective. Still other funds try to provide a degree of growth combined with current income.

According to figures of the Investment Company Institute for the first ten months of 1980, the largest category among equity funds (excluding money-market funds) were the growth-and-income funds, with 33.2 percent of all mutual fund assets. As a group, growth funds were next with 28.1 percent of all assets, and aggressive growth funds held 7.3 percent. Equity income funds held 8.1 percent of the industry's assets. Sales for the period, however, told a different story: while growth funds were in the lead position with 19.3 percent of sales, growth and income funds accounted for 17.3 percent, aggressive growth funds for 14.9 percent of sales. Income funds registered 8.3 percent of the sales.

Balanced funds. These generally have a more conservative policy than common stock funds. Their managers try to achieve a balance between holdings of common stock and of fixed-income securities such as bonds and preferred stocks of corporations. Most balanced funds rarely show as large a gain during rising markets as most common stock funds. On the other hand, balanced funds tend to drop less in a declining market, and their income from investment tends to be more stable.

In 1979, balanced funds accounted for 7.0 percent of all mutual fund assets, but they accounted for only 1.0 percent of sales during the year.

Bond funds. These funds generally emphasize income and, as described above, some are devoted entirely to earning tax-exempt income. Traditionally, bond funds have sought steady income along with safety of principal. In recent years, however, a few have come on the market that pursue "aggressive" policies, such as buying bonds that sell below par in the hopes of realizing capital gains. Funds that concentrate on high-grade bonds are considered safer than those that include the lower-grade bonds in their portfolios. However, the latter group usually offer higher income and the potential for capital gain.

Bond funds of all types held 17 percent of all mutual fund assets in 1979, but about one-third of these were assets held by municipal bond funds. Sales by bond funds for 1979 accounted for 41.4 percent of all mutual fund sales, but well over half of that figure was sales of tax-exempt bond funds.

Option income funds. This type of fund is relatively new to the industry. Their investment objective is to seek high current return by investing primarily in dividend-paying common stocks on which call options are traded on national securities exchanges. The investor's current income combines dividends with any income realized from the option transactions. These funds assume risks in the option market in order to try to increase current return to investors. A number of mutual funds holding common stocks in their portfolios also are authorized to seek option income, but usually this is a relatively small source of income for such funds.

Option funds in 1979 accounted for 1.0 percent of the assets of mutual funds, and 1.2 percent of the dollar value of sales.

Hedge funds. This is a specialized type of fund designed primarily for large investors who are in a position to take above-average risks. With a primary objective of seeking growth of capital through a broad range of techniques, these funds are authorized to use short sales, put-and-call options, and leverage to attain their goals.

Full investment service

The wide variety of new and traditional types of investment vehicles offered by the mutual funds have now placed the industry in a position to make the claim that it offers "across-the-board" investment service. Several important fund-based services are currently available.

Annuities

Several funds, in combination with life insurance companies, offer an opportunity to put savings aside in a mutual fund (such as a money-market fund or a bond fund) and then draw retirement income at a specified time from the savings and earnings that have been accumulated.

The appeal of such savings/insurance plans is greatly enhanced when the income from the savings, during the accumulation years, is sheltered from income taxes, and the income after retirement also enjoys a degree of tax protection.

Tax-deductible retirement plans

Mutual funds are authorized as investment vehicles for a number of types of retirement plans funded with tax-deductible contributions.

Corporations are authorized to set up various kinds of pension and profit-sharing plans for their employees. Corporate contributions to the plan are tax deductible and earnings enjoy tax shelter while they accumulate.

Keogh plans, which allow self-employed individuals and their employees to accumulate retirement funds with tax-deductible contributions, may also place their assets in mutual funds. Generally, the maximum tax-deductible contribution to a conventional Keogh plan for a self-employed person is $7,500 or 15 percent of yearly self-employed income, whichever is less.

Individual retirement accounts, for persons who do not participate in an employer-sponsored plan, allow contributions of 15 percent of compensation up to $1,500 a year to a retirement plan, on a tax-deductible basis. Here, too, taxes are deferred on the income while it accumulates.

In mid-1980, there were 283,000 individual Keogh Plans invested in mutual funds, with assets valued at $3.2 billion; and 137,000 IRA's funded with mutual fund shares, with assets of $646 million.

Insurance services

Several mutual fund organizations have branched out into the sale of life insurance and medical insurance policies, again in combination with established insurance companies. Under such programs, ownership of shares in the mutual fund makes the shareowner part of a defined risk group and thus entitled to group insurance rates, which usually are lower than rates the investor could obtain on his or her own.

Gold purchasing

A few mutual fund organizations use their financial know-how to buy and sell gold on behalf of their customers who seek the kind of financial security that only gold can provide. Investors usually benefit from cost savings due to the mass purchasing power of the mutual fund organization and the fact that the companies also are geared to handle safekeeping, record-keeping, assaying, insurance, and other details of gold transactions.

The convenience factor

The convenience of owning mutual funds is based on a wide variety of services that funds typically supply to their shareowners.

Among the relatively new conveniences, or those that have become particularly popular in recent years, are the following:

Exchange privileges

The exchange privilege enables a shareowner to transfer his or her money from one fund to another within the same company or fund group, often with no charge or only a small transfer fee. The attraction of this privilege has become more important in recent years as security markets have become more volatile and because there have been more frequent changes in the objectives of investors. For example, an investor who has been a shareowner for many years in an equity growth fund may wish on retirement to change to an income fund for greater stability of income. Or investors, anticipating a change in securities markets, may wish to switch out of long-term investments that involve some risk to their capital and into short-term instruments with minimum risk. That is exactly what took place in 1979 when investors switched $2,775 million into money-market funds from other funds in the same complex. The trend continued in 1980.

For all funds in general, the rate of exchanges has been increasing strongly. For example, in 1979, exchanges totalled $5.8 billion, more than ten times the dollar total of exchanges in 1974. Broadly speaking, investors used the exchanges to draw assets out of equity and bond and income funds and transfer them into money-market funds.

Check writing

A number of funds, especially those holding short-term assets, offer the privilege of writing checks against the balance in the shareowner's account for payments above a minimum amount, such as $500 or more. The money continues to earn income until the check clears the bank. There usually is no charge for the use of redemption checks, and many shareowners find them useful for making large payments that "float" in the bank clearing system for some length of time, such as checks to pay income tax installments.

Telephone transfer and withdrawal

Many funds offer expedited methods for withdrawing funds in addition to the usual withdrawals by mail. Arrangements are made by these funds to receive withdrawal instructions by telephone, provided advance authorization forms have been filed with the custodian bank. Proceeds of redemption are then transferred by wire to the bank account specified by the investor.

Standard investor services that traditionally have been offered by most mutual funds include:

Automatic reinvestment

Most mutual funds offer to reinvest automatically the income dividends and capital gain distributions payable to shareowners. This plows back the dividends or capital gain distributions in the form of additional shares, thereby building up new holdings. Currently, mutual fund shareowners re-invest approximately 72 percent of their income dividends and capital gain distributions.

Interest compounding

Some bond funds feature automatic compounding of earned interest. Dividends are earned daily and are automatically reinvested monthly to earn compound interest. How valuable this can be to the investor is shown by this example: if dividends on an investment of $10,000 at the rate of 5.5 percent are allowed to accumulate and compound over a period of ten years, the return at simple interest at the end of ten years is $5,500. But if the interest is compounded, the return can add up to $7,081.

Automatic investment plan

Arrangements can be made through the investor's bank to set up an automatic investment plan. The mutual fund receives authorization to withdraw from the investor's bank account a fixed amount at stated intervals to be invested in additional shares of the fund.

Automatic withdrawal plans

These permit shareholders to receive steady payments from their holdings at regular intervals in order to supplement income or to meet specific commitments, such as college tuition payments. Typically, the payments are drawn from dividends and capital gains, if any, and then from principal if necessary to complete the size of the stipulated withdrawal payment.

For example: a couple with $100,000 in a mutual fund set up a withdrawal plan to pay them $6,000 a year, or $500 a month towards retirement. If, in any month, total dividends and capital gains income are not sufficient to provide $500, the plan provides for dipping into capital to make up the difference. Investors should be aware that some of the money they receive under a withdrawal plan could be a return of part of their original investment.

Generally speaking, the mutual fund industry is becoming a certificate-less community. The custodian bank or transfer agent holds the investor's shares as "book shares," thus avoiding the extra expense, delay, and inconvenience involved in the handling of certificates.

The new approach to sales

The original mutual funds were primarily sold by large staffs of salespeople who earned a commission for their sales. The commission customarily was deducted from the initial funds paid in by the investor—in the case of a plan for regular investments—during the early years of such a plan. This method of compensating the salesperson acquired the nickname "front-end load."

Funds that have a sales charge are sold either by broker/dealers or by salespeople employed directly by the underwriting organization. The amount of the sales charge in the case of contractual periodic payment plans is limited by law to no more than 9 percent, and also is limited as to when the sales charge may be deducted. The sales charge in other cases is subject to NASD rules: the maximum charge is 8.5 percent and is lower for volume purchases.

No-load funds. Historically, the bulk of assets held by mutual funds have been sold under the sales commission system. However, distribution without a sales charge ("no-load") has increased dramatically. In the 16 years between 1963 and 1979, no-load funds increased their share of total mutual fund sales tenfold—from 4.7 percent in 1963 to 44.9 percent in 1978. These figures do not include money-market funds, which are generally sold without a sales charge and, as already indicated, account for a very large portion of current mutual fund sales.

A considerable number of mutual funds still are sold in the front-end-load manner. In recent years, however, the so-called "no-load" funds—where there is no sales charge at all—have become very important. Originally, the no-load funds were small ones which were started by investment counselling firms as a vehicle for grouping the accounts of many of their smaller clients, in order to make the supervision of these accounts more efficient and economical.

The "no-loads" have come of age since those early days. Today, many of the leading funds are distributed without a sales charge (including seven of the nine Dreyfus-sponsored funds). This is characteristic of the money-market funds, where a sales charge would reduce the net return to investors by an unacceptable amount. But many equity and bond funds also are sold this way. The no-load funds are sold directly to investors by the fund itself, usually by direct mail.

There are a variety of methods for acquiring shares:

Outright purchases. These involve placing an order for a specified dollar amount or number of fund shares with a dealer or distributor of fund shares. The manner is the same as in purchasing an individual security, and the buyer receives a stock certificate for the number of shares purchased, or a confirmation stating the number of shares bought and their cost.

Voluntary accumulation plans. These involve an indication by the investor, but without a binding commitment, that he or she will periodically invest additional sums of money in a fund without a definite time schedule or dollar investment figure. Usually, a minimum investment amount is required to start such a plan, and there are minimum amounts for investment of additional funds.

Contractual plans. These plans entail a commitment to invest a fixed amount on a regular basis for a specified number of years. A substantial part of the sales charge is usually deducted in the early years, within limits specified by federal law. Insurance policies are available in connection with contractual plans and voluntary accumulation plans to pay the balance due under the program in the event the investor dies before completing the plan. This insurance, which is a decreasing-term group life plan, is similar to the mortgage insurance carried by many homeowners.

Management fees

The mutual fund investment advisor receives a fee for advice and professional management. These fees are in certain cases subject to sliding-scale reductions as assets increase. The amount of the fee payable by a fund is set forth in its prospectus. In addition to these charges, a fund incurs other fees and expenses such as brokerage fees, custodian-charges, or reports to shareowners, which are essentially the usual corporate expenses of operations and affect all shareowners pro rata as in the case of any corporation. Expenses also are stated in the prospectus and are reported in regular shareowner communications.

While management fees vary from fund to fund, the cost to the shareowner industry-wide is about .5 percent a year of his or her investment. Fund expenses also can add .5 percent or so to the cost of owning fund shares.

While the long-term trend of certain of these costs have been downward, thanks to improved efficiency and the introduction in 1975 of competitive commission rates for stock transactions on the nation's securities exchanges, inflationary increases in basic costs of operations have caused many mutual fund managers to increase their management fees. Despite such increases, the cost of the mutual fund for the investor is relatively small compared with what an individual would have to pay elsewhere to have an investment managed. Indeed, estimates show that the average cost to investors for management fees and other expenses dropped from 0.67 percent per year of the amount invested in 1954 to 0.65 percent in 1978.

New markets

Mutual funds grew to their present size primarily as the investment vehicle for small and medium-size investors. However, major institutions, trust funds, pension funds, and even banks now find that these funds are convenient for investing some of the assets under their control.

In fact, in 1978, the last time the field was surveyed, 1,405,000 institutions and fiduciaries of various kinds owned shares in mutual funds totalling about $15.5 billion. This institutional stake accounted for approximately 28 percent of all mutual fund assets, including money-market funds.

Table 5-4 summarizes the importance of institutions as investors in mutual funds.

Table 5-4. Fiduciary, business, and institutional investors of mutual funds—1978.

	Number of Accounts	Value [in 000's]
Fiduciaries (banks, individuals serving as trustees, guardians, and administrators)	774,704	$ 6,689,822
Business organizations (corporations, employee profit sharing and pension funds, insurance companies and other financial institutions)	568,279	6,610,935
Institutions and foundations (religious, fraternal, welfare, hospitals, orphanages, schools and colleges, foundations)	19,591	415,299
Other Institutional Investors	42,551	1,794,476
Total	1,405,125	$15,510,532

Source: Investment Company Institute

Institutions select a mutual fund for some of the same reasons that appeal to individuals: professional selection of investments by specialists who spend *all* of their time keeping informed on market trends; diversification in a greater number of different securities than would be attainable by all but the largest institutions; superior performance records over a period of years; low costs, including no sales charge by no-load funds that often are used by institutions; instant and constant liquidity for all invested funds; and convenience of having all details of paperwork, safekeeping, and record-keeping handled by another organization.

How good are the funds?

The performance of mutual funds must be judged in terms of the stated objective of each fund, as explained in its prospectus. However, some general characteristics can be mentioned.

The securities in a fund's portfolio will, of course, be affected by broad economic and market trends. When the stock market is weak, stock funds—and especially growth funds—may suffer. When the stock market booms, these funds should show strong gains. With bond funds, as interest rates rise, the price of existing holdings of bonds tends to decline; conversely, they tend to rise when interest rates are falling. Skilled management of funds can offset the effects of market trends or broad economic cycles to some extent, but it is the exceptional fund that can buck broad economic trends consistently.

As a rule, the proper way to judge performance of a fund is to look at its record over a long period of years. Of course, there are a few speculative funds that state in their prospectuses that their goal is to concentrate on short-term speculation, and consequently it is appropriate to judge such funds on their short-term results. The vast majority of mutual funds, however, seek to achieve gains, income, or protection of capital over a long period of time, and such funds should be judged by those standards.

Mutual fund investors are paying a fee for professional management. Investors, therefore, are within their rights to expect a fund, over a period of years, to perform better than the comprehensive market averages (unless, of course, the fund is one whose stated goal is to invest in a portfolio that mirrors the market averages).

The long-term record does indeed show that the mutual fund industry has performed excellently. This becomes clear in statistics compiled by the Investment Company Institute, shown in Exhibit 5-2, which measures average performance of 33 growth-and-income funds in existence from the beginning of 1954 to the end of 1979. While it should be reiterated that past performance is no guarantee of future results, the chart nonetheless is revealing.

As can be seen, though values rise and fall, sometimes quite sharply, an investment of $10,000 made on January 1, 1955, in these funds would have grown to $74,305 by December 31, 1979. That figure includes reinvestment of all dividends and capital gains distributions into additional shares, but it also is an average that covers both good and bad years, successful funds and some not as successful, and after deducting intitial sales charges and all expenses.

The "bottom line" of this example is that the average return for the funds as a whole was 8.4 percent a year—a figure that compares very favorably with the 25-year record for other types of investments and surpasses the inflation rate, which averaged 4.31 percent for the same span.

The future: accent on professionalism

In such a volatile field as investing, it is very difficult to be categorical about the future. However, some basic trends can be clearly discerned.

One prediction that can be made with certainty is that the future will hold more uncertainty affecting investors than the eventful years we already have experienced. Today's investors have lived through jolting events every few months that affected their securities: wars, assassinations, national scandals, fuel shortages, fuel embargoes, price squeezes, skyrocketing business costs, wage costs, rising living costs, and many other "shock" events that are familiar to everyone who watches television news and reads the newspapers.

The intensity of life in today's world, the growing power of organized special interest groups, the unabated rivalry between the world's major powers, the emergence of new power centers in less-developed countries, the spread of violence as an instrument of policy, and the continuing threat of nuclear holocaust all add up to an unbelievably difficult atmosphere in which to make investment decisions. Yet anyone with savings to protect will have to make such decisions or else hire experts to make decisions for him.

In such an uncertain world, mutual funds offer several distinct advantages. One is their basic principle of diversifying investments much more broadly than most investors can do for themselves. The old saying "There is safety in numbers" certainly applies to a diversified investment portfolio. In times of turbulence, it is wise to spread one's holdings over many industries and many kinds of securities. By doing so, one has at least a reasonable chance that the broad base of the portfolio can cushion the blow.

The search for diversity in an unpredictable investment climate will also bring greater demand for the professionalism represented by the mutual funds. The staffs of the funds offer a reserve of investment experience and knowledge that investors can turn to for guidance in managing their money. Do-it-yourself investing becomes more difficult every year, not only because of the increased complexity of making investment decisions, but also because the cost savings that are available to investing institutions are not available to individuals.

As we speed towards the twenty-first century, the art of making financial decisions will not become any simpler. Mutual funds, members of an industry that devotes all its energies to seeking investment success for its clients, will play an even more important role in helping investors to make prudent use of their savings.

Exhibit 5-2.

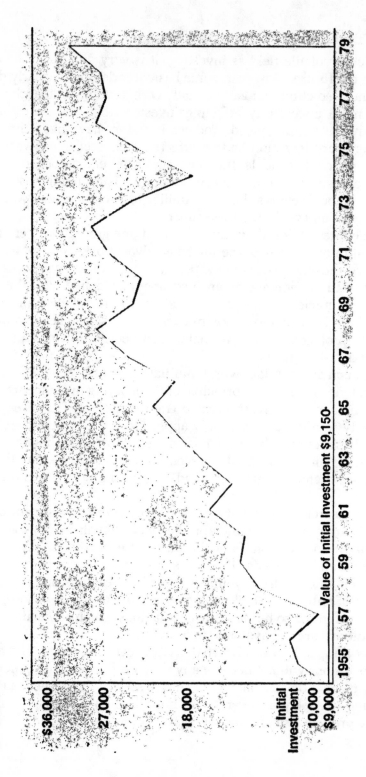

Exhibit 5-2.

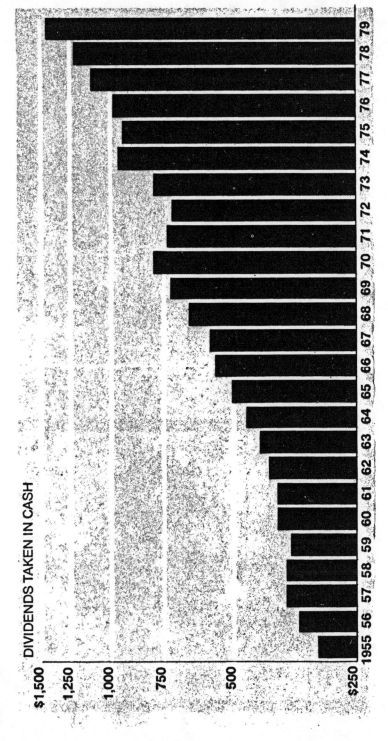

DIVIDENDS TAKEN IN CASH

Building Blocks

William Zeckendorf, Jr.

The Delmonico Hotel, located at Park Avenue and 59th Street, was once one of the best hotels in New York City, but during the real estate recession of the early 1970s it fell on hard times and was in total disrepair. The situation was so bad that either foreclosure or bankruptcy was likely. The owner of the hotel, David Phillips, was a nice gentleman in his early eighties. He was assisted by his daughter, Gladys Altman, who helped operate the hotel. They were most anxious to sell.

A good friend of mine, a very successful woman in the real estate business, obtained a contract to buy the Delmonico at what appeared to be a very low price, just under $7 million. She asked me to join her—she would do the financing, and it would be up to me to handle the conversion of the hotel into an apartment house. It is very difficult today to realize that the hotel business was so bad at that time that everyone thought in terms of converting good hotels into what they hoped would be financially successful apartment houses.

This was an extremely important deal for me to close. It came at a time when I desperately needed a new project to work on. The day of the closing, at around 10 a.m., we received a telephone call from my friend's lawyer. He said that his client had second thoughts about the deal and that she was considering not closing. After several telephone calls to her and her attorneys, we invited David Phillips to an early luncheon. We explained to him that his original buyer was not going through with the deal, but that I would take up her position and close. We agreed to meet later that day in his attorney's office with my lawyers.

At about 3 p.m., we assembled to go over the contract. There were a number of problems, the greatest of which was the fact that at that moment we did not have the funds required by the contract—namely, $250,000. The real estate broker handling the transaction, Ed Lewis, came up with a solution. He explained to Mr. Phillips that my West Coast partner, Sheldon Wilson, would come to New York during the next week to put up the necessary money, but could not do so at this time since he was in California. This was confirmed by telephone by Mr. Wilson.

During our discussions we learned that Gladys Altman was very disturbed because her German Shepherd had recently been killed by an automobile. My father, who had been sick, was living at the Mayfair House. He had as his companion a beautiful German Shepherd. The only trouble was that the dog had been trained as a police dog and would attack anyone who came into the apartment. One housemaid had been hospitalized and another one had threatened to quit and sue because of the dog. I explained the problem to my father, who quickly responded, "Yes, if you need a German Shepherd to close the Delmonico deal, you may have my dog." I thanked him and explained his generosity to Ms. Altman who was enthralled with the idea of obtaining a beautiful new German Shepherd.

In the meantime, Ed Lewis had convinced Mr. Phillips that all that was required to close the contract was a good faith note signed by me. There is no specific terminology for a good faith note—it has no legal meaning, but it said, in effect, that I would exercise my best efforts to ensure that within seven days a deposit of $250,000 was in the hands of the seller and that Ms. Altman would receive a German Shepherd by the next weekend. Both of these conditions were fulfilled—the $250,000 was furnished by my partner on the West Coast, and the German Shepherd was delivered in great style by my father, who arrived in his chauffeured limousine. The Delmonico deal was closed, and from there we went on to many other successful real estate transactions.

Had I known at the time that New York City was about to become the tourist capital of the world and that hotel rooms would become a prized commodity, I never would have converted the Delmonico into an apartment building. As it happened, however, this deal still worked out well. While I could not see what was about to happen to the Manhattan real estate market, I was bailed out by the fact that I stuck to what's become a golden rule for me—to buy only top quality property. It's a rule that's worked for me time and time again.

Advantages of real estate

Throughout the history of the United States, more fortunes have been made through the ownership of land than through any other type of investment. Real estate is attractive because of several advantages it offers over other forms of investments.

First, real estate is an asset which easily keeps pace with and often exceeds the rate of inflation.

Second, because a supply of mortgage money has generally been available from banks and insurance companies, the equity required to buy a building is usually small compared to its total value. Such utilization of someone else's money is known as leverage. Because of the investor's ability to highly leverage an investment, real estate can often be acquired with a fraction of the investor's own equity. The amount of a mortgage available to an investor is based on the value of the property, not its cost. Historically, the money borrowed was normally on a long-term basis at a fixed-rate of interest, therefore allowing increased values to accrue to the benefit of the equity owner rather than to the lender. However, at this writing, the prime interest rate has risen to a recent peak in excess of 20 percent, and mortgagees have developed new strategies to deal with inflation such as requiring some form of equity participation (an "equity kicker"), a floating interest rate, or an interest rate that is adjusted periodically.

The third advantage relates to taxes. Most sophisticated investors who are in high-income brackets consider real estate to be the best tax shelter available. Fundamentally, there are two different types of real estate investments. One type covers deals sold primarily as a tax shelter, without regard to the true economics of the real estate being acquired. These deals are normally syndicated by tax lawyers, accountants, and investment bankers—professionals who sell for the sole purpose of sheltering their customers' earned and unearned income. The major pitfall to this type of real estate transaction is that, in the event of a mortgage foreclosure, the depreciation taken to date is subject to recapture and is taxed as ordinary income.

A safer tax shelter would be a real estate transaction of the second type. Such deals are sold primarily on the basis of their economics, with the tax shelter being an added benefit. They normally produce less immediate tax or cash benefits but greater long-term appreciation.

The value of a tax shelter is usually based on the formula that $100,000 of investment produces $300,000 of tax shelter. However, in some cases, a write-off of $400,000 or $500,000 worth of depreciation—or shelter— may be achieved.

Generally, the most advantageous tax shelters occur in the field of rental housing. As a typical deal, consider a developer who builds an apartment house at a total cost of $10,500,000: $8,000,000 as the cost of the building, $750,000 as the cost of the land, $1,250,000 as interest expense during construction and $500,000 as other start-up expenses which are not capitalized (such as operating losses during the initial rental phase of the project). Assume that the building has an anticipated life of 40 years and that the developer obtains a loan of $9 million (guaranteed by the FHA). Based upon these assumptions, the following may be said:

• The developer will be able to raise 100 percent of the equity required for the project through a tax shelter sale and a deferral of certain soft costs, such as development fees. The developer can sell 90 percent of the project to a group of limited partners for $1,500,000 and, as a general partner, keep 10 percent. The limited partners would pay for their investment with 20 percent cash and the balance in notes due over 5 years. The tax shelter available to the limited partners on their investment of $1,500,000 is very high. For example, all of the partners will be able to take accelerated depreciation of 150 percent of the building costs over a 40-year life (which is 3.75 percent per year), or $300,000. In addition, the interest paid during construction would be written off over a 5-year period—or at a rate of $250,000 per year.

• Most projects have a negative cash flow for a period of time after they are completed. In this case, the $500,000 of start-up expenses are considered (for the purpose of tax computation) as losses during the years in which they occur. If the project is to be subsidized housing, the interest charges during construction can be totally deducted in the years in which they are incurred and the depreciation deducted on a double declining basis, or at the rate of 5 percent per year.

• Thus, the limited partners would be buying their investment out of tax savings. In turn, the limited partners can expect a priority return of 6 percent on their cash investment along with 90 percent of the tax benefits.

In addition to the tax benefit, leverage, and protection from inflation advantages that real estate investment offers, there is a fourth benefit. This pertains to the psychological rather than to the economic aspect of investing. Real estate is a tangible asset. People get great satisfaction in owning something they can see, interact with, and, at least to some extent, control. Stocks, by contrast, are intangible assets represented by paper certificates.

Syndications

Large-scale projects are not only for large investors. Through the formation of real estate syndicates, the small investor is able to participate in projects that he could not afford on his own. This ability to invest in larger projects represents the most important advantage syndication offers because the larger the property, generally, the better its quality. A second advantage syndication offers is the ability to avoid the day-to-day management responsibilities of a project. These responsibilities are left to the builder or professional syndicators.

Types of properties real estate syndicates often invest in are hotels, shopping centers, and office buildings. Let's take a brief look at each.

Hotels

The purchase of hotels in urban areas represents one of the best investments of recent times. In New York City, for example, the value of hotels has virtually doubled in the past two years. The principal reasons for this increase in value are the high percentage of occupancies and the escalating rates hotels enjoy today. Hotels also are a good investment because of the hedge they provide against inflation. A hotel owner is not bound by long-term leases; therefore he or she can increase rates to keep pace with inflation. On the negative side, the cost of building a hotel is not cheap. Construction costs of $100,000 per room are not unusual, and so require proportionally high rates, as much as $100 per day. Because of these high costs, properly maintained old hotels are able to remain competitive, and thus are a good investment.

Shopping centers

When properly located and anchored by two or more major department stores, shopping centers have proven highly profitable to investors. One reason is the percentage rental clauses in most or all store leases. These clauses provide additional rent as sales volumes increase and are thus an excellent hedge against inflation. There are, however, potential risks associated with investing in shopping centers, such as a deteriorating location, increased competition, gasoline shortages, and obsolescence. Generally, the shopping centers with the best location, the largest number of stores, and the best major department stores will survive and prosper.

Modern office buildings

Office buildings in well-located areas usually represent the best and safest investments in commercial real estate. They attract the most financially stable tenants which, in turn, results in better financing from the stand-point of both interest and amortization. Today, all office leases include escalation clauses to cover increases in operating expenses and real estate taxes. To protect against the down side of a bad economy as well as to take advantage of the upside of a good one, it is sound policy to lease half of the building on a long-term basis and half for a short term. Today, of-fice rates in large metropolitan areas range from $20 per square foot to as high as $35 per square foot. Ground-floor retail rents range from $30 per square foot to $100 per square foot. The escalating costs of new construc-tion prompt investors to acquire existing buildings on comparatively low yields in anticipation of re-leasing at substantially higher rentals.

Where and when to buy

When investing in real estate one should be aware of several basic prin-ciples. First, an investor always should consider whether the property is in a good location. This point cannot be overstated since location should always be considered the most important aspect in the selection of an in-vestment property. In addition, an investor must keep in mind the state of the economy, the availability of mortgages, competitive factors, and the zoning of the given area.

Very often it is best to buy real estate at a time when the economy is sluggish rather than when it is strong. In the past several years, a great amount of money has been made by people who were willing to invest when high vacancies existed in office buildings and apartment houses. During this period, very little construction occurred, ensuring that when the economy became stronger the demand for space would greatly exceed the supply. Buildings already in existence were in the best position to take advantage of a change in the market. As is true with other forms of in-vestments, the ability to choose the appropriate time to invest is probably the most important skill a real estate investor can possess.

Through the combination of leverage, tax advantages, protection against inflation, and the satisfaction of owning a tangible asset, real estate has become an attractive investment. Almost all investment bank-ing houses have real estate departments to assist clients in selecting both tax shelters and investment properties. Today the competition to acquire equities is keen, coming from financial institutions such as insurance companies, pension funds, and bank trust departments. In addition, there has been a great influx of foreign capital into the United States, due to the perception overseas that the United States is the most stable coun-try—politically and economically—for investment.

This competition for investment opportunities has resulted in the in-crease of property values at a much faster pace than both the rate of inflation and the average increase in stock market values. The financing of real estate has become very sophisticated, attracting investors who several years ago would have been reluctant to enter into this arena. As construction costs have soared, fewer new projects have been built. As a result, today's real estate market is less likely to experience a major recession than in the recent past.

Home ownership

Financially and emotionally, the most important real estate transaction for most people involves the ownership of a home or apartment. There probably is no better investment for a family than the ownership of their own dwelling. It provides security, forces savings, and is an execllent inflation hedge.

Typically, a young family starting with a small apartment or house graduates to larger quarters to accommodate an expanding family. The equity that has been built into a house or apartment because of increased values and the pay down of a mortgage will often be sufficient to buy a larger and more expensive home or apartment as a family grows and income increases. The urban or suburban dweller usually goes through five stages: the first apartment, which is small; a larger apartment or house for a family; larger still when the family income increases at ages 30 and 40; the return to the city or to a smaller house in the country when children are on their own; and, finally, a condominium or small house in the Sunbelt.

There are many financial advantages to home or apartment ownership. In the case of a home, there is generally financing available of between 75 to 90 percent of the purchase price. Unlike rent, the interest on such a loan, together with real estate taxes, is tax deductible. Proceeds of a resale and the reinvestment in a new home or apartment usually is accomplished without incurring a tax. In addition, for taxpayers aged 55 or over, the tax laws allow a once-in-a-lifetime exclusion of up to $100,000 of the profits on the sale of a home.

For city residents, there are cooperatives or condominiums. Condominiums are characterized by the ownership of an actual apartment and a participation in common elements of the building, which include corridors, lobby, basement, and land. The condominium is financed in a similar way to a home and has a separate real estate tax lot. There are few, if any, restrictions on resale or financing. Condominiums are prevalent in cities throughout the United States and have a heritage which goes back to the days of the early Romans.

Cooperative ownership, on the other hand, is limited to a few cities,

New York being the most common. While the end result of condominium and cooperative ownership may appear similar, in legal terms they are distinct. A cooperative owner possesses (1) shares in a cooperative corporation which owns a building and (2) a proprietary lease to the apartment he or she occupies in that building. When ownership of an apartment changes, the shares of stock allocable to the apartment are sold and the lease is transferred. The sale of shares and the transfer of a lease is subject to the approval of a board of directors, which can withhold its consent to protect the "integrity of the building."

By contrast, a sale of a condominium apartment does not require similar approval. However, there are advantages to cooperative ownership. For instance, the first mortgage is on the building, without direct liability to the shareholders. In addition, long-term financing of up to 75 percent of the purchase price of a cooperative is usually available from both commercial and savings banks. As an example, a $100,000 cooperative, while subject to a first mortgage on the building, can be financed for up to $75,000 at the prevailing interest rate over a 20- to 30-year period. Interest on such a loan, together with a portion of the real estate taxes assessed against the building, is tax deductible.

The most expensive cooperative and condominium apartments are today selling at up to $300 per square foot in New York and Los Angeles, and at about half that in other cities such as Washington, D.C. While this may seem expensive, it does not compare to Switzerland, Paris, or Monte Carlo, where prices can reach $500 per square foot. As in other types of real estate, the value of either a condominium or cooperative is directly related to its location with a premium for newer buildings. For both economic and political reasons, most residential buildings constructed today are condominiums or cooperatives rather than rentals. From an economic standpoint there is little justification for renting, if an individual has sufficient financial resources, and cooperatives and/or condominiums are available.

A case history

Most real estate transactions are rather mundane, and very few have the great excitement that one would expect in the corporate world. Recently, however, I participated in a series of events that were both dramatic and fascinating. The Penn Central, after selling the Waldorf Astoria, had three hotels remaining in New York: the Barclay, the Biltmore, and the Roosevelt. In total, these three important hotels in the midtown district consisted of approximately 3,000 rooms.

With my partner in this transaction, Paul Milstein, I had been negotiating for over a year to buy the Biltmore at a price of approximately $10 million. One day we received a telephone call advising us that if we really wanted the Biltmore, we should also buy the Roosevelt at a suggested price of $15 million.

Shortly thereafter, we received another call from one of the officials of Penn Central, saying that all three hotels were being taken off the market to be sold at auction. We decided to limit our bid to the Biltmore and the Roosevelt. However, in order to be certain that we covered all possibilities, we joined in a second bid with the Dunfey Hotel people, a subsidiary of Aer Lingus, who wanted to buy the Barclay. We put in a series of bids: a joint bid of approximately $34 million, covering all three hotels; a separate bid of just under $19 million, covering the Biltmore and the Roosevelt; and then a combination of other bids covering several other possibilities.

Our bid on the Biltmore and the Roosevelt Hotels gave Penn Central an opportunity to receive a still higher price based on its participation. There were about 25 bidders in total. Later we received a phone call saying that we were the second highest bidder, the top bidder being Loews Hotel Co., which had bid a total of $45 million for all three hotels. We protested because we felt that the participation clause included in our bid could easily have resulted in a much higher price to Penn Central, but we were told, "No, the trustees have decided Loews was the high bidder."

We then considered the possibility of trying to upset the bidding by going into Bankruptcy Court with a higher and better proposal. With this idea, we approached Intercontinental, a subsidiary of Pan American, since we knew it was anxious to acquire the Barclay. By this time, the Dunfey representatives had decided to withdraw from this bidding contest. My job was to negotiate with Intercontinental.

In the meantime, Paul Milstein was negotiating directly with Larry and Bob Tisch, of Loews Hotels, to buy the Biltmore and Roosevelt from them in the event they were the successful bidders. They came to an agreement, and our negotiations with Intercontinental were called off.

The Loews bid of $45 million was to be divided into two parts, the Barclay at $25 million and the Biltmore and Roosevelt at $20 million. One week before the court hearing, we were notified that the court had received an offer of $50 million, $5 million higher than the Loews bid for the entire package. We were told that this new offer came from a Middle Eastern group which included a former employee of the company which had managed these hotels. Thus, this new group was able to gain information that was not publicly available. Their bid of $50 million would clearly win.

We then went to Philadelphia and met in the courtroom. The judge ruled that the Loews group, which consisted of Larry and Bob Tisch and Mr. Milstein (I was at this time acting as advisor to the Milstein group) would have the right of last refusal; in other words, the right to match any bid made by the Middle Eastern group. The judge also ruled that, even though we claimed that this new group was using information not available to others, such an allegation was a civil matter and not a case for the Bankruptcy Court.

The lawyers for the Tisch group then immediately agreed to match the $50 million bid. The group from the Middle East went to $51 million. This went back and forth until the Middle Eastern group bid $55 million. The judge then turned to the representatives of the trustees for Penn Central and asked for their recommendation. They recommended that the lower bid of $54 million from the Tisch group be accepted since it was backed by the full faith and credit of the Loews organization, while the other bid was backed by a letter of credit of only $7 million.

We thought this was the end of the bidding. However, then the judge called a recess for lunch, and all the parties caucused. We were certain that after this recess the Middle Eastern group would once again increase its bid. We had no authority to go beyond $54 million. When we returned to the courtroom, the judge turned to the attorneys for the Middle Eastern group and asked "What is your new bid?" They explained to the judge that they wished to modify their bid, not by raising it but by raising the deposit from $7 million to $13 million. The judge then asked the representatives of Penn Central's trustee for their recommendation. They opted for the $55 million price.

At this point, the attorneys for the Loews group asked for a recess. Everybody scrambled to the public telephones and called Larry and Bob Tisch and Paul Milstein, and explained the situation. It took a great deal of time but finally Paul Milstein persuaded the Tischs to meet the $55 million bid. We went back into the courtroom and the lawyers for the Tisch group said, "We will match the $55 million bid." The lawyers for the Middle Eastern group declined to increase their offer. The hotels were purchased by Loews and Mr. Milstein, with me as a minority partner, for $55 million.

On the way out, one of the senior officials of Loews asked what we thought the Barclay might be worth. Ed Lewis, at that point, said he thought that Intercontinental would buy it for $35 million. The Loews price was $31 million. (Mr. Milstein had acquired the Biltmore and Roosevelt for $24 million.) Within two weeks, Intercontinental bought the Barclay from Loews for $35 million, and within a matter of two or three months Pakistan International Airlines Investment Corp. leased the Roosevelt at a price that would indicate a value in excess of $30 million.

This was already $6 million higher than the purchase price paid by Mr. Milstein for the Biltmore and Roosevelt, combined.

The Biltmore today has a value in excess of $40 million, so that within a period of just under a year the value of these properties has more than doubled the price that was originally paid. This has not happened very often, but it is a clear indicator that when real estate values shift, they can shift quickly and dramatically.

We came through a period not too many years ago when hotels were very difficult to sell, when their values were far below replacement costs, to the current situation where they are in great demand. This, of course, is even more true in the case of office buildings. For instance, in the past few years, we have seen Park Avenue office space rise from $10 per square foot to in excess of $30 per square foot.

The cost of money for both construction and long-term financing has skyrocketed over the last two to three years in a manner comparable to the rise in gasoline prices. The best rate on a construction loan for a new building is approximately 1 to 1½ percent over prime, compared to the 6–8 percent in effect historically. The long-term lending rate is approximately 15 percent plus an equity kicker compared to historical rates of 7 to 9 percent.

In spite of this, the real estate business has never been better, prices have never been higher, and profits have never been greater. Although inflation has had a devastating impact upon many industries, it has been good to real estate. Moreover, real estate is one of the few industries where, through the utilization of institutional planning and a minimum of equity capital, ideas and concepts can be translated into a finished product in a short period of time at a substantial profit.

Home on the Range

Brigadier General H. L. Oppenheimer

In the anthropological history of Man, 300 years is like the winking of an eye. Until 300 years ago, 95 percent of all capital, wealth, and "investments" related to agricultural land: the products of agricultural land; the implements, horses, and slaves necessary to work agricultural land; the ships and wagons to haul agricultural products; and the weaponry to seize or defend agricultural land. In those days, 90 percent of the world's population was involved in producing or processing agricultural products. Until this past 60-year period, there was not a single president of the United States who was not capable of working a 40-acre field with a horse-drawn plow. Even today, the major part of the business of at least 30 percent of the companies on the Fortune 500 list is directly involved with growing, transporting, processing, storing, financing, or retailing agricultural products. Because of space requirements, I will limit my discussion to investments in direct basic production and the land on which it is grown; to cattle instead of hamburger chains; to corn instead of distilling plants; to citrus trees instead of frozen orange juice.

The great bulk of agricultural investments in the United States is made by owner-operators whose full-time occupation is either working the land or in the direct personal management and supervision of those who do. Within the field of "direct agriculture," we shall select certain broad

categories for internal analysis themselves, and in comparison to other
types of investment. These categories will be (1) cropland, (2) grassland
for livestock, (3) citrus groves, (4) grain production, (5) cattle production,
(6) mortgages on agricultural land, and (7) chattel mortgages on livestock.

The elements that a non-operating owner, seeking diversification from
his or her main business, may want in an investment are: security, income, liquidity, a minimum of managerial headaches, tax shelter, social
prestige, and, above all in today's world, protection against inflation.
Security, at least in the minds of European investors, and with coming frequency, a majority of American investors, is *numero uno*. In accordance
with Will Rogers' oft quoted saying, "I am more interested in the return *of*
my capital than the return *on* my capital."

Time, place, and background of an individual are important in determining the respective priorities of these elements. A friend of mine who
heads the Dusseldorf branch of one of the main German banks and was a
Luftwaffe fighter pilot, says, "I cannot understand how anyone in Western Europe can make an investment move without remembering that
there are 100 Russian tank divisions poised on the border of East Germany and there is nothing that can stop them on the way to the English
Channel." This line of thinking might be labeled desire for "political
security."

Since the invention of paper currency, or the issuance of paper debt instruments by nations, there has been almost no nation within the last 100
years that has not repudiated all or a major portion of its debt either in one
fell swoop like the Roosevelt devaluation in 1932, or in a gradual attrition
by 10 percent annual inflationary nips like we are undergoing. Any bond,
debt instrument, insurance policy, or farm mortgage lacks the element of
"monetary security." A French industrialist says, "Income to support my
family comes from my business. My only reason for investment in the
United States is preservation of capital and I don't trust your dollar or
your stock market."

Method of entry

Within a single type of agricultural investment, the method of entry and
financial structure can make it impeccably safe with a worry-free low
return or considerably more speculative than a roulette wheel at Monte
Carlo. As an example, we shall review seven alternative ways of investing
in a 500-acre corn farm on the Missouri River bottom at $2,000 per acre.

Alternative A. The property is purchased on an all-cash basis and
put out on a lease with a tenant having a $5 million net worth with a 3 per-
cent net cash rent. On the assumption that agricultural land values will

continue to follow their historical pattern of increasing 2 percent faster than the inflation rate, and that Missouri is not on the edge of being invaded by the Russians, we have reasonable security against external problems and against a declining currency. The 3 percent net rent may not buy a steak dinner five years from now, but a lease is not forever, and its dampening effect will eventually be over.

Alternative B. The owners put the property out on a share-crop lease. The tenant furnishes the labor and equipment, the land owners furnish half the seed and fertilizer and get half the crop. Here, an average rate of return with a competent tenant should come out somewhere between 4 and 6 percent, but the owners are subject to the hazards of the commodity market and the weather. However, the owners also have reasonable protection against inflation, not only from the appreciation of the land, but also from the fact that grains will probably move up with inflation.

Alternative C. The owners have a direct operation in which they put in the crop; employ their own manager and labor and buy equipment; and stand all the risk of commodity fluctuation and weather. Here their return can run from a negative 5 percent in one year to 25 percent in another year, but with an average expectation of 5 to 7 percent. This takes a high degree of managerial skill, marketing acumen, and, most of all, the cooperation of Lady Luck. As far as market fluctuations are concerned, some of the risk can be leveled out by hedging on the Commodity Exchanges as will be described later.

Alternative D. Same as C, except that the buyers purchase the property with a 30 percent down payment and a 70 percent mortgage at 11 percent interest. Here, a substantial amount of efficiency and luck is needed for the crops to make the debt service. In a bad year, the buyers must be prepared to come up with substantial out-of-the-pocket cash to make the payments and avoid foreclosure. On the other hand, if they bought right in the first place, operated the property knowledgeably and efficiently, and agricultural land values continue to appreciate at a 9 percent per year compound average, then in a five-year period they might expect a 200 percent return on their original equity investment. Likewise, if they had two consecutive years of crop failures, and did not have $300,000 of additional cash to put into the property for mortgage payments, and deficiencies in operations, they would be wiped out and lose everything.

Alternative E. The investors do not buy the property at all, but lease it from somebody at a 3 percent cash rent of $30,000 per year. They make an investment in rental equipment, seed, fertilizer, advances to custom operators, and other items at $70,000. The property produces 120 bushels per acre of corn or 60,000 bushels worth $3 per bushel, or $180,000. They net $80,000 for their managerial and marketing skills. If they only get 80 bushels to the acre, or a total of 40,000 bushels and the corn brings $2.25 per bushel, they break even. If there is a drought or a partial flood and they get only 40 bushels to the acre, or 20,000 bushels and there is a premature frost so the corn has to go as silage, and they get only $1.50 per bushel, they lose $70,000. The latter is a risk they cannot hedge against on the commodity market because corn with excess moisture or damaged by frost cannot be used for physical delivery on a futures contract.

Alternative F. The investors neither buy land, lease land, nor put in a corn crop, but buy corn futures on the Chicago Board of Trade. A 5,000 bushel contract currently going for $4.04 per bushel for September 1981, having a value of $22,200, can be purchased with a $600 margin. If corn goes down 12¢ per bushel, they lose their investment.

Alternative G. The investors neither buy land, lease the land, put in a corn crop, nor purchase corn futures, but make a 50 percent loan on the farm to new purchasers with a good financial statement for $500,000 at 10 percent interest and 2 percent amortization. Their payments will be $60,000 per year. It is a 10-year loan which will have been amortized 20 percent at the end of 10 years and the balance of $400,000 will then become due. Here, they have impeccable security on the return of their investment, at least in dollars, but they may be suffering an annual attrition of their dollars by an 8 percent inflation. Hence, their actual return, net of inflation, might only be around 2 percent. However, they have complete liquidity as insurance companies are always in the market, assuming they get the proper competitive yield of the moment. Because of the lack of depreciation, obsolescence, and the extremely favorable history of agricultural mortgages over the last 50 years, these are generally preferred over urban mortgages. Consequently, the investors or lenders have complete security, complete liquidity, a fair return, but no protection against inflation.

Technically speaking, all seven of the alternatives listed above could be said to be investments in U.S. agriculture.

At the risk of boring the majority of my readers, I am going to devote the next few pages to an extremely elementary review of terminology, mechanics, and tax shelter aspects in some of the more common areas of agricultural investment. As an example, we will do a comparative and historical analysis of land and gold from the standpoint of security, liquidity, and return. Next, we will submit a comparative chart grading on a basis of zero to ten in respect to the previously mentioned investment criteria: cropland, grassland, breeding cattle, farm second mortgages, gold, race horses, movies, oil exploration, government bonds, shopping centers, and common stocks. Finally, we will review a list of criteria an absentee investor should review in the selection of an agricultural broker, consultant, or management firm.

Cropland

1. In an average season with proper planting times and proper amounts of fertilizer, above-average bottomland has these alternatives: the production of 120 bushels of corn per acre, 40 bushels of soybeans, or 30 bushels of wheat.

2. Corn and soybeans are usually planted in April and harvested in November. Winter wheat, the common crop, is planted in September and harvested in June or July the following year. Under some circumstances, a double crop of wheat and soybeans can be obtained on the same ground.

3. In some areas, extra income can be derived from winter wheat by grazing cattle on the young wheat during the fall and winter months prior to the time the wheat reaches a level of maturity where it "joints." Subsequent to this time, cattle trampling will decrease grain production.

4. Corn produces the highest cash income, but requires substantially more fertilizer than soybeans or wheat. It also requires a higher degree of cultivation and care during the growing season for maximum results.

5. The most prevalent lease over most of the Midwest is for the landlord to furnish the land, pay real estate taxes, half the cost of fertilizing and seed, with the tenant furnishing labor, equipment, and the other half of fertilizer and seed. The crop income is split 50/50. An area of bargaining is who pays the cost of harvesting and/or transportation to a grain elevator or a point of sale. This cost could be split or, in more recent years, the tenant pays it. On this basis, in 1972 and 1973, on good bottomland, the landlord's net share before real estate taxes, and assuming a good crop, would have averaged somewhere between $100 and $200 per acre.

6. Cash leases in which the landlord pays only real-estate taxes are quite rare, but would average somewhere between $30 and $80 an acre on good bottomland. Most tenants endeavor to get 10- to 20-year leases, but landlords have traditionally refused to grant anything more than year-to-year or short-term leases.

7. Example: In a normal year, on bottomland producing 120 bushels of corn selling for a price of $2.75 per bushel, there is a gross of $330 per acre. In generalized terms, the expenses would be the following: fertilizer would cost $60; labor and machine hire of plowing, planting, cultivating, and harvesting, plus fuel and oil would come to $30; seed, $10; pesticides, spraying, contingency problems, $10; real estate taxes and personal property taxes, $10; miscellaneous, $4, generating total expenses of $124, leaving a net of $206.

The split of income using the generalized numbers would be:

	Landlord		Tenant	
Income		$165		$165
Expense				
Fertilizer	30		30	
Labor & Machine	—		30	
Seed	5		5	
Pesticides	5		5	
Taxes	10		—	
Miscellaneous	2		2	
		52		72
		$113		$ 93

8. Factors affecting cropland value are as follows:
   a. Annual rainfall.
   b. Temperature or length of growing season.
   c. Topography or whether land is flat or hilly.
   d. Soil texture—whether clay, gumbo, or more permeable sandy loam.
   e. Soil fertility relative to nutrients and acidity.
   f. Depth of usable soil above rock or clay base.
   g. Presence of rock, gullies, brush, or other elements inhibiting use of equipment.
   h. Protection against flooding.
   i. Drainage to remove excess water from adjacent high ground.
   j. Proximity to concrete roads, rail, or barge transportation.
   k. Proximity to grain elevator complexes and other markets.

Grassland

We will define "grassland" as agricultural land used for grazing, but in areas either too dry, too high an altitude, or too rough and rocky to be economically suitable for cultivation. We will limit ourselves to properties at least 100 miles from any city, ski resort, lake, or fashionable recreation area, so that the effect on price from non-agricultural potential would be negligible.

We will further limit ourselves to units large enough to graze 1,000 steers during the growing season, as that would be the minimum unit to attract the large leasing operators and would be an amount that could be easily supervised by one man with three horses, a pickup, and a house trailer. In actuality, the same man could supervise up to 2,000 steers with temporary help for gathering, spraying, or special situations. Consequently, the even larger units have a greater degree of desirability and will attract slightly higher rents.

The annual rent for a given grazing season is a marketable commodity like corn or wheat, with a bid and an asked price. The price is based on a per-head basis of steers that can be grazed for a 5- to 7-month season or, in some areas, cows that can be grazed as well as winter fed over a 12-month period.

In the summer of 1978, in northeastern Nevada, for a five-month grass season on the range, not on irrigated meadows, in country that would normally be expected to produce a 175 lb. gain on a steer, the bid price would be around $38 per head and the asking price around $42. In the Blue Stem area of Kansas, in the vicinity of Emporia, where a summer steer could be expected to gain 250 lbs., the bid price was $48 for a 6½-month season, and the asking price was $52. In 1973, when the cattle market was approximately 50 percent higher, these rents ran about $15 per head higher. In the lowest point of the current cycle, around 1975, these rents ran about $5 per head less. For a landowner owning this type of property and traditionally leasing it on a cash rent for the season with no problems, no investment in cattle, no sharing of costs, no worries with the weather, and with never a vacancy, a 3 percent net return on the price of the land has always been considered satisfactory.

On the grassland, the impeccability of rent collection is also a factor. Normally, half the rent is paid in advance at the time the cattle come into the pasture, and the other half becomes a lien on the cattle comparable to a mechanic's lien in construction, which comes ahead of all other creditors, including secured bank mortgages. The cattle cannot be moved off the ranch without the remaining rent being paid, and the "pasture lien," recorded or not, gets first proceeds out of any sale.

Relating the 3 percent net rent to land values, let us take southern Wyoming in an area that requires 20 acres to run a steer for the summer. If the rent for a summer steer is $50, this amount capitalized at 3 percent would be 50 times 33⅓ or approximately $1,665. Dividing $1,665 by the 20 acres necessary to run the steer leaves a price of $83 per acre. This would be based on a ranch in which all of the acres are owned in fee. Should government grazing leases be involved, some type of proration must be worked out as to the grazing capacity of the deeded versus the grazing capacity of the government land, which is usually in the more remote, least desirable areas.

In relationship to cropland, the traditional return on capital on a cash lease is about 4 percent, possibly going to 6 percent on a sharecrop lease with its increased risks and unknown factors. The reason for the higher capitalization rate on cropland leases is because there is more risk of vacancy, increased problems of collections from tenants, a closer association with the violently fluctuating grain markets, together with the tie-in with fertilizer and energy costs. Another factor for the higher capitalization rate might be that increased cropland can always be brought into production with brush clearing, sprinkler irrigation, and other items, or increased outputs of fertilizer. Worry-free, labor-free grassland, particularly that obtained at under $60 per acre, cannot be easily duplicated.

Citrus groves

This is a $2 billion per year industry, principally in oranges, grapefruit, and lemons, concentrated in Florida, California, Texas, and Arizona, with Florida producing approximately twice as much as the rest of the United States put together. It takes four years after planting for a grove to be in production, with maximum production being hit in the 9th to the 11th year and no serious deterioration in production until after the 25th year. Good management requires the replacement of the individual damaged trees and a certain amount of replanting through the years. In California, a top 11-year-old grove of Valencia oranges will produce 450 boxes per acre worth $4 "on tree" per acre at cost of $900 per acre, which would include $150 per acre replanting and real estate taxes.

Prior to the tax bill of 1969, it was possible to deduct the entire cost of planting, which brought an enormous amount of new groves into being during the early '60s and a certain degree of over production into the early '70s. A considerable number of the groves planted during this period were poorly planned and amateurishly put together, so that in many cases they had excessive costs of irrigation in California, were planted in highly frost-prone areas in Florida, and had many other problems which made them marginally profitable and, in some cases, eventually forced their abandonment.

With the removal of their principal tax-shelter benefit, the situation has been pretty much rectified with surviving mature groves, with a reasonable record of production, now being an excellent investment. Insofar as most marketing has to be accomplished through the giant citrus cooperatives like Sunkist, reasonably accurate records of production can be obtained. Good independent appraisers are available to inspect groves as to the condition and check the books on operating costs, as well as assess historical and potential frost damage. The operation, management, and care of a grove require a great deal of skill. For this reason, groves are never leased out, as an incompetent tenant could destroy the capital investment in a one-year period. Groves will range from $1,500 to $7,000 per acre in price, with the variable dependent on location, condition of the trees, expense of irrigation or drainage, susceptibility to frost, and the type of tree planted. Net income will range from 3 percent to 18 percent, with violent fluctuations from year to year.

In a grove selling at $4,500 per acre in the frost-free, well-drained Indian River country of Florida, which has no appreciable irrigation or pumping costs, $1,500 would relate to the land value and $3,000 to the trees. Consequently, with citrus as well as walnuts, avocados, almonds, and other types of nut groves, the normal national factors of land appreciation are not nearly as applicable because a large proportion of the value relates to the trees, which are not an appreciating item. For example, if the basic values of agricultural land in Florida are increasing at the rate of 10 percent per year, a grove in an area where only 25 percent of its value relates to the land would participate in this increase only to the tune of 2.5 percent per year. In the same context, the so-called windfall potential of agricultural land going up in value for some non-agricultural use, such as residential housing, is less applicable because a value for this purpose would have to go to $4,500 per acre to justify bulldozing out the trees.

Crop production

This is the principal source of foreign exchange for the United States and, with the increasing industrialization of the rest of the world, may soon be our only competitive export. Our principal crops are wheat, corn, barley, soybeans, sugar, milo, cotton, and alfalfa. West of Kansas, production is frequently tied in with irrigation. Irrigation is usually from surface water and rivers with highly valuable irrigation ditch rights or by pumping from wells with ever-descending water tables and increasing energy costs lending this kind of farming a degree of future uncertainty. In Florida, the opposite situation exists, where excessive rainfall and drainage become the problem and pumping may be used to remove water from land into a drainage ditch. Approximately two-thirds of the U.S. grain production, including almost the entire corn, barley, and, alfalfa crops, go into livestock feeds.

The incredible advances made in farm machinery, fertilizers, and pesticides in the past 20 years have permitted 1 person on the farm to feed 50 people in the cities. In the previous 6,000 years of history, when Man first started to domesticate grain and animals, to the beginnings of the nineteenth century, it took 10 people in the country to feed 1 in the city.

To properly utilize modern equipment and techniques takes large tracts of good soil with relatively flat land with ample supplies of cheap, fresh water and adequate drainage. Poor soils without water cannot properly utilize the new fertilizers. Chopped up small tracts of rocky or hilly ground will not permit the effective use of the giant, modern equipment. High altitudes, cold winters, and short growing seasons with early frost prohibit the growing of corn or soybeans. Likewise, semi-tropical conditions with heavy weeds and insects and blight deprivations with excessive rainfall and drainage problems equally prohibit the growing of crops. The limited supply of energy sources, their increasing cost, and the political problems associated with their use may very well limit any massive futuristic schemes to convert the ocean's saltwater to fresh water irrigation and could conceivably limit most well irrigation. At today's energy costs, it is considered impracticable to lift water more than 300 feet for commercial crop irrigation, although there is a considerable amount being conducted at a 400-foot level, or greater.

In summary, when one looks at the huge expanses of Africa, Russia, Siberia, Australia, or Brazil, one might say the future competitive position of Iowa, Missouri, and, Illinois, on say, corn, may be of short duration. That is not correct. The midwestern cornbelt's soil temperatures and rainfall conditions are almost unique in the world, and the cost of duplicating, where temperatures would permit, would be prohibitively expensive.

Cattle operations

These are generally divided into three phases: breeding herds, in which cows are bred to bulls and produce calves; stocker operations, in which calves, after they are weaned at approximately 7 months of age, are run for 6 to 12 months on grass; and feedlot operations in which the male portion of the stockers and the females that are not going to be held for replacement cows are put into a feedlot on concentrated grain rations and go from there to the packing house. In the old days and in a few remaining operations, all three phases might be accomplished on a single ranch or farm. In these days of specialization, these separate operations might be thousands of miles apart. A steer calf from a cow herd in Texas might spend its summer as a stocker in western Kansas, be moved in November to a Missouri feedlot, and go on to slaughter at an Iowa packing house.

From the gleam in the bull's eye to steak on the table could be a three-year period. The gestation period of a cow is approximately 9 months, and she would give birth to a calf weighing around 70 lbs. It is weaned at 7 months, weighing 400 lbs. Animals to be retained for beef and not for breeding are usually castrated prior to weaning and cease to be "bulls" and are known as "steers." The females are called "heifers," and when they, themselves, are bred, usually at 18 months, they are known as "first calf heifers." They are classified as "cows" normally when they are bred for the second time.

Going back to our steer, he is now put on grass for a 12-month period during which he will gain another 300 lbs., thus weighing 700 lbs. at 19 months of age. He will then go into a feedlot for a 6-month period, where he will gain another 400 lbs., to weigh 1,100 lbs. He goes to a packing house and probably is graded low-choice to medium-choice. In the event he is of a superior quality and the feeder wants to shoot for the high-choice or prime market, he might be kept on feed another 2 or 3 months and come out at 1,300 to 1,350 lbs., to be graded prime. The cost of gain during this last increment is extremely high and the market for prime is quite limited, being almost exclusively in the major cities, such as New York or Chicago. Less than 3 percent of the slaughter steers coming through Kansas City Stockyards have been fed to prime grade.

The animal is "hung on the rail" where the hide has been taken off, and the head, legs, entrails, and certain other elements removed, and is now known as a "dressed beef carcass." The carcass will "grade out" at 60 to 70 percent of his live weight. At this point, an inspector from the U.S. Department of Agriculture will inspect him and stamp him as to quality, normally good, choice, or prime.

From an investor's standpoint, one can own a ranch with the cattle; one can own a ranch without cattle and lease to cattle operators; one can own cattle without a ranch and lease the ranch; or one can own the cattle on weightgain contracts with either a rancher, a ranch tenant, or a feedlot operator. Cattle can be owned free and clear with no debt, or they can be highly leveraged with 90 percent mortgages. At various ages and classifications, they can be hedged on the Chicago Mercantile Exchange futures market. The "live cattle contract" relates to the 1,000-to-1,100-lb. slaughter steer before he goes to the packing house. The "feeder contract" relates to the steer around 14 to 18 months of age, weighing 600 to 800 lbs., as he is coming off grass into a feedlot. The contract for the latter animal is for 42,000 lbs. of steers and the margin requirement is $1,800 a contract; 42,000 lbs. of steers would be approximately 60 to 70 head.

Depending on whether one is highly leveraged, whether one has a weightgain contract with a reliable rancher or runs everything alone, and whether one chooses to hedge on the futures market can make this a relatively conservative or highly speculative investment.

There are substantial tax-shelter potentials under current tax laws. Because the actual purchase of the animal has to be capitalized and is not deductible, and because bank financing is readily available, the tendency for investors motivated by tax-shelter requirements is to be highly leveraged. Because the tax input is normally with deductible "soft dollars," and the investor is usually in a very high bracket, the tendency is to gamble and not hedge, as Uncle Sam is sharing the risk.

Farm and ranch mortgages

From the standpoint of loss history and trouble-free management, these are the darlings of the insurance companies investment portfolios. One of the "big five" national insurance companies has had over 30,000 such loans on its books over the past 40 years in the states of Missouri, Kansas, and Iowa. During that period, only three properties went to foreclosure and were repossessed. All three properties were subsequently sold at a profit over the foreclosure price.

What is behind such an incredible record? First, this company never loans on "raw land" but only on agriculturally productive land. This is defined as land that has a minimum 3 percent net agricultural rental income, after real estate taxes, on appraised value. Second, it loans only 70 percent of the appraised value. Third, agricultural land in economic size units is fungible. That means 1,000 acres is not too different from 1,000 acres of similar topography in the same geographic area. Consequently, it has a "bid" and "asked" price with a high degree of liquidity within the bid-and-asked range, and its value is easily and quickly determinable. Fourth, the value of productive agricultural land increases at an average of between 6 and 10 percent per year, so there is a situation of appreciating collateral without the factors of depreciation and obsolescence that occur in developed urban properties. Fifth, there is never a vacancy. Productive agricultural land always has a tenant. Sixth, the Missouri office of this particular insurance company avoids all land that requires sprinkler irrigation and, in fact, does not like any type of irrigation, so it has minimal problems with falling water tables and uneconomic pumping costs. It likes crop farms and grass ranches where the values are based on water from the sky.

Because of this phenomenally good loss record and minimum trouble situation, competition for these loans is severe with the result that the interest rates are usually lower than urban properties. The dominant force within the industry is the Federal Land Bank, with which other lenders must compete. The second major source is insurance companies. Purchase money mortgages taken back by the sellers were, until recently, mostly seconds.

Prior to the past 15 years, the Federal Land Bank had a massive portfolio of 33-year loans at 4.5 to 5 percent interest. Its severe policy and legal restrictions on the qualifications of the borrowers were the only reasons there was any paper at all left for anyone else in the industry. Among its restrictions or policy limitations are requirements that the borrower must be a U.S. citizen, and that, if it is a corporation, 51 percent of the corporate income must come from active farming operations. While absentee owners or those with substantial non-farm income are legally permitted to receive loans, they are not greeted with wild enthusiasm by the local policy boards which make the final decisions. Consequently, this type of borrower would be lucky to get a loan of 40 percent of market value, while a full-time operator who resided in a rural area and, even better, came from a "farming background" might be given a 75 percent loan.

In recent years, the Federal Land Bank has changed its fixed rate loans to floating rates adjusted every six months which, in theory, are supposed to run 2 percent higher than the average yield on the five-year notes that it sells the public.

Generally the insurance companies stay about 1 percent over the Federal Land Bank rate. In the secondary mortgage market, a seasoned agricultural first mortgage, collaterized by land in a traditional productive area, is highly sought after by the insurance companies and has an instant market at the yields of the moment. Particularly, because of the history of refinancing over five or six years, and because of the need for operating capital or expansion, or sale, the acquisition of these mortgages at a discount is a very hot item among the insurance companies and a major source of profitability to the farm and ranch loan departments. In other words, a mortgage with a ten-year remaining life that could be bought at a 10 percent discount to give a yield of 12 percent would generate a phenomenal yield if the borrower wants to refinance or pay it off in two or three years.

Second mortgages on agricultural land represent a special target of opportunity in the investment field. First, Federal Land Banks by law are prohibited from holding them. Second, until a few years ago, insurance companies were prohibited from holding them, as were national banks. While the law has been changed, the farm loan departments of the major insurance companies, which may be the most conservative segment of the entire investment fraternity, will not make second mortgage loans except under very unusual circumstances. With the two major traditional sources of lendable funds out of this market, there is practically no secondary market in farm junior obligations even though farm first mortgages are the hottest thing around.

Coupled with this is an interesting historical situation. Until about 15 years ago, the Federal Land Bank totally dominated the market with its 33-year, 4.5 and 5 percent loans. Subsequently, the underlying land values tripled and the loans themselves were partially amortized with the result that the remaining balance of the Federal Loan Bank loan might be less than 20 percent of the current market value of the collateral. Obviously, in today's world of 11 and 12 percent interest rates, nobody is going to want to pay off a 5 percent mortgage. Its existence in a transaction is of major interest to both the buyer and the seller, and may have a dollar value at least equal to a couple of good barns. The end result is a rash of purchase money second mortgages around the industry, subordinate to very low first mortgages, but with no ready market.

The situation is just the opposite of the customary urban picture. Here, on a $1 million apartment building, one might have a $700,000 first mortgage at 11 percent interest and 6 percent amortization and a $100,000 second mortgage at 12 percent with no amortization ballooning in five years. Obviously, a slight decrease in apartment rentals might make it impossible to pay the debt service on the first mortgage, thus making the second mortgage highly risky.

A typical pattern on a $1 million ranch might be a $100,000 Federal Land Bank first mortgage at 4.5 percent, amortizing at 4 percent per year. The purchase money second mortgage is for $600,000 at 10 percent interest, 2 percent amortization with a balloon at the end of ten years. As mentioned previously, the lack of depreciation, obsolescence, deteriorating neighborhoods, and other problems besetting urban real estate do not affect agriculturally productive land, with the result that lenders do not hesitate to give very low amortization rates.

Looking at this ranch second mortgage, subordinate to a very small, low interest, first, we can see that one has an entirely different type of investment than the popular image of a "second mortgage." However, despite its soundness, there is not a ready secondary market for this kind of paper. The traditional agricultural lenders are out, and the traditional mortgage companies of the big eastern cities that deal in urban second mortgages do not understand and are nervous about remote agricultural properties. A second mortgage, as described above, that could be acquired at a 12 percent discount would generate a yield to maturity of 12.6 percent.

Chattel mortgages on livestock

The word "chattel" in Norman French means "cattle," and these may be the earliest forms of collateralized loans in history. Cattle branded with a hot iron are easily identified, have total liquidity, and were the principal form of wealth for nomadic tribes long before they settled down to raising crops. Prior to the beginning of the twentieth century, cattle paper constituted over half of the loan portfolio of every bank west of the Mississippi.

Normally, the bank lender has a recorded chattel mortgage or security agreement on the "cattle and their increase," plus sufficient feed on hand or prepaid grazing contracts to get them through a 3-to-6-month period. A calf born to the herd becomes part of the collateral until specifically released by the bank. Loans are usually for 6-month periods with an automatic renewal to 12 months. Feeder cattle in feedlots on full rations are considered more secure as the rapid weight gain increases their value, and they will be marketed for slaughter in 6 months. Cattle on full feed under close-in dry lot conditions are relatively impervious to disease, weather, and drought hazards, with a death loss generally less than .5 percent. Banks will normally loan up to 95 percent of the beginning market value provided that the feedlot operator has a reasonable record of competence. Breeding herds loans are more of a capital loan and banks traditionally do not go over 70 percent. Contrary to most loans on personal property, such as automobiles and farm machinery, the collateral on both classes of livestock loans is increasing in value through an increase in numbers and weight. On the hazard side, are "agister liens." If the rancher has not paid his feed supplier or the landlord from whom he rents his pasture, they can throw a lien on the cattle that comes ahead of the bank in most states. This is similar to "mechanics liens" on real estate construction.

While not available in any great volume, an unusual high risk, high return debt instrument might be mentioned. This is a non-recourse second mortgage on a breeding herd. The paper originates in the following manner:

1. Mr. John Doe, a New York stockbroker, has owned and operated a cattle breeding herd in the West for a five-year period as a tax shelter. The herd has a present value of $100,000 on a cash sale.

2. Because he did not want to clutter up his financial statement with the New York Stock Exchange with this as a personal liability, his first mortgage on the herd is "non-recourse." This means that in the event of a foreclosure, the lender can look only to the cattle and feed securing the note, but not to John Doe himself.

3. Within the "investor type" portion of the cattle business, if the buyers want to purchase a herd with 80 or 90 percent "non-recourse mortgage, they expect to pay, and the sellers expect to get, a 10 percent higher price than would occur if the transaction were done on an all-cash basis. During the course of the five-year operating period, Mr. John Doe has paid his original first mortgage down to $30,000. Normal bank loans on a breeding herd are for one year, usually renewable, but investor purchase money mortgages are generally for three to four years, which is another reason why the sellers can expect to get their 10 percent premium.

4. Mr. Tom Smith, another New York stockbroker, who also wants non-recourse financing, offers to buy Mr. John Doe's herd for $110,000, with $10,000 down, a $70,000 purchase money non-recourse second

mortgage at 10 percent interest, amortizable 30 percent at the end of one year, with the balance being due at the end of the second year. He assumes the non-recourse $30,000 first mortgage.

5. In addition to the cow herd, and the forthcoming calf crop, which will be collateral on this mortgage, Mr. Doe also insists that Tom Smith pay $30,000 in advance on his maintenance contracts and assigns them as additional security. He also insists that Mr. Smith pay, in advance, the rent of bulls for breeding service, plus all management and interest charges through December 31, coming to about $15,000 which, again, would be additional collateral on his second lien.

6. After about 30 days, Mr. John Doe changes his mind and wishes he had sold the entire herd for cash, and instructs his managing agent to sell his $70,000 second mortgage from Tom Smith, net of the $4,000 advance interest that he has received, for a discount that would have given him the equivalent of an all-cash sale at the beginning. This would be a discount of $10,000, or a price of $60,000 minus the advance interest of $4,000, or a net price of $56,000.

7. The manager now sells this note to a third-party purchaser, Mr. Frank Jones, for $56,000. Its yield to maturity, 23 months hence, for Mr. Jones will be approximately 22 percent.

The herd is dispersed in four geographically separated locations with four different ranchers, so the normal hazards of drought, blizzard, and bankruptcy of the contractor are reasonably spread out. The principal risk is of a market collapse causing a default upon the part of the owner, Mr. Smith. Mr. Jones' principal risk is during the first eight months of the holding period, where a market decline in excess of 20 percent could put a part of his mortgage in jeopardy. However, as soon as the calf crop is on the ground, his margin has doubled, and it would take a 30 percent drop in the cattle market to put him in jeopardy. A further consideration, here, is that Mr. Smith, the owner, is shooting for a capital gain which requires a two-year holding period, and all of the expenses of maintenance are deductible to him at the top of his tax bracket. Consequently, the odds are that he would continue to carry the herd and not default on his mortgages unless there was really a catastrophic drop in the market.

As a matter of historic interest, during the 25-year period in which Oppenheimer Industries has handled cattle loans for absentee owners of something in excess of $400 million, the banks have never lost one dollar on their first mortgage loans and the only time investors lost anything on these second mortgages was during the debacle in 1974. Their total losses did not exceed $500,000 out of total loan portfolio of approximately $20 million at that time. In that year, there was a 50 percent drop in cattle prices.

Tax shelter aspects

In general, farms and ranches have tax treatment similar to all other real estate. Buildings can be depreciated, interest on mortgages can be deducted, maintenance and management can be deducted, and certain items are subject to recapture. After certain holding periods, profits on sale will qualify for capital gain. There are however, a number of special considerations peculiar to farms and ranches.

1. "Fencing to restrain livestock" is personal property with a ten-year life and eligible for accelerated depreciation as well as the investment credit. Five-year old fencing can be depreciated at 20 percent per year at 150 percent declining balance.

2. A special circumstance relates to typical ranches that might involve 20 percent deeded land and 80 percent federal or state leased land. On these properties, the fencing belongs to the private tenant or purchaser and can also be depreciated.

3. If a run-down, worn-out farm overgrown with brush is purchased, expenditures to "restore the property to its former use" are deductible and do not have to be capitalized. New capital expenditures for "soil and water conservation" can also be deducted under very complex rules, but are subject to recapture when the property is sold at a profit.

4. Expenditures for seed, fertilizer, livestock feed, and a number of other items used to be deductible to everyone when *purchased* and not necessarily when *consumed*. Under very elaborate criteria, the 1976 tax bill divided all ranch, farm, and cattle owners into "owner-operators" and "investors."

Both groups can deduct the above items when consumed, but owner-operators also can deduct them when purchased and not consumed. One of the fascinating criteria for differentiating between the two classes of taxpayers is whether an investor had a father or grandfather who was engaged in farming even though the investor has no personal history of having done so. This may be the only item in the entire U.S. legal code in which one American is differentiated from another American on the basis of what one's grandfather did or did not do.

5. In respect to breeding herds, a cow is given a seven-year guideline life, and if she has not had a calf, which normally occurs at three years of age, she is considered to be "new in use" and entitled to double declining balance depreciation, as well as the Investment Credit. If she has had a calf, she is a "used animal" and, therefore, can get only 150 percent declining balance depreciation and no Investment Credit. Bulls are given a five-year guideline life. Once a male has been castrated, it ceases to be a breeding animal and becomes an item of inventory, qualifying neither for

depreciation nor for investment credit, nor for capital gain on sale. Breeding cattle, after a two-year holding period, qualify for capital gains but any previously taken depreciation is subject to recapture. A four-year old breeding cow purchased for $600 could be depreciated at a 25 percent rate, or $125 per year. If accelerated depreciation is taken the first year, 12-month depreciation will come to $187.50.

6. If a profit is made from one's farm, ranch, or cattle herd in two years out of five, by statute it is considered not a hobby but a business. However, if no profit is made, this does not mean that it is classified as a hobby, but the burden of proof is on the taxpayers to show that they had an economic motive; that their costs were more or less in line with the industry; that the herd has increased in value so they could show a profit by selling enough of them, and, in particular, that they are not getting personal benefit from the operation, such as charging a butler off as a farmhand, or residing in a 30-room mansion on a 20-acre "farm."

Land and gold

Sometime aroud 2000 B.C., as Man began to use bronze instruments, to get into a more concentrated agriculture, to develop urban centers, and to engage in trade, wealth and "success" were measured by one's accumulation of gold, livestock, slaves, and land. This theme persists through the bible. Historically, land and gold had certain obvious points of similarity:

1. With reasonable care, both were solid and not perishable.

2. There was a limited supply. Gold was rare and hard to produce. Agricultural or grazing land in a given geographical area or political subdivision was in tight supply, and unless you were prepared to conquer a neighboring tribe, there was no more of it.

3. Both were universally acceptable and desirable. Gold for jewelry and ornamentation; land because it produced food.

Historically, they also had points of difference:

1. Gold was compact and transportable; land was not. If you had to pull up stakes in the middle of the night, one jump ahead of a Hittite regiment, you could take your gold but not your vineyard.

3. Gold stored in a vault earned nothing; land, properly worked, produced income.

4. As a derivative of the above, gold could be used as a currency in trade. While possible, it would have been difficult swapping 100 hectares in Tyre for a ship in Syracuse. The ship seller in Syracuse may not have wanted a farm in Tyre, but he could use the gold to buy one near Rome.

5. On the other hand, the immobility of land made it ideal collateral for a loan. It could not be stolen or disappear. It also made a nice reward

for vassals or junior officers. They could not take off and join a neighboring army; they had to stay put.

What happened to these points of similarity and difference in modern times? Essentially very little, but there are certain refinements.

1. Gold for jewelry or dental fillings represents a very limited market, and its value principally comes from six countries that are willing to accept it to settle balance of payments on international trade. This situation could change.

2. Private possession can be prohibited, as happened in this country for 30 years. Modern detection devices can spot it in safe-deposit vaults, under the kitchen floor, or in airplane luggage.

3. On the plus side the complete lack of faith of every citizen in the world in his or her own country's paper currency and the conviction that a 7 percent per year inflation rate is the best that can happen and that every 15 or 20 years one can expect a sudden and surprise weekend devaluation.

4. With modern mining technology, gold production can be substantially increased if the price goes high enough. Also, the increase will principally come from such uncomfortable areas as the Soviet Union and South Africa.

5. As has been true since the days of King Midas, gold stored in a vault still earns nothing. However, the dollars that it is being priced in are shrinking in value year by year.

What has happened to agricultural land since William the Conqueror started handing it out to all of his faithful Normans?

1. Like gold, for the last 1,000 years it has been the principal security and refuge of people who fear currency.

2. Unlike gold, it has certain emotional, prestige, and cultural ties, particularly to family land, so that certain non-economic factors enter into play.

3. Between security, stability, and prestige, demand drives the price up so that a 3 to 4 percent net return is considered excellent in the United States. In Germany or France, a 1 or 2 percent net return is satisfactory. Presumably, like gold, its owners hope it will be matched by a 10 percent accretion in price due to inflation.

On one point of historical similarity there is now a major question mark. As mentioned, gold production continues and can be increased. Geographically, there is only so much surface to the earth so land cannot be increased. However, land used in agricultural production can be both taken out and added to. In addition, modern equipment, fertilizers, and irrigation have doubled production on existing land in the last 20 years. On the other hand, because nineteenth century transportation requirements necessitated starting most major cities on the best riverbottom farmland, urban expansion of these established cities is taking 2 million acres of topland out of agriculture each year.

Still, this is nothing new, and it has been going on for half a century. Increased production on existing land has matched land being taken out of production, but now new factors have been added:

1. Potential fuel shortages.
2. Skyrocketing fertilizer costs.
3. Rapidly falling water tables.

In agriculture, for a sufficient amount of money and capital, almost anything is theoretically possible. A rock mountain could be leveled; soil could be hauled in; and the soil could be brought under pivot irrigation from water piped 100 miles away. This could be done and it could produce corn at a cost of $50 per bushel.

In other words, the best U.S. agricultural land was brought into production 100 years ago. With growing population and decreasing land, more marginal arid or forested lands were brought into production with modern technology at ever increasing costs. Until the grain price increases of a few years ago, it was a rule of thumb that irrigation water could not be pumped from a depth greater than 300 feet. Increased grain prices dropped that to 500 feet. Increased energy costs brought it back to 400 feet.

If one flies over Phoenix, Arizona, and sees the miles of abandoned irrigated fields, one sees what happens when the water table goes below 500 feet. A 40 percent increase in pumping costs will put the breakeven at 300 feet.

If an extra input of $15 per acre in fertilizer will produce $20 per acre more corn on the same land with the same equipment and labor, it is worthwhile. If the fertilizer costs $21 per acre, it is not. Likewise, on better quality of land, higher inputs of labor, fertilizer, and other costs get more results than on lesser quality.

In summary, with the best quality of productive farmland being taken over by industry and suburbia, and with the costs of marginal land going up and getting less results, there is a real and substantial net reduction annually in the better agricultural land. Let us assume that it is 2 percent. Adding 10 percent for dollar deterioration, 3 percent for annual production, and 2 percent for increasing scarcity gives a total long-range investment return of 15 percent on agricultural land versus an anticipated 10 percent on gold from inflation.

From the liquidity standpoint, gold still has it. From the political security standpoint, there are questions. Back in 1933, with a stroke of his pen, President Roosevelt made it illegal to own gold, and fixed the price in paper dollars on which one had to turn it in. Furthermore, the Supreme Court backed him.

The mechanics of purchasing and storing gold:

1. You can buy 1 ounce pure gold (24 karat) Krugerrand coins and bury them in your backyard.

2. You can buy ingots or bars of gold bullion from your bank, guaranteed as to their purity, and the bank will store them.

3. Merrill-Lynch will sell you gold bullion at a fee of three-fourths of 1 percent, store it free, and issue a negotiable receipt.

4. You can purchase future delivery contracts in 100-ounce units on the New York Commodity Exchange with $1,000 margin/contract and a $50 commission.

Defining agricultural land as that which produces a minimum 3 percent net income over real estate taxes, how do you buy, lease, and manage it?

1. You select the area of the United States you want.

2. You have the local bank recommend a reputable member of the real estate board, a local attorney, and a title insurance company.

3. Cropland in Kansas, Arkansas, Missouri, and Iowa will cost you $1,000 to $3,000 per acre.

4. Grassland in New Mexico, Nevada, and Wyoming will cost $50 to $100 per acre.

5. You can put it out on a net cash lease at 2 to 3 percent, sharecrop rent it at 3 to 5 percent, or take full risk of direct operation and make annual returns of −5 to +20 percent.

6. Professional management will range from 5 to 10 percent of gross income.

In summary, gold has liquidity and no income, but should increase in value equal to the inflation rate. Productive agricultural land has more liquidity than urban real estate, but less than gold and earns 3 percent on a worry-free net cash lease. Over a ten-year period, it should go up 2 percent faster than the inflation rate, if 2 million acres per year continue to be taken for non-farm use.

Comparative investment chart

Using a broad-brush treatment, some of the rationale in assigning numbers to the non-agricultural investments is as follows:

1. Out of ten movies, the production of which is leveraged and financed by the banks, five will be failures with the banks being lucky enough to get their money back; three will have moderate returns on a strung-out basis as income from foreign sales comes in; one will be a

handsome success in which everybody from the producer to the stars to the investors will look like geniuses.

2. On oil exploration, out of nine holes drilled, three will be dry and a total washout; three will "hit oil," but not in sufficient quantities to justify commercial production; two will be marginally profitable on a long-term basis; and one will hopefully be a sufficient success to compensate the investing group for the six that were unsuccessful.

3. In Table 7-1, which compares common stocks and government bonds, note that common stocks were not given the traditional points as an inflation hedge as they have really not performed well in the past few years. Note also that common stocks were given some points on tax shelter, which government bonds did not get on the basis that certain non- or low-dividend paying stocks which plow earnings back into capital create little ordinary income, but do accomplish a certain amount of annual appreciation which would be taxed at capital-gain rates if the stock were sold. Likewise, there is some tax play involving the deductible 10 percent interest to buy such a stock which is only paying a 2 percent dividend. Note, also, that the problems of managing a common stock portfolio are considerably greater and require a higher degree of skill than managing a portfolio of gold and government bonds; thus, common stocks were given a lower grade in this column.

4. Apartment buildings with short-term leases of private tenants have a considerably lesser degree of security than shopping centers with the traditional long-term national tenants and, of course, require greater management skills than collecting rent from, let's say, Sears and Roebuck. On the other hand, in inflationary times, 20–25 year leases with anchor tenants at low rates, which may or may not have satisfactory percentage increase clauses and rarely have rents indexed to commodities or cost of living, could very well put a ceiling on shopping center salability as opposed to apartment buildings where rent might be moved up with the inflation rate, hopefully, at something exceeding the rate at which operating costs are moving up.

5. Without actual true statistics being published, based only on my reaction to the experiences of a number of my personal friends and acquaintances, it is my belief that only 1 racing stable in 50 averages a profit over a ten-year period. The 1 in 50 that hits a Triple Crown winner makes up for the 49 that have lost their shirts, plus its own nine years of "sweating it out." There may be a dozen stables in the country that consistently turn a profit, which is the result of great capital inputs and the highest level of managerial skill. The stables with 300 brood mares, staffs of trainers and jockeys, two or three winners per year, and outstanding showmanship make a go of it by getting twice as much at the

Table 7-1. Comparative investment chart, selected agricultural investments related to certain other fields based on a 0 to 10 grading system.

	Security	Liquidity	Income	Speculative Opportunity	Inflation Hedge	Tax Shelter	Social Prestige	Management Problems	Total
Cropland	8	6	2	5	10	4	9	3	47
Grassland	9	7	1	7	10	3	9	6	52
Breeding herds	4	8	3	8	7	9	4	2	45
Feeders	3	9	3	8	2	6	0	2	33
Farm first mortgages	10	9	7	0	0	0	0	9	35
Farm second mortgages	4	4	9	0	0	0	0	4	21
Citrus groves	4	5	6	5	6	5	8	3	42
Cattle second mortgages	2	3	10	0	0	0	0	2	17
Gold	10	10	0	5	10	1	0	10	46
Movies	1	1	3	10	4	10	0	2	31
Oil exploration	1	3	5	10	6	8	0	2	35
Government bonds	10	10	6	0	0	0	0	10	36
Common stocks	4	10	3	7	5	2	0	7	38
Apartment buildings	3	2	7	6	5	7	3	2	35
Shopping centers	7	3	5	4	4	7	3	4	37
Race horses	1	2	1	10	4	10	10	1	39

annual yearling sales as their less capable and less well-financed competitors. You will note on the chart that we gave racehorses a category "1" rating under managerial problems, meaning that success requires higher skills than any other investment charted.

6. Both gold and government bonds were given "0" as a tax shelter. Actually, gold, as well as discounted government bonds, can be leveraged with bank loans at 70 to 80 percent of purchase price, at probably one-half point over prime. The interest is, of course, deductible, and the gains on the bonds or gold, if held the proper amount of time, are taxable at capital gain rates. On the other hand, if we changed the investment with leveraging, we would have to change the security rating or have to open up another category on the chart.

7. In the categories of apartment buildings and shopping centers, the absentee owner is traditionally always leveraged, so we will assume 70 percent mortgages in the case of these two investments, otherwise there would be very little tax shelter. The same principle of customary leveraging applies to breeding herds, as well as feeder cattle, and, of course, movie investments, which are always leveraged, as far as private investors are concerned.

Analysis grassland versus urban as example

To quickly relate the low returns on grassland or cropland, for that matter, to the normal 12 percent cash flow, as if free and clear, that one would expect to get off such urban properties as apartment buildings, hotels, office buildings, and shopping centers, the following factors must be looked at. First, on any income-producing piece of construction, there is a legitimate 3 percent per year depreciation and obsolescence factor. Buildings get older and neighborhoods go downhill. Second, over a long period of time, even the best properties have a 10 percent vacancy factor. This comes off the top and should be a risk, giving at least a 1 percent negative potential hazard to the return, even though it might not be found in the first ten years. It would be unlikely that the combination did not exceed 4 percent per year after the middle life of the property.

Agricultural land, on the other hand, in the last ten years in the United States, has shown a 9.6 percent per year increase and seems fairly likely to at least match an inflation rate of 8 percent. Grazing land, in particular, cannot be manufactured, and it looks as if only within certain limitations can cropland be increased.

In summary, if 4 percent is subtracted from the traditional urban real estate income, and 6 percent is added to agricultural net rents, they are certainly on a par. Furthermore, secure 12 percent net returns on urban properties before depreciation, obsolescence, and vacancy factors are not that easy to obtain.

No real estate investment in the United States is more liquid than grassland in large assembled tracts. First, there is never a vacancy, even though one may not be getting the rent one wanted; second, one has total "liquidity" even though it may not be at the price one wants. However, an assembled tract of grassland with a usable fence and stockwater for cattle, with certain geographic specifications which are usually public knowledge within the industry, can always be sold at a price per deeded acre within 24 hours. The question, of course, is at what price?

These are some of the parameters:

1. Within the last two years, there has been no land of any nature whatsoever within the continental limits of the United States in tracts of 1,000 acres and up that has been bought, sold, traded, or sold at a foreclosure auction that has brought less than $30 per acre.

2. There has been no land with a usable fence around it, and stock-water for cattle, that has brought less under the above circumstances than $35 per deeded acre.

3. There has been no land that matches #2 above that has had, in addition, a public concrete highway to its border that has brought less than $40 per deeded acre.

The above are facts that can be determined by calling any of the banks making agricultural loans or any of the farm departments of any of the major U.S. insurance companies. This, then, offers a floor to the risks one might be making in acquiring grassland at, let's say, $50 per deeded acre. These floors have no relationship to the income produced but are hard facts of nature and the marketplace.

Liquidity in land or any other commodity is a function of time and price, related to sales effort and expense. At a certain price, something can be sold instantly with no effort. At a higher price, it may take a longer period and more effort. True liquidity relates to "fungibility." Fungibility is the attribute of a commodity in which one unit of measurement of certain specifications stored under certain conditions is identical to another similar unit and usually in sufficient volume that regular quoted markets are obtainable, including futures markets in which hedges can be made.

In other words, 1,000 bushels of "#2 yellow corn" relates to certain reasonably accurate government specifications as to quality, dryness, and other items delivered at a public elevator in Kansas City, Missouri, and can be substituted by law to meet a contract for another 1,000 bushels of the same commodity of the same specifications in the same location for either sale or purchase. The price on this commodity is a quoted public market for both spot cash on present market conditions or futures conditions and the range is normally a bid and ask price with a spread of about five cents per bushel. At any hour of the day, a telephone call will determine what this price for an instant sale would be in very substantial quantities.

A piece of urban real estate consisting of a developed income property, such as a shopping center, lacks this element of fungibility and consequently of liquidity. It has specific structures of variable levels of construction and age. It is located on a piece of ground, cannot be moved, and has a value in relationship to its neighborhood, competing shopping centers, potential of new competing shopping centers, and its particular position on the earth's surface. It is totally unique and cannot be substituted or exactly equated to any other shopping center or piece of real estate in the world. Its tenants have to be analyzed. Their potential of growth is an unknown, and this has to be studied in relationship to each individual lease, minimum rents, sales, percentage factors, area growth factors, and potential of future highway construction. Its analysis or evaluation is extremely complex. Shopping centers built at the wrong place at the wrong time and in the shadow of larger and newer ones may get no lease renewals and fail to make real estate taxes, much less mortgage payments.

Grassland that can run so many units of livestock in relationship to its area and that will produce a specific average gain on cattle in a specific period of time is precisely related to millions of other acres of comparable land in perhaps five other states of similar soil and climatic conditions. The variables between one tract and another are of a finite nature that can be scientifically determined with some degree of accuracy. Conditions of fencing, stockwater, and proximity to highways and railrods will cause price differentials, but the variables are easily determined by observation and are no mystery.

Within a given county in a general type of terrain, the carrying capacity is public knowledge known to all of the banks, county agents, and government representatives. Likewise, the amount of gain an animal will put on in a given season is again public knowledge. Both of these factors can be determined by a few phone calls. For example, dry non-irrigated gently rolling rangeland in the vicinity of Baggs, Wyoming, will have a bid price of $65 per acre and an asking price of $85. It would be very difficult to find any sizable pasture here at $60 per acre, but one could probably pick up several hundred thousand acres at $90 per acre.

Selecting a manager

In selecting an agricultural consultant, farm broker, or management firm, many good ones meet some of the following 12 qualifications. However, for an absentee owner who is new to the field, it would be prudent to require at least half of the following:

1. That the firm have a ten-year history of business.

2. That it have a $1 million net worth.

3. That it be able to produce a financial statement signed by a major recognized auditing firm.

4. That it be a member of the real estate board in good standing.

5. That it have a written listing from the owner it purports to represent; this is to avoid a waste of time.

6. That some evidence be produced, from either a former title policy or some other source, that the "owner" is really the owner of the land and not somebody who merely holds an option or "thinks he can buy the land."

7. That the party the owner is dealing with have some security, agency agreement or something that has been registered with the SEC. This does not have to necessarily relate to the deal at hand, but the mere fact that the party concerned had anything registered with the SEC means that there had to be a full disclosure of ownership, litigation, contingent liabilities, conflict of interest, and a considerable past history. If this information is false or there is a failure of disclosure on an SEC registration, it is a criminal offense punishable by a jail sentence.

8. Don't waste time discussing anything with anybody who is not prepared to furnish a bank reference plus a written authorization to the bank concerned to disclose and answer any questions you may have.

9. Insist that the firm you are dealing with have a fidelity bond covering its employees for dishonesty, embezzlement, bribery, and other matters of at least $1 million. Frequently, the top officers of the firm are perfectly all right, but some subordinates down the line can cause trouble.

10. Insist that the management firm, brokerage firm, or investment firm be covered by an errors and omissions policy with a nationally known insurance company for at least $1 million. This protects you against honest mistakes the firm may make but, more important is the question of whether it can get an errors and omission policy. New firms, incompetent firms, firms with a bad history will not be able to.

11. If you plan to work with an appraiser, choose one who is a member of the American Institute of Real Estate Appraisers and holds the MAI (Member Appraisal Institute) designation. This does not mean that appraisers who are not members of the institute are not perfectly worthwhile, but to get certified by the institute means that the appraiser must adhere to its code of ethics and have had a reasonable longevity and experience rating. A U.S. investor living in the neighborhood could deal

with somebody who is not a member of the real estate board or who is not a member of the institute, but a buyer living 2,000 miles away needs this protection.

12. If anybody represents you in the buying or selling of livestock, insist that he or she be registered with the Packers and Stockyards division of the U.S. Department of Agriculture, as well as bonded under the Federal Act. The USDA monitors everybody that is bonded, requires them to furnish financial statements, checks their past history for violation of its ethical code, as well as the law; once someone is registered, any violation of the rules is subject to criminal prosecution. Again, this does not mean that there is anything wrong with someone who is not bonded, but this is an added protection.

At Oppenheimer Industries, we have one additional piece of advice for our clients in the ranching business: never deal with a man who has all three of these attributes: monogrammed cowboy boots; a big, fat gut hanging over his belt; and a diamond ring on his little finger. Every time we violated this rule, it has been a disaster.

Seriously, large-scale agricultural operations dealing in people, equipment, horses, and remote terrain are very similar to military operations, and the type of managers and supporting staff are comparable to the executives one would select for troops. In this connection, I will quote a famous German field marshal of the past century:

"There are four kinds of officers: Those who are smart and lazy—they make the best commanders; those who are smart and energetic—they make the best staff officers; those who are stupid and lazy—we can find a place for them; and there are those who are stupid and energetic—these we must ruthlessly eliminate from the Prussian Army."

In summary, within the agricultural field as any other area, you have to equate the elements of security, liquidity, income, inflation, protection, tax shelter, and managerial simplicity with your financial objectives. From unleveraged grassland on 3 percent cash leases to high-risk second mortgages on cows yielding 22 percent, there is something for every investor's taste and whim. One final caveat, don't rush! When someone tells you he must have a yes or no answer in 24 hours, tell him the answer is "no." In agriculture, the aversion to rushing is widespread through all echelons, as the following story illustrates: a young bull and an old bull were walking down a Wyoming valley when they saw a group of 20 heifers on a ridge about 200 yards above them. The young bull nudged the old bull and said, "Let's run up the hill and screw a heifer." "Oh no," said the old bull. "Let's walk up the hill and screw them all."

All that Glitters

Dr. Henry G. Jarecki

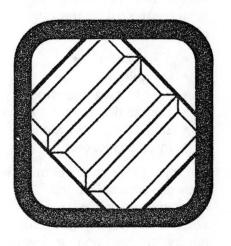

Current investor interest in gold is running at an unprecedented level and is likely to remain so. Between 1934 and 1975, Americans could not buy gold for investment. The generation that came of age during that period thus was cautious about incorporating gold into investment portfolios after it became legal to do so. Surprising as it may seem in retrospect, the first two years of gold trading in the United States were a non-event. The price fell from $197.50 an ounce to a low of $103.05 in August 1976. Trading volume averaged 3,800 lots (380,000 ounces) a day. Traders played chess on the steps of the pit, and the press mocked those who had lobbied for legalization.

Since then, widespread anxiety has arisen about inflation, recession, unemployment, fuel supplies, an energy program, and international tensions. The quest for protection against personal capital erosion has turned into a flood: more and more investors have faith in the traditional hedge against disaster, and so the amount of gold traded, the price per ounce, and the kinds of gold vehicles have climbed further and faster than anyone anticipated.

What has not climbed with equal speed has been an understanding on the part of investors, either of monetary theory, or of the kind or quantity of gold investment vehicles they may need to protect themselves against inflation, or the myriad other risks against which gold is believed to be a hedge. Although the stated policy of both the International Monetary Fund and the U.S. Treasury is to remove gold from the world's monetary system and treat it simply as any other commodity, the market and, more important, the people continue to feel that gold is money. A definition of "moneyness" and its characteristics is thus essential in developing an effective investment strategy.

Characteristics of money: how does gold stack up?

Perceptions of gold as money stretch back to the beginnings of history and have repeatedly proved to be sound. Ontologists would tell us that an object is money when it partakes of "moneyness," but that it is a paradox, for "moneyness" derives from general agreement that a given object has it. A number of objects, ranging from seashells to horses and cows, have been considered money over the course of history, but few have as many characteristics of "moneyness." That is to say, money is:

- A store of value.
- Durable.
- Easy to own anonymously.
- Easy to divide into many small portions.
- Easy to authenticate.
- Interchangeable.

Objects that have not met these criteria have been used as money but their use is more limited. For example, every ounce of gold is like every other one and gold emerges from storage in exactly the same condition as when it was deposited. Herds of cattle, on the other hand, can be wiped out by famine, flood, or disease.

The reason any object used as money must have these characteristics is to allow it to serve both as a means of exchange and as a store of value. When a given object's utility as a means of exchange or a store of value declines, two steps follow: first, that object's claim for acceptance as money comes into question and, second, there is a search—sometimes a frantic one—for an alternative. Dollars issued by the Confederate States of America lost their "moneyness" very rapidly as they bought progressively less, and they became worthless as a store of value as the survival of the issuing government became doubtful.

Other types of currency have suffered from the same malaise, although not often as dramatically or as rapidly. Gold, on the other hand, has maintained its value over the long run even when it has not been in daily use as a medium of exchange. It has done this even when its "moneyness" is formally denied, or, as at present, its "moneyness" simply is not formally accepted.

The only problem gold has ever encountered is that governments have periodically made its ownership taxable or illegal, or have confiscated private stores. Attacks of this nature or manipulations of the price by government sales confuse the investment value of gold over the medium-term and have thus from time to time moderated its acceptance as a store of value.

Its effectiveness as a hedge against inflation rests, therefore, on the experience of past generations. That experience will show the time frame within which gold is most effective as a store of value. Professor Roy Jastram's recent book, *The Golden Constant: 1560–1976,* demonstrates the close relationship between gold and commodity prices over the past 400 years and thus offers useful observations. He shows that a brick or a loaf of bread costs very much the same in terms of gold in 1960 as it did in 1560. True enough, within this long-term steadiness have been cycles of inflation and deflation when the ratio of gold prices to commodity prices has varied. Surprisingly, he shows that gold tends to *lose* its purchasing power during inflationary periods and to *gain* purchasing power during deflationary ones. Yet, even though it has been a poor hedge against year-to-year commodity price increases, it has maintained its long-term purchasing power from inflationary peak to inflationary peak. That is, commodity prices repeatedly return to the same price in terms of ounces of gold, an observation that cannot be confirmed for the prices of manufactured goods, which reflect steadily rising labor costs. Gold can thus function as an effective long-term hedge not only against inflation but also as a short-term hedge against deflation because its buying power appreciates more rapidly than anything else during such periods.

Another characteristic of gold that is important in thinking of it as an investment is that it is highly liquid. That is to say, even though there is no guarantee that it can be sold at a profit at any given moment, it can always be sold for something. From the 900,000 100-ounce contracts traded on futures markets in all of 1975, the volume of trading has recently gone to over a million contracts in a single month. One million contracts a month is equivalent to 100 million ounces a month, which equals 5 million ounces or more in a day, 3 billion dollars' worth at today's prices. Another 5 or 10 percent may trade in bullion form and perhaps as much again in coin as in bullion. Add to this leverage contracts, gold options, and mining shares, and it is obvious that the market has enormous depth. In a market this size, many millions of dollars worth of gold can be sold in minutes or less. Nor does gold's liquidity depend totally on a functioning economy. As the world's refugees and boat people can attest, gold may be the only marketable commodity in situations of extreme social disorder.

The value of gold for a sensibly diversified investment portfolio is also influenced by the fact that its price tends to run contrary to the prices of paper assets like bonds, shares, and currencies. The stock market often goes up in response to good news, while gold prices generally go up in response to bad.

A world in which gold's price is $100 an ounce can be relaxed and happy: people can live in peace and plenty. A world in which gold trades at $1,000 would be characterized by war, famine, distrust, and human misery. It is thus reasonable to keep a portion of one's net worth in gold, and still to hope very hard that the price of gold goes down.

In societies that have had more experience than the United States has had with currency depreciation, political upheaval, and economic disaster, gold has been the traditional hedge of conservative, responsible investors. Individuals, businesses, and public institutions normally keep a portion of their assets in gold. Gold is still held as a reserve by nearly all central banks. In the U.S. gold market of today similar, perhaps more sophisticated, investment attitudes are developing.

Types of gold suitable for investment

In the few years during which gold has been traded in the United States, the market has developed to the point that it offers many choices for both large and small investors. Some of these are unique to the United States. The trend is to respond to investor demand by offering investment vehicles to meet the widest range of needs.

The major categories of gold investments are *physical* gold (bullion, coins, or warehouse receipts for these) and *non-physical* gold (holding account certificates, gold futures contracts, gold options, leverage contracts, or mining shares).

The first thing the investor must decide is whether he or she wants the certainty of owning physical gold coins or bullion enough to put up with the nuisance and cost. That is, are the inconveniences of transport, insurance, storage, reauthentication, and trouble in financing the gold worth the assurance of having the actual metal and not someone else's paper promise? Broadly speaking,

• Buying *physical gold* is appropriate when the primary goal is to make a long-term investment which will require a minimum of supervision, one fears public disorder or government confiscation, or one wants anonymity; and

• Buying *non-physical gold* is appropriate when the primary goal is to use gold as a basis for leveraged trading, when one wants the benefits of moderate cost financing, when one trusts the exchange and broker from whom one buys it, and when one has both the time and inclination to keep in close touch with the market and broker.

Physical gold

Physical gold can be held in the form of bars, coins, or certificates of ownership like delivery orders or warehouse receipts. It must be paid for in full at the time of purchase. Funds used for this purpose can be leveraged only if the physical bullion is pledged to a lender. Bars and coins require storage but their advantage is that they can be held anonymously and can easily be passed from one owner or family member to another.

"Standard" bullion bar. A bar of four hundred ounces is usually traded in lots of five bars for a quantity of 2,000 ounces on the London market. Standard bars are generally left in storage in the dealer's warehouse to eliminate any problem of establishing their authenticity at the time of resale. A dealer will repurchase gold stored in the warehouse without assay whenever the owner wants to sell it.

The main risk of holding standard bars is the price fluctuation. Standard bars are totally liquid; they are traded at the twice-daily London gold fixing where the price is public and where the commission on purchases is 0.25 percent. Members and affiliates of the London bullion market and their American and Swiss counterparts are all parts of large organizations associated with international banks, and there is little need to be concerned about their credit or financial integrity. Nevertheless, the typical trading quantity of standard bars is so great ($1,200,000 at a $600 per ounce price) that trade is essentially limited to banks, governments, bullion dealers, and major portfolio managers.

Gold coins. Coins are a very popular form of physical gold because they may be owned in small units and because they are portable and easy to store or hide. The value of coins is derived from their numismatic and/or bullion character.

Numismatic coin investments are more like investments in art or antiques than investment in the metals markets because their important qualities are beauty, rarity, historical interest, and physical condition rather than gold content. Numismatic coins are less readily tradable than bullion coins because their authenticity and value must be individually established. Since the price of numismatic coins reflects this package of qualities, it is considerably above the market value of the bullion content and there is a large difference between buying and selling prices.

Bullion coins, on the other hand, while they are often very handsome, are traded for their gold content. They are minted in fixed weights and denominations; they are convenient and portable; and, because their weight and purity are widely recognized, there is usually no need to have them assayed before resale. They are thus easily resold and the premium over the bullion value is usually a modest 3–10 percent.

The most widely traded bullion coin is the Krugerrand. Its popularity is based partly on the large-scale promotional program of the issuer, partly on its ready availability, and partly on the coin's weight of exactly one troy ounce, which makes its price easy to compute. The Canadian Maple Leaf coin shares these characteristics but is minted in limited quantities and has a fineness of 99.9 percent versus 91.66 for the Krugerrand.

Other commonly traded bullion coins are the Mexican 20- and 50-peso pieces and the Austrian 100-corona coin. The U.S. Treasury began issuing one-ounce and one-half-ounce gold medallions in 1980, and other governments are also considering minting programs. American Double Eagles ($20) and English Sovereigns (£1) fall between the bullion coin and the numismatic coin categories. They are not sought for their individual numismatic qualities but may trade at premiums of 20 to 80 percent over the bullion value. Table 8-1 shows the fineness of each of these coins.

Table 8-1. Coins.

Coin	Fine Gold in Ounces	Fineness Percent
Mexican 20-peso [1959]	0.4802	90.00
Mexican 50-peso [1947]	1.2057	90.00
Krugerrand	1.0000	91.66
Austrian 100-Crown [1915]	0.9802	90.00
Canadian Maple Leaf	1.0000	99.90
British Sovereign	0.2354	91.66
U.S. Double Eagle	0.9676	90.00

Counterfeiting has to the present been a fairly minor problem, especially when coins are purchased from a reputable dealer. The penalties for counterfeiting coins that are legal tender are substantial enough to be an effective deterrent, and what little occurs is usually detectable by coin specialists.

Delivery orders. These, an innovation designed by Mocatta Metals Corp., are transferable documents of title certifying ownership of a specific numbered unit of bar gold or a specific number of bullion coins stored in a tax-free location like Zurich, Switzerland, or Wilmington, Delaware. Delivery orders are guaranteed by:

• Mocatta, which certifies it has deposited the quantity of gold described on the order in the warehouse;

• The warehouseman, who certifies that he has received the quantity described and will deliver it to the holder of the delivery order; and

• Lloyd's of London, the insurer, which agrees to compensate the holder of the delivery order if the gold described on it should ever be missing.

Delivery orders sell at a 2 to 3 percent premium. Inspection, anonymous payment of the 0.5 percent per annum storage fee, and transfer from one owner to the next have all been made easy. They should, of course, be kept in a safe place with other valuable papers.

Non-physical gold

Gold futures contracts. These are perhaps the most common way to own gold. These are executory contracts entered into on organized exchanges via commodity brokers in accord with which the buyer will buy and the seller will sell a specific quantity of gold at a prearranged price on a specified future date. The goal of most buyers in the gold futures market is to benefit from a rise in the price without the inconvenience of taking possession of the metal. The futures market makes this easy because the owner can sell the contract before the specified future date and can thus receive the profit or take the loss without having to take delivery or make full payment.

To buy a futures contract, the customer deposits margin funds in an account with a broker. With a deposit of $2,000–5,000, the customer can control a contract worth ten or twenty times as much. It is thus unnecessary to tie up large sums of money waiting for the market to move, and the potential profits per dollar invested are greater than in the purchase of physical gold. If an investor's projection of where the price is going to go is correct, the profit can be a very large percentage of the original investment, the margin. On the other hand, the potential for loss is correspondingly great. If the market moves against the investor's position, he or she will be subject to calls for additional margin which, if not met, will lead to a liquidation of the investment and a total loss of or even a loss greater than the original deposit. With a margin account, which is kept on a day-to-day basis, the investor may not get the opportunity to ride out temporary reverses.

An example: if the margin requirement on a 100-ounce contract on the New York Commodity Exchange is $5,000 and the price of gold is $600, a margin deposit of $5,000 controls a contract worth $60,000. When the price moves $1 an ounce, the investor gains or loses $100. Every dollar change in the price thus has a 2 percent effect on the investment, rather than a 1:600, or 0.17 percent, effect as would be the case if physical gold had been bought and paid for. If the market price moves as much as exchange rules permit before trading stops (currently $25 higher or lower than the preceding day's settlement price), the gain or loss on the initial $5,000 investment can be $2,500, i.e., 50 percent in a single trading day.

Another use of a futures contract is to allow an investor to benefit from the relatively low premium that gold futures command when compared to gold for immediate delivery and payment. If, for example, the price of gold for future delivery is higher than the price of gold for immediate delivery by an amount smaller than the return available from another investment, the investor may be better off buying the future gold. That is, if gold for delivery in a year is 10 percent higher than gold for immediate delivery and the investor has the opportunity to make a different investment at an 11 percent return, he or she should perhaps buy a gold futures contract on margin and use the remaining capital for the other investment rather than to buy physical gold, or to give up gold entirely in favor of the other investment.

The difference between buying physical gold and buying gold futures contracts should now be apparent. Holding physical gold requires little effort beyond the initial decision to buy it. Once the buy order is executed and a decision about storage is taken, there is nothing to do until the time comes to sell, and that may not be for 20 or 30 years. Owning a gold futures contract, on the other hand, requires the investor to keep in close touch with the market and with the broker and to decide when to undo the contract to achieve his or her short-term investment goals.

Gold options. These have the advantage that the investor can avoid the risk of margin calls or of the market moving down so far that it is necessary to sell to minimize the loss (forced liquidations). Gold options are rights, not obligations, to buy or sell a specified quantity of gold at a specified price (the "striking price") on or before a specified date.

The price of the option is called the "premium." Since the option is an obligation only for the grantor and not for the buyer, the latter has the choice of exercising it or allowing it to lapse. He may also be able to sell it at a profit on the secondary market before it expires. In any case, his maximum potential loss is limited to the original premium.

Gold mining shares. These are traded on securities exhanges and their value depends on a wide range of factors such as the past and potential production of the specific mine, the quality of the company's management, and labor conditions. The value of South African mining shares depends also on that nation's governmental regulations and political circumstances and on the exchange rate of its currency, the rand.

Factors to consider in developing a personal investment strategy

The first step an investor should take in developing an effective investment strategy is to consider his or her personal philosophy. A person with an apocalyptic view of the future will naturally have different goals from one who foresees stability restored fairly soon or, at worst, mild inflation. A person who wants to avoid foreign investment would not buy standard bars on the London market or shares in overseas mines; a person who fears possible confiscation of domestic holdings would insist on anonymity, portability, or storage in an overseas location; a person who manages a portfolio on a day-to-day basis would be more attracted to trading futures contracts or buying options than would someone whose time is fully committed to other matters. There are some general considerations, however, which can provide guidelines for decisions about the proportion of a portfolio that might be invested in gold and the kinds of gold that are best suited to various size investments.

Investors should analyze the nature of their current income and investments in order to gain maximum benefit from gold's countercycle with paper assets and from its high liquidity. A person in a business or profession that benefits from inflation has less need for investments like gold, which hedge against inflation, than someone whose purchasing power erodes with inflation. The importance of gold is further defined by an investor's age and net worth. Age is significant because of the long-term bias of gold as a hedge against inflation. Since its short-term value is affected by such unpredictable factors as the vagaries of the market, political events, and speculative activity, gold offers less benefit to older investors than to younger ones. In all age groups, investors with greater net worth need more protection against inflation, and they can afford to relinquish more dividend and interest income in favor of long-term protection.

Table 8-2 brings together age and net worth factors to indicate the proportion of gold suitable for various portfolios. It is important to remember that suggested percentages should be used as guidelines for the dollar value of the gold, not the amount one must invest to control that amount. Using 20 percent of one's funds for margin for futures contracts would involve ownership of gold worth more than the total value of the entire portfolio and would not serve the purpose of sensible diversification.

Table 8-3 suggests the most practical types of gold for investments of different sizes.

Characteristics of the American gold market

The American gold market is large, open, efficient, and versatile. Access to this market is provided by commodity and security brokerage firms, by bullion and coin dealers, and by banks. The proliferation of gold investment services offered by these institutions shows just how consumer-

Table 8-2. Percentage of portfolio to invest in gold according to age and net worth.

Age	\$0–100	\$100–250	\$250–1,000	\$1,000–5,000	\$5,000+
			Net Worth (in 000's)		
Under 20	15	20	25	30	35
20–40	15	20	25	25	30
40–65*	15	20	25	25	25
65+	15	20	20	25	25

*And institutional portfolios.

Table 8-3. Practical aspects of various types of gold.

Type of Investment	Approximate Minimum Practical Investment	Circumstances Under Which Suitable
Bullion bars	\$1,200,000	Substantial portfolios
Delivery orders	\$20,000	Investment portfolios holding \$10,000 to \$400,000 worth of gold
Bullion coins	\$650	Portfolios holding \$200 to \$100,000 worth of gold, especially when purchase or sale must be episodic because of the way money comes in or is needed
Gold futures	\$5,000–margin	Speculation; or when return on rest of portfolio exceeds gold futures premiums
Gold options	\$3,000–10,000	Speculation; or to assure future price

oriented the market is. Physical and non-physical gold in large and small quantities is widely available.

The New York Commodity Exchange is now the largest metals market in the world, and additional trading takes place in Chicago on the International Monetary Market and the Mid-America Commodity Exchange. Trading on these exchanges is by "open outcry": trades, quantities, and prices are called out across a ring. Consequently, information needed to make decisions is always open and public. Investors should keep in mind, however, that in extremely volatile markets information becomes stale very rapidly—often in a matter of minutes.

Regulatory supervision of the gold futures market is exercised by the Commodity Futures Trading Commission and by the exchanges themselves. Both are concerned with orderly trading as well as with maintaining the integrity of the industry and protecting investors from unscrupulous operators. Each exchange sets rules for trading in its rings and takes disciplinary action when those rules are violated.

Among the participants in the futures markets are floor brokers, floor traders, currency traders, hedgers, banks, and bullion dealers.

- Floor brokers are the agents responsible for executing orders on the exchange floors. Some are employed by brokerage firms; most are independent.
- Floor traders act for their own accounts in the pit and contribute to the market's liquidity.
- Gold fabricators and bullion dealers depend on successful hedging operations.
- The bullion dealers in the United States who seem to do the most business (measured by delivery on the exchanges) are Mocatta Metals Corp., Republic National Bank, Philipp Brothers, J. Aron & Co., and Sharps Pixley, Inc.
- Commodity finance banks enable the bullion dealers to buy physical gold from banks, miners, and governments and to sell futures contracts on the exchanges to hedging consumers (like jewelry manufacturers) and investors.

It must be understood that there are very few uncovered speculative shorts in the market. The shorts on the exchange are miners and bullion dealers hedging their physical stocks. The market is not, then, by any means, a paper market. As price and trade volume have increased, so have the underlying stocks (Exhibit 8-1).

Relationship with the world market

The world market interacts with the American market in many ways. As far as newly mined supply is concerned, most is of foreign origin. South African mines account for about 57 percent of annual world production, the Soviet Union for about 20 percent, Canada for 4 percent, the United States for 3 percent. But newly mined gold is a relatively small part of the tradeable supply. Above-ground stocks are estimated to be over 2 billion ounces—half in private, half in government hands. This constitutes 50 or more years of industrial consumption. Seen from this viewpoint, gold is more plentiful than water—of which there is in world storage surely less than a month's supply. Investor demand and sales thus play a larger role and new production a smaller role for the development of the gold price than is true of most other commodities.

The size and versatility of the American market attract trading from areas where investment opportunities are numerous. Many of the gold futures contracts traded on the New York Commodity Exchange, for

Exhibit 8-1. London 2nd fix and total monthly volume on U.S. Exchanges.

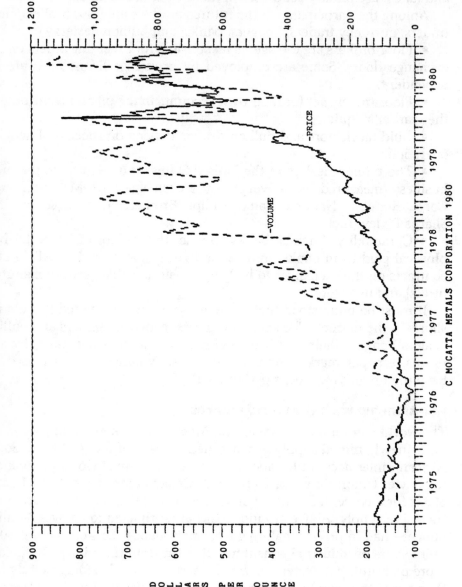

instance, are for foreign accounts, and foreign banks and dealers are active bidders at U.S. Treasury and International Monetary Fund gold auctions. Among the world's most active bullion dealers are:

• The five who make up the London bullion market: Mocatta & Goldsmid Ltd. (a subsidiary of Standard Chartered Bank Ltd.); Sharps Pixley Ltd. (a part of Kleinwort Benson); Johnson Matthey Bankers Ltd.; Samuel Montagu & Co. Ltd. (a part of the Midland Bank); and N. M. Rothschild & Sons Ltd.

• In Switzerland: Swiss Bank Corp.; Union Bank of Switzerland; Swiss Credit Bank; and Bank Leu.

• In France: Cie. Parisienne de Reescompte; and Societe Comptoir Lyon-Alemand Louyot & Cie.

• In Germany: the Dresdner Bank; the Deutschebank; and Degussa.

• In Hong Kong: representatives of Mocatta Hong Kong Ltd., and other London bullion dealers as well as a number of local bullion dealers including King Fook, Lee Cheong, and Sun Hing.

There are also substantial bullion dealers in the Mideast and, indeed, in many of the countries of the world.

Gold trading todays spans the world. The American investor is fortunately situated in terms of access to information and to a constantly broadening market. Investors who analyze their goals, develop their personal strategies carefully, and take the basic precaution of trading only through reputable brokers and dealers should find gold a valuable addition to their portfolios.

Some comments on silver

Investment in silver is conventionally paired with investment in gold because of the widely held view that the only significant difference between the two precious metals is price. Treating silver as "poor man's gold," as it is often described, however, is a poor basis for sound investment strategy under present circumstances. While silver has the same characteristics that make gold a monetary metal—relative scarcity, durability, fungibility, portability, and traditional use as a means of exchange and a store of value—there are differences between the two that affect the gold/silver price ratio and the management of investment programs.

A fundamental change has taken place since the days when silver and gold were both used simply for luxury goods and coin. At the present time, silver has important industrial uses. It is a basic component of such high-technology manufactured items as photographic and X-ray film, electronic conductors, and dental supplies as well as of traditional crafted goods like mirrors, tableware, and jewelry. About 55 percent of American silver consumption falls into the two categories of photographic use and electric or electronics use, while less than 25 percent is accounted for by silverware, jewelry, works of art, and commemorative objects. By contrast, jewelry is the single largest use for gold. Even in the United States, jewelry and the arts account for over half of total consumption, and the proportion on a worldwide basis is much higher because of the demand for jewelry as a surrogate investment in non-industrial countries.

The effect of the industrial importance of silver is that the supply-demand ratio has been out of balance since World War II with only a moment of equilibrium in 1950. In that year, silver production and consumption in the non-Communist world balanced at about 202 million ounces. Since then, production has risen to 334 million ounces, but consumption has run far ahead to 423 million ounces. The issue for investors and industrial managers is no longer whether there will be a shortfall for a given year or not, but how large it will be.

Another albeit related difference is that there are no large above-ground stocks of silver as there are of gold. Estimates of above-ground stocks of silver range from 600 million to 800 million ounces—sufficient to meet demand at its current level for less than two years. Above-ground stocks of gold, on the other hand, estimated at over 2.5 billion ounces, are sufficient to meet industrial demand at its present level for 50 years. In these circumstances, the price of silver must also perform the function of a rationing mechanism until industry makes major changes in its manufacturing requirements.

Despite the industrial element, however, the price of silver is also affected by investors hedging against inflation, that is, those who use silver for monetary purposes. One important element in this is the longstanding American love affair with silver. Not only have generations of silver-producing states' lawmakers implanted official fondness but, more recently, the love affair was fueled by the fact that silver was available for investment purposes at the time when gold was not accessible and the OPEC price hikes of 1973–74 pushed the Vietnam-era inflation into high gear. Silver thus became the first monetary metal refuge of nervous Americans.

The divergence in the upward paths of gold and silver prices during 1979 illustrates the effect of the difference between the two metals. While the price of silver rose over 700 percent, from $5.92 an ounce in January 1979 to $48.70 in January 1980, gold rose less than 300 percent, from $217 an ounce to $825 in the same period of time. The gold/silver price ratio narrowed during the year from 37:1 to 16:1.

If past history provides any clues to future price movements, it may indicate that an economic downturn can cause a diminution in industrial demand, a lower silver price, and with it an increase in the gold/silver ratio. The ratio tends also to increase in times of political crisis, when investors turn to gold as a more easily transportable and anonymous store of value. During the Great Depression, the ratio rose above 80:1; just before World War II in 1940, it reached 100:1 (based on the $35 statutory price of gold and a 35-cent market price for silver). Still, the large stocks of gold suggest that there is a greater flexibility upwards or downwards in its price while the small stocks of silver suggest that there may not be a major downward movement even if industrial consumption were to drop markedly. Silver's friends say that a large drop is unlikely because of the basic nature of industrial photography, electronics, and dentistry. There may, however, be some diminution in use in recreational photography, flatware, and jewelry in times of economic stringency.

To sum up, a silver investment partakes not only of the monetary character of a gold investment but also of the supply–demand character of other commodity investments. This means not only that price movements are influenced by considerations different from those of gold, but also that silver investment strategies resemble those for other commodities as much as they do for gold. Individual investors must keep all these factors in mind as they determine the utility of silver for their personal portfolios.

If, however, an investor should decide to add silver to his portfolio, he will enjoy as many choices as in the gold market. Futures contracts for 5,000 troy ounces are traded on the New York Commodity Exchange and the Chicago Board of Trade, and contracts for ten bags of U.S. silver coins with $1,000 face value each are traded on the New York Mercantile Exchange. Mocatta Metals Corp. offers options in both silver and silver coin bags that have the same advantages as gold and Krugerrand options. Its affiliate, Brody White & Co., offers brokerage services in gold and silver futures contracts on almost every organized market and exchange in the world.

A disadvantage of investing in physical silver, mentioned above, is portability. Thirty gold bullion coins are more easily carried or hidden than a 715-ounce bag of silver coins of comparable value. Nevertheless, secure warehouse facilities for silver are widely available and storage need not be a problem.

In short, while silver is not solely a monetary metal, it offers investors a variety of choices which may be used to diversify their personal portfolio.

Suggested Reading

Coverage of daily activity on the New York and Chicago exchanges appears in the financial sections of major newspapers, and general articles appear frequently in various publications. Among the periodicals that regularly report on the condition and prospects in the gold and silver markets are *Euromoney, Commodities,* and *Barron's.*

The World of Gold Today by Timothy Green (Arrow Books, 1973) is a readable general introduction to the subject. *Money: Whence It Came, Where It Went* by John K. Galbraith (Bantam Books, 1979), and *Money and Man* by Elgin Groseclose (2nd ed., Frederick Unger, 1961) offer good non-technical discussions of the relationship between gold and money. *The Golden Constant* by Roy W. Jastram (John Wiley & Sons, 1977) is a discussion of the relationship between gold prices and commodity prices through 400 years of English and American experience.

An interesting and valuable review of the American silver industry and the economic forces which have stimulated investor interest in coins and silver futures contracts is William Burke and Yvonne Levy's *Silver: End of an Era,* published in pamphlet form by the Federal Reserve Bank of San Francisco in 1974. Professor Jastram's study of silver, designed to complement *The Golden Constant,* is scheduled for publication in 1980. Handy & Harman's *Annual Reports on the Silver Industry* are useful summaries of activity and trend, and figures from the U.S. Bureau of Mines and other sources for both gold and silver are published annually by Fairchild Publications in *Metal Statistics.*

Everyone's Best Friend

Benjamin Zucker

Imagine yourself back in 1940, suddenly inheriting $1 million from a maiden aunt. Your friends and relatives probably would have told you to invest the money in stocks and bonds. Why not, you say, at least with 90 percent of it. With the remaining $100,000, however, you decide to splurge. Without telling anyone, you buy a full-length sable coat for $20,000, a 14-ounce tin of Russian caviar for $15, a baby grand Steinway for $2,500, a 40-foot yacht for $20,000 and, a bottle of vintage champagne for $3. Having a little money left over, you also buy a perfectly flawless, three-carat diamond for $3,000, a fabulous deep-green, gem-quality, four-carat Muzo emerald for $3,800, a wonderfully red three-carat ruby for $4,500, and a top quality, ten-carat sapphire for $2,000.

You then enroll in Yale paying tuition of $450 a year, and apply yourself to your studies. After graduating in 1944, you take off on a slow boat to the South Seas. Then, one day early in 1980, you decide to come back to New York and retire to a peaceful life in Greenwich Village, living off the fruit of the land and the proceeds of your investments.

As luck would have it, the stocks and bonds have not done all that well. But the extremes of luxury—the coat, the piano, yacht, and precious stones—have exceeded your most avaricious hopes. As shown in Table 9-1, the sable coat could be sold today for $75,000. The 14-ounce tin of caviar would be worth $300, the champagne $30. Your yacht would now go for $200,000, your Steinway, for $10,900. But the most pleasant surprise would be those precious stones. The flawless diamond would be worth $75,000, the ruby over $120,000, the fine colored sapphire $52,000, and the gem-quality emerald over $90,000.

Table 9-1. Price trends, 1940 to 1980.

	1940	1980
Full-length sable coat	$25,000	$ 75,000
Russian caviar [14-ounce tin]	15	300
Townhouse on New York's Fifth Avenue	55,000	2,500,000
Steinway baby grand piano	2,500	10,900
Yacht [40 foot]	20,000	200,000
Tuition at Yale University [per year]	450	5,585
Tattinger's vintage champagne	3	30
Gem-quality emerald [3½ carat]	3,800	90,000
Flawless diamond [3 carat]	3,000	75,000

Source: U.S. News & World Report, March 17, 1980.

How is it possible that the Good Lord rewarded luxury purchasers more than investors in Bedrock Industrial America? The answers, briefly, are revolution and inflation—or, more precisely, fear of revolution and fear of inflation. In the past four decades, it caused people who had significant disposable income to take steps to protect against the possibility of chaotic political conditions. They either rushed to consume (witness the rise of champagne and caviar), or they bought "hard assets" (witness the price rise of gems). There is no question that increases in the value of these items reflect basic uncertainty and tremendous inflation of paper money. Gem prices, however, have far exceeded the inflationary spiral of the past decades, as shown in Table 9-2.

What about the next 40 years? Impossible to say for sure, but my advice to an investor would be to place 5 to 10 percent of his or her assets in diamonds, rubies, sapphires, and emeralds. Now, even more than in 1940, there are logical reasons for doing so. The political uncertainties and problems of paper currency are as great or greater than in the past.

And a new ingredient has entered the precious stone world: increased scarcity of "gem-quality" diamonds, rubies, sapphires, and emeralds.

Table 9-2. Wholesale per-carat prices of colored stones and diamonds of fine quality. [All prices are in U.S. dollars as of December 1980 and are for dealers buying in large lots.]

Carats	Ruby		Sapphire		Emerald		Diamond	
	Gem	Fine	Gem	Fine	Gem	Fine	Gem	Fine
1	$13,000	$ 6,000	$ 7,000	$ 1,500	$17,000	$ 6,000	$50,000	$9,800
2	22,000	10,000	9,000	2,000	20,000	7,000	53,000	12,000
3	35,000	13,000	18,000	3,000	23,000	7,000	54,000	14,000
4	40,000	16,000	22,000	6,000	25,000	7,500	55,000	16,000
5	45,000	19,000	24,000	7,000	30,000	7,500	57,000	20,000
6	50,000	22,000	26,000	7,500	35,000	9,000	60,000	23,000
7	60,000	25,000	26,000	8,000	40,000	10,000	63,000	26,000
8	80,000	26,000	26,000	9,000	42,000	11,000	65,000	29,000
9	80,000	28,000	28,000	9,000	45,000	12,000	67,000	30,000
10	100,000	30,000	30,000	12,000	50,000	15,000	70,000	32,000

Diamonds

In 1976, just as my book, *How to Invest in Gems: Everyone's Guide to Rubies, Sapphires, Emeralds and Diamonds,* was about to be published, a friend of mine, a talented and methodical corporate lawyer, decided to buy a diamond for his fiancee. Being a frustrated businessman at heart, he wanted to use the opportunity to be a gem dealer for a few days and penetrate the arcane diamond world. I told him, as I pointed out in my book, that the best approach was to shop at a super-fine retail store. He protested at first, quoting Woody Allen's dictum, "In my family, the worst sin is to buy retail." He then proceeded to go to four jewelers along Fifth Avenue and three "wholesalers" on 47th Street. He eventually wound up buying a one-carat, D-Flawless diamond (perfectly white, perfectly free from inclusions) for $8,500. The stone today is worth roughly seven times the amount. What he understood after speaking to both wholesalers and fine retail stores was that a "perfect" diamond is indeed 1 out of 10,000. Most of the "wholesalers" tried to talk him out of buying a perfect stone. Interestingly enough, the retail stores had such stones available, were patient with him, and one closed the sale.

The point is that diamonds—particularly perfect ones—are terribly scarce. At the mining end, a one-carat diamond represents truckload after truckload of rock that must be sorted, crushed, grated, and processed. Approximately four tons of rock must be removed before a rough diamond of one carat can be recovered from the ground.

Diamond mining areas are basically remnants of volcanic activity within the earth which have seeped to the surface and solidified. These form thin kimberlite deposits that contain the diamond crystals. Such kimberlite deposits are scattered through South Africa, Botswana, Russia, Brazil, Venezuela, and other African countries.

The primary mining and distribution factor is DeBeers Consolidated Mines, Ltd., founded in the late 1800s by Cecil Rhodes. DeBeers has gradually tightened its control on the world diamond supply. Through its mining and marketing efforts, it now controls approximately 85 percent of all the rough diamonds in the world.

It's taken a lot of hard work. In Botswana, DeBeers financed a diamond search which took over 12 years. It began in 1953 when an African school child found a tiny, low-quality diamond crystal at the edge of a cattle feeding station. To Botswana DeBeers sent geologists who drew expensive geological surveys of the country. After two years of probing, not a single diamond crystal was found. But DeBeers was persistent. Rather than drop the project, as most corporations would have done, the company recruited hundreds of citizens of Botswana, who collected sample rock every ten yards. These were transported to South African laboratories for study. It took 12 years of searching, but a promising group of diamond crystals finally was found. This led to a pipe find of diamonds, among the four biggest mines in the world.

Wherever there are diamonds to mine, DeBeers tries to find them. However, in places like the Soviet Union, it buys rough diamonds from a consortium. Because of DeBeers' skills, the Russians—who are believed to mine 40 percent of the world's diamonds—decided to market their rough stones through DeBeers.

Once the diamond crystals are purchased or mined, they are sorted on long tables by hand. The sorters divide the crystals into low-grade industrial stones and into 2,000 grades of quality stones which, after cutting and polishing, will become "gemstones."

On the gemstone side of the business, DeBeers invites a super-select group of 350 sight holders to London to purchase "boxes." These buyers are the elite of the diamond world. Before coming to London, the buyer is informed of the value of the stones contained in the buyer's particular box. DeBeers sells $2.5 billion of diamond rough each year. It is not unusual for a box holder to go to London, hand over $3–4 million, and then send a parcel of rough, uncut stones to the cutting factory.

Over 99 percent of the diamonds cut by factories are less than one carat. (A carat is a pretty light thing: it takes 142 to make one ounce.) Once a rough stone is bought by sight holders, if it is of gem quality, it tends to be cut in either Antwerp or New York. Smaller stones are being cut in Israel and India.

Demand for diamonds is an unusual phenomenon, thanks in large measure to DeBeers. DeBeers has stated that its corporate goal is to "stabilize the price for diamonds." Thus, during recessions, it offers fewer diamonds to the sight holders, which reduces any overhang of supply. Also, DeBeers will buy any excess unsold supplies of diamonds shuffling around Antwerp, New York, or Israel. On the other hand, if diamond demand is very strong, the company will charge the sight holders more money for the boxes, which will lead, inevitably, to higher prices.

On the demand side of the equation, DeBeers spends tens of millions of promotional dollars. Its advertising made Japan the third largest consumer of diamonds in the world (after the United States and Germany), and Japan has no history of engagement rings. Now, as might be expected, DeBeers has mounted campaigns in Arabic languages as well as in German and French to try to capture the booming Middle Eastern, German, Swiss, and French markets.

Over the years, De Beers has built up over $1 billion in cash reserves and $2 billion in securities. With its allied company, Anglo-American Corp., it has at least $5 billion on hand to support diamond prices. Thus, when one goes into a retail store and plunks down approximately $58,000 for a D-Flawless, one-carat diamond, one realizes that DeBeers' financial strength will help maintain price levels. A history of diamond prices is shown in Table 9-3.

Another sort of help—the diamond certificate—has emerged in recent years. When the lawyer I mentioned earlier went into the retail jewelry store searching for an investment and a beautiful diamond, the stones he was shown were accompanied by a piece of paper issued by the Gemological Institute of America. The paper is not an appraisal, but merely a description of color, weight, and "flaws"—or, as the G.I.A. elegantly terms them, "inclusions." Exhibits 9-1 and 9-2 show two typical certificates.

The first certificate describes a round, D-Flawless diamond. That is to say, the Gemological Institute has examined the diamond and found it to be perfectly white. Nitrogen adds color to diamonds, and a diamond that is completely free of nitrogen will look like an ice cube in a glass of water on a sunny day in Bombay. It appears whiter than white. Such a stone is termed D-color. An E or F stone is very, very white, too. Still, if a D-color diamond is placed next to an E-color diamond, a trained gemologist would see a slight difference in whiteness.

That is precisely what the Gemological Institute does. For a modest fee ($80 for a one-carat diamond, $100 for a two carat, $150 for a three carat),

Exhibit 9-1.

GIA GEM TRADE LABORATORY, INC.

A Wholly Owned Subsidiary of Gemological Institute of America, Inc.

NY205650ʲ

3/27/80

DIAMOND GRADING REPORT - NEW YORK LABORATORY

IN THE OPINION OF THE LABORATORY, THE FOLLOWING ARE THE CHARACTERISTICS OF THE DIAMOND DESCRIBED HEREIN.

RED SYMBOLS DENOTE INTERNAL CHARACTERISTICS.
GREEN SYMBOLS DENOTE EXTERNAL CHARACTERISTICS.
SYMBOLS INDICATE NATURE AND POSITION OF CHARACTERISTICS, NOT NECESSARILY THEIR SIZE.

SHAPE AND CUT ___ round brilliant
Measurements ___ approx. 6.78 - 6.85 x 4.00 mm
Weight ___ ▓▓▓ carats ▓▓▓

KEY TO SYMBOLS

Extra facets shown in black.

PROPORTIONS
Depth Percentage __ 58.7%
Table Percentage __ 62%
Girdle Thickness __ very thin to slightly thick, faceted
Culet Size _____ very small
FINISH
Polish _____ good
Symmetry _____ good

CLARITY GRADE ___ Internally Flawless
Graining _____ nil

COLOR GRADE ____ D
Ultraviolet fluorescence none

COMMENTS:

Minor details of finish not shown.

GIA GEM TRADE LABORATORY, INC.

By K R ____ ;RC

GIA CLARITY-GRADING SCALE

	VVS₁	VVS₂	VS₁	VS₂	SI₁	SI₂	I₁	I₂	I₃
Flawless									
Internally Flawless									

Imperfect

GIA COLOR-GRADING SCALE

D	E	F	G	H	I	J	K	L	M	N	O	P	Q	R	S	T	U	V	W	X	Y	Z

| Colorless | Near Colorless | Faint Yellow | Very Light Yellow | | Light Yellow | Fancy Yellow |

-No Appraisals or Valuations-

(COPYRIGHT 1979) GIA GEM TRADE LABORATORY, INC.

HP 978-79

ORIGINAL

Exhibit 9-2.

 GIA GEM TRADE LABORATORY, INC.

A Wholly Owned Subsidiary of Gemological Institute of America, Inc.

NY 1023261
3/12/80

DIAMOND GRADING REPORT - NEW YORK LABORATORY

IN THE OPINION OF THE LABORATORY, THE FOLLOWING ARE THE CHARACTERISTICS OF THE DIAMOND DESCRIBED HEREIN.

RED SYMBOLS DENOTE INTERNAL CHARACTERISTICS.
GREEN SYMBOLS DENOTE EXTERNAL CHARACTERISTICS.
SYMBOLS INDICATE NATURE AND POSITION OF CHARAC-
TERISTICS, NOT NECESSARILY THEIR SIZE.

SHAPE AND CUT ___ pear shape brilliant
Measurements ___ approx. 10.67 x 7.69 x 4.31 mm
Weight ___ 1.96 carats

KEY TO SYMBOLS

pinpoint
feather
Natural shown in green.

PROPORTIONS
Depth Percentage __ 56.0%
Table Percentage __ 65%
Girdle Thickness __ medium to slightly thick, faceted
Culet Size ___ small

FINISH
Polish ___ good
Symmetry ___ good

CLARITY GRADE ___ VS-1
Graining ___ nil

COLOR GRADE ___
Ultraviolet fluorescence none

COMMENTS:

Hairline feathers in girdle and details of polish not shown.

GIA GEM TRADE LABORATORY, INC.

By _____ KT

GIA CLARITY-GRADING SCALE

	VVS₁	VVS₂	VS₁	VS₂	SI₁	SI₂	I₁	I₂	I₃
Flawless									
Internally Flawless									

Imperfect

GIA COLOR-GRADING SCALE

D E F G H I J	K L M	N O P Q R	S T U V	W X Y Z
Colorless	Near Colorless	Faint Yellow / Very Light Yellow	Light Yellow	Fancy Yellow

-No Appraisals or Valuations-
COPY

HP 1262-78

a G.I.A. expert will place your stone in a light box with 15 diamonds lined up like soldiers, in a top down position. The gemologist will say something like, "This stone is less white than a G-color but whiter than an H." It will then become an H-color diamond. Diamond dealers have such sample stones on hand and they, too, provisionally grade their own stones.

Table 9-3. History of diamond prices. [These prices are for internally and externally flawless diamonds of D-color, in a round brilliant cut diamond.]

	Weight in Carats	Value per Carat	Total for Diamond
1968	3	$ 3,000	$ 9,000
1970	3	4,000	12,000
1972	3	5,000	15,000
1974	3	11,000	33,000
1976	3	14,000	42,000
1978	3	18,000	54,000
1979	3	50,000	150,000
1980	3	54,000	162,000
1968	2	2,000	4,000
1970	2	3,000	6,000
1972	2	3,500	7,000
1974	2	8,000	16,000
1976	2	11,000	22,000
1978	2	15,000	30,000
1979	2	44,000	88,000
1980	2	53,000	106,000
1968	1	1,400	1,400
1970	1	1,500	1,500
1972	1	1,900	1,900
1974	1	5,000	5,000
1976	1	6,500	6,500
1978	1	10,000	10,000
1979	1	41,000	41,000
1980	1	52,000	52,000
1968	½	700	350
1970	½	800	400
1972	½	900	450
1974	½	1,300	650
1976	½	1,500	750
1978	½	2,500	1,250
1979	½	4,000	2,000
1980	½	8,000	4,000

The proportions of the stone also get clearly stated. The table size on the D-Flawless diamond in the first certificate is 62 percent. That is to say, it is 62 percent of the height of the stone. Diamond dealers like a table of 53 to 62 percent. This will give the stone a good proportion, a lot of brilliance, and aesthetic allure.

The second certificate covers a more average stone. It is a very slightly included 1.96 carat, pear shape diamond, with the inclusions sketched out.

The most important factor after color is clarity. If the diamond is perfectly free from inclusions, it is called flawless or internally flawless. If the inclusions are minor, the diamond is called very, very slightly included (VVSI), then very slightly included (VSI), slightly included (SI), and finally an imperfect stone.

At first, old-time diamond dealers hated the idea that a non-profit, scientific organization like the G.I.A. would presume to tell them what a gem-quality stone was. The trade had always described fine diamond colors as "blue-white" or "river" diamonds. They described very pure diamonds as "clean," while impure diamonds were known as "pique." The past 20 years have led to more sophisticated scientific measurement, and the retail storekeeper can now show the customer a diamond accompanied by a certificate. However, much of the romance of diamonds started to disappear as dealers, instead of describing a stone as beautiful, well-made, or of exceptional color, would refer very precisely to a "G-color, 1.06 round diamond, very slightly included." On 47th Street there is a saying that today you are "dealing in certificates as opposed to beauty." And in the long run, this technocratic emphasis may bleed diamonds of some of their aesthetic appeal.

To the investor, however, it has opened whole new worlds. It is now possible to "computerize," for example, what an F-Flawless, round diamond sold for in the past, and set up a grid of past price movements. Not only that, once one buys, one can cable the description of the stone to Hong Kong, for example, and the Hong Kong dealer can make an offer on the stone, with an exceptionally clear picture of what the diamond looks like without physically seeing it.

Diamonds have become fungible in much the same way that gold is, but not quite. First of all, the shape of the diamond is important in its investment consideration. Diamonds can be cut into either round shapes, emerald shapes, pear shapes, marquise shapes, or other, more exotic shapes. If the piece of original rough has a carbon spot at one end, very often a pear shape will be chosen by the cutter. Basically the job of the cutter is to try to envision the biggest, purest stone that can be faceted from the rough. This skill requires a particular kind of geometric imagination. The cutter must be able to visualize the diamond crystal from all angles. And since the flaws are sometimes hidden within the stones, it also pays to have a certain amount of luck. In a pear shape, marquise, or emerald cut, proportion is extremely important.

At least 90 percent of investment diamonds tend to be, as of this writing, in round stones. The ideal proportions for round stones have been carefully worked out and are fairly simple to apply. If the stone is being purchased purely for investment, it is safer to buy a round diamond. The other shapes, however, can be extraordinarily beautiful, and if there is a hope of wearing the stone, the other shapes should not be eliminated.

Virtually all stones better than G-color and very slightly included or purer are being certified by G.I.A. at present. The result is that tens of thousands of stone certificates exist. It is not surprising, therefore, that there are computer print-outs of price lists for diamonds.

The market, however, is far from huge. I would estimate that only 75 diamonds in the one-carat size and D-Flawless category are cut each year. The number would be the same for two-carat D-Flawless diamonds, three-carat, and so on up to ten carats. What this means is that the total volume of perfect diamonds available for purchase would be approximately $5 million for one-carat D-Flawless, $11 million for two-carat D-Flawless, and so forth. These are small numbers compared to the $4.5 billion worth of all diamonds sold annually at the final distribution level.

DeBeers' position on investing in diamonds is guarded. While its advertisements mention the words, "Diamonds are forever," they do not state outright that diamonds are a good investment. Also, two markets have developed in the diamond world: (1) the world of jewelry originally sold by DeBeers, cut by master cutters, mounted into exquisite settings and purchased by the public to commemorate the important moments of life such as engagement, marriage, birth, or birthday; (2) the investment world, where very often the stone is simply regarded as a store of value and is not worn.

Diamond jewelry is rarely sold except in an estate or distress situation. Investment diamonds, however, are held specifically with the idea of being offered for sale. If all the D-Flawless diamonds sold in the last two years were suddenly put on the New York market, there is no question that a sharp price drop would occur. While this represents a danger to the would-be investor, most diamonds are purchased with the idea that they will go up in value, and a buoyant market seems to feed upon itself.

Because of this worldwide acceptance of diamond certification, and because a growing number of investors are aware of the appreciation that has taken place in gem-quality diamonds, the near-term outlook for diamonds should be strong. Less than .5 percent of all diamonds, however, constitute genuine investment quality. As a result, while an investor is paying much more for a top-quality D-, E-, or F-color flawless diamond, this means that such a stone is much more liquid in the future.

The place to buy and the place to sell top-quality diamonds is the same—the reputable, top-quality retail store or auction house. If you know the quality of the stone you want, D-, E-, or F-color, and the degree of purity you would like, there is no harm in price shopping. The seller of a diamond should be willing to point out to you the nuances of the particular stone, whether it fluoresces (if the stone does, one should deduct approximately 5 percent of its value), the beauty of its polish, and so on.

Moreover, if the stone is truly a gem, the retail store is more than willing to buy it back. I am always struck by the fact that Harry Winston, Van Cleef, and other fine jewelers advertise in the newspapers to buy gems even more often than they advertise to sell them. Dealers are constantly on the lookout for fine estate jewelry. The commercial range of stones—the Js, Ks, Ls and other colors—are not as easy to sell.

Auction houses, which sell certificated stones, have become big businesses, and there are fine ones in New York, Geneva, Zurich, Hong Kong, and elsewhere. If a diamond is of truly top quality, a reputable auction house will give you guidance as to the best market at which it should be sold.

Diamonds of gem quality have come of age. No longer are they a blind item. They can be described carefully, weighed, and measured. Their beauty and value are appreciated throughout the world. Moreover, although their prices have risen extraordinarily in the last ten years, it is my belief that they deserve a place in an investment portfolio.

Rubies

When you enter the world of ruby, you return to the time of Marco Polo, that extraordinary gem dealer who bought and sold gems in the time of Kubla Khan.

The key to ruby's allure is its incredible scarcity and beauty. As early as the seventeenth century, Jean Baptiste Tavernier, the French gem merchant who purchased stones for Louis XIV, wrote, "When a ruby exceeds six carats and is perfect, it is sold for whatever is asked for it." Tavernier had seen it all—the treasures of the Indian Mughal and Deccan rulers in Bombay and Jaipur, the gem markets of Istanbul and Venice. A ruby was rare, even in his day.

For every 50 gem-quality diamonds, there is only 1 ruby of equivalent gem quality (sapphires and emeralds are also 50 times as rare as diamonds). I would recommend that the gemstone investor put one fourth of his or her money into diamonds, one fourth in rubies, one fourth in sapphires and one fourth in emeralds.

"A rose is a rose is a rose," Gertrude Stein tells us, but red is not always red. Ninety percent of a ruby's value lies in the depth and purity of its shade of red. In 1979, at a Christie's auction in Geneva, a four-carat, rich, red ruby mounted in a ring was expected to fetch $40,000 per carat. However, its color was so unique, and its brilliance so great, that to the astonishment of the gem merchants present, it was whisked away for a total of slightly over $400,000.

What is the perfect shade of red that gem connoisseurs and investors should look for? Geologically, a ruby is aluminum oxide. A tiny admixture of chromium oxide makes it red. If the aluminum oxide has an admixture of titanium oxide or iron oxide, the stone will be blue, yellow, green, purple, or pink. These are grouped under the generic term of sapphire. In other words, the ruby and the sapphire are identical in chemical composition. The shade of red depends upon the strength of the chromium. A fraction of a percent too much chromium and you will get a brownish-red stone, not beautiful and not particularly valuable. Too little chromium and you get a watery, light-pink stone.

The gem merchant's shorthand for a perfect shade of red color is "pigeon blood red." This is a 2,000-year-old term used by Indians and ruby merchants to describe the shade found in the very center of the red spectrum. It is the red, unmistakenly vivid in its purity, found in the blood of pigeons. In the West, the intense red shade of Happiness Rose corresponds to pigeon blood red in gem rubies. Less than 1 in 20,000 rubies have this shade. Rubies from Burma occasionally have just the right combination of aluminum oxide and traces of chromium that gives this vivid red color.

It takes many years of comparing shades to develop a connoisseurship in rubies. The essential method a gem merchant uses is to lay one ruby alongside other rubies. By constantly comparing, one's eye adapts to the different nuances. This connoisseurship is difficult to attain, of course, and one normally needs the advice of a guide when deciding on a substantial purchase of rubies.

Rubies from Burma traditionally are regarded to have the purest shade of red. Rubies mined in Ceylon are a more pink variety and are called "Ceylon red" in gem dealers' shorthand. A slightly violet shade of red called "Siamese red" or a brownish shade of red, the Thai ruby can often be exceedingly brilliant. Last in esteem would be the African ruby, a still more brownish shade of red.

The origin of a colored stone—that is to say, the country in which the stone was mined—can often be determined by the nature of the inclusions within the stone. For the investor, if a Ceylon ruby has the characteristic Burma look, its value is regarded as nearly identical to what it would be had it come from Burma itself. The happiest constellation of quality, however, still remains a stone of rich pure Burma color, coupled with a Burma origin.

When I entered the gem world after graduating from Harvard Law School, my first reaction was that I had entered an insane asylum where 50 or so dealers had a shared madness. It seemed incredible to me that such dainty bits of crystals should vary by factors of tens of thousands of dollars depending upon the depth of the shade of red. But my father, Charles Zucker, reassured me, "It's been this way for hundreds of years." To my amazement, when I put stones on the white blotter paper used on the wholesale level for grading, and invited my corporate lawyer buddies to view the rubies, they always preferred the stone that was the purist red over the brownish or pinkish gems. They knew the most beautiful one— even though they had little idea of its dollar value.

As with diamonds, it is important to go to a top-grade retail store to choose a ruby. If you see only one with no standard of comparison, it is difficult to make an evaluation. Important stores tend to have wide selections.

The market for rubies is so limited compared to diamonds that I would estimate that no more than seven top-flight, four-carat gem rubies are available for purchase at any given moment. These will be scattered throughout the retail and dealer merchants. At the important auctions, one can sometimes find a top-flight gem ruby. The four-carat stone that sold at Christie's for $100,000 per carat was the finest in at least five years. This very scarcity, however, makes rubies a good balance to the more numerous and more liquid gem diamond.

Where are gem rubies found? It is a peculiar gemological phenomenon that as you dig deeper into the ground, the purity of ruby color becomes weaker. With stones in the gem world, the old days were the good days. The shades of old Burma rubies are a much more intense red than stones found today. Also, as the mining goes deeper into the ground, gemstones tend to be smaller in size. This, incidentally, is also true of diamonds, sapphires, and emeralds. The large, incredibly fabulous gemstones like the Hope Diamond, the Bismarck Sapphire (both in the Smithsonian), and the fabulous emeralds of Iran were all mined before the turn of the century.

Because the Burma ruby mines have been worked for over 2,000 years, it is not surprising to realize that the output at present generally is of very watery color and miniscule size. The Ceylon ruby mines were worked even before the time of Marco Polo. There, too, most of the fine rubies have been taken from the ground. The Thai mines, after only 40 years of extensive exploitation, are already showing signs of exhaustion, and the quality of African rubies has been very disappointing for the would-be investor.

On the supply side, therefore, rubies are reaching a critical point. The rewarding "mines" are the various jewelry centers in the United States. Here, one can still find estates with gem-quality rubies that were purchased around the turn of the century and later. Once these rubies are sold over the coming years, I believe the supply of gem rubies will virtually disappear.

With such a limited supply, why is it that rubies under eight carats tend to command less of a price per carat than diamonds? The answer is twofold. First is that DeBeers has built a great sense of confidence in the diamond. Second, and more importantly, it takes a much greater skill to appreciate the nuances of color in a ruby than the nuances of whiteness in a diamond.

However, the G.I.A. recently began to sell a machine that qualifies and describes the shade of color in gemstones, and the American Gemological Laboratory has devised a system to divide the shades of ruby into its component color parts: red, pink, orange, brown, and so on.

As a result, I believe that the ruby is where the diamond was 40 years ago. Once an accurate certification system is developed, "investors" and all purchasers will have more confidence when buying the stone. At that time, given the extreme scarcity and the fact that people inherently love color, I would think that ruby prices will be much higher than the even incredibly high level at which they are today.

While 90 percent of a ruby's value is in its shade of color, 10 percent lies in its purity. All colored stones, with virtually no exceptions, have inclusions. If the stone is very included, light will not be able to bounce around within it and return to the eye of the observer. While such a stone may be a good color, it will be regarded as "dead," in the language of the trade.

Buying rubies has always involved a high degree of aesthetics. When it comes time to sell, it is extremely important to take the stone to either a fine retail store or an auction house. There are perhaps no more than 100 people in the United States who can fix a firm price on a gem ruby. Auction houses and fine retail stores are always on the lookout for such stones. By buying the gem ruby, you are letting yourself in for a purchase of incredible beauty, but it is not one that will be instantly salable.

Sapphires

Blue has always been central to the human imagination and the blue shade of sapphire is the most prized. In fact, the word sapphire, or *sapir*, is a synonym for *sippur,* the Hebrew word for story. Mystical Jews use the word *sefirot* as the emanations of God in the universe. Sapphires have always been regarded as the secret message from beyond. Persians believed that the world rested on a giant sapphire.

Knowing the history of sapphire and what it has meant to different cultures, it is not surprising that a superb, pure-colored blue sapphire from the wonderful Kashmir mines in the Himalayas fetched over $30,000 per carat at a 1979 auction.

As with rubies, the purity of the color accounts for 90 percent of a sapphire's value. Blue skies are not always blue skies, and for every shade of blue sky, there is a corresponding shade somewhere in a sapphire. Pride of place in sapphire color goes to 1862, when a rock slide on the high slopes of the Zanskar (Himalayas) range of mountains exposed sapphire-bearing rock. For about 50 years, extraordinarily pure blue gems were mined. The blue in the Kashmir sapphire became proverbial. Its intense richness does not change in sunlight or artificial light, unlike Burma or Ceylon sapphires, which tend to lose color, or what the gem dealers call *bleed color,* in artificial light. The color of Kashmir sapphires is so beautiful that the term Kashmir is applied to Ceylon or Burma stones if they have this shade. Gem connoisseurs in India state that this pure blue Kashmir color resembles the blue hue of the peacock's feathered neck. Scientifically, it is also the blue in the center of the blue spectrum, a blue without traces of green, grey, or violet.

Before the Kashmir mines were known, two sources of sapphires existed in Burma and Ceylon. The Burma mines (where sapphires' color tends to be a more royal blue) were known as far back as Marco Polo's day. Also, Ceylon had a "magic mountain" of sapphires in the center of the island. Rains washed the stones from the secret source down through the river where they were and, to this day, are mined as one would pan for gold.

Like rubies, sapphires can be mined only by painstaking hand tools. Dynamiting or bulldozing the rocks would destroy the fragile crystals. Ceylon sapphires often tend to have a greyish shade of blue. However, although the Kashmir and Burma stones are purer in color, Ceylon stones are exceptionally lively and brilliant.

The Ceylon and Burma mines are virtually exhausted. Very few crystals that yield a five-carat or more weight are found these days, and exceptionally few of these crystals have a top, intense color. Therefore, the supply is almost exclusively from either the old Indian collections found in Bombay today, or secondhand estate pieces within the United States or Europe. A top-flight, superb sapphire that sold for $1,300 per carat in 1970 would sell for over $25,000 per carat today.

Sapphires tend to come in larger sizes than rubies or emeralds. Rubies of over 6 carats are exceptionally rare. In museums and in extraordinary private collections, one can see top-quality sapphires of over 25 carats. With the Middle East's love of things grand, any fine-quality sapphire of 2 carats, in the past two or three years, has been vigorously sought after by the world gem merchants. Traditionally, sapphires sold for one-fourth to one-third the price of rubies. The ratio holds today, but I believe that the gap will narrow.

A person who wants a large gemstone is virtually forced to buy a sapphire, as top-quality rubies and emeralds of over 5 carats are excessively rare. A great many sapphires have been discovered in Australia and cut by the bushel in Thailand. Thai sapphires also have been discovered at several mining sites. The problem with Australian and Thai stones is that they have a blackish or greenish color.

When one goes to a fine retail store, one may be shown a layout of the range of color in sapphires. One's eye is immediately drawn to the pure blue of Kashmir, Burma, or Ceylon stones. The Thai or Australian samples do not hold up. Unfortunately, many practically pure black-blue sapphires have been sold over the telephone by unscrupulous people who claim that this is the "most intense color." A 10-carat blackish-blue sapphire can sell for $100 a carat in the resale market, whereas a gem 10-carat Ceylon sapphire can sell for $15,000 per carat.

Color connoisseurship is thus all-important. The idea of the beauty of a fine sapphire can be gotten by visiting the Smithsonian Institution, which houses the pure blue Bismarck Sapphire. Occasionally one can also see the very fine Kashmir stones in Art Nouveau or Art Deco pieces that were made around the turn of the century.

Sapphire inclusions can indicate the country of origin. Unless they interfere markedly with the brilliance of the stone, the inclusions should not be considered a detriment or "flaw." A Gemological Institute certificate for sapphires (as for ruby) at present states only whether or not the colored stone is genuine. The cost is $30. It does not give a quality judgment as to color or purity. However, the recent development of color analysis systems will mean that, in the future, sapphire color will be easier to describe over the telephone and by letter.

As sapphire supply is so rare, a future rise in price is indicated. If one has a pure Kashmir, Burma, or Ceylon sapphire to sell, a fine retail store will snap it up. Auction houses, too, with their facilities for reproducing a sapphire in color in the sales catalogue, are eager for such stones. At present, auction houses typically charge the seller 10 percent for the privilege of selling the stone, and the buyer also pays 10 percent upon successful purchase of the stone.

There are no "bargains" in sapphires any more than in rubies, emeralds, or diamonds. Either you pay a retail markup for advice as to which stone to buy or you pay the "fever" markup at auction. Purchase by telephone without seeing a stone has not been the traditional avenue of success.

The love for sapphire and the wearing of sapphire goes back to the Bible, extends through all of Islamic history, flourished in the courts in India and Europe, and exists today in undiminished vigor. Because of the decline of supply and the dissemination of information, I would think that the sapphire, along with the ruby, would complement the diamond purchase for the precious stone investor.

Emerald

Over the years, emeralds have driven women wild. They have driven men even wilder. Colombia and all of South America were discovered and first charted by Pizarro and Cortez, who were searching for the Inca's emerald mines. In the early 1500s, the fabulous Colombian emerald mines, the Muzo and El Chivor, were found. Before that, the only emerald had been a rather dark, lifeless stone from Egypt.

There is something in the human imagination that loves the emerald's organic green color. Dozens of these deep green crystals were shipped to Europe. The top stones, however, found their way via the Philippines to the princely kingdoms of India, where the highest prices were paid. To this day, the Chinese refer to emeralds as "the Philippine stone." After a period of approximately 60 years, the Colombian emerald mines started to run out and were eventually abandoned until the late nineteenth century, when they sporadically yielded more gemstones.

Women love emeralds. One of the most beautiful emeralds I ever saw came up for auction in 1972 at the Enid Annenberg Haupt sale. A fabulous 34-carat stone, it had a richness of green color that was accompanied by a translucent quality. One could look into the emerald as though one were peering into a deep green pool. Turning the stone from side to side opened fresh vistas of color. The stone seemed to be alive within. Enid Haupt had purchased it at a 1968 auction for $6,000 per carat. In 1972, when she decided to "simplify her life" by selling the stone, it fetched $10,000 per carat. Today at an auction, it would bring well over $50,000 per carat.

Colombian emeralds from the Muzo mine often have a slight hint of blue-black to the green. It gives them an incredible and serene royal appearance. El Chivor stones are yellowish green, having a fire-like appearance.

Stones that were mined in the sixteenth century and cut and mounted into jewelry have an intensity in color that is different from the slightly more watery appearance of the modern-day Colombian emerald. These early stones, called "Old Mine" emeralds, are the aristocrats among aristocrats. One can occasionally see "Old Mine" pieces in American estate jewelry. The stone might have been mined in the sixteenth century, sold to an Indian prince, and then, perhaps, in the early 1900s, purchased by Tiffany's and mounted in a ring. Today, such a stone would be taken out of the old-fashioned mounting, repolished, and put into a new setting. In a three-carat size, such a stone can easily fetch $30,000 per carat.

Africa, Rhodesia, Zambia, and South Africa also produced significant quantities of emeralds. The Zambian emerald tends to have too much black to appeal to the connoisseur or investor. The Rhodesian emerald, discovered in 1955, tends to be less than a carat and a less intense shade of green. Because of their brilliance, however, these stones were much sought after by jewelry manufacturers. Smaller Rhodesian emeralds were used for bracelets, rings, pins, and cluster rings. Because the stones were small, Rhodesian emeralds did not, at any time, take the premium position in the emerald world.

Emeralds from Brazil, another important source, are often opaque and soapy. Brazilian laboratories are extremely skilled and are able to cut the material so that a Brazilian emerald tends to be well proportioned and, at first glance, quite attractive. The problem, however, is that it often contains open veins that have been oiled to improve the color. The tremendous bargains that one may buy from a "street merchant" in Rio often lose their color as the oil evaporates over the years. Colombian material, with its fewer surface scratches, does not pose such a problem.

As with rubies or sapphires, it is necessary to have a layout of emeralds to truly see the nuances of top color. People often ask, "Does the fact that synthetic emeralds (or sapphires or rubies) are so abundant lessen the value of genuine emeralds?" Synthetic colored stones have been mass-produced since the turn of the century. But any reasonably competent jeweler, using a loupe or microscope, can spot the veil-like inclusions that differentiate between synthetic and colored stones. Moreover, the widespread nature of synthetics has created a taste for the "real thing." The problem in purchasing "investment" emeralds is not synthetic versus genuine. The true problem is description and connoisseurship with the shades of green. Emerald color is even more subtle than ruby red or sapphire blue.

All emeralds are at least moderately included. The French term these inclusions with Gallic grace, "Jardin" (garden). The inclusions seem to accentuate the emerald's organic quality. If you are looking for flawless-ness, forget about rubies, sapphires, and emeralds. They will all contain inclusions (don't we all?). Concentrate on diamonds.

Green is the color of the prophet in Islam, and some market observers credit that fact with the explosive rise in emerald prices over the past four years. At the same time, top-quality emeralds are also exceptionally popular in the United States, as well as in Europe and Japan. Because of the scarcity of pure green emeralds, and because of the ever-increasing demand for gem-quality stones, the emerald, along with the diamond, ruby, and sapphire make for an exciting investment and purchase.

Again, when it comes time to sell a gem emerald, auction houses or fine retail stores would seem to be a logical avenue along which to pro-ceed. Photographs of fine emeralds tend to be lifeless. But once one sees the emerald in the Smithsonian or the ones in the "inquisition necklace," one can readily understand people's yearning for gem emeralds.

Conclusion

Diamonds, which have been thoroughly researched and can be accurate-ly graded and described, have a long history of acceptance throughout the world. Colored stones—the rubies, sapphires, and emeralds—are much scarcer and much less liquid. Their history, however, is even more an-cient than diamonds, and the four stones together would constitute a balanced portfolio.

During the Depression, prices of diamonds and colored stones fell by 50 percent. There are no significant tax advantages to investing in precious stones. Museum gift transfers are under close scrutiny and should be treated warily and with advice of counsel. If major diamond mines or colored stone mines are found, we may assume a fall in prices, at least for the short run. While diamonds probably would be stockpiled by DeBeers, rubies, sapphires, and emeralds boast no cartel to absorb such an over-supply.

On the other hand, even though people have been scratching at the earth for thousands of years, ruby, sapphire, and emerald mines are in-credibly few in number. Precious stones are central to fairy tales, folk tales, and novels. They are the substance of dreams and a source of vast pleasure to those who own them. I hope that you buy and wear gems. I also hope that you never have to sell them.

Acknowledgments

I would like to thank Daniel Friedenberg, John Flattau, A. Phillip Goldsmith, Sam Beizer, Jan Mitchell, Michael Varet, Bernie Zucker, and my wonderful father, Charles Zucker, for their assistance in writing and researching this chapter.

In the gem world I was helped by the encouragement and advice of Luzer Kaufman, Bernard Grosz, Willie Rosenfeld, and Cap Beesley. The staff of the Gemological Institute of America also was of great help.

Bibliography

History of gems and jewelry

Desautels, Paul. *Gems in the Smithsonian Museum*. Washington, D.C.: Smithsonian Institution Press, 1972.

——————. *The Mineral Kingdom*. New York: Grosset & Dunlap, 1974.

——————. *The Gem Kingdom*.
These provide an excellent overview of the mining areas and methods employed as well as descriptions of important gem material. Excellently written by Paul Desautels, the dean of gem museum curators.

Goitein, G. D. *Letters from Indian Merchants.* Berkeley: University of California, 1974. This is a series of letters which were written by Jewish pearl and stone dealers who traveled to India in the eleventh century. Their correspondence with relatives and fellow stone dealers in Cairo proves that things have not changed too much in the gem-trading world in the past thousand years.

Hackenbrach, Yvonne. *Renaissance Jewels.* Parke-Bernet Publishing Co. This is a brilliant study of the height of jewelry making, namely, the Renaissance. It is also a most beautiful book on jewelry.

Heiniger, E. and J. *The Great Book of Jewels.* Greenwich, Conn.: New York Graphic Society, 1974. This is a remarkable study of the principal gems in the world in private and public collections.

Lenzen, Godelhard. *History of Diamond Production and the Diamond Trade.* London: Barrie & Jenkins, 1970. This book is the best history of the diamond trade. It is an unparalleled, detailed study of the ups and downs in past diamond pricing.

Investment

Moyersoen, Jean-Francois. "Executive Report on Investment Diamonds." An excellent survey.

Zucker, Benjamin. *How to Buy and Sell Gems.* New York: Times Books, 1979. This is a revised version of a primer that I wrote in 1976 under the title, *How to Invest in Gems* (Quadrangle). It contains updated price lists and a flavor of the wholesale and retail markets in the gem world.

Jewelry business

Jewelers Circular Keystone and *National Jeweler* are periodicals that give the reader an up-to-date picture of the business world of jewelry.

Technical data

Gubelin, E. J. *The Internal World of Gemstones.* Zurich: ABC Edition, 1974. This is a technical handbook on gem inclusions. Dr. Gubelin is a most remarkable man. He is a gem merchant, scholar, and photographer. The book is extraordinarily beautiful.

Liddicoat, R. T., Jr. *Handbook of Gem Identification.* Los Angeles: Gemological Institute of America. This concisely explains the gem identification and authentication processes used by the G.I.A.

Analytics Manual describes the system to analyze precious stones that was developed by C. R. Beesley of American Gem Labs.

Gems & Gemology, a quarterly published by the Gemological Institute of America, contains many fine articles on technical developments in the gem world.

Mining the Mints

Max Leibler

Coins

The subject of investing in rare coins has received a good deal of attention lately. Part of this attention is predicated on the fact that rare coins have turned out to be an excellent hedge against inflation. Fifteen years ago, you could purchase a cup of coffee for one silver dime. During the interim, coffee has increased in value, with today's cost averaging 35 cents per cup; however, the same silver dime today will buy three cups of coffee. Fifty years ago a new

Ford with no accessories could be purchased for 30 $20-gold pieces; today, the same number of $20-gold pieces will purchase a fully equipped Cadillac. These examples clearly demonstrate that precious coins have out-paced inflation.

This interesting hobby has become an investment medium for non-numismatists as well as those who collect coins for enjoyment only. In many instances, investing in rare coins has been found to have a greater profit return than investing in gold bullion.

More persons probably would utilize this investment alternative if they had a greater familiarity with the coin market and an understanding of investment patterns of the investor and collector.

The development of numismatic awareness is a process which requires the investor to place a high degree of reliance on reputable dealers.

We will later discuss choosing a reputable numismatic agent to protect your coin investment.

The numismatic public can be divided into three categories: namely, collectors, the advanced collectors, and the investors.

The collectors, or beginners, learn to look for adventures in the coin field and, through buying and selling experiences, begin to feel their way into the hobby. The advanced collectors, on the other hand, are aware of better grade coins and are more discerning about purchases. And finally, there are investors who are solely interested in rare coins for what they hope will be a profitable resale.

Auctions, the pulse of the coin market, provide a major means of diagnosing the current state of the market, revealing overall trends over given periods of time. The auction market's pulse beats loudly and clearly, leaving a permanent record for all collectors to follow.

To expect nothing more than financial remuneration from the ownership of numismatic rarities, however, is short-changing oneself. The rare coin you may own can be a keystone in history and learning about that history can become an exciting dividend of ownership. It also has a pedigree as significant as that of a thoroughbred animal and probably has been handled and appreciated by its former owners through the years. Remember, you are merely the temporary custodian of your coin collection. Coins endure, which further enhances their value.

Evaluating coins

The science of coin investment frequently appears to be an esoteric and highly complex field to the novice. However, rudiments of coin investment may be simply stated and understood. The value of a given coin is determined by it face value, instrinsic value, and numismatic value.

Face value is defined as the amount of standardized monetary value assigned to the coin; that is, the U.S. $20 Double Eagle has a face value of $20.

Intrinsic value is defined as the current market value of the metal(s) of which the coin is composed. The U.S. $20-gold piece contains .9675 troy ounces of fine gold, which makes the current intrinsic value over $350.

Numismatic value is defined as (1) the rarity of the coin, that is, how many of a given coin are known to be in existence, and (2) the condition of the coin; that is, its relative state of preservation in relation to its initial mint state. To determine rarity and condition, the coin industry has designated systems of evaluation which are accepted throughout the industry by reputable dealers. The U.S. $20-gold piece may have numismatic value of anywhere between $100 and many thousands of dollars. This is in addition to its bullion value.

Table 10-1 typifies the relationship among face, intrinsic, and numismatic values for a select sample of copper, silver, and gold coins of both rare and common specimens.

Table 10-1. Face, intrinsic, and numismatic value.

Date	Metal	Condition	Face Value	Intrinsic Value*	Numismatic Value
1857	Copper	Proof	$ .005	$ .02	$ 3,000
1959	Copper	Uncirculated	.01	.01	.03
1815	Silver	Uncirculated	.25	3.00	5,000
1841	Gold	Proof	2.50	50.00	100,000
1926	Gold	Uncirculated	10.00	200.00	2,000

*Subject to change due to market fluctuation.

Collecting trends

A balanced collection for purposes of coin investment represents one that includes coins in the highest possible state of preservation, thereby possessing a high degree of future liquidity and salability.

In 1965, for example, cupro-nickel coinage was adopted for the dime and quarter because the value of silver in the United States coins had exceeded its face value. Since Gresham's Law—"bad money drives good money out of circulation," (1550)—continues to be operational, the ensuing flood of debased coinage inevitably caused a rise in silver coin prices. Therefore, silver coin hoarding has taken place, and at the same time millions of dollars worth of silver coins have been melted for both private and industrial use, which has *decreased* the amount of potential numismatic material available. This same argument may be made for gold coins. In fact, a top numismatic authority, Walter Breen, has estimated the mortality rate of U.S. coins to be approximately 98 percent for better-date gold, silver, and copper coinage. These coins were lost, damaged, or melted.

Table 10-2 shows the mintage of several rare copper, silver, and gold coins along with the approximate number known to be in existence today. The numismatic significance of these coins is clearly evident by an investigation of their rarity.

Changes in the coinage laws and the subsequent decrease of "good money" in circulation for the several reasons discussed above have developed a concentration in rarity. This has supported the transition of numismatics from primarily a recreational pursuit to a viable and highly profitable investment alternative.

Table 10-2. Mintage of rare coins versus number known.

Date	Denomination	Mintage	Number Known
1811	Half cent	63,140	150
1802	Half dime	13,010	50
1873CC	10 cents	12,400	1
1876CC	20 cents	10,000	15
1823	25 cents	17,800	15
1856D	Gold 1 dollar	1,460	30
1822	Gold 5 dollars	17,796	3

This transition is undoubtedly the most difficult concept for a novice to appreciate. Perhaps an analogy would be helpful. Investments in real estate represent solely an investment in intrinsic value; at the opposite end of the continuum, investments in various artistic media represent solely an investment in rarity and aesthetics. Investment in coins may be seen as a compromise between the two extremes. While coins do have an intrinsic value, their profitability is also a function of rarity and condition, which is more predictable and reliable and therefore less affected by subjective appreciative factors than art.

Liquidity

A factor concerning many collectors and investors is the ability to readily convert their collections to cash. Throughout the United States there is an extensive network of coin dealers whose activities are coordinated through the use of teletype networks and other timely reporting mechanisms. The sophistication of this system allows for easy resale of numismatic properties.

In numismatic rarities, you may find drastic differences in the price of the same coin. This is because some dealers tend to "overgrade" their coins, that is, they may warrant a coin as being in better condition than it really is, so as to charge more than the coin's true value. It is, therefore, important to *know your dealers.*

Normally, before a rare coin is actually offered for sale, it is examined and cataloged in detail. A photograph is usually made to establish a "history" of the particular coin. Coin dealers, among themselves, have a virtual "lending library" of fakes for reference purposes. In addition to the day-to-day access to the coin markets, at least 50 large and prestigious auctions are held each year. Auctions provide a method of dispersal of high quality specimens and collections. They continue to feel the pulse of the coin market and are also a major means of diagnosing the current state of the market.

Coin investment provides the collector with a non-perishable, low-maintenance commodity. And, while theft is a concern for collectors, coins can be efficiently and privately housed in a safe deposit box, the cost of which is tax deductible. In addition, insurance costs very little and is offered by several insurance companies.

Many coin designs have artistic value in addition to rarity. Artists of note have rendered representations of U.S. history on coins as well as on canvas. With the advent of the Bicentennial commemoration, investors had an unusual opportunity to become involved with coins during a period when both their value and historic relevance were highlighted. For the Bicentennial, the U.S. Mint developed a remarkable number of items to commemorate our nation's founding, including proof and mint sets available in silver and lesser metals.

One need not be a sophisticated collector with particular wants to fill in empty spaces in a collection. Anyone who appreciates fine art, whether in painting, sculpture, or graphics, and also is interested in the economic potential of rare coins, should take the time to achieve at least a certain familiarity with them.

As a hedge, rare coins historically have offered excellent protection in periods of inflation, devaluation of currencies, and serious economic recession. For centuries, rare coins have been purchased for investment purposes as well as for sheer collecting pleasure.

Investment factors

In evaluating the standard criterion of an investment strategy—namely that of supply and demand—it is obvious that the supply of rare coins is fixed and is shrinking in proportion to the number of collectors who simply hold these coins, perhaps for many years, with no intention of selling.

Many persons today are placing coins in Keoghs, IRAs, and other forms of pension funds. This makes the coins inaccessible and unobtainable for many years.

Coins with rare dates and mintages tend to remain in short supply. The demand factor is compounded by an estimated several million collectors, and their number is growing annually: the U.S. Mint has a mailing list of one million collectors. Thus, while a rare 1930s $20 gold piece uncirculated condition, has a current intrinsic gold value of over $400, the numismatic value of this coin in today's market is $39,000. This is an unusual example when compared to a current market price of about $550 for the more common uncirculated $20 gold pieces. Interestingly, this same 1930s $20 piece in 1966 had an intrinsic gold value of $35 and numismatic value of $2,000. Then, the more common uncirculated $20 gold piece had a market value of $80.

In a recent article on coin collecting, author Rita Reif mentioned the experience of a Baltimore banker, Louis Eliasberg. Before his death in 1976, Mr. Eliasberg had reported that his coin collection, one of the finest ever assembled in this country, had been appraised in 1975 at $15 million to $18 million. He said that after subtracting costs from the minimum appraisal figure and dividing the results by 41 (the number of years he had been a collector), he had enjoyed a minimum return of 119 percent a year. In fact, he told a group of numismatists that the value of his collection had "doubled in 18 months."

Ms. Reif also reported that a March 1976 auction of a portion of the fabulous Garrett collection brought a total of $2,308,710, establishing a record for single-owner coin sales, and that the collectors, dealers, and investors she interviewed were optimistic on all vintage American coins. She noted that some silver coins minted before 1860 set records that were double the values registered in 1973. Another portion of the Garrett collection was offered by a Los Angeles gallery in November 1979. That sale brought in over $7 million, thereby setting yet another new record for a single coin collection. In New York, $1 million was recently bid at another auction for a collection of coins which cost its owner roughly $12,000 in the 1940s, a gain of nearly 10,000 percent, or 100 times the amount invested.

The process of beginning a coin collection, or upgrading an existing one, can be aided immeasurably by consultation between the client and an advisor. They can explore the many varied options available to the collector or investor. As in all investment pursuits, the quality of advice received can significantly affect the return on investment. Sample portfolios which feature profitability records of representative coin investments over the past 15 years are shown in Exhibit 10-1. The *Red Book* and "Gray Sheet"—the standard guides for U.S. coins—were used as references. We chose *not* to highlight the exceptionally profitable coin but rather to illustrate the increase in value of an average collection of common coins over a 30-year span. The several portfolios so presented represent a cross section of gold, silver, and copper coins.

We have all seen charts and graphs depicting extraordinary profits generated by unusually rare dates, newly discovered coins, or appreciated rarities. And we might add such profitability does exist in coin investing. But, from investment experience, we have been conditioned to expect that the "windfall profit" is the exception rather than the rule. The thoughtful coin investor does not rely upon these exceptions when developing an investment strategy.

In presenting the following sample portfolios, we attempt to demonstrate the profitability of a variety of small collections. In this manner we can highlight those factors which influence a coin's value. This survey will also demonstrate the general upward trend of coin investment and the value of a diversified collection.

The following terms are used in describing the grade or quality of numismatic coins:

Proof coins are made especially for collectors from highly polished dies are fully struck to bring out the coin's design.

Uncirculated coins are made for circulation but are preserved in their near-to-perfect form.

The first illustrative portfolio, Exhibit 10-1, tracks the profit progression of an average collection of silver and copper coins.

Over a 30-year period, uncirculated coins have outpaced proof coins, 9,870 percent versus 6,512 percent. A number of factors impact on the value between proof and uncirculated coins. However, with other factors held constant, the explanation of the different profitability of uncirculated versus proof coins is increased collector demand for uncirculated coins. Uncirculated coins were made for use as coinage in general circulation, while proofs were made expressly for collections. In this instance, coins made for the collector are valued less highly than those minted for public use but which have been kept in a high state of preservation.

During the 1949 to 1979 period, uncirculated silver and copper increased in value by 16.5 percent compounded annually, while the proof portion of the portfolio increased by 14.8 percent compounded annually, which certainly is an extremely high rate of return.

For persons interested in gold, Exhibit 10-2 shows a gold portfolio for comparison with the silver and copper collection.

Note that the relationship between the profitability of uncirculated and proof coins is the reverse of that demonstrated in the silver and copper portfolio. Proof gold has outpaced uncirculated gold by a factor of nearly five over the past 30-year period, 7,500 percent versus 1,608 percent. The reason for the different values is the same as described in the silver and copper collection, that of rarity. Few proof gold coins were struck and, therefore, recent trends in numismatic awareness have designated proof gold as the "rarest of the rare." Also, the intrinsic value of all gold coins has increased due to the increase of bullion value in this 30-year period.

Earlier we described in detail the relationship between the intrinsic value of a coin (the market value of the bullion in the coin) and its numismatic value (defined by rarity of a coin and its state of preservation). We concluded that the numismatic value is significantly higher and has been least affected by the reversal of the price of gold.

Exhibit 10-1. Silver and copper coin portfolio. The following coins were used for our analysis: 1865 2¢; 1870 nickel 3¢; 1862 silver 3¢; 1873 half dime; 1876 10¢; 1892 10¢; 1875 20¢; 1876 25¢; 1892 25¢; 1876 50¢; 1892 50¢; 1873 Seated Liberty $1; 1876 Trade $1; and 1880 Morgan $1.

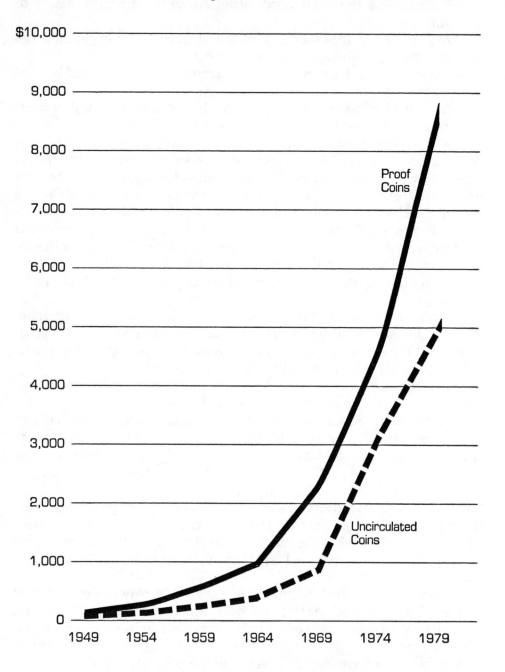

Table of values for Exhibit 10-1.

	1949 UNC	1949 PF	1954 UNC	1954 PF	1959 UNC	1959 PF	1964 UNC	1964 PF	1969 UNC	1969 PF	1974 UNC	1974 PF	1979 UNC	1979 PF
1845 2¢	1.	11.50	3.	13.50	7.	40.	16.	85.	27.50	130.	100.	165.	200.	385.
1870 NIC 3¢	2.75	8.	4.	11.	6.50	20.	12.	50.	21.	75.	55.	80.	110.	200.
1862 SIL 3¢	1.75	10.	5.	11.50	9.50	22.50	26.50	60.	52.	135.	120.	300.	225.	400.
1873 ½ 10¢	1.75	6.	3.	8.50	7.	25.	20.	62.50	40.	135.	130.	175.	250.	325.
1876 10¢	2.50	5.	3.	6.	4.	15.	10.	35.	35.	80.	125.	140.	200.	325.
1892 10¢	2.	4.	3.75	7.50	6.50	25.	12.	40.	25.	77.50	70.	140.	120.	300.
1875 20¢	7.50	17.50	20.	27.50	35.	52.50	80.	130.	175.	260.	500.	575.	1000.	1250.
1876 25¢	2.	4.50	4.	7.	5.50	22.50	14.	42.	45.	80.	230.	300.	375.	450.
1892 25¢	3.50	6.75	5.	9.	8.	30.	17.	57.50	40.	115.	190.	275.	260.	460.
1876 50¢	4.	9.	5.	12.	9.50	37.50	21.	60.	52.50	115.	300.	325.	400.	500.
1892 50¢	4.	11.	8.	14.	16.50	50.	25.	75.	95.	140.	375.	400.	525.	650.
1873 $1 Seated Liberty	9.50	14.50	17.50	32.50	29.	75.	45.	100.	125.	350.	525.	700.	725.	1350.
1876 $1 Trade	5.	15.	12.50	27.50	22.50	57.50	32.50	100.	110.	340.	360.	600.	500.	1400.
1880 $1 Morgan	2.75	10.	3.	13.50	2.75	50.	2.	85.	5.	220.	10.	360.	45.	650.
Index:	50.	132.75	97.25	201.	169.75	522.50	333.	982.	848.	2252.50	3090.	4535.	4953.	8645.

Exhibit 10-2. Gold coin portfolio. The following coins were used for our analysis: 1887 $1; 1905 $2½; 1902 Indian $2½; 1859 $3; 1905 $5; 1908 Indian $5; 1905 $10; 1908 Indian $10; 1907 Liberty $20; and 1908 $20.

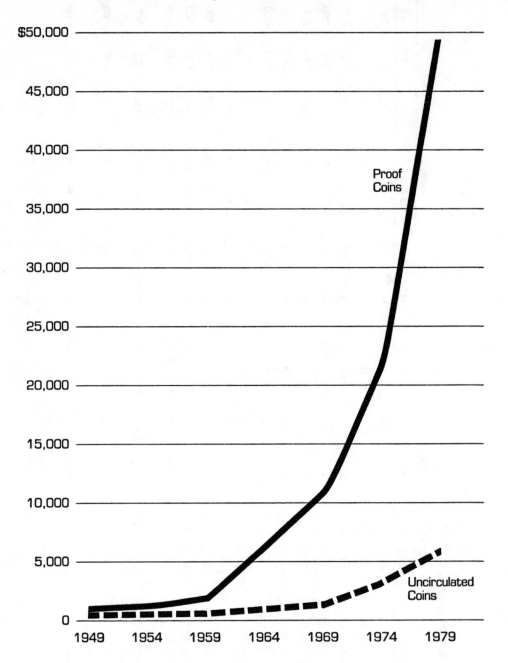

Table of values for Exhibit 10-2.

	1949		1954		1959		1964		1969		1974		1979	
	UNC	PF	UNC	PF	UNC	PF	UNC	PF	UNC	PF	UNC	PF	UNC	PF
1887 $1	14.	20.	14.	20.	35.	52.50	90.	150.	145.	300.	285.	675.	625.	1500.
1905 $2½	15.	25.	15.	25.	24.	75.	55.	250.	65.	400.	150.	1000.	250.	2000.
1908 $2½ Ind	9.	20.	11.	20.	18.	55.	35.	500.	60.	600.	150.	1000.	220.	2250.
1887 $3	30.	550.	45.	55.	100.	140.	300.	900.	375.	1300.	1100.	2150.	2250.	6000.
1905 $5	17.50	50.	17.50	50.	19.	100.	32.50	350.	60.	475.	115.	900.	210.	2750.
1908 $5 Ind	15.	30.	25.	50.	22.50	120.	35.	675.	80.	750.	160.	1500.	350.	4500.
1905 $10 Ind	37.50	70.	35.	75.	33.50	185.	47.50	600.	70.	850.	200.	1500.	260.	5000.
1908 $10 Ind	37.50	60.	35.	65.	40.	180.	60.	1200.	100.	1350.	250.	3000.	475.	7000.
1907 $20	75.	225.	75.	250.	67.50	600.	85.	1800.	110.	2500.	375.	3750.	325.	8500.
1908 $20 SFG	80.	110.	75.	120.	75.	500.	67.50	87.50	120.	2400.	375.	5000.	350.	10000.
	330.50	660.	347.50	730.	434.50	207.50	807.50	6512.5	1185.	10925.	3160.	20975.	5315.	49500.

Careful examination of the portfolios will support our conclusion that numismatic value offers a reasonable opportunity for growth and return on investment. A new investment strategy requires a tremendous amount of study, but no technique can really be successfully mastered until tried in the marketplace.

How to choose a numismatic agent

We stress the investor's need for careful selection of a coin agent who can provide guidance in evaluating and predicting numismatic trends and aid in designing collector strategies to maximize the profitable return on those trends.

Perusal of *Coin World*—the leading trade journal for numismatics—will demonstrate the growth of numismatic firms. The discerning reader is often distressed by the similarity in marketing techniques and by the technical terminology used by the advertisers. Each company offers accurate grading, genuine coins, fair or bargain prices, and the all encompassing "satisfaction guaranteed."

It is not the purpose of this study to question the reliability or professionalism of any firms. We are well aware that in any investment medium there are those firms which are more or less competent and more or less profitable. In light of these factors, we should like to provide some general guidelines for the reader in choosing his agent.

In order to make this distinction, it was necessary for us to make some educated assumptions about the investment needs of the reader. We assume numismatic investors are:

• Looking for a firm with the highest level of professionalism in the numismatic field, one which can offer personalized advice and knowledgeable value projections.

• Expecting a reciprocal relationship with a company that is prepared to monitor the status of their collections and provide continuing advice on overall profitability.

• Interested in a firm that provides comprehensive services, such as advice on possible tax implications, estate planning, and integration with other investment pursuits of the investor.

Contingent on these assumptions, we would offer the following advice in choosing a numismatic agent:

• Avoid firms whose marketing and sales approach is designed to capture the novice collector on the fringe of numismatics. (These companies typically sell non-numismatic items only peripherally related to the coin market.) This type of company does not meet the needs of the serious investor because of its diluted focus. The science of numismatics requires deliberative and uni-dimensional emphasis. Diversification necessarily diminishes this concentration.

• Avoid a coin dealer who claims expertise in every phase of numismatics. As with any complex investment medium, coin agents typically have an area of specialization. You do not want to purchase ancient coins from a dealer whose main interest is U.S. coins.

• Avoid companies that do not offer or seek a continuing relationship with investors. The development of profitable collections as we have mentioned previously, requires ongoing involvement. In addition, dispersing your business across the market can deprive you of auxiliary services and advice available as the result of the relationship with a consultant you have learned to trust.

• Avoid companies whose inventory is of lower quality coins. Not only do these companies offer less profitability, but their choice of specialty might serve as an interpretation of the firm's worth. An indication of the stability of their operation can affect the general quality of the services offered.

Conversely, here are positive criteria one should seek in choosing an agent:

• Choose companies whose sole and primary objective is the provision of expert advice in the field of numismatics.

• Choose companies that specialize in the acquisition of high quality coins. (In the event your collection requires the acquisition of lesser calibre coins, such a firm will be in the position to acquire them for you.) The reverse is not necessarily true.

• Choose companies that are interested in dealing with a select group of investors whose collections they can continually monitor, appraise, and develop. (This is in addition to providing advice in the areas of taxation, retirement plans, and other advisory services pertinent to the collector's interest and aims.)

• Choose companies that stipulate their interest to aid in disposal of part or all of your collection, as you may decide. In so doing, such firms confirm to you their confidence in the profit potential of the coins they are selling.

• Finally, analyze the credit, integrity, and business experience of the agent and choose companies whose access to the field of numismatics will ably represent your interests. (This criterion is normally met through their ads in reputable journals, attendance at prestigious auctions and conventions, possession of teletype and other sophisticated monitoring devices, and the general calibre of their clientele.)

Broadening your knowledge of numismatic coins

Having selected a coin dealer whose firm provides this quality of service, the deliberative investor may then choose to develop his or her knowledge of the field of coin acquisition in order to play a more active role in the collection's development.

Various resources are available to assist the collector in learning more about this fascinating field. We mentioned that the numismatic agent selected should be the investor's most significant resource in providing information relevant to numismatic investment, in general, and various collector strategies, in particular. In addition to this ongoing relationship, the investor may find supportive knowledge through familiarization with trade publications, involvement with other investors or hobbyists, and attendance at coin shows and auctions.

The knowledge thereby gained will enable the collector to become more familiar with the jargon of the numismatic agent. As in any investment medium, terms used by professionals for the sake of quick and convenient reference to describe transactions may be confusing. This specialized language can be learned by the beginner, and we would encourage the novice collector to ask as many questions as necessary to feel comfortable with the purpose and security of the investment.

This familiarization process with numismatics will be most rapidly achieved through the selection of a professional agent. There are no absolute rules in coin collecting. Any numismatic principle is "right" only if it fits your investment and collection needs. An adept numismatic agent will encourage an investor to examine the many options available and aid the investor in making those decisions that best fit his or her specific investment needs.

We have defined the field of numismatics, demonstrated the investment potential available, and communicated the challenge and gratification experienced by the collector/investor. Numismatics provides personally rewarding satisfaction for the well informed investor, indeed, as much an aesthetic experience as an economic one.

Suggested reading

Coin World is the weekly newspaper of the coin collecting and investing field and boasts a circulation of over 100,000. It contains advertising from virtually all of America's leading dealers and a feature called "trends," which is a retail price guide of most U.S. coins. A one-year subscription costs $15 and can be acquired by sending your check, name, and address to *Coin World*, Subscription Department, P.O. Box 150, Sidney, OH 45365.

A Guide Book of United States Coins, the standard "Red Book" of U.S. coin values is published once a year and is in its 33d edition. A copy costs $3.95 and is available at your local coin shop. Remember, it is just a guide. Actual coin prices might be higher or lower.

Photograde is the easiest of all the grading (condition) guides to use, and for this reason, I recommend it to all novices. It won't help you differentiate between Almost Uncirculated and Uncirculated coins, but it will give you a better idea about coin grading. You can buy a copy for $2.95 at your local coin shop. Over 250,000 copies have been sold.

Coin Dealer Newsletter, a Monday morning report on the coin market called the "Gray Sheet," is published weekly. C.D.N. is the most accurate price guide of rare coins. A subscription costs $45 per year from *Coin Dealer Newsletter,* Box 2308, Hollywood, CA 90028.

The Dictionary of Numismatic Terms is a guide to the standard definitions of descriptive terms used within the numismatic hobby, as established by the Numismatic Terms Standardization Committee. A copy costs $1 and can be acquired by writing to the American Numismatic Association, P.O. Box 2366, Colorado Springs, CO 80901.

The Numismatist is published by the American Numismatic Association. *The Numismatist,* a monthly numismatic journal, is devoted to articles on coins, tokens, and paper money along with dealer advertisements. Persons may join the ANA for $17 for the first year and $12 for subsequent years. Information and application forms may be obtained from ANA, P.O. Box 2366, Colorado Springs, CO 80901.

High Profits from Rare Coin Investment by Q. David Bowers is the premiere book on how to invest in rare coins and has sold tens of thousands of copies. It is available for $6.95 from Bowers and Ruddy Galleries, 6922 Hollywood Blvd., Suite 600, Los Angeles, CA 90028.

Stamps as an investment

As an inflationary hedge, stamps may well be in a class by themselves. Collectors who have fared best are those who have specialized in scarce stamps in top-notch condition. On August 29, 1977, at the Robert A. Siegel auction in San Francisco, a U.S. air mail stamp—printed in error with an inverted airplane in the center of the stamp—was sold for $62,500. The same stamp without a printing error is worth approximately $100. A first issue of a U.S. five-cent Franklin stamp, issued in 1847, in unused condition, was recently valued at $3,500 dollars.

Stamps, in short, are not for kids anymore. As Table 10-3 vividly demonstrates, rare stamps have become an important inflation hedge, a store of value with international recognition and marketability.

Table 10-3. Performance of selected U.S. stamp issues versus Dow Jones Industrial Average, London gold price, and cost of living index (CPI), 1925-1980.

Scott's Cat.	U.S. stamp issue	1925	1980[1]	Approximate Percent Increase
1-2	1847 First Issues [set]	$ 180.00	$ 18,000.00	10,000
230-45	1893 Columbian Expo [set]	45.33	11,169.00	24,050
285-93	1898 Trans-Miss. [set]	23.83	4,827.00	20,000
323-27	1904 La. Purchase [set]	2.13	442.00	22,000
C 3a	1918 24c Biplane [invert]	750.00	115,000.00	15,200
	Total	$1,001.29	$149,438.00	14,800
	Gold price [London][2]	$ 20.67	$ 512.00	2,300
	DJIA[2]	159.40	838.74	425
	Cost of Living [CPI][3]	52.50	230.00	338

1. Scott Specialized Catalog prices, 1980 Edition, published in the fall of 1979. Prices are for average condition mint stamps. The premium for superb stamps of U.S. nineteenth century can be at about 200 to 600 percent of the catalog price.
2. As of December 31, 1979.
3. 1967=100. Officially called U.S. Consumers Price Index.

Nor do the gains show any evidence of ending. In April 1980, a one-cent British Guiana stamp, purchased as a hedge against inflation ten years earlier for $280,000, was auctioned in New York City for $850,000, the highest price ever paid for a single stamp. The stamp is one of a kind. Dated 1856, it was printed in the then-British colony in South America by the postmaster of Demerara (now Georgetown) when a supply of new one-cent and four-cent stamps failed to arrive from Britain. Each of the locally printed stamps was initialled by the postmaster or one of his assistants as a measure against possible forgery. Several of the four-cent stamps survive, but only one known original of the one-cent stamp survives.

The stamp is nothing much to look at. Crudely printed and badly stamped, it is little more than an inch across and cut in an octagonal shape. It was discovered in 1873 by L. Vernon Vaughan, a Demarara teenager who came across it in a trunk in his attic. He sold it for $1.50. It has been rumored that in 1929, its owner, Arthur Huid, was approached by someone who had come across another of the one-cent stamps. Mr. Huid was said to have offered the man twice the $32,000 he paid for the stamp in 1922, and then to have burned the new stamp so that his stamp would be unique.

Pricing

There are no bargains in stamps. One must be prepared to pay superior prices for superior items. Moreover, it is not easy to estimate the price of a stamp any longer since the premium paid for quality may be twice the regular price.

The uptrend in prices is due to many factors, one being an influx of money from European and Middle Eastern dealers and investors. Funds also have come from U.S. investors who seek inflation havens, as well as from those who have become disenchanted with the securities markets. In addition, a growing number of investors are joining dealer-sponsored syndicates to play the stamp market, assembling portfolios of top-drawer merchandise. Individual tax-deferred IRA and Keogh programs also are discovering philatelic investments for their funds, further contributing to the growth of the market.

While investors talk of the concept of leverage and yields, comparisons of return on investment on stamp portfolios—when compared to return on investment from stocks and bonds—may be misleading. The market for selling stamps differs from that of stocks and bonds in that the buyer and seller of stamps, even at a public auction, must be prepared to assume at least a 10 percent selling cost. Moreover, although some collector/investors may find financing sources for their purchases, financial leverage for philatelic material is usually not available from the standard lending institutions. Such leverage is normally available to the securities investor, which may result in a rate-of-return gain that is greater than the comparative return from a stamp investment.

Philatelic prices have been rising for most of the century and have been an excellent investment in both good and bad times. Since the 1960s, they have shown an annual compound rate growth exceeding 15 percent. Presently, we are in a rapidly rising sellers market and it is unlikely that stamps will greatly depreciate.

But newcomers to the field of stamp collecting and investing are often at a loss as to where to begin building their collections. Most dealers suggest that the beginner specialize in one certain area. Concentration of U.S. air mail, dollar-value, and commemorative issues printed since 1890 is highly recommended. The investor/collector should concentrate on material classified very fine or better. Prices can vary by as much as 1,000 percent depending on such criteria as clarity of the picture or the number and evenness of perforations. If even a single perforation is missing, the value of the stamp could be reduced by as much as 50 percent.

Many stamp items are priced under $100, and the new collector should consider starting at that price range rather than purchasing a single classic item for several thousand dollars.

As in any investment medium, a caveat is in order. The result of price increases has encouraged counterfeiting. It is estimated that forgeries may amount for as much as 10 percent of the dollar volume of philatelic sales. Thus, questionable material should be submitted for inspection to organizations in the field, such as the Philatelic Foundation in New York City or the American Philatelic Society in State College, Pa. These organizations specialize in the authentication of stamps. A nominal charge is made for this inspection.

The collector/investor's need for careful selection of a philatelic agent who can provide guidance in evaluating and predicting trends must be stressed. The agent should provide assistance in designing the investor strategies to maximize the profitable return on those trends.

It's a big and growing market. According to the U.S. Postal Service, which has had a big say in philatelic progress, more than 16 million Americans collect stamps. Because of this interest, and the price gains it has spawned, stamp catalogues are often outdated as soon as they are printed. Careful study is thus a prerequisite for anyone interested in investing in stamps.

Problems

There are other problems an unsophisticated investor may encounter. For example:

• Dealers have been known to purchase large amounts of new issues, stage phony auctions to force prices up artificially and then publicize the "increases" in the philatelic press.

• Stamps do not earn interest. Appreciation is based on capital gains.

• Rare stamps need to be kept at relatively stable temperatures and humidity and should not be left lying around the house. If someone in your family uses one of your rare stamps to mail a letter, you're out of luck.

• Because dealers normally charge a 10 to 20 percent commission for their efforts, investing in stamps is not likely to be an in-and-out deal.

• It is important to know where to buy and sell investment-grade stamps, and this takes learning a bit of history about the business.

The best place to start acquiring this connoisseurship is with the Scott catalog, the bible of stamp collectors, which has been issued yearly since the 1880s. Every stamp ever issued in the world is included. Market values are listed for used and unused stamps. Buyers and sellers can refer to the Scott numbers when communicating, rather than an awkward description or title of the stamp. Copies of the catalog are available from:

Scott Publishing Co.
530 Fifth Avenue
New York, NY 10036

Acknowledgment

The author wishes to express his deep appreciation for the tireless and creative assistance of Richard Bagg, Ph.D., for his many excellent comments, criticisms, and suggestions and for making available much of the research on which the numismatic section of this chapter is based.

Belly to Belly

Leo Melamed

. . . and Joseph said unto the Pharaoh, "There are to be seven years of great plenty throughout the land . . . after that there will be seven of famine. . . ."

Thus, with a minimum of fanfare, Joseph laid the groundwork for the commodity futures market, undertaking, on a grandiose scale, history's first recorded buy hedge. Amazingly enough, it became a model for hedging theory that is still applicable today.

In fact, although uses and techniques have dramatically changed since biblical times, Joseph's basic application of forward hedging is the central reason why modern U.S. futures markets are not merely arenas for speculation. Indeed, futures markets today are an important and integral part of the U.S. and world marketing systems, providing the best, and sometimes only, means of shifting inherent risks from the producer to the speculator, to the ultimate benefit of the consumer.

Yet the basic reasons for futures markets, the fundamental benefits derived from them, and their importance to our national economy are seldom discussed. Speculative opportunities or tales of fabulous fortunes won or lost are all you are likely to encounter in the press. Well, after all, economics is a dry science, and there are not many people who will be turned on by an analysis of the system of price insurance or price discovery which is provided by futures markets. Even in Joseph's day, I am sure that more Egyptians were interested in how to make a buck as a result of the Pharaoh's dream than in discussing the beauty of Joseph's hedging plan.

Without question, futures markets have catapulted themselves to the forefront of the financial world and offer some of the most exciting vehicles of investment available anywhere. During the past dozen or so years, futures transaction volume on U.S. commodity exchanges has grown tenfold, rising from 6.4 million contracts in 1965 to a 1979 record of 75.9 million.

During this period, the scope of futures experienced a metamorphosis which is still hard to fathom. In less than a decade, futures markets shed their traditional and exclusive agricultural base and embraced virtually every important form of financial and monetary instrument. Their dramatic and explosive change included expansion into meats and live animals—itself a break with the "sacred" principle that futures could not be successfully applied to non-stored items—into metals, precious metals, and finally the giant leap into foreign currency and interest-bearing instruments—the so-called financial futures.

As a direct result of their growth and expansion, and particularly as a result of their dramatic successes with monetary and financial instruments, futures markets became a "respectable" vehicle of finance. Indeed, the New York and American Stock Exchanges, those sacred temples of investment which only a few years ago considered futures something akin to snakebite, have instituted futures market divisions within their respective institutions.

Moreover, futures markets today and the opportunities they offer are topics of conversation from one end of the world to the other, and many different world centers are considering opening futures markets of their own.

Brokerage firms, bond houses, security dealers, and banks—groups that heretofore never considered these markets—are actively seeking membership in commodity exchanges or other means of connecting themselves to their investment opportunities; financiers, financial institutions, and broker-dealers the world over are seeking an understanding of these markets and the means by which to participate; at least two federal agencies are squabbling about jurisdictional prerogatives over these markets (a dubious distinction); almost monthly, a seminar or workshop is conducted somewhere pertaining to the use of futures markets; every major newspaper, as well as every financial periodical, has expanded its coverage of futures markets; a host of new advisory services and special advisory publications have been created—with more to come. Little wonder, then, that the average investor with risk capital is avidly interested in what happens on these markets and how to become involved.

Yes, futures markets have grown in geometric proportion and their expansion is inevitable. In fact, as a result of the explosive financial instruments section, futures markets are probably on the threshold of a quantum jump in volume. Thus, it is timely and appropriate to offer a word or two of caution to all would-be participants: futures market speculation is treacherous and not for everyone; there are and always will be more losers than winners; anyone who approaches these markets with a cavalier attitude, as one might an occasional minor investment, is doomed to failure. These markets require study and thought. They also require risk capital, which, if lost, will not materially affect one's life style. Above all, these markets are not for the faint of heart.

On that score, many would argue and insist that futures can not and should not be considered an investment. Certainly they are correct in terms of classical definition. *Encyclopaedia Britannica* tells us that "investment" is the "process of exchanging income during one period of time for an asset that is expected to produce earnings in future periods." When I consider that at 11:03 a.m. on a recent day a friend of mine purchased 50 contracts of Swiss Francs and at 11:29 a.m. the same day sold them out at a loss of $24,000, it is indeed hard to look at the transaction as an investment. Even if my friend had been right and had in those 26 minutes earned the same sum he lost, it would still be difficult to view the transaction as an investment in terms of the traditional definition.

On the other hand, few would argue that you are considering an investment if you feel that the Swiss Franc will rise in value against the dollar over the next 12-month period because Switzerland's rate of inflation will be substantially less than that of the United States. If you purchased actual Swiss Francs and deposited them in a safety deposit box for the next year, did you not, if fact, make an investment in Swiss Francs?

The point is that we are used to a definition of "investment" that implies a duration longer than 26 minutes. But does the time element itself change the nature of the act? Are we not in either case doing the same thing, that is, attempting to increase the value of our estate by exchanging dollars for something else. Hopefully, the "something else" will increase in value relative to the dollars we have spent acquiring it. Clearly, if we buy real estate in the hope that five years from now it will net us a large profit, we are investing. But if 26 minutes after our purchase, oil is discovered on the premises and we are offered a large profit immediately, have we now changed the nature of our original purchase if we accept the offer?

I doubt it. Whether we hold on to our purchase for 5 years or 26 minutes, the purpose was the same. If it was an investment in one case, it is an investment in either case. Besides, the world is no longer the slow-paced place it was once. The world has shrunk, and, with it, our concepts of time. A century ago, it took months to travel from New York to San Francisco; today it takes several hours. A decade ago, a complicated mathematical theorem could take weeks to prove; today less than 10 minutes. Such almost incomprehensible changes in our lives have had an incalculable effect on our investment strategy. Why, 100 years ago if someone in the States invested by purchasing the Mona Lisa, it would be months before someone in France could offer the investor a profit; certainly, the art investor then had no intention of making a profit in terms of minutes. But today the same investment could show a profit in the length of time it takes to make a telephone call; is it, therefore, not to be considered an investment? Clearly, time alone should not be the only criterion of what is or is not an investment.

Still, futures must be differentiated from most other forms of investment. Although the time element is the most striking difference, there are other distinguishing characteristics. For one thing, the futures investor is seldom the recipient of the physical property in question; nor does the investor want it. Physical delivery, in fact, is one of the inherent fears of the uninitiated would-be futures traders. I recall that when I first began trading commodities while attending John Marshall Law School in Chicago, my father's biggest fear was that his son's antics would one day result in a big truck backing a carload of onions onto our porch. "They rot, you know," he would remind me and walk away shaking his head.

Of course they rot, and for that and many other reasons, futures speculators do not as a rule take delivery of the product, be it onions or Swiss Francs. Delivery is left to the merchants who participate in that particular business. A futures speculator knows that whether one is long or short, one should liquidate one's position before delivery. The investment is geared to capitalize on the market fluctuations between the time of entry into the market and the date of maturity of the contract. Thus, the investment is inherently of short duration; most contracts mature within a year or two of the date they are born. Moreover, most of the action occurs in contracts with only a few months of life remaining.

Investment in futures does not identify a specific item, such as it does in real estate or art. All futures, at least until delivery, are fungible. You buy or sell a contract of silver, coffee, or cattle, but you cannot inspect the item. In fact, the item may not yet exist, and it does not matter which unit or carload is yours since the specifications are created to make them all the same. Not only is quantity of one contract the same as the next, the quality of each contract is the same as well. In this respect, it is, therefore, safer to deal in futures than it is to, say, buy diamonds or coins. Not only need you not worry about storing the physical item, you need not worry whether your product is chipped, warped, or damaged or whether it is as good or better than another quantity of the same product.

Furthermore, when dealing in futures, it is erroneous to believe that you actually purchased or sold the commodity in question. You didn't. When you trade in futures, you are simply establishing a price at which you may take or make delivery of a specific commodity. Naturally, you always have the option of receiving or delivering the actual item in question, but it is an option you will undoubtedly not exercise. After you enter the market, if you are a speculator, all you will really be doing is trying to sell it out, before maturity, at a higher price than you paid (if you can) or buying it back at a price lower than at which you sold it. You, therefore, do not have to pay for the item at the time you go long or have the item in your possession at the time you go short.

Which brings us to another distinction of futures investment. Since you do not have to own the commodity in question in order to sell it, you can go short in futures easier than in most other forms of investment. This means that you can utilize with equal ease both sides of the street. You need not invest only when you believe an item will go up in value, as is traditionally the case in most forms of investment. You can invest as easily when you believe the price of an item will fall in value. Of course, when you are short, you must buy back before maturity or you will be required to deliver the item; otherwise, you will be in default. Appropriately, an old saying in commodities reminds the short seller that "he who sells what isn't his'n must buy back or go to pris'n."

Recently, there was a scandal on the New York Mercantile Exchange involving thousands of contracts for potatoes. The shorts defaulted because they had sold more than they could deliver. This type of default rarely occurs, but when it does, it gives an erroneous impression of futures markets and casts a doubt on the whole system. Actually, every exchange and the Commodity Futures Trading Commission (CFTC), the federal agency governing futures markets, has the capability to prevent most defaults. Such situations are usually the creation of a concerted effort on the part of individuals to "squeeze" or "corner" a market for the purpose of manipulating its price above or below its market value. Such actions, either by shorts or longs, are against the law and subject the wrongdoers to severe penalties, as was the case in the Maine potato incident.

Still another major characteristic of futures is the leverage available to the speculator. Everyone knows you can invest in many things on "margin." That is, you can buy or sell something without putting up the full price. But in futures, since you do not actually buy or sell the commodity, your leverage is much greater. In fact, in futures, margin is a misnomer where it is applicable. In futures, "margin" in reality is a security deposit; it is an amount sufficient to protect the brokerage firm handling the account from the next immediate adverse price swing in the given market.

The reason this amount is necessary is because futures markets uniquely operate on a "no debt" system. Every brokerage firm dealing in the market must settle up each day in cash with the exchange clearing system for all of its customers' market positions. The "settlement" is based on the closing prices of each commodity each business day. So your brokerage firm must settle with the exchange daily for the position you hold in the market. The brokerage firm, therefore, must have some of your money in case your position goes against you. But the required security deposit is actually very small compared to the real cost of the contract. Most margins are anywhere from 1 to 5 percent of the actual purchase price.

As a result, the leverage for the speculator is spectacular. For example, as I write, gold is about $370 an ounce (who knows what it will be when these words are read). But you can purchase one contract of gold (100 ounces) on a futures exchange (the International Monetary Market or the COMEX) for $3,000[1] margin. (Actually, most brokerage firms will require at least $5,000.) Even at $5,000, at this gold price level, your leverage is seven times greater than in the physical market.

But leverage is a two-edged sword. In a positive sense, it allows someone of modest means to participate in investments from which he or she would otherwise be excluded. At the same time, it causes many speculators to take on positions far greater than they should. In a similar way, the latter false sense of risk also affects floor traders on the exchanges because they trade all day without seeing the actual losses or profits until the next day. I have often thought that if I had to pay someone $10,000 in cold cash for a bad trade I made ten minutes before, I would not be so quick to make the next trade. Actually, we do not deal in cash until the close of the market, and then only on a net basis, so that we do not see each and every loss or profit resulting from our continuous buys and sells during the trading session.

Finally, one additional major difference of this form of investment is that you do not receive any interest or dividend on your money. Your profit, if any, will be based only on the price difference from when you bought to when you sold or vice versa. This is true even if you invest in the financial futures sector and deal in something like Treasury Bills. In futures, you will not be investing for an interest income on your purchase as you will when you purchase an actual Treasury Bill; nor will you be banking a dividend paid by the corporation whose stock you purchased. In futures, you put up money in the hope that you will come out with more than you started, or at worst break even. Appropriately, professionals sometimes repeat an instructive commodity saying: "I hope to break even today; I need the money."

I have often been asked what advice can I give a newcomer to this difficult arena of investment. Most of the time I have responded by saying, "Think it over again—maybe you shouldn't." But usually such warnings go unheeded. After all, we all like to think that we will succeed. Besides, the lure to quick fortune is a much bigger force than my words of caution could ever be. There is no denying it; futures markets today are the last frontier where someone with limited risk capital has a chance at a big strike; in all other fields it takes big money to make big money.

Not that you can enter futures with a couple hundred bucks—far from it. Still, it doesn't require a couple of hundred thousand either. How much do you need? That depends. First of all, as I already mentioned, it must be risk capital (RC); in other words, money, which, if lost, will not affect how you eat or dress or whether you can meet your rent or alimony payments. Obviously, you should have a secure income and other investments that are of a minimal risk nature. Second, how much you have to lose (and that is exactly how you must reason) will determine the type of position and size of position.

In my opinion, it takes a minimum of about $25,000 RC to start in futures. Any lesser amount substantially diminishes the chance of success in the fast pace of today's markets. At the same time, I must admit that I would defend everyone's right of access to the market regardless of the amount of his or her RC, as long as such participants understand that their risk of loss is enormous. After all, I have seen many investors succeed in pyramiding large profits over time, even though they began with an amount far below what I would consider prudent.

Such cases are, of course, the exception, but they do illustrate that no one has the right to pass a law or otherwise categorically exclude anyone from the attempt. This belief is further underscored by the fact that I have seen many investors with large pools of RC fail miserably and lose it all. The point is that the money itself is not enough. The market is the ultimate "equalizer." It doesn't care if you are rich or poor; it doesn't ask if you are white or black. The market is only concerned with whether you are right or wrong and whether you have the psychological temperament to meet the challenge of failures as well as the fortitude to hang in when successful.

What is as important as risk capital is that you know something about what you are doing and adhere to some prudent market rules. If you do start with the minimum amount of RC, you should limit your positions to no more than one or two contracts at a time, and you should stay away from the highly volatile markets.

Basically, there are two main methods of trading for the "outside" investor. The simplest is by opening a discretionary or managed account with a firm of your choice. That means that your broker will have the discretion, on his own judgment, of when and what to buy or sell for you. You can, of course, close your account whenever you wish, but normally you will not be involved in the decision-making process in this type of arrangement. It is, therefore, imperative to choose a broker and firm that has a decent track record. It is equally important to determine in which market the broker excels, and to limit your account to those markets. If your account executive (AE) has shown a faculty for the currency markets, then for heaven's sake do not agree to sugar or soybeans. On the other hand, if your AE is a cattle or corn specialist, then do not agree to gold or silver.

Even before you open your account do a little studying about the market in which you intend to invest. Pick up a book or manual (your broker will usually provide some on request) and learn the facts that make the market go up and down. Learn some of the history of the specific commodity in question. Learn some of the statistics and language so that you can ask your broker intelligent questions. This will not only keep your broker alert, but it will also make you feel better.

Another thing to remember is that you need not always be "in" the market. One of the greatest failings of futures participants is that they over-trade. Most brokers are honest and conscientious, but nonetheless they earn their money from commissions. The more you trade, the more the commissions mount and the more exposure to the market you have. You have absolutely zero chance for success if you are constantly in one or another position. Talk to your broker or AE about that; say that you do not mind missing some of the market moves or gyrations and that you would be happy if you only entered a limited number of times a year. Ask for an opinion on market moves that might involve major price shifts. Every commodity will have several major bull and bear swings each year. Try for those and leave the minor ups and downs that occur daily to the professionals who devote a large portion of their day to the market. Otherwise, you will surely be eaten up either by commissions, by the times your broker is bound to be wrong, or both.

The second method is more or less a professional approach. This means that you will make the final decision regarding when and what to buy or sell. It will, therefore, require a good deal more knowledge on your part about the market. It will mean studying and staying abreast of new factors as they unfold. It will also mean keeping track of all daily market gyrations. But by far, this method can be the most rewarding over the long haul. Naturally, even with this approach, the broker you choose will be of prime importance. Again, the broker's track record and specific market expertise are paramount factors in your chance for success. But since you will make the final decision each time, two things will happen: first, you will learn from your own mistakes; second, when you figure a market correctly, you will get a psychic thrill that is second only to sex. Maybe the latter reason is more important than the former.

Whatever your approach, there are salient rules that must be followed or you will not have a chance. The most cardinal of all: be a lover, not a fighter. Every professional knows that in the long run only the lovers make money. What do I mean? A lover is someone who follows a love's direction. If the market is moving up, be a bull or stay out of the market. If the market is moving down, be a bear or keep away. Do not be a fighter who has to buck the direction of the market and take a position opposite the immediate trend. Fighters like to pick the "top" of a bull trend to go short or find the "bottom" of a bear trend to go long. How do they know it is the top or bottom? They don't. When they are right, they make it big, but their chances are not good in the long run. Lovers have a much better chance.

Being but frail human beings, all of us, including the best of the professionals, will forget this principle on occasion. When we do, it is usually with devastating consequences. I should know, because I recently forgot. It all started several months ago in the cattle market. I had been short as the cattle market was dropping.

After a time, I liquidated my positions and took my profit. So far so good. But—as fate would have it—my getting out of the short side did not impress the cattle market. Cattle futures kept sliding lower and lower. This upset me; after all, I could have stayed short and made more money. (I should have remembered another good rule that "a little out of the middle" is good enough.) Pretty soon I was convinced that the cattle market had gone too low and was now due for a major bull market. Thus, I became a fighter and went long in an attempt to pick the bottom.

I was wrong. Cattle went lower. I aborted the attempt and took my losses. Several days later, at still lower cattle prices, I tried again. Again, the same result. I now was an active fighter, trying each day at a new lower level to find the bottom. But the market was always weaker than I anticipated. By the time the bottom had actually been made, I was weak from the battle and the losses. I was also afraid. So when the market did turn around, I had only a fraction of the long position I should have had and was psychologically so worn out that as soon as I had a small profit, I was too quick to take it. As a result, I missed one of the biggest cattle bull markets in history. The market, as I write, has gone up some 16 cents ($6,400 per contract) in a matter of a few weeks, and I hardly made any money in the process.

This is one of the best classical examples of why it does not pay to be a fighter. After all, I was right about the eventual cattle market. In fact, it was a better bull market than I had anticipated. But because I started to buy long before the bottom had been reached, I ruined my chances to make money. Had I waited until the "up trend" had been established and then become a "lover," I would have participated in one of the best market plays of the year. (Alas, it is tough to be human and make the same mistakes again and again—there ought to be a law.)

A second principle, which is as important as the first, is to "run quickly." Much has been written about taking losses when you are wrong, but not enough can be said about it. Everyone has probably heard about the rule "not to meet a margin call." Meaning: if you are losing in the market to the point you need to put up more margin money, don't; liquidate your position instead. Well, I would not necessarily be that hard and fast about it, but it is not far from the truth. It takes courage to admit you are wrong and that the money you have lost is gone, but that is one of the first things you must learn in futures if you are going to succeed.

The key to successful futures trading is to limit your losses. If you learn to do that, the profits will take care of themselves. As will become obvious to anyone watching futures markets for even a few weeks, the price gyrations in one commodity or another are momentous. Each price swing is another opportunity. Obviously, you cannot capitalize on all of them and you cannot expect to be right in every attempt.(There is an appropriate Jewish saying: You can't dance at every wedding.) Let us suppose that you are right 50 percent of the time in the positions you do undertake (that is a darn good average). However, if your losses equal your gains, then the commissions will make you a net loser. Moreover, you must strive to be successful even if you are right only 40 percent or even 30 percent of the time. Obviously then, you must make greater profits the times you are right than the losses you incur when you are wrong.

Thus, it is imperative not to let a losing position get out of hand. As soon as you think you are wrong; or as soon as you or your broker begin to doubt the reason for your purchase or sale; or as soon as your position shows a loss greater than you are willing to take; or as soon as your own good sense or rule of thumb tells you that you should run for cover, then do just that—run for cover. The sooner the better. Remind yourself that some of the time you will be on the right side of the market.

Those are the times you will stay with your position and let the profits run. The difference between winners and losers in the field of futures is not that the winners are more often right than the losers; it is that the losers never want to admit when they are wrong. Such traders remind me of the guy who fell out of a 50-story window; as he was passing the thirtieth floor, he was asked how he was doing. "So far so good," he replied.

All of us professionals have one rule or another which guides us when we are wrong. If we don't, we are quickly forced to find a different field of endeavor. I remember an old and wise trader who once told me that his rule was quite simple. The night that any market position caused him the loss of one moment of sleep, he automatically liquidated the position the next morning. His chart, he said, was in his stomach. His stomach was a good trader.

Which markets you choose to trade and how many at a time are also important considerations. As a professional, I will trade almost any market in which I get an idea. In fact, at times, I have held positions in as many as a dozen markets at a crack. But I emphatically do not recommend such an approach to anyone who is not professionally on the floor of an exchange every day or otherwise is not fully connected to every market he or she enters in order to have immediate access. As a matter of fact, most professional exchange members usually limit their largest commitment to one or two markets at a time and take only minor positions in others. In other words, the majority of professionals feel they have expertise in one or two areas and concentrate primarily on those markets.

If that is the professional approach, it certainly must be the approach of "off-the-floor" or non-professional investors. Choose one or two markets that, either by virtue of your background, education, or immediate interest, suit you best. Concentrate on those markets and ignore those that you know little or nothing about. Above all else, do not trade or take positions in markets that have relatively low daily volume. Such markets are illiquid and will expose you to unwarranted dangers. By definition, illiquid markets have large price gaps between transactions and, what is worse, they are difficult to exit. Every professional trader knows that the most important question about a given market is not whether you can get "in" but whether you can get "out."

For me and many other professionals, as well as a host of newcomers to the field of futures, there is a special interest and attraction to the emerging financial futures sector. Obviously, many more investors feel they know something about interest rates, foreign currency, or gold and silver than about agriculture. Certainly, financial news gets a good deal more print and media attention than any other; many of us, therefore, get the impression that we know something about this field of investment. As a matter of fact, that is not necessarily the case, but how can I argue with the public's view of itself? At any rate, these new futures markets have attracted a large following of investors who heretofore never traded in commodities.

When the International Monetary Market (IMM) was spawned by the Chicago Mercantile Exchange in 1972,[2] it officially ushered in the era of financial futures markets. Today, a few short years later, financial futures are the hottest items on the futures scene. Transaction volume in this sector already rivals volume in agricultural futures, which are over 100 years old and which have themselves witnessed phenomenal growth. Today, financial futures markets are on the verge of becoming international in scope and application.

Scores of new contracts, new concepts, and new applications are being considered for financial futures by virtually every commodity exchange; many colleges and universities are initiating courses of studies for this new field of investment; most major brokerage firms either already have or are gearing to have a special financial futures division within their firm; special training programs are under way for account executives; dozens of studies are being conducted on the variety of uses offered by these futures contracts for every segment of business. In short, unless the world suddenly experiences a major change of direction brought on by events that are not predictable, financial futures will capture the limelight for investment opportunity in the coming decade.[3]

Not only are financial futures inherently exciting and interesting; not only is there an abundance of daily information available to the investor; not only are their uses applicable to virtually every form of commerce or business, but also one glance at their recent record of price movement makes it amply clear why the opportunities they offer are so attractive. Take the record of some foreign currency movement during the first nine months of 1979.[4]

• *British Pound* (IMM) (Present minimum margin: $1,500 per contract.)

In early February, Pounds were at the 1.95 level, from which they rose and reached the 2.30 level by the end of July—a rise equal to $8,750 per contract; Pounds then fell and by the middle of September were at the 2.15 level—a fall equal to $3,750 per contract.

• *Japanese Yen* (IMM) (Present minimum margin: $2,000 per contract.)

In early February, Yen were at the .5400 level, from which they fell to the .4650 level by the end of April—a decline equal to $9,375 per contract.

• *Deutsche Mark* (IMM) (Present minimum margin: $1,500 per contract.)

In the middle of March, Deutsche Marks were at the .5600 level, from which they fell to the .5350 level the middle of May—a fall equal to $3,125 per contract; from this point, they rose to the .5700 level by late September—a rise equal to $4,375 per contract.

• *Swiss Franc* (IMM) (Present minimum margin: $2,500 per contract.)

In early January, Swiss Francs were at the .6850 level, from which they fell to .6000 by the middle of May—a fall equal to $10,625 per contract; the Swiss Franc then bottomed and returned to the .6500 level by the end of September—a rise equal to $6,250 per contract.

Or take a look at price movements in the interest rate sector during this same span.[5]

• *Ginnie Mae* (GNMA) (CBOT) (Present minimum margin: $1,000 per contract.)

In late May, GNMA's were at the 85.50 level, rising to a high of 89.00 by early July—a price rise of $3,500. They then dropped to the 83.00 level by the middle of September—a swing of $6,000.

• *U.S. Bond* (CBOT) (Present minimum margin: $1,000 per contract.)

In early May, U.S. Bonds were at the 88.00 level and rose to 99.50 by the end of June—a rise of $4,500 per contract. From this level, they returned to the 88.00 level again by early September—again, a $4,500 swing.

• *90-Day Treasury Bill* (IMM) (Present minimum margin: $800 per contract.)

In early May, T-Bills were at the 90.40 level; by the end of June, they had risen to 92.20—a rise equal to $4,500 per contract. They then "topped" out and fell to the 89.60 level by early September—a fall equal to $6,500 per contract.

Such a review makes it abundantly clear why these futures markets have captured the attention of so many investors and why so many more are flocking to the scene. It's a similar story in the gold and silver markets. Naturally, by strict definition, these are not financial futures. But you would have a hard time convincing a majority of the public that the price movements of these precious metals are not directly related to the value of the dollar or the world's inflation problem. And what breathtaking price movements they have been:[6]

• *Gold* (IMM & COMEX) (Present minimum margin: $3,000 per contract.)

In March, Gold was maintaining a 260 level, from which it rose to the 320 level by the end of July—a rise equal to $6,000 per contract. Gold then broke quickly to the 285 level—a fall equal to $3,500 per contract, and then began its rise to the 380 level, which it reached by the middle of September—a rise equal to $9,500 per contract.

• *Silver* (COMEX & CBOT) (The minimum margin for Silver rose substantially during the course of 1979, from $1,500 to $20,000 on September 30.)

Silver began the year at 6.50 level, from which it rose to the 9.00 level by the end of May—a rise equal to $12,500 per contract; after consolidating at the 9.00 level, it began its spectacular rise and reached the 16.00 level by the end of September—a rise equal to another $35,000 per contract.[7]

If you compare any of the foregoing price movements with the movement of any given stock, security, or that of the Dow Jones or Standard & Poors 500 Average during a comparable period and for the comparable dollar of investment, it is obvious that financial futures offered the investor far greater opportunities. Oh, but the risks were equally great. You must not assume, as one is prone to do, that you would have profited from every major rise or fall in the futures market. You cannot even assume that you would have caught the right side of a majority or even half of the given opportunities. As professionals, we know that if we are fortunate enough to have capitalized on even one of the many spectacular swings, we have done well indeed. Besides, as the investor, you must realize that often you will be on the wrong end of some of these price shifts and, thus, cannot assume that just because opportunities are there, you will do well if you participate.

A friend of mine, a professional trader and an extremely capable "fundamentalist,"[8] was very bullish on silver at the beginning of 1979. He was, of course, right and profited greatly from the upward silver price movement during the first four months of the year. But later in the year he became afraid that U.S. recessionary forces would affect all commodity prices and would force them down. Thus, he liquidated his long silver positions around the nine-dollar level, took his enormous profits (over $2 million), and began to look for indications of a "top." He who seeks finds. That is, he found dozens of imaginary reasons why silver had reached its high and, therefore, why he should be "short."

None of his reasons proved right. Silver continued upward to price levels beyond anyone's expectations (and who knows at what price this upward motion will cease). As a result, this story has a sad ending and serves to illustrate the point I was making. My friend lost all the profits he made earlier and then some. This is a good example of how difficult it is, even for the professional, to capitalize on what in retrospect looks like an easy and highly lucrative market opportunity. Sure, I can cite happy examples as well, but the point I am trying to make is that the opportunities offered by futures are much harder to capture than they appear on paper.

On the other hand, for most investors, the fact that opportunity exists is the only and most important aspect. Most investors who have applied themselves to these markets fully understand the risk involved: they are, nonetheless, attracted simply because the reward can be great. That is true not merely of the financial futures markets but also of the agricultural as well.[9]

- *Soybeans* (CBOT) (Present minimum margin: $2,500 per contract.)

From the 6.60 level in January, the November option rose to the 7.10 level by the end of February—a rise equal to $2,500 per contract; it then consolidated at the 7.00 level and rose to the 8.20 level by the end of June—a rise equal to another $6,000 per contract. From this level, it fell back to the 7.00 level by early August —a fall of $6,000 per contract.

- *Wheat* (CBOT) (Present minimum margin: $1,250 per contract.)

The December Wheat option staged a dramatic rise from the 3.40 level in April to the 5.00 level in late June—a rise equal to $8,000 per contract; from this level, it fell to the 4.20 level by early August—a fall equal to $4,000 per contract.

- *Sugar* (C & S) (Present minimum margin: $1,800 per contract.)

In middle February, the October Sugar option was at the 9.50 level, from which it fell to the 8.50 level by the end of April—a fall equal to $1,120 per contract. It then rose to the 10.00 level by the middle of September—a rise equal to $1,680 per contract.

- *Cattle* (CME) (Present minimum margin: $1,200 per contract.)

The December Cattle option began the year at the .6500 level and rose to the .7300 level by the middle of May—a rise equal to $3,200 per contract; it then fell to the .6000 level early in August—a fall equal to $5,200; it then went into a major bull market which brought it to the .7400 level by the middle of September—a rise equal to $5,600 per contract.

- *Hogs* (CME) (Present minimum margin: $900 per contract.)

The major move in Hogs in 1979, a bear market, began in the middle of March. The December option fell from the .5100 level to .3300 by the end of July—a fall equal to $5,400 per contract.

- *Pork Bellies* (CME) (Present minimum margin: $1,000 per contract.)

The February option fell from its early May level at .5500 to .3800 by the end of July—a fall equal to $6,400 per contract; bellies then rallied from that level to the .5100 level by mid-September—a rise equal to $4,900 per contract.

No doubt about it, the opportunities are mind boggling. Moreover, there is every reason to believe that such price swings will continue to be prevalent during the '80s decade. Every economic guidepost seems to indicate that commodity prices, in both the financial and agricultural sectors, will experience volatile price movements up and down during the foreseeable next several years. The futures markets are thus positioned to offer investors almost the only feasible means for participation in these potential opportunities.

The big futures markets are in Chicago. What New York is to the securities business, Chicago is to futures. That is true of both the agricultural markets as well as the financial. While the reasons for this are manifold, they are primarily bound up in the fact that Chicago was the traditional transportation center of the United States. Once born there, these markets took root and remained in Chicago where they grew and prospered.

Today, the Chicago futures exchanges—composed of the Chicago Board of Trade (CBOT); the Chicago Mercantile Exchange (CME), which includes the International Monetary Market (IMM) and the Associate Mercantile members; and the Mid America Exchange—account for between 75 and 80 percent of the annual U.S. futures market business. The Commodity Exchange (COMEX) of New York, that city's largest, captures somewhere between 15 and 18 percent of the futures markets. The rest of the futures business is divided among seven other U.S. commodity exchanges: AMEX Commodities Exchange; Board of Trade of Kansas City, Missouri; Minneapolis Grain Exchange; New York Cocoa Exchange; New York Coffee & Sugar Exchange;[10] New York Cotton Exchange; New York Mercantile Exchange; and New York Futures Exchange (NYFE). Each of these lists a variety of futures contracts which, from time-to-time, become "hot" items in the world of futures.

In conclusion, there is one overriding thought I would like to leave with all present and potential futures market participants. There is no magic formula for success. Don't look for one nor listen to someone who claims to have it. The investor must approach these markets in a business-like fashion and must apply proven business rules and common sense. Do not depend on luck and do not consider these markets as something akin to gambling. Factors that cause the markets to go up and down have little to do with the rules of chance or probabilities. Ignore the claims of "hot tips" or "inside" information. Such claims in futures markets are a near impossiblity.

Basically, price is determined by rules of economics and supply/demand equations. Oh sure, many of the market gyrations seem to be random or make little sense; often a given market will rally or fall for a reason which, in retrospect, seems silly; sometimes you will hear that the cause for a recent drop in price was attributed to a concentrated effort by "professional shorts" or vice versa; sometimes you will be told that the market is being subjected to a squeeze by special groups or by foreign investors; sometimes you will hear accusations of manipulation; sometimes you will be caught by forces resulting from unfounded rumors.

In all such cases, if you are on the wrong side of the market and forced to take a loss, it will seem unfair and contrary to the sound principles of economics which, in your belief, should govern. But I know of no free market which is not, to one degree or another, subject to the same or similar market forces. You must remember that in futures you are indeed dealing with future expectations, often in supplies that are not yet in existence. That factor alone makes these markets much more vulnerable to intangible and imagined fears, anticipations, and predictions; by their definition, these markets are volatile as well as subject to emotional responses. It is axiomatic, therefore, that daily or intermediate price swings of futures markets are often unpredictable and treacherous.

One of the best illustrations of the unreasonable nature of these markets occurred at the outbreak of the "Yom Kippur" war between Israel and Egypt in 1967. All futures markets immediately responded with swift and large upward price movements. (It is generally believed that wars increase the demand for and reduce the supply of commodities.) The pork belly market was no exception, and it immediately skyrocketed up "the limit"; the belly pit was swamped with brokers and traders bidding at the permissible limit price, but there was nary a seller in sight. At that moment, one of the traders, an extremely capable pork expert who, for many good fundamental reasons, was heavily short the market, came down to the "floor" from his office; he ran over to the belly pit and, in an emotional outburst, shouted at the top of his lungs, "What's the matter with you guys, have you gone crazy? Don't you realize that neither the Jews nor the Arabs eat pork?"

Emotion, rumor, imagined expectations, unexpected world events, adverse weather conditions, the concentrated influx of many orders to buy or sell, and many other similar causes will often result in pushing a given futures market up or down in contravention to the dictates of conventional economics. But such causes are generally of short duration and of relatively small consequence. With very few exceptions, the prices of all markets in the long run end up at levels that are determined only by the available supply of the given product and the demand for it. The in-between, intermediate or "contra-trend" price shifts are what make these markets so difficult, so challenging, and, at the same time, so rewarding. At contract maturity in 1967, the Mideast War made no difference to the eventual price of pork bellies; our local pork expert was right after all.

Whether you have the capital to withstand the inconsequential, whether you have the determination and fortitude to stick with your beliefs when you are right, whether you have the aptitude and psychological stamina to admit when you are wrong, and whether you have the discipline to follow strict business and market rules are the principal factors which, in the final analysis, will determine your success or failure in this most challenging form of investment.

Notes

1. The required minimum margin is up to the exchanges and may be changed from time to time depending on the price volatility of the commodity. A brokerage firm may require a higher amount than the published minimum.

2. The main theoretical thrust in favor of a futures market in foreign currency came from Professor Milton Friedman, Nobel Prize-winning economist. It was his influence, logic, and distinguished credentials which gave me the courage and belief that such a market was important and could work. Although there had been one small attempt at currency futures before the IMM, it was Professor Friedman who convinced me that the timing was right in 1972. The system of parities under Bretton Woods, he argued, had to be abandoned and the world would soon switch to the more realistic system of floating exchange rates, a system that would eventually benefit by a futures market in currency. He was right, and, therefore, my efforts in instigating a financial futures market proved successful.

3. The unmistakable trend of their explosive growth is sufficient to bring one to this conclusion; yet there are other good reasons. Already many different financial instrument contracts are on the drawing boards or in the federal application stages; of singular significance is the fact that some exchanges are in the midst of studying the revolutionary concept of stock-index futures. The potential of such "index" futures is overwhelming. If the technical and regulatory problems inherent in such contracts can be overcome, the use of futures markets as a financial and business tool would once again be dramatically expanded.

4. Each example used is based on the December 1979 option of each given commodity; dollar calculations are made on a one-contract basis and include only the major price shifts during the first nine months of 1979.

5. See footnote 3. In interest rate futures, as interest rates rise, the futures contracts fall in price, and vice versa.

6. See footnote 3.

7. Please note that the foregoing, as well as later examples of price movements, merely represent the history of the first nine months of 1979. In this volatile era, by the time these examples are read they may indeed look stale and insignificant in the light of subsequent market developments.

8. The two basic approaches to trading are technical and fundamental. Technical refers to the use of charts and the application of chart theory; fundamental refers to the use of supply and demand facts and statistics.

9. Dollar calculations are made on a one-contract basis and include major price shifts during the first nine months of 1979.

10. The New York Cocoa Exchange and the New York Coffee & Sugar Exchange are about to be merged.

How High Can It Go

Barrie M. Damson

The old song, "There's No Business Like Show Business," could also have been titled, "There's No Business Like the Oil Business." No industry in America is more filled with the adventure, risk, romance, danger, and the potential sudden fulfillment of one's economic fantasies than the oil business when a "gusher" comes in. The only problem with this scenario is that it does not always happen that way.

How good can an investment in the oil business be? Well, look at Texaco, Mobil, and Exxon. When one buys the common stock of these and other majors, in some large measure one is betting that the expertise of these companies as oil finders will increase the value of the investment. If the president of any of those companies invited us, as individuals, to invest $5,000 with the company directly into every well the company drills, many investors would run to their savings accounts for the privilege of doing so.

It is interesting to note, however, that when two large oil companies (Continental Oil and Sun Oil) sponsored public drilling programs in the early 1970s which raised over $75 million, they were not particularly successful. In contrast, many of us have heard of people getting rich after drilling with an unknown "ABC Oil Company" of Odessa, Texas—the point being that size does not necessarily assure success in this business.

The purpose of this chapter is to provide the reader with the benefit of this writer's 15 years' experience in the oil industry. During that period I have met countless oilmen and financiers, examined thousands of drilling prospects, drilled hundreds of wells (including the fourteenth-deepest well in the world, which unfortunately was also the fourteenth-deepest dry well in the world), and sponsored public and private partnerships through Damson Oil Corp., which to date have expended on drilling in excess of $100 million.

History of funding

The history of the oil funding business begins in the mid-1960s with the emergence of two types of public partnerships. King Resources, a Denver-based operation, engaged in drilling activities. The public invested as limited partners in partnerships sponsored by King Resources. Almost overnight, investors were hearing about these partnerships, and numerous brokerage houses were selling limited partnership interests to their customers. When the smoke cleared, several hundred million dollars of partnership interests had been purchased in a relatively short period of time. Moreover, King Resources stock rose from $3 to over $100 per share. During its relatively short history, the King Resources operation was drilling more wells in the United States than most of the major oil companies, and it had a larger drilling budget than any of the independents.

At the same time, another company known as Clinton Oil Corp., based in Wichita, Kansas, came on the scene. Rather than offering drilling partnerships, Clinton organized limited partnerships to purchase producing oil wells. These partnership interests were subsequently exchanged tax free for stock of public companies which were also organized by Clinton. Once again, stockbrokers were able to attract hundreds of millions of dollars to these ventures and, as in the case of King Resources, both the Clinton partnerships and Clinton common shares became overnight favorites in the investment community.

How and why these two situations occurred, developed, failed, and ultimately reemerged as strong producing oil companies may some day make the subject of a fascinating book. For our purposes, they are important as the first large-scale investment vehicles that introduced the two types of public investment vehicles for oil drilling and oil property acquisition that are so popular today.

The early results of the King and Clinton activities were quite dramatic. Whether the returns were real or imaginary depended very much on what particular partnership an individual investor was in, whether he or she was able to get in and out at the right moment, whether he or she was referring to stock interest or limited partnership interest, and so forth. What these ventures did accomplish was to create an environment that excited not only brokers and customers, but also investment bankers and other independent oil companies. Both groups immediately recognized that an industry was starting to blossom that would permit other oil companies access to public capital markets for oil funds.

It was at this point that certain "horror stories" began to surface vis-a-vis the funding world. Those of us in the oil business have heard tales of how certain promoters would sell more than 100 percent interest in a well and would hope (perhaps even ensure) that the well would be dry. (Shades of the Zero Mostel movie, *The Producers*.) A more famous story was of an oil operator who sold interests in his well; when he ran out of money he would find other investors to continue to drill. Each investor owned an interest in the well only down to the depth his or her money allowed the operator to drill. This was a case of whether one's money was getting in when the operator hit the right depth. More common sins of the business involved overcharging for equipment and services, restricting investments to single-well deals rather than participations in blocks of acreage, or building pipelines to take oil or gas from the investor's well but not allowing the investor to participate in the profits from such pipelines.

Perhaps the worst example of misuse of investor funds involved a friend who invested not only with our company but also with an oil company whose money-raising activities were quite successful for many years. Our friend visited us one afternoon and commented on the fact that, after he stopped investing with the other company, his cash distributions decreased substantially. We told him that this could be for many reasons including the possibility that the oil wells might be declining in production. He pointed out that the distributions had decreased in every one of the programs in which he had previously invested and he believed this was just too much of a coincidence.

We agreed to review the information he had received from the operator, together with the check stubs, and the next day he appeared with several files concerning his investment. We immediately noticed that the check stubs contained an item known as "equipment rental income," and that soon after his investments had stopped, so had almost all of the income under this particular item. Certainly it was an unusual situation. We asked if he knew any other participants in the particular programs in which he had invested. Sure enough, a close friend of his had not only invested in the earlier programs, but still continued to invest. He was able to secure the friend's check stubs and realized that the income he was no longer receiving was still continuing as an item of income for his friend.

We advised him to take the next plane to the other company's head-quarters and secure the services of a local attorney. In a relatively short period of time, he returned with a check from the oil company representing his full investment. Subsequently, other investors discovered that the operation was being mishandled. After a government investigation, the company is no longer in the funding business.

This is an unfortunate story because it impacts negatively on the entire funding business, but we are pleased to note that the industry has matured since then. Today, most of the companies that are raising funds from the public are experienced and well-governed oil companies which recognize the benefits of securing outside capital without having to issue their stock or notes to borrow such capital. They also recognize that they must provide the investor with a reasonable opportunity to make money while they receive reasonable (but not unrealistic) compensation both in the form of fees and interests in the production for sponsoring and managing these partnerships.

Present status of funding

In 1979, public subscriptions for drilling programs exceeded $804 million, which was an increase from $540 million raised in 1977. It is estimated that private partnerships provided another $500 million in 1978. This represents over 10 percent of the $9 billion exploration and production budget for independent oil companies. Another area of funding which is growing is the income partnership, where individuals invest in purchasing producing properties. In 1979, over $246 million was raised from public investors for this type of investment. Today, major national brokerage houses, regional brokerage firms, financial planners, and independent oil companies themselves are soliciting subscriptions from the public to assist them in their drilling and production purchase activities. The market is a large one and continues to grow with typical public programs having anywhere from 200 to 800 investors and minimum subscriptions of $5,000.

Over 50 oil companies offer public partnerships, ranging in intent from 100 percent exploratory programs to the "balanced program" in which a portion of the money is used for exploratory or high-risk wells and a portion for lower-risk or development wells. Program size or capitalization of such a partnership normally runs at a minimum of $1 million to as much as $50 million. Drilling is conducted in all parts of the United States with primary activity centered on the Gulf Coast, Louisiana, Oklahoma, and the Rocky Mountains.

Regulation of the industry has also increased and improved. The Securities and Exchange Commission takes responsibility for reviewing (although not approving) the public offerings of sponsoring companies. The prime responsibility of the SEC is to ensure that adequate disclosure has been made so that the investor can at least have sufficient facts on which to make an intelligent investment judgment. State authorities, known as the "blue sky commissions," look at the prospectuses and clear them on a different basis. The various state agencies determine whether or not, in their opinion, an offering is a fair and reasonable one for the citizen of a particular state. In this regard, California, Michigan, and Texas take an active and leading role among the various commissions.

Another organization, an industry group known as the Oil Investment Institute, also plays a role. This writer was elected president of the Institute for 1980 and has been encouraged by its development and growth. Although the O.I.I. is not a policing unit—nor can it enforce policies for all its members—it enables the companies, big and small alike, to assemble in one group and review the problems of the industry and of the individual members. It is a forum for discussion and today includes members of the investment community as well as the oil industry. It has been able to meet with key government and political figures to discuss the problems and potentials of the business.

In a word, it appears evident that the management of public partnerships in the oil industry has matured through the process of time, stronger government regulation, higher oil prices, the participation of leading investment firms, and the financial growth of participating companies.

The investor, however, is more concerned with two bottom-line matters—tax savings and return on investment. Conducting a partnership for drilling or income purchasers requires strong corporate disciplines. The investor who puts money down today is not at all interested in the return or tax savings the investor obtained in the past or may obtain in the future. It means that the oil company must perform within a relatively short period of time for each individual partnership and that last year's hero can easily be this year's failure. Keeping all of the above in mind, our investor is faced with the dilemma of trying to determine where to make an investment.

Examination of funds for investment

Many years ago when we founded our company, we had the services of one secretary in New York and one engineer in Texas. We also had a photograph of a good friend, Ben Stanton, who at that time was married to the daughter of the head of production of Paramount Pictures. As a joke, Paramount put Ben in an western movie starring Clint Eastwood, and there was Ben, dressed in a cowboy outfit, telling Clint, "They went thataway." We asked Ben if he would send us a photograph in his outfit and if he would endorse something humorous on it. He wrote words to the effect, "Thanks for finding oil on the ranch. With best regards, *Tex* Stanton."

When any oil promoters came to our unpretentious office in New York City, they would be confronted with this unusual photograph on the wall with Stanton's inscription. We would then ask them if they knew "good old Tex Stanton from Midland, Texas." If they said, "Yes we know good old Tex," it was a fast and easy way to determine whether or not it made sense for us to do business with them. Unfortunately, investors cannot visit the oil fund sponsors with a lie detector to determine which one is the best with which to invest.

One of the important factors to consider in determining whether or not to invest with any general partner is the question of conflict of interest. When is it that the general partner and the investor are on the same side of the equity fence? If the period of time between the investment and the time that the general partner and the investor are on the same side of the equity fence is too long, we consider that there is a lack of mutuality of interest. Putting it another way, if the investor is taking substantially all of the risk and the general partner comes in for a substantial portion of the revenues, we consider that type of program lacks a mutuality of equities.

Another way of approaching the matter is to analyze how much the general partner receives even if a program is unsuccessful. Today, however, most program sponsors are limited to a certain percentage of subscriptions for their "upfront compensation" as well as the percentage they can receive in any production without taking a financial risk in the program.

Some of the specific questions that should concern an investor are:

1. How much is the general partner investing at risk? If the investor pays to drill a well (and therefore takes 100 percent of the risk), the general partner's obligation to pay to complete the well, although a monetary one, has a considerably lower risk attached to it.

2. What are the sharing arrangements? The general partner understandably receives a larger share than would be indicated by the direct investment because his or her activities deserve compensation. However, the investor should evaluate whether company A is taking more for its sponsored partnership than company B sponsoring a similar partnership.

3. Is there liquidity for the investor? In recent years, liquidity has become very much a part of oil company partnership offerings. Investors are able to sell back their shares of proven reserves for cash to the general partner on an independently engineered basis. Partnerships that do not

contain such a provision certainly are less desirable from the investors' viewpoint.

4. What is the "front-end load" (i.e., sales commissions) and is any portion being contributed by the general partner? The lower the front-end load, the more money goes into the ground for the purpose of drilling. In this regard, there exists a wide difference in the approach of the various sponsored partnerships. Most require the investor to bear all or a substantial portion of the front-end load. Note that a reduction of 2 percent of the load on a $10 million offering would mean an additional $200,000 to be potentially applied to drilling.

There are other factors an investor should review. The legal entity is a good starting point. The drilling program can be either a joint venture or a limited partnership. For investors wishing to limit their risk, the limited partner role makes sense. Risk is limited to the amount invested plus any undistributed profits. A joint venture could easily entail far more financial obligation for the investor and, unless there is a valid reason for creating a joint venture, the limited partnership is preferable.

Program design is another aspect that deserves close examination. A drilling program can be totally high-risk exploration "wildcatting," or a somewhat lesser-risk exploration, or a balancing of investment in exploratory wells and lower-risk wells known as development wells. Oil industry statistics show that only 1 wildcat in 10 finds any oil or gas and that only 1 in 40 or 50 finds a field that is a significant commercial success. An investor, therefore, must have a strong stomach to invest in a wildcat program. There also have been exploratory programs that cannot be classified as wildcats but rather are controlled exploratory drilling. These types of wells usually are seeking oil and gas in emerging areas somewhat near to production, or at least close to other wells that have been drilled. This allows the geologists and engineers to develop a subsurface "picture" that offers a degree of control, versus the drilling of wells in areas where no production or very little drilling has taken place.

A more conservative approach concerns the lower-risk development well. This type of program usually consists of acreage the operator has been able to acquire from other companies that have developed wells in the area and are now willing to "farm out" drill sites to third parties. The question an investor must ask himself is, why did the original oil company "farm out" the well sites when they seem to be of low risk? Usually it is because terms of the "farm out" and the consideration of the original oil company are attractive enough that it makes better sense for the originating company to dispose of a portion of its interest. It should immediately be clear that if such a farmout is attractive to the originating oil company, it will probably be marginal for the company obtaining the "farm out." In addition to the considerations being paid to the originating oil company, if the investor must also share whatever oil or gas is found with the managing oil company, then it may well be a "high risk" situation when it comes to obtaining a real return on investment even though the likelihood of drilling success is high.

A third approach is a balanced program in which the sponsoring oil company seeks to blend a mixture of higher-risk wells and lower-risk wells in order to assure the investor of some degree of return on investment. This seems to be acceptable to both the oil company and the investor, but an even more desirable approach, at least in theory, would be a several-year commitment by investors for controlled exploratory drilling and a few wildcat wells. It would provide maximum upside potential and, by continuing an investment program over several years, would allow the investors to participate in the statistical averages of the oil business. This is another way of saying that, if one is drilling valid exploratory prospects with a strong oil company over a period of years, one should be able to obtain a satisfactory-to-substantial return on one's investment on a *pretax* basis.

Finally there is a form of oil and gas investment that completely eliminates the uncertainties associated with drilling. Oil and gas income programs have become popular in recent years because of the fact that domestic oil and gas prices are substantially below world prices. The concept here is for an investor to participate in direct ownership of domestic reserves that provide current income and potential appreciation in value. These partnerships purchase *existing* oil and gas production. Risks are low and participation is considered suitable for all classes of investors, not just those who invest in oil and gas for tax shelter purposes.

The general partner, which in most cases is an oil company, is often able to provide economies of scale and efficiencies of operation that can increase production above historical rates. In addition, the purchaser may be able to offer secondary and tertiary programs to enhance recovery and life of property. Development drilling on the purchased properties is often associated with such properties and provides further upside potential. Thus, price and technological factors may combine to increase the value of purchased properties. Tax benefits for income programs are not a motivating factor for investment. Distributions are classified in part as return of capital and are therefore deductible from other ordinary income. Generally, in income programs, about 50 percent of distributions are deductible.

Publications

Several publications can be helpful to individuals interested in investing in oil funds. The *Oil & Gas Journal* (published weekly by Petroleum

Publishing Co., 1421 S. Sheridan Road, Tulsa, Oklahoma 74101—Annual subscription rate: $21) is considered to be the overall information publication dealing with all phases of the industry in all parts of the world. *Oil Industry Comparative Appraisals* (published by John S. Herold, Inc., 35 Mason Street, Greenwich, Connecticut 06830—Annual subscription: $260) covers most of the oil companies and annually evaluates them primarily on a basis of reserves and assets. *Oil/Energy Statistics Bulletin* (published by Oil Statistics Co., Inc., Babson Park, Massachusetts 02157—Annual subscription: $165) also focuses on oil companies and their performance, keeping abreast of current industry activities and the stock market action of these oil companies. *Investment Search, Inc.,* (P.O. Box 706, Annapolis, Maryland 21404) publishes three types of research reports evaluating oil companies that manage oil and gas drilling funds. These publications focus on the analysis of the structure, performance, and track record of the individual companies and their respective funds. They are helpful tools for individuals intending to invest with these companies.

Tax and econominc considerations

It goes without saying that the prime reason for the appeal of drilling programs is the significant tax advantages they offer. The amounts the government allows to be deducted against current income emanate from intangible drilling expenses. Intangibles are those costs that have been incurred in connection with the services and supplies used in the drilling and completion of a well such as salaries to the individuals, payments for chemicals, and mud and are deductible to the investor. Tangible items, such as the casing in a hole, are not deductible except in the event that the well is dry, and then all costs associated with the well become deductible. Tangible items in a successful well will be capitalized and amortized over a period of years.

In the typical drilling program, approximately 80 to 90 percent of the initial investment can be deducted from taxable income in the first year. There is also a provision that allows for pre-payments of drilling costs so that deductions can be taken even though actual drilling may not occur until the following year. However, there are strict guidelines as to the manner in which these pre-payments may be made. Thus, an investor in a 50 percent tax bracket, having made a $10,000 investment and obtained an 80 percent deduction, will have had $4,000 (50 percent of 80 percent) of the cost recouped by the saving of tax dollars which otherwise would have been paid to the government. The actual investment is thus only $6,000. If the same person is in a 60 percent tax bracket, the investment will amount to $5,200; in the 70 percent bracket, it would be $4,400.

It should also be noted that income generated from successful wells will be partially sheltered by the depletion allowance. This statutory depletion allowance, which is based on percentage of production, can be several times greater than the cost of a well.

Another economic fact to keep in mind is that if an investor in a 50 percent tax bracket puts $10,000 into a stock and it doubles in value, the investor receives a return of 2 to 1. If the investor invests the $10,000 in an oil well and receives $20,000 back over the life of a well, this is a 3.3 to 1 return on the net investment. This does not consider the tax benefits of depletion and depreciation, nor the negative impact of income taxes on taxable income. Naturally, the reader should consult a lawyer or accountant to review fully the tax implications of this type of an investment.

The new look in an old business

One day in the mid-1960s, we walked through an old and partially abandoned oil field in North Texas. Oil was selling for approximately $3 a barrel at that time and very few of the hundred or so oil wells in the field were producing more than a few barrels a day. The owner of this dilapidated operation had been in the oil business all his life and had developed a fine sense of humor. As we strolled through his field he turned to us and said, "This field can make you rich." We asked how he expected it to make us rich and he replied, "When the oil hits $20 a barrel."

Had we listened to him at the that time, and had we been able to continue to operate the field while waiting for the price to change, his prediction certainly would have been correct. Today the price of crude is well over $20 a barrel. Many fields in the United States and throughout the world, which at one time were uneconomic or marginal, today are enjoying a rebirth with extensive reworkings and development wells being drilled to produce oil, even at low rates of production.

There is a new risk/reward ratio in the oil business. It revolves around the new economics and takes into account both the substantial increase in the price of product and the substantial increase in the cost of drilling. For example, a gas well drilled in 1972 cost our company approximately $400,000 to drill. If we sold gas at 20 cents per 1,000 cubic feet (which would have been the sale price at that time), the total revenues for a well with 2 billion cubic feet of recoverable gas would have equalled the drilling costs. In 1979, if that same well cost $1.6 million to drill but returned $2 per 1,000 cubic feet (which our company is receiving on many newer wells), total revenues would amount to $4 million. This would provide a gross profit of $2.4 million.

Looking into the future, we estimate that this same well in 1986 will cost $3.5 million to complete; gas should be selling then at $5 per 1,000 cubic feet, which would mean that total revenues would amount to $10 million and gross profit would be $6.5 million. The point to recognize is that there is a widening gap between the cost of drilling and the revenues we expect to receive. It means that returns today and in the future should be substantially greater than what they were in the past.

An investment in a drilling fund presupposes that sufficient oil and gas reserves will be found in the future. We have all heard that the United States is running out of oil and gas, which would augur badly for the types of investments discussed here. As a matter of fact, the United States remains an attractive area for new discovery. The U.S. Geologic Survey in 1975 estimated that, in addition to reserves already identified of approximately 75 billion barrels, another 60 to 150 billion barrels remained undiscovered in the United States. Today the United States is producing approximately 4 billion barrels a year, so these known and potential oil resources are 38 to 63 times the current annual rate of production. Insofar as natural gas is concerned, the U.S. Geologic Survey estimates that there is approximately 440 trillion cubic feet of gas in the country that has been identified and from 320 to 650 trillion cubic feet of undiscovered reserves of natural gas. The United States is currently producing approximately 20 trillion cubic feet of gas per year, which means that theoretical future supplies of gas also amount to 40 or more times current production rates. In a word, then, the United States has produced vast amounts of oil and gas and contains abundant reserves likely to be discovered in the future.

A substantial portion of the oil and gas reserves that have been found in the United States were discovered through the efforts of independent producers, of which there are at present some ten thousand. Indeed, almost 90 percent of the "wildcat" wells have been drilled by independents. This group has historically discovered 75 percent of the significant new fields found in the United States, which account for almost half of total new reserves. Unlike many other important industries where there are few, if any, small companies, independents play a signficiant role in the U.S. oil industry, and the individual investor can participate with these companies in the search for new oil and gas. It is an exciting challenge and one I look forward to each day of my business career.

Shooting from the Hip

Tennyson Schad

The prominent New York print dealer, Lucien Goldschmidt, tells of having sold 300 Eugene Atget photographs in the 1950s for one dollar each. Fine quality vintage photographs by the great French master today sell for $2,000 to $8,000. Contemporary masters, whose works now sell for $750 to $10,000, were getting $10 to $25 for their prints only 15 to 20 years ago—when they were not giving them away. Except to the cognoscenti, photography was a curiosity in those days; a passion for some, a business for none.

As late as 1968, Peter C. Bunnell, then associate curator of photography at the Museum of Modern Art in New York, wrote in *Art in America*, "Today there is a genuine interest in collecting original photographs; however, for many this remains a difficult concept to grasp." Bunnell deplored "the relatively low price of a picture by even an established master and the apparent absence of personal pride in ownership as in some of the other arts." The works of younger photographers, Bunnell reported, could be purchased for $25, those of more established masters for $50 to $100.

Two years later, in 1970, the magazine *Creative Camera* complained with some petulance that "the lack of . . . an outlet for the work of non-commercial photographers means that they must either prostitute their pictures or sink into a withdrawn world of insecurity and obscurity." In the vain hope that the words of Peter Bunnell somehow could breathe life into the moribund market, the magazine republished his *Art in America* article. A grand, but utterly futile, gesture.

Helen Gee, an intrepid patron of photography, loved and lost with the Limelight Gallery, a coffee shop/photography gallery in the Greenwich Village of the 1950s. She showed everything—everything, that is, but a profit. In 1969, the Witkin Gallery opened in New York City and became the first viable gallery of photography. LIGHT Gallery, devoted to contemporary photography, opened there in 1971. Helen Gee's avuncular advice to me at the time was monosyllabic: "Don't."

LIGHT was located at 1018 Madison Avenue, in a small but prestigious building that housed fine painting galleries. Our landlord, an art maven of sorts, was more than apprehensive about the prospect of a photography gallery in his building, but it was 1971 and the real estate market was in trouble. The lease, laced with injunctions against processing and selling film, selling cameras and the like, bespoke his concern. But the landlord was not the only one confused. One Saturday afternoon, as the elevator ascended to the third floor and the doors opened, one matron was heard to observe to her companion in a confidential whisper, "This is where the young hairies get off." Photography as art, quite clearly, had not arrived.

The public's apathy was understandable. To most people, the photograph was a medium for recording information and documenting events, both public and personal. Family photography albums overflowed with snapshots of the rituals of childhood, of graduations, and weddings. *Life* magazine's photographs told generations of Americans about earthquakes and wars, of adventure and heroism, poverty and despair. Through photographs, we documented our times; we learned more about our world and about ourselves. The concept of using photography as a means of expressing an artist's personal vision was alien and inexplicable to many.

Increasing interest

As Peter Bunnell observed in 1968, ". . . our major universities generally ignore the medium and give no real insight into the enormous vitality and significance it has had in shaping our vision. Students especially sense this lack but find few places to turn for guidance. . . ." But even as Bunnell spoke, a significant change was under way. Between 1964 and 1967, the number of students in photography instruction programs grew from 14,000 to 26,000. Three years later, it had exploded to 79,000. The number of colleges and universities offering photography courses, a mere 268 in 1964, grew to 627 in 1971. At the University of Illinois (Champaign-Urbana) alone, the number of students studying photography or cinematography multiplied from a covey of 132 in 1966 to a horde of 4,175 four years later. Today, photography programs proliferate on American campuses. In most, students study photography as a means of personal expression.

During these years, public attitudes began to shift, too. Collectors of paintings, prints, and sculpture developed an awareness of photography as an art form. Major universities and museums shifted considerable energies into developing basic collections of historical and contemporary photography.

In the marketplace, most interest was focused on nineteenth-century material, which was limited in supply and similar in style and subject matter to conventional art and thus easier for collectors from other media to deal with. Although the market was small, prices soared, a fact trumpeted by the business press. Almost without exception, every story referred with awe to a triple play that started in 1973. A dealer purchased a nineteenth-century daguerreotype of Edgar Allan Poe for $9,250 at an auction, promptly resold the prize for $18,000 to another dealer, who in turn peddled Poe to Chicago collector Arnold Crane for $35,000 or more. Readers swooned, the caper became legend, but no commentator ever asked how much cash actually had changed hands in the transactions. History also failed to note that the principals were not exactly strangers. Well, it made a good story. It also made a market.

The work of the early twentieth-century masters was in demand during this period, too, but little was available. The market for contemporary photography, meanwhile, was lethargic at best. (As used in this chapter, "contemporary" refers to the work of photographers whose major images appeared after 1940.)

Slowly but surely, however, this too changed. In the latter part of 1977, the market for contemporary photographs came alive; by the end of the decade, it had become a major part of the business. The development was unavoidable. The availability of earlier material was diminishing, and, more importantly, universities were spewing out thousands of students for whom contemporary photography was a passion, an integral part of their lifestyle. Whereas older generations customarily had restricted their critical appraisals of photography exhibitions to a bemused and noncommittal "that's interesting," today's photography generation fills gallery guest books with lengthy critiques. These people can analyze and appreciate photography the way very few of their parents could appreciate fine painting.

As with most movements in history, a single event or a single person captures the public's attention and signifies history's momentum. In contemporary photography, the catalyst was the courtly and indefatigable septuagenarian, who plants trees: Ansel Adams. Adams' dramatic Western landscapes of monumental scale have long appealed to a wide and diverse audience. In late 1975 it was announced that Adams, who prior to that time had probably sold more photographs than any other photographer, living or dead, would take no more orders for his photographs after December 31, 1975. The retail price of Adams' photographs, $500 in mid-1975, was raised to $800 on September 1, 1975. Galleries and individuals queued up to buy.

Adams' photographs thus having been "limited" in number, the free market took over. Gradually, his better-known images began to edge up, then gallop up in price. In May 1979, Ansel's best-known image, *Moonrise, Hernandez, New Mexico,* was sold at an auction for $6,250. Also during that month, Edward Weston's *The Shell* set a record auction price for a single twentieth-century photograph. The record didn't last long.

During the summer of 1979, demand for Adams' prints began to intensify in anticipation of his major retrospective at the Museum of Modern Art, opening in September. Then Adams' cherubic countenance appeared on the cover of the September 4, 1979 issue of *Time* magazine, and the stampede began. On September 28, at Christie's New York auction for the benefit of the Friends of Photography, *Moonrise* went for $12,000, a new twentieth-century print record. Soon after it sold for $15,000, another record. Then on December 19, at Sotheby Parke Bernet, a larger version of *Moonrise* went for $22,000, another new record for a modern photograph. (To be sure, auction prices vacillate. For example, a standard *Moonrise* sold at that same auction for only $8,000. In 1980, profit takers overloaded auctions with Adams' prints, affording a rare opportunity for below-market buys. Dealer prices for *Moonrise,* however, remained firm between $15,000 and $18,000.)

That Ansel Adams should be the Moses of the medium, leading contemporary photography out of obscurity, was considered inevitable by many. Adams' constituency reaches far beyond photography and touches millions who revere his "America the Beautiful" vision of the West. Many who have purchased Adams' prints have never bought, and may never buy, another contemporary photograph. Yet within photography, the Adams chronicle is not without irony. Some contemporary commentators consider Adams for all his greatness to be of another time. To them his landscape theater, while breathtaking and technically astounding, is anachronistic. Still, whatever the point of view, all photographers and dealers alike should make obeisance to Ansel Adams.

The Christie's auction on September 28, 1979 was singular for another reason: most of the prints were donated by contemporary photographers, some of whom have yet to establish national reputations. Surprisingly, the prints sold very well, in some instances for more than the same images were bringing in neighboring galleries.

As the 1980s began, buyers bid photographs to dizzying heights, and record-breaking crowds flocked to photography shows at major museums throughout the country, demonstrating the extent to which photography has captured the imagination of the American public.

And in ten years the public's attention had shifted radically from nineteenth-century photography to photography of the post-1920s. While nineteenth-century photographs are of substantial historical and artistic importance, prime material is difficult to come by. In my judgment, expert guidance is required if you wish to buy nineteenth-century work today. Much of it is fully priced, and there are indications that prices have stabilized. Of course, over the long term, the finest examples of nineteenth-century photography will be a good investment.

The masters of the early twentieth century have not played a major role in the photography boom because relatively few of their key works are available. Photographs by Alfred Stieglitz, Paul Strand, and Edward Weston are important to any photography collection. But work by Stieglitz is almost unobtainable. I doubt that there are more than several hundred Paul Strand prints presently on the market, and very few of those are examples of his finest work done in the first quarter of this century. There are fewer Paul Strand prints than there are copies of *Moonrise*, yet that single Adams' print sells for substantially more than the average Paul Strand. In addition to Edward Weston photographs printed by Weston, there are many examples of his work printed by his sons, Brett and Cole. The latter are of interest to anyone who admires the work of that great master, but they are not recommended as investments.

Contemporary photography

This chapter will deal primarily with the subject of contemporary photography, the work to which I am personally committed and the area where I believe the more attractive—albeit more speculative—investment opportunities exist. Contemporary photographs, from a marketing point of view, fall into two categories: photographs by artists who are dead or have ceased printing, so that the number of their prints have been definitely determined; and photographs by living artists who continue to work and to print and whose final bodies of work have yet to be defined.

Collector market

The swelling market for photography has piqued the interest of investors, many seeking alternatives to the stock market. As long as the equities market fails to protect the investor against the erosion of capital through inflation, the investor, the theory goes, will seek out tangibles that increase in value and will at least keep pace with inflation. Photography is now mentioned as such an alternate investment, along with gold and silver, art, antiques, classic cars, or stamps. Even pension funds are jumping on the collectibles bandwagons. (I understand that some are even collecting bandwagons.) And that esteemed arbiter of public taste, Time-Life Books, has published *The Encyclopedia of Collectibles*. Photography is dealt with in the volume entitled, ''Photography–Quilts.''

Buying photography or any other tangible has pitfalls as well as promise. The prudent investor certainly knows that collectibles are not income-generating investments. They don't earn money or bear interest, they must be insured and stored, and they are essentially illiquid. Yet in times of inflation and uncertainty in the equities market, many investors will take their chances that prices of collectibles will spiral merrily upward.

As a result, many investor dollars have already been diverted from the stock market to photography, but I hasten to place that remark in perspective. The photography market is quite small, probably less than $15 million per year. (My guess is that one week's take in Las Vegas would corner the entire photography market; I don't know exactly how much that is, but then neither does the Nevada Gaming Commission.)

Whatever the size, the diversion is unmistakable. One dealer informs me that some of his clients arrive with checks drawn on their brokerage houses, news to gladden the heart of any dealer, provided the investors intend to stay. Investors hopping into and out of photography with short-term money will only disrupt a relatively small market. And when the stock market improves, and they try to unload and put their money back into equities, I doubt that they will be presenting their brokers with checks drawn on their dealers. Instead, there will be a lot of disappointed sellers complaining about the perfidy of it all. Photography is not the gold or commodities market. There are no short-term plays. Stay in or stay home.

There are two kinds of photography investments. The first is the collection of photographs for long-term capital appreciation and, one hopes, some esthetic enrichment along the way. The other is a means to avoid taxes. Before we discuss the former, a few words about the latter.

In the past three years, I have heard of a number of ''tax shelter'' deals where the investor purchases negatives from an artist for a little cash and and a large non-recourse note. According to the promoters, the idea is to buy tax write-offs many times your investment. My advice: proceed cautiously. First of all, most deals will probably never pass IRS scrutiny.

Second, even if they could be properly structured, in many shelters the appraisal of prospective revenues from exploitation of the artwork far exceeds reasonable expectations. The typical tax deal I have seen has had no socially, or artistically, redeeming value. The only art they advance is the art of tax avoidance.

A second tax-oriented arrangement, involving "tax donation" packages, is more difficult to criticize. It works like this. The donor purchases from a "packager" the work of a given artist for an amount ranging from one-quarter to approximately one-third the current retail value of the artist's work. The idea is to hold the work for a minimum of one or more years, and then to donate it to a museum. The donor gets a handsome write-off, and—in these days of skimpy museum acquisition budgets— it's a windfall for the museum. Assuming—and it is a tall assumption—that only museum-grade artwork is involved, these packages are a boon to all concerned. Nevertheless, the IRS is beginning to sniff around these deals, sensing something other than the eleemosynary spirit. Also, some packagers, in the eagerness for "product," are purchasing work of substandard quality. Thus, before you jump into these particular waters, obtain an independent appraisal and an unequivocal opinion from competent tax counsel.

If you are interested in investing in photography with an eye to something more than next year's tax return, there are a number of ways to proceed. Although the photography investor and the photography collector are two different breeds, the successful investor should have a touch of the collector. The collector is motivated by a strong esthetic commitment to photography, a person who purchases photographs not as an investment but to satisfy some other need. The collector knows the medium, and knows what he or she likes. Occasionally the collector buys and cares not for the price. The investor draws upon, but does not necessarily rely upon, the advice and counsel of others. The two best-known collectors, Arnold Crane and Sam Wagstaff, were driven by a passion—and their collections are worth many times their investments. There is a moral here.

Dealing in photography is a capital-intensive business. No matter how successful a dealer may be, he or she is always thirsty for additional funds. If you know a dealer you respect and trust, you may want to discuss the possibility of a co-venture in the purchase of a collection of photographs. You can be repaid either in photographs or from the proceeds received upon resale. Such participation can be rewarding financially and esthetically, but the investor should proceed carefully and retain a security interest in the photographs purchased.

Understanding photography

Investing in art or photographs requires more time and intelligence than other investments. It is not like calling your broker, pricing Krugerrands, or buying a Queen Anne chest of drawers. There are many dos and don'ts, and you will need to learn fast or have access to superb advice. If you know a dealer, have infinite respect for his or her intelligence, and would trust that dealer with your life, you are in pretty good shape. Even so, you should become familiar with photography and its collecting. An excellent primer is *Photographs: A Collector's Guide,* by Richard Blodgett, published by Ballantine Books, 1979. While I do not subscribe to some of Blodgett's esthetic characterizations, that is a minor point. He is a journalist, not an art historian. The book was researched and written with unusual intelligence, clarity, and objectivity. Two other helpful books are *The Photograph Collector's Guide,* by Lee Witkin and Barbara London, New York Graphic Society, and *Collecting Photographs,* by Landt and Lisl Dennis, E. P. Dutton.

Blodgett offers cogent advice on selecting a dealer. He observes, quite correctly, that

> . . . each dealer tends to espouse a specific point of view and to steer customers in a direction befitting that view. For instance, a dealer specializing in contemporary photographers is not likely to recommend the purchase of nineteenth-century stereographs or of contemporary works by photographers represented by other galleries . . . . But picking a dealer tends to be a highly subjective process, like choosing a dentist or an attorney. The recommendations of other collectors, the professionalism of the dealer, and the dealer's quoted prices (versus prices listed by other dealers for similar items) should all have a bearing on your choice. Ultimately, though, the most basic points are whether you get along with the dealer, can establish a good working relationship, and feel the dealer offers quality pictures of a sort you most like. A word of caution: Don't spend a lot of money with a single dealer until you are absolutely sure of the dealer's integrity. And always try to stay in touch with one or two other dealers in order to maintain a broader view of the market and have a sense of the prevailing price levels."

The aptness of Blodgett's advice was demonstrated by a certain enterprising private dealer who used to purchase photographs at close to retail, then sell them at grossly inflated prices to her husband's professional associates. Now I understand the full import of the parental injunction, "Marry a professional man."

And a further word of caution: avoid dealers who talk about how much money they have made and how much money you may make by investing in photography. Chances are they are trying to make more—off you. I recall, parenthetically, the Rev. Ike of car dealers, who plied his trade with considerable enthusiasm and fervor. He would ask anyone who would listen, "What would you rather own, a Rembrandt or a Duesenberg?" Since the listener was sitting in his showroom, the question was somewhat rhetorical. "Well, just as Rembrandts ten years ago were worth $100,000 and now are worth $1,000,000," he would intone, "Duesenbergs in ten years will be worth $1,000,000." Such blatant appeal to an investor's greed is insidious. Sure, he may have been right. But he may have been wrong as well. Ignore the hype. As with any other investment, buy the best photographs you can afford. Let the dollars take care of themselves.

Also, take with a grain of salt newspaper and magazine articles that hail photography as "the hot collectible." The individual success stories cited are generally correct, but when strung together they give the impression that untold riches will be yours if you put your money in photography. In the latest article of this genre to come to my attention, the writer, a respected journalist, reveals that "profits can range up to 1,000 percent on photographs held only a few years." Sure, some buyers of Ansel Adams prints in 1976 made profits on that scale, and others have also done handsomely, for prices have on the average better than tripled in the past eight years. But investors in any medium are certain to be disappointed when they build their expectations on such success stories. It is inane and totally unjustified to extrapolate tomorrow's prospects from yesterday's performance.

Before you invest, whether or not you have already found a dealer you are comfortable with (there are fine dealers throughout the country), learn about the esthetics of the medium. It's not only good investment advice. Learning how to look at and appreciate photographs can be a most exciting adventure. A good place to start is to read several books that deal with photography generally. Many have been published on single artists, but there is a depressing paucity of books that give the reader a feeling for photography generally. John Szarkowski's *Looking at Photographs,* Museum of Modern Art, is important. Beaumont Newhall's *A History of Photography* was for years the standard text. Although it is outdated and the basic edition does not deal with the all-important period since 1950, it nevertheless presents a lively and informative overview of the history of photography that can be indispensable. To fill in the gap since 1950, I recommend *Mirrors and Windows,* by John Szarkowski, Museum of Modern Art. Another Szarkowski book, one some think is his best, is *Photographer's Eye,* Museum of Modern Art. *Photographers on Photography,* by Nathan Lyons, Prentice-Hall, is a highly regarded book in which photographers talk about their work. It may be out of print, but it's worth reading if you can get a copy.

Reference to three Szarkowski books is not only a concession to the lamentable dearth of intelligent criticism, but an accolade as well. Szarkowski, director of photography at the Museum of Modern Art, is without question our foremost commentator on contemporary photography. Many consider him the ultimate arbiter of what is, and what is not, important. Others roundly criticize the "narrow" vision of the medium that he espouses without apology. The carping would most likely cease if others would speak out with equal authority and intelligence. Whether you agree with him or not, he writes with formidable intellect, insight, and charm. You can not read Szarkowski and not be affected.

To learn about pictures, major museum shows are another good place to start. If you can't see the show, get the catalog. Look closely, too, at exhibitions in local museums and galleries. Talk to dealers and curators about pictures. Try to find what they look for and to understand their sensibilities. You don't have to accept their judgments as your own, but at least learn from them. Seek out, too, if you can, someone with a substantial background in the history of photography. I emphasize history, for too often prospective collectors align themselves with local camera store dealers, baby photographers, and the like. They know how to *use* the camera, and may be very good at it, but chances are they don't know any more about the esthetics or history of the medium than you do. Also, don't hesitate to take a class in photography where you will have an opportunity to talk and learn about pictures.

In this learning phase, a trusted dealer can be helpful as well, suggesting reading materials and showing you work. I had intended to pass on to you a list of major contemporary photographers, drawn from a consensus of dealers. Alas, I cannot. In preparing this chapter, I asked a representative sampling of dealers around the country a hypothetical question: if someone were to solicit your advice in investing $100,000 in contemporary photography, which ten photographers would you recommend? Tne results were distressing. Of the seven galleries from whom replies were received, only three gave lists that, though heavily weighted with their own artists, as one would expect, were sound and balanced. The other galleries merely indiscriminately volunteered the names of the artists whose work they represent or carry. I consider myself reasonably savvy on the subject of contemporary photography, but I had never heard of some. Others I wish I had never heard of. The list was unusable.

I make the point not to undermine your confidence in your dealer or to impugn his or her intelligence. It's simply to remind you that dealers are in business, and some of them feel less responsibility to the buyer than they do to transferring photographs from their inventory to yours. If you are knowledgeable about photography and have convictions of your own, your relationship with your dealer can be rewarding. Many dealers will work long and hard to learn your tastes and to guide you in a reasonably disinterested way. I might add that the owner of the gallery is often less objective than his younger, less jaded, lieutenants.

Choosing photographers

As you develop a feel for photography, start your own list of photographers you wish to collect. Include on your list acknowledged contemporary masters and some of the younger photographers who may be the masters of tomorrow. All the photographers in your collection should be persons who have made or who are making substantial innovative contributions to the medium.

Don't be afraid to consider the works of photographers that initially seem unappealing. Intelligent new work often jars our preconceptions of what art should be. But remember that even Beethoven offended many in his time and Marcel Duchamps and Pablo Picasso, to name but two, ruffled many a collector's sensibilities before they were embraced by the art buying world. The analogy may appear inapt or even presumptuous, but the point is still valid. Only the intelligent collectors are taking chances today.

Your list will undoubtedly include contemporary masters who no longer are printing. Many of the photographs in that category are fully priced by today's standards, either because of market demand or dealer pricing in anticipation of the demand. Nonetheless, bargains can be found. Be certain to select photographs that are of high quality. That will require shopping around. The reasonableness of the price will depend upon the stature of the photographer, the quality and importance of the photograph, and the quantity of that photographer's work generally available. You may also wish to compare that photographer's prices to those of other masters of similar stature. It would be possible to rank (with some imprecision) the photographers in this category and to give general ranges within which each photographer's photographs should sell, but I would prefer to defer to a more objective observer, given my strong personal predilections and interests. You will feel confident to make your own ranking soon enough. The better works of photographers in this category sell for prices that range, roughly, from $1,000 to $4,000.

Your greatest opportunities will be found among working photographers. They continue to make new photographs and to reprint earlier work. As a result, their prints are not yet fully valued. Adams' major prints sell at prices from three to over ten times greater than those of his contemporaries, master photographers in their own right, whose work has yet to be limited. This extraordinary disparity among artists of comparable stature suggests that a correction will eventually occur. Just how the reader believes the market will reconcile that enormous disparity is to define the difference between an optimist and a pessimist. As a professional dealer and an amateur seer, I believe there are possibilities for substantial appreciation as the market broadens to include other artists.

There are lingering misconceptions about photography as art in the minds of those for whom the merits of a photograph are determined not by the uniqueness and the clear expression of the photographer's vision but by the apparent "beauty" of the photograph. Most of us are literate rather than visual. We are often struck by the unique verbal expression of an old idea or by the clear verbal expression of a new idea. It expands our perceptions of ourselves and the world around us. Although visual art does that as well, often we cannot see as we can read. The language is different and unfamiliar. We tend to like what we have seen before. We are seduced by superficial visual statements, ones we would reject as cliche if expressed verbally. Much of the photography we "relate to" today may well embarrass us tomorrow as our visual sophistication grows. We will, as we become more familiar with the infinite possibilities of the photographic medium, reject many simple visual statements and look for insights and revelations as we do with the written word.

In that connection, there are certain photographers or schools of photography that the investor should avoid. Every school or style of art or literature has its leaders and its followers. "Derivative" art is work that is imitative or in the style of other masters. One gallery director, when asked what was wrong with "derivative photography," illumined the issue with a noncontroversial analogy. "After James Joyce wrote *Ulysses*, it would not have been difficult or noteworthy for another to have written a book in the style of James Joyce." Once the feat has been accomplished, the innovation made, emulation, no matter how skillful, is without artistic significance. Many have difficulty understanding the point. My daughter's first grade class was asked, as an exercise, to do drawings from paintings by modern masters. It was the classic opportunity to test the standard canard, "My kid could do it." Having "copied" a painting by Paul Klee, one extraordinarily perceptive first grader (not my daughter!) commented, "He must be famous. He did it first." That says it all.

Even the critics often fail to recognize that basic truth. Some years ago an esteemed art critic hailed a relatively unknown photographer as a new master. The review rhapsodized, if memory serves, how the photographer's work was reminiscent of Stieglitz, of Strand, of, in short, all the twentieth-century masters. If that critic had been writing about his forte, painting, he surely would have declared the work derivative. Avoid modern photographs that appear to have come straight from the dark-rooms of Alfred Stieglitz, Paul Strand, or Walker Evans some 40 or 50 years before. Hang them on your wall if you like, and you may have a splendid decoration. A work of art, you ain't got.

That does not mean that artists do not borrow from one another. Of course they do. Every artist, musician, or writer borrows a little from what has gone before, using the ideas of others to state something new and very much his or her own. But the derivative artist merely takes the ideas of others and restates them, often skillfully. Without the infusion of that certain creative newness, the photograph, however beautiful, has no true artistic and, therefore, investment value. The more you read and know about photography, the more easily you will notice when a photog-rapher's work emulates an illustrious forebear. That is why the question, which so often seems silly to many, "When was it made," is so important in the arts. Of course derivative work is not endemic to photography. One need only walk through the painting galleries of New York to understand what "derivative" truly means. But in painting, the galleries and the buyers know it is derivative, and prices reflect it. You will be well-served to know it in photography.

The investor should also be wary of the faddish or voguish photo-graph. Today many buyers are beguiled by photographs of celebrities. The public taste seems to disdain the portrait of a nonentity by a celebrated photographer, preferring instead the portrait of a celebrity by a nonentity. Judging from recent auctions, the likes of Greta Garbo, Marilyn Monroe, Winston Churchill, and Georgia O'Keefe appear to be leading the celebrity sweepstakes. I can only surmise from that interest that a lot of people are opening restaurants and barbershops. Some of the portraits stand on their own as great pictures. Many do not. The current "trading card" mentality of photography buyers in my judgment is short-lived.

The same seductive quality is inherent in those ultra slick fashion photographs. Their superficial allure makes it difficult for many to discern their intrinsic worth. Fashion photography, without question, can be art. Edward Steichen, Richard Avedon, Irving Penn, Paul Outerbridge, and others proved that. But even they made less interesting fashion (or more commercial) photographs that cannot be considered as among their best work. Do not stray too far from the straight and narrow in this genre unless you trust your own eye and instincts. While beauty may be in the eye of the beholder, value often is not.

You should also know that fashion photographers work in studios, generally with assistant photographers. Beware of unsigned photographs

attributed to the "studio" of some never-to-be-forgotten fashion
photographer. The photograph may, or may not, stand on its own as a
photograph, but unless it was made by the big man himself, ignore it.

I would also think twice about "nostalgia" photographs. Don't spring
for a $700 photograph of the 1930s simply because it pictures an old cor-
ner drug store, dad's old Essex, and a guy with a straw boater. Use your
head and your eye, not your memories, when you buy photography.
Lucky Jackson Pollock. No one has ever bought a Pollock—or an Aaron
Siskind for that matter—out of nostalgia.

Quality

After you have decided which photographers you would like to collect,
seek out the best examples of their work. Your reading and conversations
should give you a feel for that. If you are imbued with confidence, try
building a collection suited to your own specific tastes. You may,
however, wish to play it conservatively by selecting photographs that are
generally considered among the artist's best work, or at least most
popular images, for example those selected for exhibits and for publication in books on photography. Historically, that is where most buyers put
their money and those are the photographs that have done best in the
market. (I hate myself for saying this, for too many artists are defined by
their work selected for publication and exhibition by others often less
knowledgeable.)

Master photographers, as with other major artists, create bodies of
work. (They are not unlike children.) Some of them are extraordinary,
others less so. For example, Paul Strand in New York City in the first part
of this century created a number of photography's landmark images. Also
important are his photographs of Maine and the Gaspe Peninsula. On the
other hand, some of his later work in Africa, made primarily for publication, is of less importance to a collector. So, too, with Edward Weston,
whose images made around his home in Carmel, California stand among
the twentieth century's most important photographic achievements. On
the other hand, some of his photographs made in the southern United
States in connection with *Leaves of Grass*, while good, have not contributed in a major way to the history of photography.

Even within the major bodies of work by photographers, certain images most clearly state and distill the artist's vision. Other photographs
come close and yet others may be considered almost as sketches. Walker
Evans made an extraordinary photograph of a hotel in Saratoga, New
York. Other photographs made by Evans of that hotel, that same day, are
good but can't touch that one image. Also know that great photographers
are capable of frivolous or just plain bad pictures. Those photographs,

albeit "vintage" and signed, do not necessarily have investment value. Try to buy the best-made prints of the finest examples of the photographer's work. While a photographer's best-known photographs are generally the most important, great images are often overlooked by history. This is true, of course, in music and literature as well. An experienced collector will often seek out less well-known images that nevertheless rank among the finest work of that photographer. That is an exciting and important part of collecting, but as an investor you may wish to play it more conservatively.

Noted collector Sam Wagstaff prides himself, justifiably so, in seeking out unknown images by unknown photographers. That's risky business unless you have a great eye and Sam's reputation. Ironically, many of his photographs have substantial value only because he selected them. Otherwise they would have passed unnoticed. You should do so well!

The photographs you purchase should be signed by the photographer. It is the ultimate assurance that he made and approved the photographs. Generally, a photographer will not sign prints that do not measure up to his or her standards, but will not always destroy the prints. Even photography has its Right to Life movement. Within the last few years, a cache of unsigned Aaron Siskind prints was offered to dealers in New York and elsewhere. They did not have the look of better Siskind prints. The prints had apparently been thrown out, but not destroyed, by Siskind years ago.

As photographs increase in value, we also find an increasing number of "press prints," i.e., copies of prints made solely for the purpose of publicity and reproduction in periodicals, shamelessly being extracted from the desks and burrows of editors of America's most prestigious journals. They are not signed and are inferior. Often they are stamped on the back, "For Reproduction Only." More than one brouhaha has broken out in an august auction hall over the issue of unauthorized prints, and it will doubtless happen again.

A signature is also important to guard against forgeries. To date, the photography market has been relatively free of forgeries. But just as everything from phonograph records to Renoirs has been either pirated or copied, we can expect the same in photography. As one noted dealer pointed out, photography has not been bedeviled heretofore by forgery simply because it hasn't been worth the effort.

Only recently, in the middle of the Ansel Adams explosion, we were offered an Ansel Adams "print" that had an unmistakable dot pattern in it, meaning it had been mechanically reproduced. The "treasure" had been ripped out of a book and mounted on board. Someone had affixed a rather clumsy forgery of Ansel's distinctive signature. The buyer is well advised not to purchase photographs that are unsigned unless they are otherwise authenticated.

Just to demonstrate, again, that nothing in this world is simple, there is an exception to this rule. A number of master photographers did not sign many of their prints back in the days when they could not sign checks either. Paul Strand, W. Eugene Smith, and Minor White, among others, died leaving a quantity of unsigned prints. The estates have either signed by proxy or otherwise authenticated the prints as original finished prints. That authentication is important to the investor. Today's photographers are much more aware of the market, and the investor should have an ironclad rule not to buy an unsigned print by a living photographer.

The "economy," "jumbo," and "giant" size syndrome has also affected photography. Prices of photography will often vary according to the size of the print. This is a modern phenomenon of dubious justification or merit. (I can imagine each dealer trying to cope with some consumer regulation mandating the posting of a price per square inch.) In photography, bigger is not necessarily better. The size of a photograph should not be determined by the whim of the buyer but by the artist. Most photographers feel that a specific image should be a certain size. If the image is made larger, or occasionally smaller, it may lose coherence or presence. On the other hand, where there are no strong esthetic considerations governing the size of the print, the artist will often print to a larger format.

In recent years there has been a trend toward larger 11- by 14-inch, 16-by 20-inch, and 20- by 24-inch prints. The 16- by 20-inch *Moonrise* sold at auction for $15,000, its larger 24- by 30-inch version for $22,000. The trend is attributable in part to an awareness that many buyers think bigger is better. Nonsense, but one cannot deny that some photographs are almost transformed and assume an extraordinary presence in large format. Another factor is that today many collect photographs to exhibit on walls rather than to store in black boxes.

Much has been written about the importance of purchasing vintage prints, that is, prints made by, or under the supervision of, the photographer, at or about the time the negative was exposed. This is a good rule of thumb with respect to work prior to 1940 or so, especially where the paper and chemicals used by the photographer in making the original print are no longer available. Modern prints in that case will have a different feel and look. Vintage platinum prints made by Paul Strand 60-plus years ago are extremely rare and very valuable. Because of the importance and rarity of the original prints, silver prints made by Strand in the 1960s of those earlier masterpieces are also valuable, but much less so.

The vintage print rule, however, breaks down with contemporary photography. A print made today by Harry Callahan from a negative exposed in 1948 or 1949 may be as good as or better than a "vintage" print. And Frederick Sommer has few peers as a master printer. In assembling a recent exhibition of his work, we had two prints of several of his photographs. The prints had been made as many as 25 years apart. All were magnificent, but the more recent ones, in very subtle ways, were in fact superior. While it is doubtlessly true that many persnickety collectors will insist upon a vintage print, that insistence will in many cases be a personal preference rather than an esthetic or investment choice.

It is also written that a photograph has less value if it is printed by someone other than the photographer. That axiom holds only if the photographer customarily makes his or her prints. If such a photographer were to permit another to print a portfolio or special edition, those prints would have less value. Perhaps the best-known example is Andre Kertesz, who, due to an allergy to chemicals, has not made his own prints for many years. Vintage prints made by him years ago are very rare and precious, but modern prints made by his printer under his direct supervision sell briskly at approximately $1,000 each and are a very viable investment. "Direct supervision" generally means that the photographer approved and signed the print. Prints made by others without direct supervision would suffer in value, but presumably they would not be signed either.

A posthumous print is worth very little as an investment. Berenice Abbott has for years printed the photographs of Eugene Atget, whom she had known in Paris. Her posthumous prints sell for a fraction of the price of a vintage Atget. Recently, Joel Snyder and his Chicago Albumen Works printed photographs by Eugene Atget using the same albumen process that Atget had used. The prints, which sell for $300, are very beautiful, but have no certain investment value. I have also seen posthumous prints made by persons who had no sensitivity to the work of the artist. It would be unusual for those prints to have any value at all.

Quantity

The issue that has most concerned collectors and, therefore, photographers and dealers over the years is that most prints are not limited in number. Collectors have always worried that a negative can yield a limitless number of copies. For the first 70 years of this century, the problem was of only academic concern. With no market to speak of, photographers did not limit their images (indeed, many times they did not even bother to sign them.) But with the advent of the 1970s, buyers asked with increasing frequency, "How am I to know that the photographer will not run amok and turn out thousands of these prints?" The question, although naive, is fair. After all, lithographs, engravings, etchings, and other graphics have always been limited. But print editions historically were limited because of the physical limitations of the processes, not to create a sense of rarity. (I am not certain that holds true today.) A photographic negative has no such limitations.

There is another major difference as well. The lithograph or etching is carefully planned before the stone or plate is made, and the actual print-making process is more mechanical than creative. On the other hand, the photographer uses the camera as the artist uses a sketch pad. His first prints are more than likely exploratory. Moreover, in photography, print making is less a mechanical process than an integral part of the creative process. The distinction was well drawn by John Szarkowski in an article that appeared in *Aperture*, Summer 1970. Szarkowski wrote,

> Collectors of the traditional graphic media generally don't understand that a photographic print is a much less predictable product than a print from an engraving or etching plate, or a lithographic stone. While the older processes are based fundamentally on yes or no signals, the photographic negative is almost infinitely plastic, capable of yielding a very much broader range of response than the traditional multiple media. This fact argues against the arbitrary limitations of an edition, for the photographer's own understanding of his negative may be enriched (or impoverished) by time—and the chance of his being able truly to duplicate an earlier print is very slight indeed."

Examine the archives of a master photographer. You will find hundreds, if not thousands of prints, but rarely more than half a dozen of any one image—all after a lifetime of work. Although today some photographers are required to make substantially more prints to meet market demands, their manner of working has not radically changed. A photographer still makes one, or two, or perhaps three prints of the better images of his or her latest body of work, but seldom more. But that body of work may be comprised of 20 to 100 photographs (quite different from a graphic print portfolio of perhaps ten prints). Very few, if any of those photographs, will be strong enough artistically to be considered among that photographer's major works. As the photographs are sold in galleries, the photographer will make additional prints to meet the demand. Printing photographs remains a slow and tedious process, a chore most working photographers abhor.

For the finer print makers, it may take days or even weeks to produce a satisfactory print. Once Emmet Gowin found it necessary to cancel an order for a print when he found, after countless attempts over a period of months, that he could not make another print from the negative that was acceptable to him. Most photographers will not sign or release a print that does not meet their standards.

For other photographers, however, the print-making process is of lesser importance. They are more interested in an objective presentation of the information in the negative than in altering, augmenting, or enhancing the image revealed by the negative. Those photographers could, if so inclined, make multiple prints of their photographs. But it would be extremely unlikely for them to do so except to fill orders. Photographers generally do not enjoy printing old photographs any more than a certain child likes to clean her room. No photographer is willing to spend the time and money to print large numbers of photographs in anticipation of future sales. Which photographs would be printed? To whom would they be sold?

The concern is basically an empty one, yet photographers and dealers have been reacting to the issue in a number of strange ways. In 1973, a young and highly regarded LIGHT photographer, whose works had yet to find a market at $150 a print, decided to limit each of his photographs to editions of three and raise his prices to $350 per print. Instant rarity, however, did not breathe life into the incipient market. Why? If buyers do not want the print at $150, they are unlikely to be persuaded to buy it at $350 simply because it is now limited in number. Limitation, if any, must follow demand, not precede it.

At one time, a photographer offered to sell a unique print to a private collector and destroy or retire the negative. The purchase price, of course, would be many times the unlimited-print price. While the proposer was solemn, the proposal was silly because the value of a photograph is determined, in the best of all worlds, by the public's demand for it. The demand is whetted by public exposure, through exhibitions and publications. (As we know in Judeo-Christian circles, it is not unusual for one to covet one's neighbor's photograph.) Few collectors are so self-assured and confident of their visual taste and acuity as to make their own independent and unverified selections.

The idea of limiting prints to deal with collectors' ideas of rarity (and to free photographers from the drudgery of multiple printings) remains a foreign and uncomfortable concept in photography. Many photographers view limitation as not only artificial but totally unnecessary. Prior to recent years, it was rare for as many as 10 or 20 copies of even the finest examples of a photographer's work to be in existence. Nevertheless, a small number of photographers have for years limited their work to relatively small editions. But many photographers who earlier had favorably considered the idea are now reluctant to do so in the face of the increased demand for their better prints. (Sic transit limitation.)

Dealers and photographers have devised other, more natural, ways to effect limitation. Ansel Adams did not number or in any way limit the number of his prints. He let John Q. Public do it when he announced he would not take orders after December 31, 1975. His example will undoubtedly be followed by others. Dealers and photographers are also using periodic price increases to control or limit the demand for a photographer's work. Heretofore, a living and working photographer's work was priced uniformly. Today, however, we are finding that an artist's better and more popular photographs sell at substantial premiums. A similar tactic being used by dealers is step-pricing—that is, after a predetermined number of any given print is sold, prices for that print are increased by a fixed amount.

It is unlikely that any of these methods actually limit the number of prints being sold by a photographer. The reverse appears to be true. While higher prices undoubtedly are a deterrent to some, rising prices are a strong stimulus to others who sense that they must buy now if they are to include that photographer's prints in their collections.

Paradoxically, while the photography market wrestles with the question of limitation, the legitimacy of the issue is being sorely tested by the market. Limitation of the number of prints appears to have no effect on the prices of a photographer's work unless the immediate demand for the work exceeds the number of prints immediately available. Ansel Adams again is the perfect example. *Moonrise, Hernandez* sold in 1979 for over $15,000, although, by an educated guess, 850 copies of that image have been made. But there are many fine, but lesser-known Adams photographs of which very few prints have been made. The market is saying either that limitation is not an issue, or that 850 copies is sufficiently limited to maintain demand for *Moonrise*.

Nor has the limitation issue slowed demand for Andre Kertesz' *Chez Mondrian* and *Satiric Dancer*, each of which has sold at least several hundred copies. Modern prints of these images, made by a printer other than Kertesz, sell for approximately $1,000 although *Chez Mondrian* recently went at auction for $2,100. Kertesz has not limited any of his prints, nor does he intend to. The market apparently is aware that Kertesz is in his eighty-seventh year. But those who know this passionate, yet enigmatic master know that if anyone can resist the ravages of time, it is Kertesz, if only to dash the mercantile aspirations of collectors and dealers alike. (He also has more beautiful photographs to make.)

Portfolios

Any collector is at some time or another going to be tempted to buy a portfolio of photographs. The average portfolio contains 10 to 15 prints by a single photographer. The advantage is that the price of the entire portfolio will generally be about one-third less than the cumulative value of the included prints. A number of fine portfolios have been published and are good investments. But shy away from portfolios that include weak images or photographs that are printed with less care and quality than others by the same artist.

Occasionally, a portfolio by a lesser-known photographer is offered at a very low price compared with that photographer's single print prices. If you like the portfolio, buy it, but understand that it is unlikely that the photographer has any appreciable market for his or her prints at the single print retail price. It is a long shot, but every young photographer must start somewhere, and you may catch a rising star.

All portfolios are numbered, but the number generally means only that the portfolio itself is limited. The photographer is free to print and to sell additional prints of any of the photographs in that portfolio. Two exceptions to the rule come to mind. Negatives to the photographs included in certain of Ansel Adams' portfolios were retired by Adams. That is a moot point to collectors today, since Adams has ceased taking orders for any of his photographs. And Aaron Siskind retired the negatives to the photographs in his Seventy-fifth Anniversary portfolio.

Color photography

Another concern for investors is color photography. In the past five years, photographers have been using color with increasing frequency. Modern black-and-white prints are printed archivally and will last for many generations under proper care without fading. The processes most used to print color photographs, however, are not archival. The most stable process, Cibachrome, is not favored by most photographers because of its high contrast qualities and garish color characteristics. I understand there are good reports on the new Fuji process but I am not aware of any photographers presently using it.

Most photographers today employ the dye transfer process or the Type C process. Type C is favored because you can make one print at a time inexpensively and easily. The dye transfer process requires making color separations and black-and-white matrices from which a print is made. A single eight- by ten-inch dye transfer print today costs upward of $250 to make. Succeeding prints are substantially less expensive.

Much has been written about the stability of the two color processes, but the information is inconclusive. Some claim that dye transfers will last 50 to 100 years without deterioration if properly cared for, and one photographic lab is willing to guarantee its dyes for 50 years. Those guarantees do not apply, apparently, if the work is constantly displayed. Type C prints are believed to be less stable than dye transfers, with a stable life of five to ten years before some fading can be expected. Others state that with curatorial care the life will be much longer.

A third process, Polaroid's Polacolor 2, is of particular fascination to some photographers today. The large format 8- by 10-inch and 20- by 24-inch Polaroid prints are of awesome clarity and richness of color. The prints are reasonably stable while in storage, but will tend to fade as will other color photographs if displayed over a protracted period of time.

Proper care of color pictures is important. They should not be exposed to daylight or fluorescent light. Heat, humidity, and air pollution also affect color stability. (But, in the interest of perspective, these factors affect our longevity as well.) It is not advisable to display color photographs for more than a few months at a time. Some museums are considering the acquisition of refrigeration units that can be used to store color prints at the proper low humidity and temperature. (I expect to read any day now of some incurably ill tycoon being flash frozen—taking along, of course, his collection of color photographs.)

All of this sounds quite complicated and uncertain. However, the lack of permanence of color is not unique to photographs. Says Polaroid: "Color photographs, on the whole, are inherently much more light stable than many watercolor dyes. . . ." Watercolors are vulnerable as well. Many photographers today are working exclusively in color, and that work will one day be of considerable historic and artistic importance. For that reason alone, color photographs are worth consideration for investment.

Where to buy

Once you have decided what photographers you wish to buy, you should know where to buy. Start with a good dealer who will offer helpful guidance. The dealer may be able to offer you buying tips and opportunities and to assist you in setting your purchasing priorities. For example, a friend mentioned the other day that he had purchased several photographs from a highly regarded contemporary photographer whose work, in my judgment, is radically overpriced. It is not likely that the photographer's prices will come down, but neither are they likely to substantially appreciate for some time. The rest of the market will have to catch up. My friend could have spent his money to much better advantage by purchasing the works of other equally important, if not more important, artists whose work is presently being sold for substantially less. Remember that dealers and photographers set prices, *not* a free market.

Price is an indicator, but not a determinant of quality. Some photographers would prefer to sell a few prints at a very high price and others choose to sell more prints at a lower price. It is a matter of style and philosophy. Personally, I believe you have got to make a market before you can take advantage of it, but ego often cannot be denied when it comes to pricing. If the work of someone you judge to be a master is selling at prices that seem low, and the work is of good quality, buy it!

Auctions will be another source for your collection. They can be rewarding for the sophisticated buyer, but for the novice they can be tantamount to skipping through a mine field. Some photographs will be extremely good values, some will appear to be good values, and for others the buyer will pay through the nose.

Photography auctions are fast growing in importance, but the breadth of work available is narrow and will remain so until the market for contemporary photography grows larger. Any collector who scans auction catalogs to acquire a sense of who is important in contemporary photography will be badly misled. Some dealers use auctions to give their artists visibility. Others hold back, preferring not to play an active role in "making a market."

Do not enter the auction hall unless you know the prevailing prices of the prints in which you are interested and you have examined the photographs at the preview to determine their condition and quality. (You will be well served to keep a record of dealer and auction prices.) While auction prices are erratic, they are nevertheless important indicators. Every auction house makes available the prices at which items were sold. The need for knowing the prevailing prices was vividly demonstrated at the Sotheby Park Bernet auction in December 1979 when an 11- by 14-inch modern print of Andre Kertesz' *Chez Mondrian* went for $2,100. That same print was generally available in New York at the time for $850.

With unique prints or master photographs of which very few prints are known to exist, prior prices are only a guide. You should decide beforehand how high you are willing to go. It is easy to lose one's sense of perspective in the heat of the bidding.

With the increase in activity at auctions, many fine prints are being drawn to auction and the quality of the work is getting consistently better. Occasionally, dealers will try to unload their photographic turkeys at auctions, very gratefully taking whatever the fates will award. Remember, if the dealer does not want it, chances are you do not either. Those cheap prices are not always a bargain. Buy a photograph because it is good, not because it is cheap.

The importance of previewing prints at an auction cannot be overemphasized. Occasionally, a photograph, otherwise prized, may have a crack or a bend or a nick that substantially affects its value. You do not have time to examine the print during the auction. While the auction catalog will note if there is apparent damage to the photograph, only personal examination can permit you to judge the extent of the damage and its effect on market value. Other buyers are not often as fastidious as you may be.

The preview also allows you to check the quality of the photographs that interest you. Even great photographers occasionally make bad prints. Edward Weston, for example, made extraordinarily lustrous prints most of the time, but he also initialed and dated a print that had been given many years ago to a friend of mine as a wedding present. One day my friend mentioned that he had a photograph by Edward Weston in the attic, and I told him he had a real prize. I visited him some months later and the "prize" was hanging in the kitchen. The print, a squash, was the worst printed Weston I have ever seen. The moral of the story is clear. Do not buy without closely examining the prints. Also bear this in mind when photographs by masters go for peanuts at auction. It does not mean that the market has no appreciable interest in a major artist.

You know by reading the newspapers that auctions are a good place to make headlines. Many skeptics, among whom I am numbered from time to time, suspect that dealers unabashedly bid up prices of the work of photographers in which they jointly share an interest. Dealers know, of course, that buyers like movement, and if one can give public enthusiasm a little goose, it may become a frenzy. Such hijinks may happen occasionally, but they will be more amusing than distracting if you have a feel for photography prices and the ranges within which specific artists trade.

There is a more rational explanation of why auction prices vary from sky high to dirt cheap, even for quality material. Usually there is a considerable amount of money chasing a very limited number of prime and rare photographs, and record prices result. It is that material, otherwise unavailable, that draws the auction crowds. Other master photographs, offered for sale in galleries throughout the country, may therefore be overlooked, and it is not uncommon to see fine examples going for low or wholesale prices. Thus, the auction can present real buying opportunities for the canny buyer, especially for the work of younger photographers who, while they may have national reputations among museums and scholars, have yet to be discovered by collectors. These disparities will disappear as the auction market and buyer awareness broadens.

Occasionally, prints by a well-known photographer are over-exposed. When *Moonrise, Hernandez* went for $15,000 in 1979, many thought the prices would continue to escalate. *Moonrise* was offered at four additional auctions in New York that fall. At the third it was booed, good naturedly, and slipped to $11,000. At the next auction it dipped further to $8,000. But that is also the auction at which a larger version of *Moonrise* fetched $22,000, setting a record for a modern print at auction. In 1980, auction houses in a gross miscalculation overwhelmed the market with more Adams prints than the auction crowds could absorb. His prices staggered through 1980. It was a good time to buy, in my opinion, for, in the face of it, dealer sales and prices for his work remained firm.

The erratic bidding tells us that market support at art auctions is not broad based. Two bidders in the room can give you a $15,000 price. If one of them remains home with chilblains, the print might not reach its reserve. A smart buyer knows there often is a tomorrow. What is the real price of a *Moonrise?* There isn't one, except that price agreed upon by buyer and seller.

How to sell

Illiquidity is the bane of all collectors who choose tangibles as an alternate means of investment. The collector has two reasonable alternatives for selling, through or to a dealer or at auction. The growing number of auctions is beginning to create a legitimate secondary market. At most auctions today, the seller receives 90 percent of the sales price, 10 percent being retained by the house in commission. The buyer generally pays as commission a premium of 10 percent over the purchase price. Thus, the seller can often liquidate master photographs with reasonable ease at a price close to full retail.

Auctions presently are held periodically only in New York and Los Angeles. That undoubtedly will change. Photographs must be submitted approximately 90 days prior to the auction date. Unless you must liquidate, you are foolish not to place a reserve price on any photographs placed at auction, that is, a price below which the photographs may not be sold. If the photograph remains unsold, you can await a better day or do a little negotiating directly after the auction. Your success at auction will depend upon the quality of and demand for the photographs you offer. On balance, selling at auction is the preferred method of selling a relatively small number of quality photographs.

Another way to liquidate a collection is to place it on consignment with a dealer. Depending upon the marketability of the work and the amount of active selling required, the dealer will ask a commission ranging from 20 to 50 percent upon the sale of the work. The higher commission is not unusual where the dealer will handle a collection or a body of work and publicize and make a market for it. In that situation, the collection is dealt with on the same basis as a represented artist. On the other hand, where a small number of prints are involved, the commission will range from 20 to 40 percent depending upon the quality and marketability of the prints and on how well you know the dealer. If you are a good client, a sensible dealer will work with you to liquidate your holdings with the fond expectation that you will reinvest all or part of it in his or her gallery.

Leaving work with a dealer on consignment involves obvious risks. Be certain to get a receipt that clearly describes the works to be sold and at what prices. Also, to avoid confusion, mark your prints in a manner that does not harm the photographs (ball-point pens are murder). Some galleries have thousands of prints to deal with.

Selling your photographs to a dealer is more of a problem. Unless you need the money immediately, you are best advised to sell on consignment or sell at auction. The photographs would have to have extraordinary intrinsic value and marketability for a dealer to be willing to pay as much as 50 percent of current retail price, and then will probably want to pay you over a period of time if a substantial amount of money is involved.

Photography's future

Now you know the good news: photography has in the past ten years grown at a rate that has astonished even its most ardent exponents. The bad news: it is not easy to put together a good collection and it often is not easy, as we've discussed, to get rid of it.

As for photography's future in the next ten years, I have no crystal ball. I know that investment-oriented people relate to projections, deriving assurance from lines drawn through haphazardly placed dots on a chart. But the market, unfortunately, rarely accommodates. I can only share with you my visceral feelings, which are essentially optimistic, irrespective of price trends among other art forms, and "collectibles" in general, for the following reasons.

Photography, in the way it touches and involves us, has a very special meaning and relevance to our culture today, particularly to the younger generation. As members of that generation achieve some degree of affluence, they will undoubtedly swell the collector base that, despite the frenzy in photography in the past five years, remains relatively small.

Photography is also attracting many collectors who heretofore have or would have turned to paintings and prints. Major works by contemporary artists in those media today are well beyond the reach of all but the more well-heeled collectors. With few exceptions, the finest examples of twentieth-century photography, even rare landmark images, sell for prices well below those of paintings of little merit or investment value. The multiple works of major printmakers also are priced well beyond most photographs by significant artists. Thus, photographs offer an attractive alternative to art collectors.

Of course the number of artists today who are working in photography is also burgeoning, just as the exploding market in prints and paintings coaxed countless artists back into the studios in the 1960s. They will produce an ever-escalating number of prints that may have a moderating effect on prices. If history is any guide, while many more fine photographs will be made, the growing market will also encourage the making of a torrent of bad or meaningless photographs, and tomorrow's buyer will have to be even more discerning. Through it all, prints by masters will be in short supply, and as silver paper becomes difficult if not impossible to obtain, silver prints themselves will become rarities—nature's way of solving the limitation issue.

Suggested artists

I realize I have left you hanging. Which artists do you buy? The question is fair enough, but as you know, I am a dealer. So, head or tails, I lose. Either a legion of artists unmentioned in this article, prints under their arms, march in ranks over my prostrate body out the door along the length of 57th Street looking for another gallery, or I get a stack of hate mail calling me a self-serving so-and-so. Neither alternative has any appeal to me.

Nevertheless, a little constructive guidance may be helpful. Some photographers today are being collected avidly and, to me, foolishly, while other important photographers are being overlooked. My principal criterion for selecting the following photographers is the importance of each artist's full body of work and its impact on the evolution of the medium. Their work in particular deserves your attention if you are to be conversant with contemporary photography. It is not, however, a "shopping list." A few photographers, some already enshrined in photography's pantheon, have been excluded because they made only a limited number of important images. Collection of their key images is eminently deserved, but their work as a whole does not qualify them for consideration as artists of the first magnitude.

You should know that some of the artists represented or collected by my gallery are mentioned, others are not (self-interest does have its bounds). I have tried to be as objective as my passions will permit.

Please bear in mind that we are dealing here with photographers whose major works were made after 1940. Thus I exclude those earlier twentieth-century photographers whose works have been central to the development of contemporary photography, among them, Eugene Atget, Brassai, Walker Evans, Andre Kertesz (whose monumental career already spans 68 remarkable years and who continues as an exceptional photographer), Dorothea Lange, Moholy-Nagy, Man Ray, August Sander, Edward Steichen, Alfred Stieglitz, Paul Strand, and Edward Weston.

Among the "old masters" of contemporary photography, in alphabetical order, I would include Ansel Adams, Richard Avedon, Bill Brandt, Harry Callahan, Henri Cartier-Bresson, Robert Frank, Arnold Newman, Irving Penn, Aaron Siskind, Eugene Smith, Frederick Sommer, Weegee (Alfred Fellig), and Minor White.

Some of the new masters, whose work first achieved critical recognition in the 1960s, are Diane Arbus, Paul Caponigro, Lee Friedlander, Robert Heinecken, Ray Metzker, Duane Michals, and Garry Winogrand.

The 1970s produced a bumper crop of photographers, some of whom have already had a profound impact on contemporary photography. Other observers will assuredly quarrel with some of the names included. Critical judgments require the perspective that only time can give. But for your guidance, the works of the following photographers are worthy of consideration: Robert Adams, John Baldessari, Louis Baltz, Thomas Barrow, Hilla and Bernard Becher, Michael Bishop, Linda Connor, Robert Cumming, William Eggleston, Emmet Gowin, Jan Groover, Les Krims, William Larson, Nicholas Nixon, Edward Ruscha, and Stephen Shore.

And in the 1980s we will see many more artists producing important new work. There are already fully a dozen standing in the wings.

With all the attention given contemporary photography today, it is unlikely that an important young artist will go through his career unnoted. That was not always the case. We are still discovering photography's past. Only recently the work of Paul Outerbridge achieved public recognition. Two other photographers of the 1940s and 1950s whose photographs have been generally overlooked are Louis Faurer and William Klein. Those bodies of work appear to be of substantial historic significance. And recently an assiduous researcher, Sally Stein, uncovered in the Library of Congress archives work in color by Farm Security Administration photographers who were active in the rural United States in the 1930s. Those photographs may cause us to reappraise the history of color photography.

By giving you names of photographers whom I consider of special significance in the development of contemporary photography, I do not intend to suggest that they are the only photographers worthy of collecting. If that were the case, many of the photographs in my personal collection would never have been purchased. There are many other important artists to be considered.

As with the stock market, certain artists are "hot" and very good investments at the present time, but their work, I believe, will not stand the test of time as the level of photography connoisseurship is raised. But place my observations in perspective, because market value is determined not by quality or actual worth but by the public's perception of quality. Thus, while scholars, critics, and the discerning public will decry the appalling tastes of the market at large, it is that larger market that will determine market value. Also be aware that a good number of the artists I have mentioned are not yet actively collected, but I believe that their artistic achievements will in the future be recognized in the marketplace.

For those who wish to invest in art, photography is a very exciting vehicle. But remember: the best investor is an informed one. If you buy with discrimination and taste, you should not be disappointed.

Pleasure and Value

Robert D. Schonfeld

In the spring of 1886, a struggling Parisian art dealer, eager to capitalize on the ravenous appetite of American millionaires for imported culture, arranged with the American Art Association (one of Sotheby Parke Bernet's predecessor firms) to exhibit 289 paintings by the contemporary artists he represented. The AAA, financed by a son-in-law of R.H. Macy, and located in New York's most fashionable neighborhood on Madison Square, would be just the place, he reasoned, to establish a beachhead. Unable to pay the 30 percent duty on paintings which had an uncertain value, the AAA convinced U.S. Customs to allow them into the country under bond.

To put it mildly, the exhibition was a disaster. Only 15 pictures were sold for a total of $17,150. In its review, the *New York Times* commented: "The three hundred oil and pastel pictures (at the AAA) . . . belong to the category of art for art's sake, which causes more mirth than a desire to possess it."[1] The prevailing taste was for Barbizon school pictures, especially landscapes heavily populated with sheep or cows, which were easily priced at $1,000 per animal. By the turn of the century, the unit cost of lovable bestiary drawing room decorations had doubled.

In the meantime, the canvases—which were providing giggles for the press—had been taken back to Paris by their dealer, Paul Durand-Ruel.

Undaunted, he returned soon thereafter to open his own gallery on lower
Fifth Avenue. While the strange-looking paintings continued to confuse
and bemuse the art-buying public at large, a small group of wealthy collectors took immediate interest. They included Mrs. H.O. Havemeyer and
Mrs. Potter Palmer, who were able to buy large canvases for less than the
price of a cow or two. The contemporary art they bought is now on
display in museums throughout the country. You can find the pictures
above the brass plaques that read "Renoir," "Degas," "Monet," "Seurat"
and other such names.

Works of art as an investment

Thus began a success story not very different from the one that could be
told by the original stockholders of a company like Xerox or Revlon. The
impressionists are the blue chips of the art market, and as with their Big
Board counterparts, analysts in recent years have been emphasizing selec-
tivity. Artists are human beings and therefore not immune from hang-
overs and fights with their spouses; the quality of their output varies. The
impressionists produced a tremendous volume of work; in recent years, it
has not been surprising to notice a widening discrepancy in price between
the bulk of more commonplace examples and the much rarer, important
paintings. In such a market, where values are already very high, there is
sometimes a gap between the expectations of sellers and the response of
the buying public, especially when the merchandise being offered is not
"fresh," for example, has been on the market frequently. The slope of the
price line, while still healthy, is definitely slowing as buyers succumb less
to the need for status, and respond more to a desire for value when spending a minimum of, say, $50,000 for a painting. These are signs of maturity
in the market.

By the same token, it is a well-established fact that in a market with
diminishing supply, outstanding works will fetch a premium. On July 3,
1979, a Matisse, *Le Jeune Marin I*, sold at Christie's in London for
$1,605,600, while a Renoir, *Le Pecheur a la Ligne*, sold on July 4, 1979 at
Sotheby's in London for $1,360,300.

The strength of the modern paintings market extends beyond the Impressionists. In the 1973–75 period, speculation, combined with the
recession, depressed activity in School of Paris and surrealist painting.
However, the recovery is complete and price levels for Dufy, Vlaminck,
Pascin, Magritte, and Man Ray, among many others, reflect an influx of
new and affluent buyers from America, Europe, South America, and
Japan.

With such international participation, it is worth noting that at
Sotheby Parke Bernet's Madison Avenue gallery, over 60 percent of the

purchases in these areas have been by Americans since 1975, even in the face of a growing currency disadvantage. The same disadvantage has produced very high prices for works of artists such as Foujita and Klee, whose respective followings are markedly Japanese and Swiss/German. Watch the forward markets for the yen, the Swiss franc, and the Deutsche Mark for early warning signals of a reversal.

Stories like the one about Durand-Ruel and his new artists, which titillate the nerve endings of investors and collectors everywhere, have been repeated throughout history. King Charles I bought contemporary art by an artist called Rembrandt. In our own lifetime, the artist William N. Copley was able to realize nearly $7 million from the sale of his collection of surrealist paintings, acquired in many cases directly from the artists out of love for the works. The ability to combine taste and financial acumen with a shrewd reading of the temperament of the times has traditionally been a rare combination of personal attributes. Unlike the financial markets, which generate mountains of research, the art market is notorious for mystery and a lack of decision-making criteria.

Now, however, investing in art has come out of the closet, or, more aptly, out of the mansion. With the ongoing search by financial services organizations to discover new investment vehicles and the "Europeanization" of American attitudes towards tangible assets, artworks have acquired a new legitimacy as investments. This is not to say that concern over prices in the art market, and advice about investing in art, are phenomena of the 1970s. Consider the following:

> The increased value of art as a commodity . . . is evidenced by the statistics of the art market . . . exhibitions of works of art have become lucrative and popular . . . and sales of pictures at auctions have produced unprecedented sums of money.

This is not a quote from *The Wall Street Journal*. It appeared in Henry Tuckerman's *Book of the Artists*, published in 1867.

Seven years before that, Harriet Beecher Stowe advised her readers in *American Women's Home Magazine* that: "Housewives should invest 20 percent of their expenditures for the purchase of pictures." Ms. Stowe was a little bit aggressive albeit in the context of a household budget, rather than an investment plan. The rule of thumb, which seems to be gaining credence in the United States, is 15 percent of one's net worth, exclusive of real estate and other major tangibles, such as boats or airplanes. *Business Week*, in its Investment Outlook issue of December 25, 1978, published a chart entitled, "How to build an estate that can resist inflation." In the portion captioned, "What to do at age 60," it suggested that 15 percent of one's assets be placed in tangibles, "for security and appreciation." *Barron's,* in its Index of Investor Confidence for the first quarter of 1979, found that one in four households surveyed has antiques; one in five owns fine art.

In spite of these precedents and research, the merest mention of the idea of investing in art still evokes strong emotional responses in many quarters. Conversations bemoaning the passing of the old days, when art for its own sake was good enough, when Big Steel was only getting bigger and candy bars were a nickel, are difficult to avoid these days. But today's aggravation is tomorrow's nostalgia. Think about the Hershey bar you had yesterday before your tennis game. It cost 30 cents (suggested retail price). In 1962, it cost 5 cents. Assuming the same compound rate of increase (11.1 percent), your pregame energy jolt will set you back $2.46 at the turn of the century, but it does not really matter, because by then you will not be able to afford to rent the court. Unless, that is, you have managed your money intelligently. Just as in sports, the best offense in investing is a good defense. An investment in works of art, as we shall see, is ideally suited to this function.

Although economists change their minds about the future as often as *Vogue* models change their clothes, there seems to be a consensus that inflation is a permanent fact of life. We do not mean any disrespect to the serious and earnest discipline of forecasting; we only mean to say that economic life is becoming ever more confusing, and more than a little bit frightening.

The first reaction to fear is defense. In this observation, we find the primary motive for investing in works of art to be protection of value. The media world of catch phrases and easy reference has dubbed artworks as "alternative investments," a description which can only lead to more confusion. Alternative means "instead of." Traditional portfolio structure, especially for high net worth individuals, is based on diversification, with each component performing a specific function *complementary* to the others, resulting in a unified strategy. It is no small irony that both money management and the artistic process are judged to be successful when unity of concept and execution are achieved.

The greatest difficulty in accepting works of art as an investment probably lies in the fact that such things have no direct relationship to the performance of an economic system. Their value is not based on an anticipated flow of earnings, discounted back to the present, as equities (at least partially) are; it is not based on crop reports or point and figure charts, as commodities are. More like gold and large gemstones, works of art are tied only to raw measures of supply and demand, and even then in a way that no doubt seems bizarre to the financial professional, as supply is virtually unrenewable (barring the occasional major discovery), and demand is highly inelastic for the highest-quality objects in a given category. With this in mind, we can dispense with the notion that investments in works of art perform countercyclically to the financial markets. It would be more accurate to say that *attention paid* to investing in works of art by the media, investors, and money managers in general runs countercyclically to the fortunes of the financial markets. The hard-core cognoscenti of art investment are quite steady in their participation, precisely because they comprehend the complementary nature of the asset.

Before going any further, I should make an important distinction. There is art, and then there is art which is suitable for investment. As with other classes of investment, there are some strict criteria, to be discussed later on, which unsubtly move an object from the former category to the latter. The art market is very much a two-tier market. The bottom tier, massive and broadly based, consists of hundreds of thousands, maybe even millions, of items of personal property, which change hands through auctioneers and dealers every year. Nearly all of these items, while qualifying as works of art, are essentially decorative and/or personal in nature, and sell for under $1,000. The top tier, narrow and elite by any definition, consists of the highest individual achievements of mankind throughout history. In this chapter, it is these things I am referring to when we speak of investment-quality works of art.

In case there is not enough confusion already, let me add to it by saying that the above distinction applies to a conservative investment philosophy, which is in keeping with the fundamentally defensive function of the asset. For the investor with a speculative streak, unraveling the mystery of what's undervalued in the art market can provide the same thrill as buying frozen concentrated orange juice futures because the arthritis in your knee tells you it is going to snow in Florida.

Investing in art is not a new idea. For thousands of years, the finest objects in the world have moved back and forth across mountains and oceans as the spoils of war, or as shrewdly obtained diplomatic perquisites (such as the Elgin Marbles). The stabilization of international boundaries and the Industrial Revolution paved the way for collecting that involved a heavy commitment of capital. If the great J. P. Morgan could be asked today what he thought of this new idea of art as an investment, he would probably smile patronizingly, and then, with a sweeping wave of his arms, taking in his own vast holdings which have since formed the basis of so many great collections, public and private, say, "What the hell do you think I was doing all those years?" Mr. Morgan would surely be among the first to remind those with narrow vision that an intentional financial decision is the other side of every acquisition of a work of art, and that, especially at the top of the top tier, such a decision must be made in the context of the availability and "mix" of one's assets.

Since Morgan's day, investing in art has steadily widened its constituency. The market itself has undergone major changes which permit greater access and more informed participation. For example, it is now a relatively simple matter to consult with established experts. The auction houses, dealers, museums, and universities are all staffed by people who can knowledgeably discuss specialized areas of interest. Periodicals abound with detailed articles, and libraries are bursting with books on everything from Swedish silver to Etruscan grave markers. The proliferation of well-financed, reliable dealers is especially valuable to the more experienced collector/investor who may be looking for that maddeningly elusive, final object to round out his collection. For beginners, too, the dealer's shop can be an hospitable place for learning and encouragement.

The tremendous growth of the auction business, especially in the past decade, has given the art world a liquidity that is truly remarkable. The Sotheby Parke Bernet Group of companies alone held over 700 sales in 1979. Awareness of such liquidity, and the fact that auctioneers will, in certain circumstances, give advances to consignors, opens whole new vistas of investment strategy. That "ugly weaving" you found in the attic, which was identified by the auction house experts as a sixteenth-century Flemish tapestry, can be converted into a CD, a call option, or anything you and your financial advisors think is right, in as little as a week if an advance is obtained, and it is usually no more than three months from the moment of discovery to the time a settlement check appears in your mailbox. Furthermore, auction houses in recent years have been matching a trend that is manifest in the financial services industry, namely, full service. This kind of vertical integration makes the major auctioneer a logical partner for the financial planner in the total management of a customer's assets.

The greatly improved quality of appraisals, and the reporting in various media of prices realized, have made it much easier to establish values. Although the auction market, like the securities markets, operates by open outcry, due to the heterogeneous nature of works of art, there is no bid and asked market. Thus the task of establishing value of "reading the market" becomes central to the entire exercise. More about valuation later on.

The effect of these important changes has been to make the art market more accessible. It is available to those with diverse financial requirements. Art is even acceptable as collateral for loans.

Works of art are a legitimate component of net worth and are justifiable as an element of investment strategy. Having arrived at that conclusion by observing actual experience, let us now turn to some definitions, then to some criteria that will be useful in seriously considering an investment in art.

Definition of art

To begin with, what is fine art? If you ask this question of ten people, you will probably get ten different answers. For our purpose, which is the establishment of investment criteria, Webster's definition serves nicely: "The conscious use of skill, taste, and creative imagination in the production of aesthetic objects" and "works so produced." To this we might add the need for inspiration which precedes conscious application. It is the constituency's judgment of the aesthetic content of an artist's work that places the work relative to everything else clamoring for the same recognition. Paintings and sculpture are fairly easy to fit to this description. To draw it for utilitarian objects, think of the simple chair, the very embodiment of the maxim that form follows function. The stacking chair found in classrooms and meeting halls all over the country would have difficulty qualifying for our definition. But the original Charles Eames stacking chair would come closer, and an American Chippendale chair with hairy paw feet, carved knees, and other elaborate decoration is an unquestionable product of individual vision and skill.

The further something is removed from the creator, the less likely it will qualify as a work of art. This raises the sticky question of limited editions. The easiest way to deal with the confusion in this area is to follow this rule: if the edition in question was produced by the artist with his own hands, or *directly* under his supervision (as in the case of bronzes cast by skilled foundrymen), and is limited to a reasonable number (i.e., for sculpture, six), then you are dealing with a legitimate limited edition. Every work of fine art is not unique. Prints, for example, are indeed "multiple originals" produced by transferring images from a metal plate, woodblock, or stone slab on which the artist has created an etched, engraved, carved, or lithographic image. Following is a description of the basic printing techniques:

- Relief: (wood cuts, wood engravings, linoleum cuts) where areas are cut away to provide the raised printing surface.
- Intaglio: (engravings, drypoints) where lines are incised directly, or indirectly (etching, aquatint) in a copper plate or other surface which carries the ink.
- Planographic: (lithographs) a process of drawing on a stone or plate with greasy crayon; when the stone is moistened with water, the

greased area repels the water but accepts ink. Thus, the image is transferred to dampened paper pressed on the stone;

- Stencil: (serigraphs, screenprints, silkscreens, pochoirs) all made by squeezing ink through the uncovered or cut-out areas of a prepared screen or mask.

By whatever method, the finished work is the inked impression taken from the master image. It must be emphasized that the print as art is not a copy or a reproduction of a painting or drawing or any other primary medium. It is the only output of the artistic event.

Selecting an area

The first step is to select your area of primary interest. By limiting and defining your tastes you can begin to acquire an in-depth knowledge of the market. Many important prints sell for tens of thousands of dollars. Pablo Picasso's *La Minotauromachi* etching, for example, fetched over $125,000 at auction recently. However, most prints by Picasso, Klee, Matisse, Miro, Braque, or Leger sell for under $10,000, while most graphics by contemporary artists—Stella, Johns, Rauchenberg, Ruscha, Warhol, and Rivers, for example—bring from $500 to $5,000. Moreover, quality original prints are available from a number of talented young artists at prices of $200 to $500.

Although prints are an excellent starting point for the new collector, the same risks, caveats, and investment guidelines apply as for other areas of the art market. Beware of all claims, and apply the criteria of edition, size, signature, and originality very stringently, and you will be on your way. If you are unable to get satisfaction on these points, you are no longer dealing with investment-quality objects. There is no shortage of "limited editions" which are limited to the number of well-meaning but misguided individuals who return the coupon before a certain date. A single break in the chain of investment criteria will disqualify the object as an investment. If you go ahead and buy it nevertheless, you are no longer an investor. You are either a collector or an accumulator, the difference being that the former specializes in, say, Staffordshire pottery or eighteenth-century English walnut furniture. The collector studies, and is known for a willingness to be overtaken by the terminal, thrilling disease of search and acquisition. Doctors and lawyers have abandoned their practices, husbands have left their wives (and vice versa) in pursuit of everything from Greek hair ornaments to farm vehicle seats. One couple who lived on the third floor of an apartment building and were unable to control their passion for collecting manhole covers, one day found themselves living in a duplex with their downstairs neighbors.

Accumulators are much more calm and casual. They buy more for decoration and instant gratification. To them, there is no sin in mixing a mouse
in with the crystal elephants.

A collectible, then, is anything you collect: swizzle sticks, pot-bellied
stoves, stacking chairs. All collectibles are not works of art, and therefore
do not suit our purposes. And please, don't ever think in terms of "in-
vestibles." Whoever invented that term deserves to spend the rest of his
or her life going from one swap meet to the next.

What is an antique? According to U.S. Customs, an antique is anything
100 years old before date of importation. However, on your next trip to
the country, if you venture more than a mile off the Interstate, chances
are good that you will encounter one or a series of buildings trying
desperately to look rustic, with a sign, usually in gold-painted gothic
script, which announces "Antiques" (be even more careful if the sign
says "Antique Shoppe," or something similar). Inside, assuming the collector or the accumulator within you has gotten the upper hand, you are
likely to find 1920s vintage telephones, Depression glass, Mickey Mouse
watches, and some "We Luv You Beatles" buttons sharing space with old
Coca-Cola bottles and dismembered bisque dolls. The point here is that
whether or not something is an antique is not relevant to its investment
potential. Age and value do not run on parallel scales. Some objects can be
thousands of years old and worthless. Others, like Tiffany lamps, for example, can be relatively recent and quite expensive; the finest and rarest
examples now fetch more than $100,000 at auction.

Having made some basic distinctions, we can now ask another simple
question: what is the art market? It should be obvious by now that we
have been using the term "art market" loosely; not out of disrespect, but
because the commercial endeavor of selling valuable personal property
takes in much more than Old Master paintings and Louis XV commodes.
The market includes jewelry, rare books, baseball cards, used Dior
dresses, smoked pipes, and sometimes even refrigerators and electric
razors. The size of the art market (or the art and antiques market, or the
personal property market) is impossible to estimate accurately due to the
large number of significant privately owned firms. Auction houses reporting volume of sales in the 1978–1979 season are shown in Table 14-1.

During the 1977–1978 season, the total value of oil paintings, watercolors, and drawings which sold for £1,000 or more was £105,968,000
(+32 percent), compared with 1976–1977 total of £80,522,200 (+17 percent). According to the Art Sales Index, the volume of pictures sold in the
1976–1977 season for more than £1,000 each was £80,522. In 1977–
1978, the figure was £105,968, up 32 percent. (Source: *The Art Sales Index
Art Market Survey, 1975–1978,* edited by Richard Hislop, April 1979.)

Table 14-1. Volume of sales at auction houses.

Auction House	1976–1977	1977–1978	1978–1979	1979–1980	Percent Increase
UNITED STATES [$ millions]					
Sotheby Parke Bernet*	$ 79.0	$112.0	$147.3	$247.8	68.20
Christie's (not including Christie's East)	8.0	33.0	56.0	113.0	101.79
William Doyle Galleries	6.0	8.0	12.1	15.2	25.62
Plaza [estimated]	4.0	10.2	14.0	*16.5	18.00
Phillips			9.5	12.9	35.79
Butterfield & Butterfield		4.0	5.0		
Robert Skinner		3.2	5.0	7.5	50.00
Adam A. Weschler and Son		3.5	3.9	4.0	3.89
Robert C. Eldred		3.6	4.0	3.0	25.00
C. G. Sloan's		5.0	5.5	6.0	9.09
Garth's		1.5	2.0	2.5	25.00
Morton's		1.6	2.6	6.0	135.29
*Includes total North American sales		$185.6	$266.8	$434.4	62.8
WORLD [British Pounds]					
Sotheby Parke Bernet		161,097,000	181,500,000		12.66
Christie's		89,106,000	110,358,000		23.85
Phillips		23,866,000	30,051,000		25.91

Sources: The Gray Letter, July 16, 1979, P.O. Drawer 2, Tuscaloosa, AL 35402; The Gray Letter, August 13, 1979; The Gray Letter, July 21, 1980.

By any measure, the art market is a small business compared to the financial markets, a fact that supports our contention that investing in art should be a highly specialized diversification involving a small portion of portfolio value, to be undertaken only after larger segments of net worth are secured in traditional capital placements.

The art market has four main components:
1. The working artist.
2. The private collector, investor, or accumulator.
3. The dealer, auctioneer, or agent.
4. The institution or museum.

The artist provides a continuing source of supply. While there will never be any more Van Goghs, there is every reason to believe that somewhere, sometime, a new figure will achieve greatness in his or her own way. Much the same way that new industries—such as semiconductors or pollution control—have grown out of seeds sown in the past, so new schools of art emerge from previous traditions. And much the same as certain companies dominate their new industries, so individual artists will dominate developing stylistic trends. The odds for success are about the same as those for a new franchise idea, or the possibility of becoming a movie star; roughly one in a hundred artists will achieve even moderate commercial success.

Private purchasers, whatever their ultimate motives, provide depth, breadth, and velocity in the marketplace. They reflect changes in taste and changes in the economy. No amount of hype or promotion can force a trend on buyers over a reasonable period of time. To be sure, an aggressive merchandiser can influence purchases over a very limited period of time (remember the Nehru jacket?). But eventually, the will of the buyer holds sway; the final option to buy or not to buy is the buyer's alone.

The dealer, auctioneer, or agent keeps the market in motion. They are the indispensable middlemen without whom very little would be accomplished. The dealer's markup may be 100 percent or more; most auctioneers charge 10 percent to both the buyer and seller. The services they sell are invaluable: bringing buyers and sellers together, maintaining liquidity, and offering advice, guidance, and uniformity in the transaction process. In this sense, art merchants are very much like stockbrokers, and the auction room is as close to a trading floor as the art business can come.

Museums fulfill a twofold function. By displaying in a systematic way the best objects obtainable, they define standards of quality and, at the same time, educate the public. The more successful a museum is in accomplishing these functions, the more objects will be withdrawn from the top of the market, thereby increasing the value and demand for the "best of the best" (which is also "the best of the rest"), and at the same time creating the need to discover fresh, innovative work that will stand the test of time. This need redirects the market's attention to the artist, the broker, and the buyer, creating a system that is circular and self-sustaining.

Why people collect

Having provided ourselves with a frame of reference and a scorecard so that we can tell the players in the game, a brief look into the motives for collecting and investing in art would be useful. The reasons people collect things are probably best left to psychiatrists, but, lacking their insight, we can nevertheless observe a genuine pleasure in bringing together a group of objects. Whether it is comic books or Japanese tea ware, collectors have an emotional urge that compels them to assemble things of a certain kind. This subjective response—the psychic dividend—is both the starting point and the special aspect of investing in art.

There are also those whose decision whether to buy a work of art is determined solely by investment considerations. There are others who desire to possess a particular piece for purely emotional and aesthetic reasons and who can afford to indulge their fancy to the extent necessary to buy it. These are two extremes of the spectrum. They are both somewhat dangerous, and fortunately, whatever one may be led to believe, they seldom actually exist. Between the two extremes is a broad mass of collectors and other purchasers of works of art, who consider both the financial and the aesthetic points, and who give more or less weight to each according to their preferences, but who never altogether ignore either one of them.

Let us consider the characteristics of some different types of buyers, to examine how they might balance the two considerations. In my own experience, the client who says, "I have a certain sum available. My broker tells me that I should diversify into art. Tell me what to buy—I don't mind what it is, as long as I get a good return on my money," is mercifully apocryphal. What is more likely to happen is that, when shown a selection of possible pictures, the buyer will rapidly show signs of strong personal tastes and preferences, of definite likes and dislikes of which he or she may not even have been aware, never having given any conscious thought to the matter. The client is likely to end up buying things that he or she really likes, and be very happily involved in the decisions. Even large pension funds, museums, and corporations which are putting huge sums of money into works of art are not doing so with a purely investment motivation, to the neglect of other considerations. Certainly, as trustees or custodians of other people's money, they have a fiduciary responsibility to consider the investment implications of their purchases. Properly advised, they are using the funds at their disposal to build collections of great taste and discrimination—indeed, it is often this quality of the collections that enhances their value.

Equally apocryphal is the client who sees a particular item and who determines to buy it at the first opportunity, regardless of cost, considering any talk of the investment merit or otherwise to be profane.

How many of such people would insist on buying it now, if they were reliably advised that they would be able to buy the same piece at a substantially lower price a short time later? They might deny it, but postponing the purchase in such circumstances is a decision in investment strategy. Further, in the back of many collectors' minds is the knowledge that at some time in the future their collections may have to be sold, for financial or other reasons.

If you are uncertain about what you like, the process of discovery can be quite fulfilling; it can also lead you to some very good investment opportunities. Consider Old Master paintings. Old Masters, like scotch and opera, are an acquired taste for most people. As with drink and song, they become more interesting with experience. One family I know does its shopping together and then takes a vote before plunging into the market. The children, I am told, especially enjoy this democratic method of collecting. Unburdened by cultural prejudice, a fun-filled Dutch household scene, or the soft and reassuring beauty of a Madonna and child, reflects their own experience and point of view. Allegorical subjects, often difficult and full of dense and tangled meaning for adults, are essentially fairy tales, that is, lowest common denominators with which children identify easily. A still life of flowers by Ambrosius Bosschaert is a delightful burst of color. And what child would have any difficulty being absorbed directly into a rollicking Isaac van Ostade winter scene, with its sledding, skating, and general merrymaking?

A lot of work has been done by adults to make Old Master paintings accessible to children, and, yes, even to grownups who never learned to like Chivas Regal or La Boheme. Before, the only way to see important works of the Masters, in any number, was on the European Grand Tour. Not to be confused with a golf tournament, this extravagant method of travel was originated by the British titled class and adopted by wealthy American families. One much-publicized objective of this trip was to make a match between their daughters and suitably titled noblemen, who were meant to lend cachet to their fast-acquired riches. Another objective, also designed to add respectability, was to buy art. Lots of art. The most famous and most successful of these acquisitors, J. P. Morgan, bought thousands of objects that subsequently formed the basis of the Metropolitan Museum of Art, the Morgan Library, and numerous important private collections.

Authenticity

Not that everything that crossed the Atlantic was a masterpiece. Worse, not everything was what it was said to be. Just calling a painting a Rembrandt didn't make it so. Visitors to galleries and private collections before the turn of the century might have been impressed and respectful standing before an array of pictures labeled Van Eyck or Botticelli, but for the most part, they did not know or care what they were really seeing. Fashion also guided attributions in the absence of anything more reliable. Beginning in the late eighteenth century, emigres to the United States brought with them, in addition to the necessities of life, their art. Whether it was just one small picture or a large collection, the new arrivals understood the value of art, both aesthetic and material, and they wanted it with them for both reasons. One such collector, who gave his name as

Comte de Survilliers, settled in Bordentown, New Jersey, in the second decade of the nineteenth century. Among the paintings in his collection was a small still life of flowers, attributed to Jan van Os. As it turned out, the Count was really Joseph Bonaparte, abdicated King of Spain, and brother of Napoleon. The painting probably came from his uncle, Cardinal Feche of Rome, whose own collection was well known. The taste of the period was for the work of Van Os, and so, in the absence of primary documentation, the picture was attributed to him. When it changed hands in 1912, the attribution remained intact. But when it returned to the market in January 1979, tastes had changed, and, more importantly, scholarship had progressed to a point where the label of Jan Breughel the Elder fit it comfortably and incontrovertibly. Under these conditions, it brought its most recent owner $410,000.

During the twentieth century, as paintings became more valuable and public exhibitions in the United States increased, study of Old Masters expanded dramatically. Political, social, and economic upheaval in Europe played havoc with the market and drove some of the Continent's greatest experts to America, among them Max Friedlander, connoisseur of Flemish painting; Irwin Panofsky, a specialist in Italian paintings; Wolfgang Stechow, von Blanchenhagen, Lotte Brandt Phillips, and many more. Among their important contributions was the expansion of a critical literature on Old Masters in English. Some of what was written by other, more self-styled "experts" did more harm than good, though, and the lesson learned time after time still needs to be taught today; when you buy an Old Master painting or drawing, especially if you are doing so for investment and your expenditure represents a significant portion of your capital, do not buy an impressive-looking piece of paper signed by a professor or a "doctor." *Anyone* can express an opinion about a picture. Ask for credentials, consult the literature, and seek a consensus of opinion from recognized experts who do not have a vested interest in your potential purchase. Above all, become involved with the paintings yourself. The "sixth sense" you will develop with time and concentration will be your surest guide to value as well as pleasure.

The United States, especially the melting pot of New York, has become a very good market for Old Masters. The universities, museums, collectors, and economy have all combined to produce a marketplace that operates successfully on its own; at the same time they work to broaden the base of international trade. The growth in the size of the market, both in terms of dollars and number of objects, has been steady since the late 1940s. Since the late 1960s, the market has continued to expand, with supply and demand for the most important works becoming more inelastic each year. (One of the more interesting ironies is that "priceless" works, when they do come on the market, seem to have no difficulty establishing a price. Since 1963, when Rembrandt's *Aristotle Contemplating the Bust of Homer* was sold at Parke Bernet for $2,300,000, the firm's index of Old Master paintings rose from 48 to 255, not adjusted for inflation. Using the same rate of increase, the *Aristotle* would be worth approximately $12,000,000 today.

Happily, for those of us of more modest means, the market for Old Masters offers a wide variety of opportunities to please both the eye and the pocket. Compared to other sectors of the art market, values can be very good indeed. For instance, a very good example of the works by Carl van Falens, a seventeenth-century Dutch landscape artist, can be purchased at auction for under $10,000 (and sometimes under $5,000). Van Falens was related to the Wouwermans family, well-known painters whose works today can fetch $50,000 and more at auction. The same $5,000 or $10,000 would buy a corner of a Picasso, or the legs of a Chippendale highboy.

In general, Dutch pictures of the seventeenth century reflect many of the same mercantile values as we have in modern life, a factor that accounts to a large degree for their popularity with the successful upper-middle class in Europe as well as in America today. Unlike religious pictures, which are cumbersome in size, or meaning, or both, these images, mostly small and easily transportable, are a celebration of secular life. This appeal across time has not been lost on the art market, and the very best things, when available, are very expensive. There were many good painters and they produced many good pictures. Another affordable example is Pieter Molyn, a student of Jan van Goyen, whose works are still available for as little as $3,000–$5,000.

These are not "hot tips"; they are examples of value that can be found with a certain amount of application. As the market for Old Masters continues to grow, lesser-known artists of quality will come to the public's attention. Like the financial markets, the price performance of your own purchases will be a function of timing, assuming, of course, you have observed the other rules given elsewhere in this chapter.

Remember, too, that the art market does not go only one way. It can and does go down, and one way in which it does so is in response to changing fashions. Eighteenth-century British portraits are worth a small fraction today of their value in the early decades of this century when Americans with quickly made fortunes would pay huge sums for the legitimacy of title and patina of time.

The pendulum swings and opportunities present themselves as forgotten Masters reemerge. The great Vermeer was almost totally ignored for

200 years after his death, while Georges de la Tour, even though he was painter to the King from 1630 to 1640, and even though his important paintings are routinely appraised for more than $1,000,000, was only "rediscovered" in the early twentieth century.

A detailed discussion of even a small portion of the huge and diverse market for Old Masters is beyond the scope of this chapter and far beyond my own expertise. Many experts, however, say that large segments of the market are undervalued. I am not going to point them out to you. That would be too easy and would rob you of the fun. If you don't become a serious investor, perhaps you will become a collector, and if you get bitten badly enough by the collecting bug—and can afford it—you may become a serious collector, and thus by definition, an investor. You will not clip any coupons but you will be paid dividends of pleasure at least as great.

American furniture

Some guidance in striking a balance among appeal, affordability, and availability may be culled from a brief look at the market for American furniture—chairs in particular. Almost 30 years ago in a book called *Fine Points of Furniture*, Israel Sack, the dean of American furniture dealers, made the following observations in response to concerns that prices for fine American antiques had risen too high:

> What will happen when more wealthy people will begin to realize that this country produced as fine furniture as any made in any other land? Who can predict, as [a] collector friend did in 1914, that prices of fine American antiques will never go higher? More and more museums are preserving and appreciating American-made pieces. The market is getting larger and the rare pieces come to light more infrequently. It is not an isolated condition. If you consider the recent development and awakened interest in American literature, painting, architecture, and music, it is not hard to see that we are merely on the threshold of a great new era.

Mr. Sack's insight has been dramatically confirmed. Conveniently, the postwar baby boom has provided a bedrock-solid demographic base for all things American. By the end of the Chippendale period in America, around 1780, the population of the colonies was between 1.5 and 2 million. The finest furniture was produced in just five major cabinetmaking centers: Philadelphia, Newport, Boston, New York, and Charleston. Today, Americans number more than 200 million, the craftsmen are gone, and the furniture they made has disappeared into museums, private collections, dealer's inventory, town dumps, and attics up and down the Atlantic seaboard. But the American public's fascination with its past continues unabated, and competition for the most outstanding examples is strong from all parts of the country. The greatest hope for beating the odds against this degree of rarity rests in the attics of America. Unlike jewelry, which is not bound to be forgotten, furniture is often relegated to storage as prevailing taste and customs change. Many a windfall has befallen the keen rummager who knows what to look for.

With an ever-growing constituency, an ever-diminishing supply, and faith in the future of the nation, prices can only continue to escalate. Eighteenth-century American furniture, which was not cheap when it was made, is universally acknowledged for its design interpretation and quality. It is every bit as fine in its own way as French furniture of the same period. Like French furniture, American examples reflect their time and place very accurately.

By the third quarter of the eighteenth century, it was clear that American Queen Anne and Chippendale furniture had a unique character. It didn't matter that Queen Anne had died in 1714 and that Thomas Chippendale never made an American piece of furniture; they served perfectly well as namesakes for styles that achieved a unity of scale, line, and decoration unequaled in their English counterparts. The carving on a fine American chair of this period seems to arise from the wood and flow with its lines. By contrast, an English chair will seem broad and heavy, the carving laid on. This reflects a genuine rococo influence on the part of English craftsmen. (The Chippendale style itself may be seen as a rococo development of Queen Anne. In the English case, the frame of the chair is used as a background for the decorative carving, whereas in America, the same influence was not felt and the resulting products were therefore more fluid and elegant.) In addition, the type of wood and its color, finish, and pattern of the grain are all elements of quality that distinguish American chairs and contribute to their value.

This stylistic information is a strong hint as to why American Queen Anne and Chippendale chairs can be worth 1,000 times more today in 1760 dollars than when they were made, and why certain contemporary furniture, such as sleep sofas, have no possibility of achieving the same appreciation: one is a work of art, the other not. If the chair is the most perfect expression of form following function, then the Philadelphia or Newport Queen Anne or Chippendale chair is the perception of the form's essential nature, imparting to it an aesthetic component that becomes a prime determinant of its value.

Condition, as we have said, is a prime determinant of value. Obviously, the better the condition of a piece, the more desirable it is. However, a chair with repairs, or one in somewhat damaged condition, but completely original in all its parts, will compete with and often surpass in value a chair in superb condition, but which has been significantly altered by the non-contemporary restorations of an important component, such as its legs.

This is an appropriate place to lodge several other caveats that are best dealt with by taking the advice of an expert. Fakes are the most obvious pitfall. Fakes, as opposed to reproductions, are intentionally misrepresented as being genuine period pieces. Many are so skillfully made that only someone with a firm academic and practical grounding in the field could uncover them. A much less venal variation on this theme is pieces which are unintentionally misdated, misidentified as to geographical origin, or misattributed. A piece wrongly attributed to John Goddard of Newport could command a premium of approximately 400 percent above a similar but anonymous piece from, say, New York.

Such mistakes may be encouraged by false labeling and/or counterfeit bills of sale. Labeled, signed, or completely documented American furniture is extremely rare, and the temptation to enhance the value of more ordinary period pieces is strong indeed to the less scrupulous. One can play the sleuth with labeled chairs by carefully inspecting the tone of the wood around the label. It should be slightly lighter where the edges of the label have worn away.

Finally, the historical significance of a piece will substantially influence its value. This is so in varying degrees. For example, a chair known to have been made for and used by George Washington will be worth more than one known simply to have been owned by him, which in turn will be worth more than one in which the father of our country was known to have sat. All of these chairs will be worth more than one that he never came close to.

Let us examine a selection of Queen Anne and Chippendale chairs sold in our galleries between 1972 and 1975. William W. Stahl, Sotheby Parke Bernet's vice president in charge of American furniture and decorative arts, has compiled this selection together with his estimate of what each lot would bring at auction today.

Date	Presale Estimate	Hammer Price	Current Estimate	Compound Rate of Growth [Based on Median Current Estimate]
1/29/72	$15,000–20,000	$13,000	$40,000	15%

Important pair of Queen Anne side chairs, Philadelphia, circa 1730. Plain design but quite early. Walnut (desirable wood for this type of chair). Pair more valuable than singles.

Date	Presale Estimate	Hammer Price	Current Estimate	Compound Rate of Growth [Based on Median Current Estimate]
5/15/75	$1,500–2,000	$1,400	$2,000–2,500	11.1%

Queen Anne side chair, Philadelphia, circa 1750. Carved mahogany (less desirable than walnut in this type of chair). Transitional crestrail, no carved shells.

Date	Presale Estimate	Hammer Price	Current Estimate	Compound Rate of Growth [Based on Median Current Estimate]
1/30/75	$8,000–10,000	$5,400	$10,000–15,000	18.3%

Queen Anne side chair, Newport, circa 1750. Walnut. Plain design but early. Rounded stiles (very desirable, would not expect more complicated carving on a chair of this period). Purchased cheaply during '74–'75 recession.

Date	Presale Estimate	Hammer Price	Current Estimate	Compound Rate of Growth [Based on Median Current Estimate]
1/29–31/75	$4,000–6,000	$9,500	$10,000–12,000	2.98%

Queen Anne side chair, Philadelphia, circa 1750. Maple. Intact label of William Savery. Transitional crestrail. Old and probably original finish. Exceptionally high price paid in 1976 not fully absorbed by passage of time.

Date	Presale Estimate	Hammer Price	Current Estimate	Compound Rate of Growth [Based on Median Current Estimate]
10/72	$20,000–25,000	$29,000	$40,000–60,000	8.09%

Important pair of Chippendale side chairs, made for George Washington, Philadelphia, circa 1780, carved mahogany. This is an exceptionally good example. One chair from this pair sold in the landmark Reginald Lewis sale in March 1961 for $7,000, more than twice the presale high estimate of $3,000. Even at this premium, the chair more than doubled in value in 11 years. Another chair from the same set was added to make the pair noted above.

While eighteenth-century American furniture is reaching record prices at every sale, it is not overvalued. Barring a genuine national economic disaster, these pieces and ones equivalent to them should continue to appreciate in value at rates similar to those indicated in the preceding chart.

For the investor or serious collector of more modest means, Mr. Stahl suggests an investigation of American furniture of the American Empire period (1815–1835). Pieces by Duncan Phyfe, the leading craftsman at the turn of the century, are already out of range of most buyers but many handsome pieces of very high quality of his contemporaries, such as Michael Allison and George Woodruff, can still be purchased for $5,000 to $10,000.

We have gone to some lengths to blur the distinctions, to encourage the recognition that there is no black and white, but many shades of grey. Buyers of works of art have complex motives; the often-cited extremes of motivation seldom exist.

Guidelines for buying

Our first cardinal rule for investing in art can thus be stated as, "Buy what you like." After all, works of art are expressions of human experience and it would be a disservice to stuff them into a dark vault. The exceptions, works purchased purely for investment, should be loaned to a museum or otherwise placed on public display. Finding the right one is part of the service provided by auctioneers and dealers. Once found, the museum should provide insurance under its blanket policy, security, and temperature and humidity controls, not to mention an appreciative public. The tax advantages of a full or partial lifetime gift, or a gift from your estate of the loan, should also be carefully investigated by you, your financial and legal advisors, and the museum.

Within the framework of the percentage of your net worth you have allocated to art investment, the next rule is to buy the very best available. If the best available is not that good, pass. Furthermore, if your investment budget for art is $10,000, understand that you will not be investing in impressionist paintings or medieval enamels. A balance must be struck between what appeals to you and what you can afford that is of investment quality. If you are unable to reconcile these criteria, you should stick to being a collector, not an investor, which as already mentioned, is a wonderful thing to be.

Our third rule is to seek expert advice. You wouldn't buy or sell stocks or bonds without the benefit of it; don't subject yourself to the vagaries of the art market without it, either. If you do, you are taking a patently unreasonable risk and you might as well be stuffing your money into a slot machine.

While we're at it, here are the other major risks in the art market: buying in haste and buying "bargains." There's plenty of time. Don't let anyone rush you. Prepare for an auction by reading and talking to people with experience in the field. Go to the presale exhibition. Handle the objects. Try to develop a feel for quality. If you are sincere and consistent, it will come. Go back to the dealer's shop several times. Ask him to hold the piece for you. Get a photograph of it which you can show to others. If it looks like a bargain, beware. A Durer etching for $250 just is not going to be the best of its kind, no matter how elaborate the story about the little old lady who is selling it because she needs money. A colleague of mine tells the story about a Louis XV carved beechwood armchair which came on the block at an auction. The auctioneer was struggling for $200. Although our friend had not first looked at the chair, he thought that at that level, there was no way he could go wrong. He was able to buy the chair for $350. When he picked it up, the first thing he noticed was that it swayed on its legs in every direction, like a drunk with his feet nailed to the floor. A cabinet maker was able to sober it up for $400. However, our friend was handed the eighteenth-century part of the chair in a brown paper bag, and told that the legs were just too full of worm damage to support even the most dainty derriere. Next came some fabric for $100 and upholstery at $300. His $350 antique had become a $1,150 reproduction. Bargains are expensive.

Assuming the chain of investment criteria is still unbroken for you, we can now proceed to the central task of deciding what something is worth. The value of a work of art relies upon four basic considerations: quality, condition, rarity, and historical importance, which includes provenance, or the history of ownership of the object. Quality means a formal aesthetic examination resulting in an opinion as to the skill of execution of an object. The finest Ming vase will lose as much as 40 percent of its value if it has a hairline crack. The next chip will remove still more value, and so on. Rarity means just that. How many Leonardo da Vincis are there? How many are left in private hands? What is the likelihood they will come onto the market? Historical importance can be a significant factor on its own, as in the case of collecting autographs of the signers of the Declaration of Independence.

In no sense is the art market a "sure thing." Risks abound, and prices go up and down. In addition to responding to general contractions in economic growth (negative G.N.P.), segments of the market can also lose value when fashions change, and when the market corrects itself in response to overspeculation, as with average-quality impressionist pictures following the Japanese buying frenzy of 1973–1974. But remember this: things that are the best of their kind will always attract competition, and are therefore among the best insulators from the slings and arrows of modern economic life.

If you have been faithful to all of our rules, you have a pretty good shot at making a well-informed investment in the art market. When the truck pulls up in front of your house and your Queen Anne gilt-decorated red japanned double-domed bureau bookcase is unloaded, your responsibilities are not over, though. There is tax and estate planning to do, appraisals and insurance to get, security to see to, and so on. But that is another story.

Works of art are assets. They have value; they can be exchanged for other assets. That beat-up old chair with the springs popping out that came from Grandma's house in Philadelphia could be an eighteenth-century Queen Anne armchair worth $100,000. The ugly porcelain swan that's been hiding in the back of the china closet since Uncle Ed brought it back from the war could be worth $50,000.

The threats we all face to our financial well-being are so complex and beyond our control that it would be negligent not to take every measure possible to protect ourselves. Taking account of your tangible assets can be a very pleasant surprise. Your net worth can be greater than you think, and, by extension, your financial options can be significantly expanded. A woman found what she called "an interesting old piece of wood" in her house. Sotheby Parke Bernet experts identified it as a rare Carolingian ivory. Sold at auction, it brought $470,000. The director of a boys' home in Manchester, England, badly in need of funds, inquired about the value of a painting that had hung in a back stairwell for over 100 years. Sotheby Parke Bernet experts in New York immediately identified it from a photograph as a lost masterpiece by the nineteenth-century landscape painter, Frederic Edwin Church. The epic picture, entitled *Icebergs*, brought the boys' home $2.5 million, less expenses.

Knowing the value of *all* of your assets is the first step in any responsible investment program. There needn't be any disservice done to artistic sensibility in the process. On the contrary, the more carefully and professionally you manage your works of art, the more likely they will survive and continue to give pleasure and insight to future generations. Table 14-2 shows a list of the areas you might consider looking into. Table 14-3 shows how Old Masters have compared to the Dow Jones Industrial Index since 1950.

Table 14-2. Comparing collectibles.

Type	Description
American paintings	National market; collector base broadening; reputations still being made
American furniture & decorations	Eighteenth-century "classics" can reach $350,000 but no top in sight. Still possible to find exceptional examples of later styles
American folk art	Booming; a weathervane made $23,000; shop carefully for value
Antiquities	Masterpieces $1 million and more; many areas still under-valued; good pieces available for $500–5,000; watch out for fakes
Armor	Only if you own a castle
Art Deco/Art Nouveau	Somewhat faddish; strong dealer support
Books and manuscripts	Extreme rarities unaffordable for most; still many fertile areas with active markets, such as American first editions
Coins	Condition crucial to value; buy extremely fine or better for investment
Contemporary art	Least exposure to test of time; for the venturesome and those with the wall space
English furniture	Undervalued relative to American examples of equivalent period
European porcelain, works of art, tapestries	Difficult areas for the uninitiated but worth the time
French furniture	Best pieces over $300,000
Impressionist and modern paintings	The blue chips; big names, big prices, big competition
Islamic works of art, rugs	Subject to politics; rugs recovered from the Iranian revolution
Japanese works of art	Highly specialized and complicated; good values make it worth effort to seek expertise
Jewelry	One of the best investments; relatively high liquidity; get a certificate for your stone
Old Master paintings	Broad appeal, widespread in quality; best of the best have been in museums for a long time
Photographs	Market still seeking its level; some "names" undervalued, some overvalued
Prints	Good starting point; much data available
Stamps	Condition crucial; very broad market
Vintage vehicles	Romatic; expensive upkeep; rallies fun
Wine	Drink or speculate; limited secondary market

Table 14-3. Index of Old Master paintings (1970 = 100).

Year	Old Master Paintings		Dow Jones Industrial Index[1]	
	Basic	Adjusted for Inflation[2]	Basic	Adjusted for Inflation
1951	14	21	15	23
1952	16	24	17	25
1953	20	30	17	25
1954	23	34	26	39
1955	23	34	33	49
1956	27	39	36	52
1957	28	39	33	46
1958	32	44	46	63
1959	34	46	55	74
1960	37	49	51	68
1961	44	58	63	83
1962	50	65	58	76
1963	48	62	70	90
1964	71	90	84	107
1965	86	107	96	120
1966	93	112	81	98
1967	84	98	96	112
1968	92	103	104	116
1969	97	102	92	97
1970	100	100	100	100
1971	112	108	110	106
1972	123	115	130	122
1973	158	136	113	97
1974	163	125	86	66
1975	162	116	125	90
1976	148	101	153	105
1977	194	124	134	86
1978	255	150	137	80

Notes

1. The Dow Jones Industrial Index has been adjusted to allow for the re-investment of gross dividends.

2. The adjustment for inflation is based on the Consumer Price Index [CPI-U]. Source: U.S. Bureau of Economic Analysis.

Sources: Paintings Index, Sotheby Park Bernet Inc.; Dow Jones and Co., Inc.

Acknowledgments

The author gratefully acknowledges the indispensable guidance and assistance provided by the following Sotheby Parke Bernet personnel: Frederick H. Scholtz, Executive Vice-President and Chief Operating Officer; C. Hugh Hildesley, Senior Vice-President; W. Stahl, Jr., Vice-President, Department Head, American Furniture & Decorative Arts; Marc E. Rosen, Vice-President, Department Head, Prints; Brenda J. Auslander, Vice-President, Department Head, Impressionist and Modern Paintings & Sculpture; Jeremy L. Eckstein, Art Market Analyst.

Notes

1. Wesley Towner, *The Elegant Auctioneers* (New York: Hill & Wang, 1970).

A Noble Endeavor

Nancy Hoffman

The pursuit of art has always been considered a noble endeavor. The cavemen, moved by life and nature around them, painted a kingdom of animals in broad sweeping gestures on cave walls. Even in prehistoric times people had the impulse to surround themselves with beauty, celebrating life in art. The Egyptians regaled themselves with art in life and death. When Egyptian royalty were buried they were accompanied by art, jewels, and treasures. The Greeks built temples to the gods

and walked the earth rejoicing in the arts: sculpture, painting, architecture, poetry, and music. From Roman times to Romanesque and Gothic, art celebrated life, nature, sport, and spirit. Art flowered in the Renaissance and has continued to blossom and grow through the centuries.

From the moment mankind developed the ability to make marks, pictograms, and pictures, there arose within the desire to own, possess, collect. This passion, incurable and unstoppable, sometimes even incorrigible, is why collectors collect. It is the passion of connection with a work of art that sparks the collector's first acquisition and, more often than not, sustains a desire to collect throughout life.

The art world has never been larger than it is today. There are contemporary art centers in Los Angeles, San Francisco, Houston, Chicago, among other places in this country. In New York alone, there are approximately 300 contemporary art galleries listed in the Gallery Guide, a special pocket-size guide with maps of the gallery areas. *Arts, Art in America, Artnews, Artforum, Portfolio* are among the many magazines covering the contemporary art scene in America and abroad. Art investment funds are growing. A credit card for art acquisition, The Collectors Card, enables the art purchaser to finance art purchases. Art is available to more people through the media. Collecting is no longer an activity limited to the elite; art has become a household word. Then who collects? The captain of industry, the young lawyer, the post office employee, the decorator, the aspiring author, the elementary school English teacher, the housewife, the tennis champion. Young and old—anyone who simply cannot live without art!

In ancient times the only people in a position to acquire works of art and support the arts were royalty. As early as the second century B.C., the Romans began to collect art, as purchases and through the spoils of wars. Art became a symbol of power, prestige, and status in ancient society. When Caesar presented works of art to the city or to palaces, they were received as special treasures. As early as the first century A.D., a law was passed governing the preservation of works of art. What has survived of ancient Rome is its art, not its trade, commerce, or business. In this country today, big business (corporations), not royalty as in Rome, is the main holder of wealth. In 1967, an organization called the Business Committee for the Arts was established with $22 million in corporate support to finance projects in the arts. In 1970, the Business Committee for the Arts received $110 million, in 1973, $144 million, and in 1976, $221 million from corporations to support the arts. It is a long history from the Romans through the Medicis and their support of Michelangelo's works to the present-day collector.

Can one define the contemporary collector? There is no one definition for this creature we call the "collector," but there are several groups or categories: the scholar-connoisseur, the art lover, the accumulator, the decorator, the gamesperson, the investor, the social climber, the herdsman, the do-gooder, and the artist-befriender.

The scholar-connoisseur buys with knowledge and a system focusing on specific periods of an artist's work or specific periods of art history. The art lover collects for pleasure, inspired by the passion of connecting with a work of art. The accumulator does just that, accumulating objects without focus on a period of history or kind of work. The accumulator may buy contemporary paintings, nineteenth-century English silver, Louis XV French furniture, and American Indian blankets. Each work is important and equal to the accumulator. The decorator buys with a beginning and end in mind: to fill the walls and create an environment. When the walls are full, the collection is complete. The gamesperson collects for the sporting event of collecting—the hunt, chase, and conquest of an important work.

The investor collects for the joy of buying an artist's work at low prices and selling at high prices. During the time the investor holds the "stock" in art, he or she has the added dividend of living with the works of art. The social climber is swept away by the enthusiasm of friends who own and collect art. The impetus to buy comes from another member of the herdsman's peer-group or social pressure. The do-gooder collects, believing that it is possible to contribute to society and do some good by supporting the arts. The do-gooder often buys works of art for donation to museums, sits on museum boards, and contributes financially to a museum or museums. The artist-befriender buys art with several purposes in mind: to help the artist financially, as an introduction to and connection with the artist, and as an entree into the art world.

Buying art provides a means of self-expression and adds a depth and dimension that would otherwise not exist in the collector's workaday world of standardization. We live in a world of frozen foods, prefabricated houses, modular construction, computerization, and systematized everything; art is at the opposite end of the spectrum from everything instant, ready-made, and standardized. Some people call collecting art a passion; others say they have been bitten by the bug. Whatever you call it, once you start collecting art, it is hard to stop.

A thought expressed by most collectors is a feeling of necessity of owning art (it is no surprise that Aline Saarinen called her 1958 book on collectors *The Proud Possessors*). One woman told me: "I want to buy something the day I die! When I connect with a work of art my blood starts perking. Collecting is a necessary part of my living." One man said, "I buy art and I travel, those are the two things I do. I buy art because it's fun. I get my thrill from ceasing to be an outsider for a moment and becoming an insider—a person in harmony with a creative mind."

A woman I spoke with said: "For one year I didn't buy a pair of stockings so that I could buy art. It is wonderful to do without something for something else."

When asked how his collecting began, one man said: "When I was a child I collected coins, stamps, baseball cards, paper cups. I had collections of things. I would suspect that that instinct runs through life. It is quite possible that collectors are simply born collectors."

One woman explained that she began collecting art as soon as she could afford it: "I started to collect right after I got married. My first purchase was a $15 print about 40 years ago. My mother was very dramatic and loved beautiful things. Beauty meant a great deal to her. She couldn't afford to buy art. Several years ago I discovered a contract dated 1905 between my mother and a dealer in which she agreed to buy a round oak dining room table and two small pictures at a few dollars a week. Although she couldn't afford the pictures, she couldn't live without them and had to buy them. This is how I feel when I buy art. I fall in love a little bit each time I connect with a work of art."

Many collectors begin buying art at a young age with first purchases of prints in the $5–15 range. One collector who studied art in high school became interested, involved, and intrigued. While he was engaged, he took his fiancee to museums because they were both interested in art and museum going was the most pleasurable free activity in New York at the time. This interest in art shared by the couple blossomed into a major commitment throughout their life together. From their first purchase of a print for $15, through a series of Andy Warhol flowers to a John deAndrea life-size sculpture, this couple has always taken risks.

In this new era of collecting, since 1960, art has become a public pastime, not just for the collector who haunts the galleries and artists' studios for new works, but for people who enjoy spending their Saturdays and Sundays strolling through galleries and museums. In New York there are four main gallery areas: SoHo, 57th Street, Madison Avenue, and Tribeca (the triangle below Canal Street). SoHo is a landmark cast-iron district South of Houston and North of Canal Streets where artists' lofts, light manufacturing warehouses, and galleries coexist. SoHo galleries are often ground-floor spaces, old warehouses that have been emptied out, renovated, and painted white. They are open, informal, and inviting.

The second gallery area is on 57th Street between Park and Sixth Avenues. The galleries are above street level from the second floor on up as high as the buildings go. These clean white spaces often are divided into different viewing galleries and exude an air of establishment and formality. Along with the third gallery area on Madison Avenue, 57th Street galleries exist in the heart of Manhattan's high-rent shopping district. The fourth and most avant-garde area is Tribeca, where the galleries look like those of SoHo: large, open, wood-floored, high-ceilinged, white spaces. With the alternative spaces (non-commercial exhibition spaces, often grant supported) such as the Clocktower and P.S. 1, Tribeca is the bastion of the avant garde.

Strolling through galleries is often the way collecting begins. "The best way to begin is to look at art—lots of art. That's the only way to develop an eye, the ability to discriminate, and select works of greatest quality. Then ask questions, find people you trust and when you have confidence, begin to buy art." Over and over the concept of looking at art, as much as possible and in many styles, was given as the key to learning and collecting successfully.

Collectors can buy directly from the artist in the studio or, as is more often the case, from the dealer in the gallery. As in all businesses, the gallery from which the work is purchased, the "label" is important. Galleries of quality represent artists of quality. In buying a horse, you want the owner to guarantee it is a thoroughbred. The same is true for the collector buying a painting. You want it to have a good pedigree.

In the past, prior to the late 1950s and early 1960s, most collectors would buy from one dealer with whom they often had a close relationship. Since the 60s, with the proliferation of galleries all over the country, collectors no longer buy from just one dealer. Some buy from a few dealers over the years, others buy from many. One collector informed me that he never buys a work of art for over $10,000 from one dealer without having it appraised and authenticated by another.

The role and function of the art dealer is as diverse as the definition of the contemporary collector. The dealer works directly with the artist, the collector, the critic, the museum curator and/or director, the general public. The dealer sells art, catalogues and documents works of art, arranges exhibitions for artists at other galleries and museums in this country and in Europe, educates the public, builds careers, appraises paintings, holds exhibitions in his own gallery, ships works of art all over the country.

Most contemporary galleries work on a consignment basis. The artist consigns his or her works to the gallery. When a sale is made the artist is paid a commission ranging from 66.6 to 50 percent, and the gallery receives the balance. For its commission the gallery covers all or some of the expenses involved in mounting an exhibition: advertising, photography, framing, shipping, announcement cards, catalogues, promotion, installation.

The galleries generally begin their season in September and end in June, corresponding to the academic calendar year. It has been the tradition for galleries to close for vacation for the month of August. During the past few years, as the art business has become less seasonal, more and more galleries remain open year-round.

Most contemporary galleries schedule one-man exhibitions during the season on a three- or four-week rotating basis. Some galleries have 5 one-man shows a season, others have 40. Each gallery has its own "style" or "look," though the artists' work may not look the same; the gallery expresses a particular and specific personality and esthetic through the dealer's selection of artists.

The nature of the art gallery has changed since the first gallery opened in New York approximately 150 years ago in 1832. This was a private gallery run and built by Lumman Reed. He was a retired grocer who housed his private collection in the gallery and eventually gave his paintings to the New York Historical Society. From 1853 to 1854, Thomas Jefferson Ryan built and ran a gallery located on the second floor of a Broadway building. Like Reed, Ryan housed his collection in the gallery. He was devoted to Christian art and ultimately gave the collection to the New York Historical Society.

Also during the mid-1800s, James Jackson Jarves traveled through Italy for ten years looking for and buying Italian primitive paintings, which he called "gold background" pictures. Among the artists in his collection were Sassetta, DaFabriano, and Pollaiuolo. When he returned to America, having invested $60,000 in his collection, he offered the paintings to several museums with the hope that the entire collection might go to a museum in Boston or New York. Jarves received only one bid from Yale University for the collection he had lovingly assembled and personally selected over the years. For a mere $22,000, one-third the cost of the collection, Yale acquired these Italian treasures.

Isabella Gardner was a Boston woman with an early interest in and taste for European art. She gave her collection to a museum that now bears her name, the Isabella Gardner Museum. Mrs. Potter Palmer of Chicago was interested in French painting at an early date. She gave her collection of nineteenth-century French paintings to the Art Institute of Chicago, making it one of the richest repositories of nineteenth-century French painting in this country.

Approximately 100 years ago in the late 1800s, a major change took place in collecting in America. Lord Joseph Duveen influenced this change when he came to America from Europe. Duveen had three galleries, one in New York, one in Paris, and one in London. He traveled back and forth between the galleries, often bringing French, English, and Italian paintings from Europe to sell to American collectors.

Joseph Duveen started in the art business when he was 17 in 1886. He began his training working first with his father Joseph Joel in London at the family shop on Oxford Street, then with his Uncle Henry in New York, the American partner in the firm of Duveen Brothers, dealers in furniture and objets d'art. He was not interested in dealing in objets d'art and furniture, but in fine paintings and sculpture. At an early age he began to buy European masterpieces, paintings, and sculpture to resell to clients.

During his first trip to New York in 1886 after visiting his uncle's shop, Duveen realized that he could take advantage of a special moment in American history. The market was ripe for art. Men who had made millions from the land, the railroads, mining, and department stores were ready to buy art and be educated. With the money they had earned they had already begun to buy French paintings of the Barbizon school and English "story" pictures. Duveen set about changing this taste for sweet pictures and directed these collectors to the great masters of Europe—from Italian primitive paintings to French and English paintings of the eighteenth century. He sold the European masters to Andrew Mellon, William Randolph Hearst, Samuel H. Kress, Henry Ford, John D. Rockefeller, J. P. Morgan, Jr., Henry C. Frick, and P. A. B. Widener, among others.

In 1928 Duveen sold Rembrandt's painting, *Aristotle Contemplating the Bust of Homer,* to advertising man Alfred Erickson for $750,000. When the stock market collapsed, Erickson sold the painting back to Duveen in 1930 for $500,000 and finally repurchased it again in 1936 for $590,000. In 1961, the Metropolitan Museum of art paid Erickson's estate $2.3 million for the painting.

Duveen himself was instrumental in the creation of the National Gallery in Washington as well as in the creation of the Frick Museum in New York. For both buildings Duveen selected the architects. He was responsible for the sale of many of the paintings that both museums house.

From the early 1900s until World War II, the primary emphasis of American collecting was still on European art, not on contemporary American art. Paris was the center of the art world. Gertrude Stein and her salon of artists reigned supreme. After World War II the emphasis changed and shifted. Americans became more interested in acquiring American art and less interested in acquiring European art. Slowly the center of the art world moved from Paris to New York.

During the 1950s, there was a handful of galleries in New York. The same names appear over and over: Sidney Janis, Betty Parsons, Peggy Guggenheim, Sam Kootz, Knoedler. There were few galleries and few collectors. The activity of collecting was a pastime for the monied class only, the privilege and pleasure of the elite.

In the 1960s, several phenomena contributed to the multiplying of galleries, the growth in numbers of collectors and the interest in American art. One of the key stimuli was Pop Art, which depicted everyday common objects in painting and sculpture and, therefore, was understandable and appealed to a larger audience than earlier, more abstract styles. European travel was more easily available to more people, bringing with it the possibility for exposure to art of many centuries, as well as to the tradition of investing large amounts of capital in art and tangible assets. The publication of fancy, well-illustrated art books brought art in reproduction to a larger public.

More people had more money from profits realized in the stock market to indulge in art, as well as in other leisure activities and pleasures. More people considered investing in art as a hedge against inflation and protection against the fluctuation of the relative strength of the U.S. dollar. In the 1960s, as through history, art was considered a luxury and, thus, desirable. Because people enjoy living with beautiful things, the market exists and flourishes.

During the 1960s, many of the major European collectors began to buy American art actively, spurred on by the rise of Pop Art—a particularly and peculiarly American style—as well as by the devaluation of the American dollar. Several of the European collectors have continued to buy and support American art as styles have changed and grown since the 1960s. Among the movements Europeans have supported during the 1970s are Photo-Realism, Minimalism, and Pattern Painting, to mention just a few.

From the 1960s to the 1980s there has been constant growth in all aspects of the art market. New galleries are opening each season, while artists are earning their livelihood from their art. New museums are opening. Collectors collect with rigor, some of them even building special gallery wings onto their houses. Auction news makes the front page of the *New York Times.* The art world has become a sprawling network, larger and more varied than ever before.

As evidence of an expanding market of collectors and investors in art, Salomon Brothers published a study to show how tangible assets outdistanced financial assets in 1979. As shown in Table 15-1, during 1979, silver jumped 62.5 percent, stamps 60.9 percent, gold 55 percent, Old Masters 22.1 percent, and common stocks 5.3 percent.

People tend to view auction prices as a kind of market indicator for the season whether in contemporary art, impressionist painting, or Japanese pottery. They use auction price results to determine whether the market is soft or strong, whether it is a time to sell or buy.

During periods of inflation, interest in collectibles rises as it did in 1973–74, a record-breaking period for contemporary art auctions at Sotheby Parke Bernet in New York, which showed sales of $23.2 million; 1979 ran a close second, with sales of $22.3 million and some record-setting prices in the modern and contemporary art areas. Among the record prices set in 1979 were: Piet Mondrian's *Large Composition in Red, Blue & Yellow,* sold for $800,000; Franz Kline's *#3,* for $240,000; Morris Lewis' *Aleph Series I,* for $170,000; David Smith's *7 Hours,* for $80,000; Jim Dine's *The Studio,* for $55,000; Robert Motherwell's *View Number 1,*

Table 15-1. Tangible assets vs. financial assets.

| | Compounded Annual Rate | | | | | |
	68–79	Rank	68–78	Rank	1979	Rank
Gold	19.4%	1	16.3%	3	55.0%	3
Chinese ceramics	19.1	2	18.0	1	31.1	4
Stamps	18.9	3	15.4	4	60.9	2
Rare books	15.7	4	16.5	2	7.8	11
Silver	13.4	5	9.1	11	62.5	1
Coins	12.7	6	13.0	5	10.0	9
Old Masters	12.5	7	11.6	8	22.1	5
Diamonds	11.8	8	12.6	6	4.0	14
Oil	11.3	9	11.8	7	6.2	12
Farmland	10.9	10	10.6	9	14.2	6
Housing	9.6	11	9.2	10	13.7	7
Consumer Price Index	6.5	12	6.1	13	10.5	8
Foreign exchange	6.4	13	6.2	12	8.8	10
Bonds	5.8	14	6.1	14	3.3	15
Stocks	3.1	15	2.9	15	5.3	13

Source: Salomon Brothers, 1979.

for $40,000; Ellsworth Kelly's *Four Panels: Green Red Yellow Blue,* for $54,000; Frederic Edwin Church's American landscape *Icebergs,* for $2.5 million.

The year 1980 was a record-breaker for auction prices in modern and contemporary paintings. In May at Christie's, New York, six new records were established for the impressionists in one auction of the Henry Ford collection: Van Gogh at $5.2 million for *le Jardin du Poete, Arles;* Cezanne at $3.9 million for the *Paysan en Blouse Bleue;* Gauguin at $2.9 million for *La Plage du Pouldu;* Degas at $660,000 for *Etude de Nu;* Modigliani at $600,000 for *Nudo Seduto* and Boudin at $480,000 for *la Plage.* A few days later at Parke Bernet in New York several new records were established for contemporary artists: Roy Lichtenstein's painting *Oh Jeff . . . I Love You, Too . . . But* sold for $210,000, $110,000 higher than his previous auction record six months earlier. Other records set were: Francis Bacon's *From Muybridge—Studies of the Human Body—Woman Emptying a Bowl of Water, and a Paralytic Child on all Fours* for $180,000; Ellsworth Kelly's *Green Black* for $57,500; Robert Motherwell's 1967 *Untitled* painting measuring 116 × 140 inches for $55,000, and George Segal's *The Photobooth,* for $47,000.

The contemporary auction in May 1980 at Christie's, New York, broke a record. It reached a total of $2.6 million, surpassing the earlier Scull sale total of $2.1 million, and broke several auction record prices, among

Exhibit 15-1. An index of art inflation.

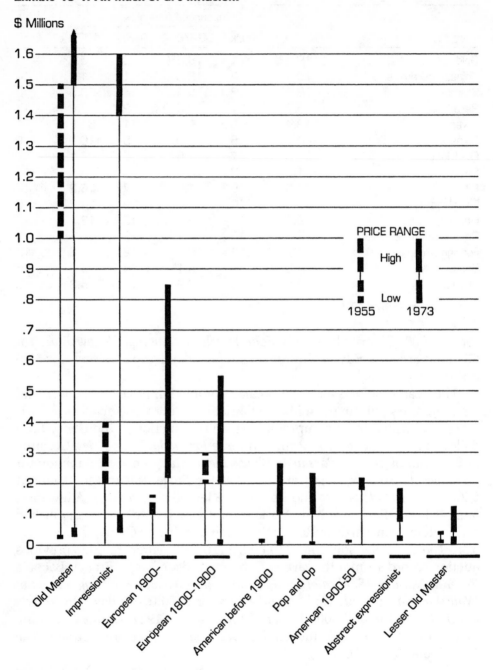

Source: Fortune Magazine, May 1974.

them: Jackson Pollock's *Four Opposites* sold for $550,000, Barnet Newman's *Primordial Light* sold for $250,000; Morris Louis' *Beta Khi* sold for $180,000, and Frank Stella's *Abajo* and *Wake Island Rail,* each sold for $85,000.

Apart from the auction record prices, other record sales occurred privately and through dealers in 1980. One of the most dazzling was the sale of Jasper Johns' painting, *Three Flags,* to the Whitney Museum for $1 million, the highest price ever paid by the Museum for a post-World War II painting. That painting was purchased originally for $900 in 1958.

During the lively 1980 art season the Picasso show at the Museum of Modern Art in New York broke museum attendance and catalogue sales records. At least partly as a result of the show, Picasso's prints rose 10 to 20 percent in price during the 1980 season. For example, a complete suite of Vollard prints, which would have sold for $250,000 in 1979, was priced at $350,000—375,000 during the 1980 season.

Shown in Exhibit 15-1 is an index of auction prices for art since 1955, charted by *Fortune Magazine* in 1974, indicating an upward inflationary trend.

Another record-setting contemporary art auction was the 1973 Parke Bernet sale of the Robert and Ethel Scull collection. Repercussions still resound from this event, which brought certain notoriety to the collectors. During the 1960s, the Sculls had acquired a large collection of Pop Art at low prices. The Sculls bought well and invested wisely. When their Pop Art collection was sold, the prices were high and profits enormous. A Jasper Johns painting, *Double White Map,* purchased in 1965 for $10,000, was sold at this auction for $240,000, one example of the profits realized. Naturally, the proceeds of the auction went to the Sculls, minus the auction house commission on the sale. None of the profits based on the appreciation in price and value on the works went to the artists. It is this fact and the public underlining of it that prompted an active movement on artist's resale rights, whereby the artist has the right to a certain percentage of the resale price of any and all of his works. This law has not been passed or enforced throughout the United States. It has, however, been passed in California. The fight for passage still goes on.

Buying well, as the Sculls did, does not always mean buying at a low price and selling at a high price. Buying well often means buying the best. Today, as throughout history, some collectors express this sentiment and believe that no price is too high for the best painting or sculpture or drawing. There is always a market and resale value for the best. This is not always the case for a work that is less than best. Some collectors borrow money from a bank to finance such purchases. Others finance the purchases on a time-payment installment plan with a gallery. Some galleries will allow the collector to buy a work of art over time, establishing a specific payment amount and schedule per month, without charging the collector interest. And now there is the "art card," with which a collector can finance art purchases.

Altruistic motivations for buying art do not preclude the pleasures of making correct decisions where investment is concerned. According to one collector, "If you want a huge bankbook you buy stocks. You can have all the stocks you want, but you are much better off with your art. The interest and dividends of looking at art in your home, living with it privately are enormous." This collector has some of his money in the stock market as well as in art, and rarely trades from his collection. In a unique situation of owning three works of the same period by one artist, he decided to sell an earlier work of 1971 to finance his purchase of a newer work by the same artist. The painting he purchased in 1971 for under $800 sold in 1976 for $25,000.

This jump in price can be attributed to many factors. The best painting of its period, it had become a "classic" Photo-Realist work. The painting had been purchased at the outset of the artist's public and sales career, when his works were just beginning to appear on and be sought after by the New York Market. In the five years between the time of purchase and the time of resale of this work, New Realism—or Photo-Realism—had become a style or movement collected by many with almost insatiable appetite. The very nature of the New Realist paintings—precise, pristine, carefully painted works depicting the urban landscape and environment or objects of everyday—means that the artist spends a long time on each painting. The works become rare objects, and prices went up as the market expanded. During the five-year period between purchase of the painting and its resale, the artist's work had become well known in this country and in Europe. Articles had appeared about his work in art magazines. Some of his paintings had been reproduced in books. His work had been collected by museums. All of this exposure and authentication contributed to the appreciation in value of the painting.

One woman said to me on the subject of investment: "My husband collects stocks. He's very creative, but one (stocks) does not substitute for another (art)."

One investment-minded collector told an interesting story about a Lalique vase he acquired on a buying trip accompanied by a dealer friend. The collector bought the vase for $800 from one dealer and resold it immediately thereafter to his dealer friend who had accompanied him on this trip for $950. In a matter of minutes, he had realized a profit of $150.

Most financial investors find investment in the art market somewhat of a mystery. To dispel this mystery, Sotheby Parke Bernet began an advisory program a number of years ago. More recently, Citibank embarked on an art investment program available to a select clientele willing to commit a minimum of $1 million to the art investment fund. For 2 percent a year, Citibank manages this investment program and employs Sotheby Parke Bernet to suggest art works for purchase.

Since the 1950s, art prices have multiplied geometrically 10 to 50 times, and in some cases 1,000 percent when a collector may have gambled at an early date on a young artist who became an international superstar. The rise in art prices, even at an average of 10 percent over the past 20 years, is a bit better than the average price gain for stocks. A Parke Bernet staff member concludes that art outdistances stocks because of its multiple appeal—that is, the combination of value with aesthetic pleasure. It is difficult to display stock or bond certificates.

The demand for art as investment accelerated after the Goldschmidt collection of impressionist works was sold at auction in 1958 for $2.2 million. Recent auction sales at Parke Bernet confirm this position: sales for 1977 were $79 million; for 1978, $112 million; for 1979, $147 million. Some individuals who sold entire collections at auction during the 70s have fared well: in 1971, the Norton Simon Collection realized $9.8 million at Parke Bernet; in 1977, the Geraldine Rockefeller Dodge sale realized $7.5 million at Parke Bernet; in 1979, the Sonnenberg Collection realized $4.9 million, and the Baron Von Hirsch estate in London realized $13.4 million.

The best that can happen in buying art is that you make a right decision. The work or works you purchase appreciate in value and you make money reselling these works, or you make money by donating a work (or works) to a museum at current market value and taking a tax deduction. The tax benefits of donating works owned for more than a year to nonprofit institutions can amount to deductions of up to 30 percent of adjusted gross income for up to five years. The psychological rewards of ownership and gifting are many and different from the profit motive.

Unlike any other market, the art market has a limited and diminishing supply of great works. If you buy great works only, there is always a demand for them and, more often than not, at a higher price than you originally paid. Naturally, blue chip paintings, like blue chip stocks, command relatively high prices. The strength of the prices has been demonstrated over time. These prices are not likely to decline over a short period of time.

The worst that can happen in acquiring art is that your collection does not maintain its value and declines in value. This is the gamble one takes in buying art, particularly by artists who are not yet considered "blue chip." Ralph Colin, vice-president of the Art Dealers Association, commented in *The Wall Street Journal* that 99 percent of art now available will never be worth more than it is worth today, and much will be worth less.

While art never loses its total value, prices do fluctuate with changes in taste and in the economy. Prices can peak due to an oversupply of work by a particular artist, as is the case for Chagall, Dufy, and Vlaminck. Owning a work by a big-name artist does not guarantee a big price tag on a resale. The price of the work, be it painting, drawing, print, or sculpture, is determined by several factors: who made the work, how characteristic it is, desirability of the period during the artist's career, when it was made, size, subject, condition, presence of signature, pedigree (previous owners), provenance (exhibition record), previous price history, where and when it is being sold. Art is not easy to sell like stocks and it provides no income while it is held. There are three ways for the collector to sell art: through a dealer, through an auction house, or privately. Depending on what the work is, the best way will at times be through a dealer and at other times through an auction house.

Another risk for the beginning collector is that of being drawn to art that is "in vogue" and, therefore, already in a high price range. When the time to sell arrives, the work is often out of style and prices have dropped. A recent article in *Money* puts it this way: "Since no one every really knows what a work of art is worth until after it is sold, investing in collectibles offers no guarantee of financial security. Collectibles don't pay dividends or interest as stocks, bonds or savings accounts do, and they need to be insured."

Stories of interesting purchases, risks, and riches abound in the art field. Ben Heller, a former textile executive turned art dealer, purchased a Jackson Pollock painting, *Blue Poles,* in 1966 for $32,000, and sold it in 1973 for $2 million to the National Museum of Australia. In 1977, a group of California investors bought a set of Edward S. Curtis photographs of North American Indians for $60,000 and sold it three days later for $85,000. A New York art dealer found a painting hidden away at an English country antique store for $392, which was later authenticated and attributed to Domenichino; it is now worth $200,000. In 1889, a period of vogue for nineteenth-century painting, a Meissonier painting measuring 3½ by 4¾ inches sold for $7,100 at auction in New York. During that same season a collection of 25 impressionist paintings, including Renoir, Degas, Sisley, Pissarro, and Boudin, sold for the same price. Today the Meissonier French Salon painting is probably worth around $20,000 and any one of the 25 impressionist paintings more than $100,000.

The price explosion applies to prints as well as original paintings. A 1904 etching by Pablo Picasso, *Le Repas Frugal,* sold originally for a few dollars a print in an edition of 30. During the 1950s, the prints sold for

$175 each, and in 1973 one of the prints brought $179,000 at auction in Switzerland. A 1964 Jasper Johns lithograph, *Ballantine Beer Cans,* sold originally for $200 and is now valued at more than $12,000.

Some people are lucky enough to reap the financial rewards of serendipitous finds of art. At a church auction in 1942, a Massachusetts teacher bought a watercolor portrait for $350, which he sold at auction in 1977 for $22,000 after it had been authenticated as a work that primitive artists R. W. and S. A. Shute painted around 1835. A New Jersey salesperson auctioned a family heirloom after finding out that it was a fourteenth-century painting by the Italian Angelo Gaddi and realized $55,000 on his inheritance. A Connecticut businessman purchased an Andy Warhol painting of a can of Campbell's beef noodle soup, *Nineteen Cents,* in 1962 for $1,300 which he sold for $95,000 at auction in 1977.

As with the stock market, everyone has a story to tell about art investment or otherwise. There is a story of a minister whose first purchase was a Marilyn Monroe painting by Andy Warhol. An architect beginning his practice who could not afford to buy art found himself commissioning a piece for which he paid $25 a month over a number of years. A letter carrier who put all of his earnings into art decided he could not live without a $5,000 painting of a nude woman atop an animal by Mel Ramos, for which he paid monthly over three years. A collector, whose daughter had a poster of a visionary landscape painting by Bill Martin, came upon the real painting after years of knowing it in reproduction and bought it on the spot. One collector whose favorite beverage is water discovered a painting of that subject, *A Glass of Water,* by Ben Schonzeit, and purchased it immediately. Another collector who owns a soft sculpture by Claes Oldenburg, *Ghost Toilet,* which is often giggled at by visitors to the house, feels that the sculpture is a deeply moving and poignant work "like a crucifix." Another collector bought a life-size sculpture of a horse made of mud and sticks that she did not want her husband to notice right away, so she placed it in a rarely visited upstairs bedroom rather than in the dining room on public view. She had to have this horse. All of these people had to have, possess, live with the works that spoke to them.

From the cave paintings of animals in Lascaux, France, to the contemporary mud and stick horse, from the Greek statue of a nude discus thrower to the modern-day nude atop an animal, from the visionary landscape of the Renaissance to the visionary landscape of today, mankind has celebrated life in art. From prehistoric times to the present day, the passion to dwell with beauty and art has inspired men and women to collect, has enriched their lives, and has ennobled the human spirit.

An International Market

James J. Lally

The Chinese art market has been in the news lately, and much has been written about the spectacular rise in prices paid for Chinese works of art, particularly for Chinese ceramics over the past 15 or 20 years. As one might expect, the rise in price levels has been accompanied by a rise in the volume of trade and a steady increase in the number of buyers and sellers. Nevertheless, one important feature of the Chinese art market is the fact that it is not at all as large as one might expect, either in dollar volume or in terms of the number of participants. The net total of all Chinese art sold at auction by the Sotheby Parke Bernet Group worldwide during the fiscal year ending in August 1979 was approximately $22,000,000 (an increase of 20 percent over the total for 1978). This figure does not account for the entire world market, but Sotheby Parke Bernet, acting as agent for buyers and sellers, handles a larger volume than any other participant in the market, by quite a wide margin. The total number of buyers and sellers at Sotheby Parke Bernet sales annually is less than 5,000 individuals and institutions.

The events in the Chinese art market which are widely reported in the news are naturally the sales of the rarest and most expensive pieces. This gives the impression that all Chinese art is very expensive. In fact, this is not true. A few rare and exceptionally fine or beautiful pieces are very expensive indeed, but the majority of the Chinese ceramics and other works of art sold today are much less expensive. Approximately 80 percent of the Chinese art lots offered by Sotheby Parke Bernet worldwide are sold for less than $2,000, and nearly 60 percent are sold for less than $750.

The Chinese art market is an international market. The arts of China are recognized around the world as being an important part of the artistic heritage of all mankind. Important museums and serious collectors are active in the Chinese art market in every major country around the world. This widespread demand factor gives the Chinese art market a great deal of depth and diversity, and the ease of jet travel and worldwide communications have simultaneously tended to even out price levels and reduce price differentials in various trading locations.

Demand for Chinese art has increased considerably, on a worldwide basis, throughout the 1960s and 1970s. The American market in particular has shown steady growth. In the 1950s during the Korean War era, the arts of China were very much out of favor and, in fact, an embargo on the import of Chinese goods had a serious negative impact on the market. But the 1960s and 1970s have seen a warming of relations between America and China, and demand for Chinese art has increased steadily. The volume of Chinese art sales at Sotheby Parke Bernet, New York for the 1979–80 auction season was more than 70 percent higher in dollar volume than the preceding season.

The most significant development in the Chinese art market during the past two decades has been the strong re-entry of Far Eastern buyers, not only in their regional trading centers, but around the world. During the late 1960s and early 1970s the Japanese in particular began buying more frequently outside of Japan and in increasing quantity. During the 1970s other Far Eastern buyers became more involved and more active in the world market. This activity has accelerated noticeably since 1975, and the phenomenal growth of the turnover at Hong Kong sales is clear evidence of this important trend. Sotheby Parke Bernet held no regular sales in Hong Kong—or in any other location in the Far East—until 1973, but by 1978 the Hong Kong sales were established as a regular biannual event and represented close to 20 percent of the total net Chinese art sales worldwide for Sotheby Parke Bernet.

Variety of objects

A wide variety of different objects and works of art are bought and sold in the worldwide trading which here is being referred to as the Chinese art market. This diversity is, perhaps, an obvious point but it is also fundamental to the nature of the market. All of the studies and statistics regarding the Chinese art market which have been published to date (including those here) relate to and deal with Chinese ceramics only and therefore are of questionable utility for other sectors of the market. Even the ceramics sector is extremely complex and diversified, and the statistics and studies tend to deny or at least obscure all the complexity and diversity, which is an everyday fact for collectors and dealers. In order to give a clearer picture of the major components of the Chinese art market, I will describe briefly the different sectors of the market and the nature of the trading activity in each.

Ceramics

The largest sector of the Chinese art market is ceramics. This is true both in terms of physical volume and dollar volume. Ceramics prices are the leading and dominating factor in the Chinese art market. The market for ceramics is as diverse as it is widespread, and therefore it is very useful to look at different sections of the market and to review the recent history and different trading characteristics of each section.

Ming porcelains are the most widely traded and the strongest section of the Chinese ceramics market today. The Ming dynasty (A.D. 1368–1644) porcelains, and particularly Ming blue and white, are so well known as to have almost become a cliche, but their importance in Chinese art history and the history of ceramics around the world remains unchallenged. Every museum with rooms devoted to Oriental art must have representative ceramics from the Ming period.

Beginning collectors, or even occasional buyers who may not be collectors of Oriental art, are drawn to Ming ceramics first, and for many serious collectors the ceramics of the Ming dynasty are the most desirable and the most important ceramics of all. Despite a shortage of the best-quality material, prices for the best Ming porcelains are currently as high as they have ever been. Demand for the best-quality Ming ceramics is so very widespread that it is difficult to envision a significant short-term decline in this segment of the market without a decline in the market as a whole.

The demand and the price levels for the ceramics of the Qing (Ch'ing) dynasty (1644–1912) are also very high at this time. There is a universal demand for Imperial Qing (Ch'ing) ceramics and the wares made for Chinese use, but the interest and trade in the ceramics made for export during the Qing (Ch'ing) dynasty is limited almost entirely to the Western (i.e., American and European) buyers. The most sophisticated and the most active buyers of the best Imperial Qing (Ch'ing) ceramics are Hong Kong Chinese, but in recent sales, other Chinese buyers from Taipei and elsewhere in the Far East have begun to give the Hong Kong Chinese stronger competition.

Song (Sung) (A.D. 960–1280) ceramics are the classic wares of Chinese ceramic history and their appeal is truly universal. There are several major collectors of Sung ceramics in America, and no museum with a serious interest in Oriental art can ignore this category. The Japanese buyers are always a major factor in the market for Song (Sung) ceramics, particularly in the case of the robust Cizhou (tz'u chou) wares and the finest of the celadons or any of the many types of tea bowls or wares that might relate to the tea ceremony. In recent sales, the Hong Kong Chinese have been dominant in the bidding for the brightly glazed Jun (Chun) wares, and for the finest Ding (Ting) Yao white wares, which are often referred to as the earliest true porcelains. The Hong Kong Chinese collectors' interest in other sections of the Song (Sung) ceramics market has not been a major factor in the past, but there are signs that this may be changing. In every sales location, there are very wide price differences between the less important Song (Sung) pieces and the finest examples, but the prices paid for the rarest and best Song (Sung) ceramics have always been quite high in relation to the market as a whole.

Tang dynasty (A.D. 618–906) and earlier ceramics, particularly the famous glazed pottery horses and other tomb figures, have been popular among Western collectors for many years. The recent, continuing archaeological work in China and the several major traveling exhibitions of the new archaeological finds, which have been sent around the world by the Chinese, have greatly reinforced existing trends toward increased collecting interest in Tang dynasty and earlier ceramics. The new archaeology has also contributed to the trend toward more serious and sophisticated collecting in this area. Early ceramics, such as painted Neolithic pottery dating from the second millenium B.C. and the tomb pottery of the Han dynasty (206 B.C.–A.D. 220) or the olive glazed stoneware called "proto-yueh" and the other wares of the Six Dynasties (A.D. 265–589) period were all too esoteric for most collectors and were not widely appreciated as recently as 15 or 20 years ago. As collectors' attitudes have changed and our knowledge of these wares has increased, museum curators and collectors have become more aware of the historical importance and relative scarcity of these earlier pieces, and they are now very much in demand. The thermoluminescence technique for scientific dating of the Tang and earlier pottery wares, first introduced in the late 1960s and widely used ever since, has also had a positive impact on the confidence of buyers in this area and has contributed greatly to price stability and growth.

Bronzes

Another very important sector of the Chinese art market is archaic bronzes. The majority of the works of art traded in this part of the market are archaic bronze vessels, excavated from tombs of the Shang, Chou, and Han periods (1200 B.C.–A.D. 200). Prices for major bronze vessels are strong and reasonably high right now, but it is a remarkable fact that prices for archaic bronzes have not increased at the same rate as ceramics prices. Archaic bronzes are thus less expensive, in relation to the market as a whole, than they were 20 or 30 years ago. One important problem in this collecting area is the serious shortage of the best-quality material. There is a much smaller supply of fine-quality archaic bronze vessels than there is of fine ceramics.

Other early Chinese works of art and archaeological artifacts—such as bronze mirrors, chariot fittings, belt hooks, and small animal bronzes such as shroud weights in the form of animals and birds—have commanded high and steadily rising prices over the past ten years. There has been significant museum buying in this area, but it seems likely that many private collectors who might be wary of the conservation problems of archaic bronze vessels, or who find the bronze vessels too difficult to display and live with, are much more interested in the smaller archaic pieces. There have been very high prices paid, by Japanese and American buyers particularly, for gilt bronze sculpture and other fine small archaic works of art. Prices in this segment of the market appear to have risen faster than prices for archaic bronze vessels, despite the fact that the issue of supply is a serious problem in this area as well.

Sculpture

Chinese sculpture has become much more popular during the past two decades. Prices have recently begun to increase quite sharply as a result of wider interest and more sophisticated buying among Western buyers and increased participation from the Far East. Except for the well-known Tang dynasty and earlier tomb figures, the subject of most Chinese sculpture is Buddhist or other religious figures. The style is often highly formalized and repetitive. As a result, Chinese sculpture has historically had limited appeal for collectors and buyers other than museums, particularly in the West. The gradual trend toward a more sophisticated and more scholarly approach to Chinese art collecting in the West has certainly enhanced the market for Chinese sculpture, and this appears to be a continuing trend. Chinese sculpture from early periods has strong appeal for Far Eastern buyers, particularly the Japanese, and the increasing prosperity of the Far East should reinforce the rise in Chinese sculpture prices.

Minor Arts

There has recently been a rapid growth in collecting interest in a wide variety of Chinese works which are generally referred to as the "minor arts." The term minor arts is commonly used to refer to works other than ceramics, jades, paintings, and early sculpture or archaeological material and so includes objects in various materials and techniques such as lacquer, cloisonne enamels, painted enamels, carved bamboo, carved rhinoceros horn, glass, textiles, and hardstones. One important reason for the increased interest in collecting in these various fields is that Chinese ceramics have become too expensive for many buyers to contemplate forming a serious or extensive collection. It is still possible to buy the very best pieces in many of the minor arts categories without ever paying more than a few thousand dollars. While prices in the low-to-mid five-figure range are now not uncommon in some categories, the six-figure prices, which we are now quite used to for the finest pieces in the top range of the ceramics market, are unknown in the market for the minor arts.

One major collecting area in the minor arts that has developed rapidly is Chinese snuff bottles. These small (seldom over three inches) containers have been produced all over China since the seventeenth century, and they are made in every conceivable material and with every type of carved, enameled, painted, and applied decoration. Snuff bottles were treated as curiosities or were disregarded entirely by collectors until about 20 years ago, and at auction rooms they were sold in lots of five or ten or more at a time for very little money. Today the study of snuff bottles is well advanced, and there is a strong international snuff bottle collectors' society. The better-quality and rarer snuff bottles routinely sell for thousands of dollars each. A fine eighteenth-century imperial glass snuff bottle with enamel decoration was sold in 1979 by Sotheby Parke Bernet for a new world record price of $50,000, more than double the previous record.

Other sections of the minor arts have long been recognized and sought after by museums and private collectors. Chinese lacquer, particularly carved cinnabar lacquer of the Ming dynasty, has long been an important collecting area. Cloisonne enamels are also an area that is well established. There is a serious shortage of major early pieces in the market for lacquer and enamel wares, but prices for the better pieces that have come to market recently have been quite high.

The market for bamboo carvings is still quite new and developing, but there have been major scholarly works and museum exhibitions recently, and it appears likely that interest in bamboo carvings will continue to grow. Rhinoceros horn carvings are particularly popular in the Far East, and prices have been rising recently. Chinese glass, often referred to as "Peking glass," has also become increasingly popular among collectors over the past ten years, and prices for the earlier and better pieces have risen significantly. In all of these areas, a great deal of art historical research remains to be done.

Another area of increasing collector interest is the general category of "scholar's table articles"—objects such as brushpots, inkstones, seal paste boxes, brushrests, waterpots, seals, table screens, and other items related to painting and calligraphy. These items may be porcelain or jade but most often are in the minor arts category, and, as a general rule, the minor arts pieces that have some relation to this scholar's table category are the more sought after and more expensive pieces.

Textiles also might be included under the minor arts heading, and textile collecting has increased significantly over the past ten years, particularly in America. Several important museum exhibitions have been staged recently with scholarly, well-illustrated catalogues. Private collectors are buying Chinese textiles not only for display and decorative purposes but also as a serious collecting field, so that now the date and relative rarity of a textile can be every bit as important as the quality and condition in determining the price. Price levels for the earlier textiles in good condition have been rising steadily.

Jade

Jade carvings, which have been collected for centuries in China, have long been popular in the West. Nevertheless, jade prices have not kept pace with ceramics during the past 10 to 15 years. It is not too long ago that the best jades were as expensive as or more expensive than the best ceramics. In fact, during the 1959, 1960, and 1961 auction seasons, the most expensive Chinese art object sold at auction by Sotheby's in each year was a jade carving. Today ceramics routinely outpace jades in the major sales. While six-figure prices for important ceramics are seen at auction many times every year, even the most important jades seldom sell for more than $100,000, and many fine carvings are sold for much less.

One significant trend in jade collecting today is the growing interest in early and archaic jades. As collectors have become more aware of Chinese art history, the date of a jade carving has become a much more important factor in determining its price. Excavated archaic jades dating from 1200 B.C.–A.D. 200 (Shang dynasty–Han dynasty), which were formerly of interest to very few collectors outside of museum circles, are now much more widely understood and sought after. In recent auction sales, the archaic jade prices have risen sharply and the traditional museum buyers, while still active, are meeting stiff new competition from private collectors. The post-archaic jades of Ming and earlier dates are also increasingly sought after, and recent prices in that segment of the market have risen faster, in relative terms, than prices for later jades other than jewelry jade. Nevertheless, there are many problems encountered in dating early jades accurately. The study of Ming and earlier jades lags far behind the study of Ming and earlier ceramics. The basic agreement on chronology of style and the general consensus on proper criteria and correct prototypes for dating which now exists in the field of Chinese ceramics is still a long way off in the case of Chinese jades. This uncertainty factor clearly has a significant impact on the level of activity in the jade market and on the price levels in those segments of the market where dating is essential to the determination of scarcity and value. Recently, the increased archaeological activity and growing scholarly interest in earlier jades has had a positive effect on the market, but there are still serious problems to be overcome.

The question of dating is very often not as much of a problem for later (e.g., eighteenth- and nineteenth-century) jade carvings. All so-called Ming and earlier jades, particularly the archaic jades, have relatively little value unless the carving is authentic. For later jades, there is still a premium for eighteenth-century carvings, but the size of the stone and the quality of the carving are often much more important considerations in determining price. It is not at all unusual for a nineteenth-century or even a twentieth-century piece which is carved from a fine, pure stone to fetch a higher price than an eighteenth-century carving of similar size and type which is carved from a darker, less desirable stone. Although different colors of jade have been more or less popular among collectors over the years, a stone of even color without impurities or mottling is always preferable. White jades are particularly popular today and the purity of the stone is always a very important factor in deciding the price of a white jade carving. Bright green jadeite is the most popular and the most expensive type of jade in the market now. The intensity and clarity of the color is much more important than the date of the carving in determining the price of the best jadeite. Green jadeite is currently very popular among jewelry buyers, and any carving in which the stone is of good color, or even has a patch of good color, may be sought after as a rare material and may be considered more as a gemstone than a work of art. Sometimes the stone is cut up for jewelry and sometimes it is not, but fine-quality jadeite is currently the most expensive kind of jade. A pair of large jadeite table screens (17¼ inches high), less than 100 years old but of very good bright green color in some areas, were sold by Sotheby Parke Bernet in Hong

Kong for HK $1,400,000 (U.S. $297,500) in 1976, still the world auction record for Chinese jade.

Painting

Chinese paintings are not a new field of collecting by any means, but it is only very recently that major public sales have met with any real success. There has been rapid growth in the Chinese painting market over the past five years, but it is still a very small part of the total picture. The main obstacle to growth is the uncertainty factor. A great deal of organized art historical research is now going on, but the area to be covered is vast and complex and the work has really only just begun in the West. Even in the case of well-known artists, it is often very difficult to obtain a consensus among art historians, and it is not uncommon for well-respected experts to disagree on the date or attribution of well-known paintings in museums here and around the world.

Nevertheless, the art historical research continues and the opening of China is sure to give researchers greater opportunity and better resources. Significant progress has been made during the past 20 years, and the pace of study and the rate of progress has been steadily accelerating. There are now many more well-educated, serious, and sophisticated museum curators and collectors in the field of Chinese paintings than ever before. This growth of interest and participation has brought about a significant increase in the number of serious auction sales, and the better-quality paintings have sold for much higher prices in recent sales. A fine Ming painting by a well-known artist was sold at Sotheby Parke Bernet New York in November 1979 for $110,000, the current world auction record for a Chinese painting. The buyer was an American private collector, but the underbidder was an American museum. American museums are more active in the Chinese painting market than they are in any other area of Chinese art.

The market for Chinese ancestor portraits and other decorative Chinese paintings (i.e., paintings that may or may not be early in date and that are anonymous or of uncertain attribution) is very active now, and prices are quite high in relative terms, although seldom over four figures. There is no indication that prices for paintings in this category may go down, but over the long term, they are unlikely to appreciate as rapidly as prices for other paintings.

The greatest potential for price appreciation, for real growth, is in the area of early Chinese paintings. The paintings of the Song (Sung), Yuan, Ming, and Qing (Ch'ing) dynasties (twelfth to nineteenth centuries) by known artists are currently more expensive than anonymous or unattributed paintings, but they are still far less expensive than good Chinese ceramics of the same date.

If the Chinese painting market can reasonably be expected to develop and mature over the next two or three decades in the same way that the Chinese ceramics market did over the past 20 or 30 years, then this is clearly a time of great opportunity. It must be emphasized, however, that the market for early Chinese paintings is currently an area of great uncertainty and maximum risk.

The fastest-growing part of the Chinese painting market today is modern and contemporary paintings. Far Eastern buyers are very active in this area. American museums and private collectors have shown a growing interest, which is enhanced by the steady opening up of China to more and more tourists. Since dating is seldom a problem and attributions are significantly less difficult, buyers have much more confidence and the rising prices clearly reflect this confident attitude.

Modern and contemporary Chinese paintings are now available for purchase in China. The authorities have permitted a large group of paintings to be bought by one overseas company in at least one instance, and a great many individuals have been able to buy one or a few paintings. Prices quoted for modern and contemporary paintings in China are, as a rule, quite a bit higher than prices for comparable paintings available on the auction market outside China.

Supply of works of art

When the current Chinese regime came to power in 1949, the flow of Chinese works of art to the West was gradually cut off. Over time, many antiques and works of art that had been in private hands were gathered up by the government. During the 1970s, as new channels of trade with the West began to develop, a carefully controlled and limited selection of these pieces was made available to dealers and tourists. Until late 1979, a policy of restricting trade to later decorative material was carefully enforced, and no ceramics or other works of art dating from before the nineteenth century could be taken out of China.

Recently, there has been a gradual loosening of this policy, and some earlier pieces, such as minor Tang pottery tomb figures, have been made available to tourists, usually at prices quite a bit higher than retail prices for comparable pieces in the West. Other minor works of art, jades, and some pre-nineteenth-century porcelains have been made available as well. None of the pieces released to date is of the very finest quality. The supply has been quite small and the prices have been, as a rule, at or above the current market level for comparable pieces outside China. It seems very unlikely that the Chinese might sell rarer and finer ceramics and works of art regardless of price, but in the event that any important works of art were made available, there is no doubt that the prices asked would be as high as or higher than prevailing world market levels.

In the area of Imperial porcelains, jades, and non-archaeological works of art, it is not at all clear that a significant number of fine pieces could be sold without seriously depleting the national museums. In this context it should be remembered that a great majority of the Ming and Qing (Ch'ing) ceramics, paintings, and works of art from the former Peking palace collections are now in Taiwan, in the National Palace museum. There is certainly a large supply of archaeological material available in China, such as Han or Tang pottery and bronzes, including a vast quantity that is still unexcavated. The best of the archaeological finds would certainly be kept as part of the national heritage, for museums, and to continue the politically important and lucrative programs of traveling museum exhibitions outside China. Any archaeological material that might be made available for sale would certainly be carefully controlled and priced in keeping with conditions prevailing in the world market.

Prices and value

Prices for the finest and rarest Chinese works of art are currently very high, and it is useful to remember that this was not always true. In fact, price levels for Chinese art remained extremely low, compared to today, for over 20 years after World War II. Prices began to climb slowly around the mid-1950s and continued to rise at a moderate but steady pace until the late 1960s. A steep rise began in 1969–70 and continued at an accelerating pace through the early 1970s until, by 1973, prices for certain selected categories in the ceramics market increased 100 percent or more in just six months' time. Quite a bit of speculative buying took place during this period and the market finally hit a peak in the spring of 1974, which was followed by quite a severe fall in prices during the latter part of 1974 and early 1975. The recovery was remarkably rapid, however, and most prices returned to levels very near the peak of 1978–79. By 1979–80, several sectors of the market began to show prices edging above previous highs. Table 16-1 shows how different Chinese ceramics have compared in value since 1950. Table 16-2 shows the value of Chinese ceramics in comparison with the Dow Jones Industrial Average. Table 16-3 compares the return on regular investment in Chinese art with that of investment in the Dow Jones Industrials.

As has already been mentioned, the entry of Far Eastern buyers into the world market is one of the most significant factors determining the recent history of the Chinese art market. The increasing participation of

Table 16-1. Indices of Chinese ceramics (1970 = 100).

Year	T'ang	Sung	Ming	Ch'ing Export	Ch'ing Domestic	All Ceramics
1951	2	28	4	21	21	12
1952	2	26	5	20	20	12
1953	7	22	5	21	21	12
1954	11	19	6	16	16	12
1955	12	26	7	20	20	14
1956	9	22	14	23	23	18
1957	12	20	15	33	33	20
1958	13	20	16	36	36	21
1959	15	30	14	43	43	25
1960	16	44	25	55	55	34
1961	22	52	32	68	68	43
1962	28	61	40	66	66	48
1963	33	68	44	62	62	51
1964	44	79	41	83	83	58
1965	31	79	62	73	73	64
1966	50	79	70	100	100	77
1967	59	106	82	110	110	90
1968	81	105	81	110	110	93
1969	129	113	95	99	99	103
1970	100	100	100	100	100	100
1971	103	280	155	191	191	178
1972	341	528	213	235	235	285
1973	337	483	103	352	352	619
1974	279	212	431	153	153	304
1975	256	164	171	76	76	156
1976	210	313	268	124	434	255
1977	283	379	357	151	534	328
1978	370	488	537	158	679	450

Japanese buyers in the late 1960s and early 1970s was an important part of the price boom, and the Japanese pulled out quite rapidly at the time of the "oil shock" in 1974, contributing greatly to the fall in the market. Today, the Japanese are not as important to the overall market as they were ten years ago, and Far Eastern participation has broadened considerably. The Hong Kong buyers are now just as important as the Japanese in some sectors of the market, and there is rapidly growing participation from Taiwan, Singapore, Bangkok, and elsewhere in the Far East. At the same time, the American market is growing and broadening very rapidly, and

Table 16-2. Indices of Chinese ceramics (1970 = 100).

Year	Chinese Ceramics		Dow Jones Industrial Index[1]	
	Basic	Adjusted for Inflation[2]	Basic	Adjusted for Inflation[2]
1951	12	18	15	22
1952	12	18	17	25
1953	12	17	17	25
1954	12	17	26	38
1955	14	20	33	48
1956	18	26	36	51
1957	20	28	33	46
1958	21	28	46	62
1959	25	33	55	73
1960	34	45	51	67
1961	43	56	63	82
1962	48	62	58	74
1963	51	65	70	89
1964	58	72	84	105
1965	64	79	96	119
1966	77	92	81	96
1967	90	105	96	112
1968	93	103	104	116
1969	103	110	92	98
1970	100	100	100	100
1971	178	171	110	106
1972	285	264	130	120
1973	619	543	113	99
1974	304	239	86	68
1975	156	112	125	90
1976	255	173	153	104
1977	328	210	134	86
1978	450	268	137	82

Notes
1. The Dow Jones Industrial Index has been adjusted to allow for the re-investment of gross dividends.
2. The adjustment for inflation is based on the Consumer Price Index.

major sales in London, New York, or Hong Kong are drawing an increasingly diverse and sophisticated audience.

Although it is dangerous to rely too much on generalizations and stereotypes, American and Japanese buyers tend to be more active in the market for archaeological material and earlier ceramics, up to and in-

Table 16-3. Yield for regular annual investments in Chinese ceramics.

		Chinese Ceramics	Dow Jones Industrials	
			Gross Dividend Reinvested	Net Dividend Reinvested
If $1,000 were invested each year since [a] 1960 and [b] 1970, the accumulated value at the end of 1978 would be:	[a]	$85,978	$28,652	$21,798
	[b]	16,214	10,489	9,188
If the objects were sold at the end of 1978, the sum realized after allowing for expenses would be:	[a]	77,380	28,652	21,798
	[b]	14,593	10,489	9,188
This represents an average annual compound growth rate of:	[a]	13.8%	4.4%	1.5%
	[b]	11.7%	3.8%	0.5%

Notes: 1. The figures for Chinese ceramics allow for the expenses of dealing as follows:
   a. On buying, it has been assumed that the 10 percent buyer's premium was in force through the period and an appropriate deduction has been made from each $1,000 investment.
   b. On selling, a 10 percent deduction has been made from the value of the fund to allow for the seller's commission.
   2. No allowance for expenses has been made for the stockmarket investments.
   3. The Dow Jones figures for reinvestment of net dividends assume a tax rate of 70 percent.

cluding Sung, Yuan, and early Ming (fifteenth-century) wares; Hong Kong and other Far Eastern buyers tend to prefer the later porcelains, particularly the Imperial wares, and are strong bidders for Ming porcelains, particularly pieces bearing the mark of the reign. American buyers are very active in the entire painting market; Hong Kong buyers tend to prefer modern paintings. Japanese buyers are generally not interested in jades other than archaic jades. American buyers are interested in all jades, and Hong Kong buyers are very keen on the later jades, particular pure white nephrite or brightly colored jadeite.

Condition

Another generalization that might be made about regional markets is that Western and, to some extent, Japanese buyers are more tolerant of damages or repairs, while the Hong Kong or overseas Chinese buyers are extremely demanding in matters of condition and will discount heavily for any damage or flaws or will even pass over damaged pieces entirely. At any rate, the condition of a piece is always an important consideration, particularly in terms of the current and possible future valuation. As prices have risen, the difference between the price of a perfect piece and the price of the same piece in damaged condition has widened considerably. The statistics for resold pieces show that price levels for damaged pieces have often moved erratically and have increased much less rapidly, or, in some cases, not increased at all. This is particularly true of Ming and Qing (Ch'ing) porcelains. The buyer's expectations and the rules of the game are often quite different for archaeological material and earlier wares, but the fact remains that some discounting occurs whenever there is a problem of condition involved. The diminishing supply of the best-quality material may change this state of affairs in the long run, but at the moment any change in this basic attitude appears very unlikely or very long range.

The impact of condition (i.e., state of preservation or amount of damage) as it relates to value is necessarily an area of serious concern for collectors who are thinking about the investment potential of Chinese works of art. For collectors who are more concerned with aesthetics, the fact that even minor damage can have a major impact on prices might be regarded as very good news indeed. The collector who is attempting to form a comprehensive collection or acquire specific rare examples will simultaneously find the range of possibilities expanded and expenses lowered by considering damaged as well as perfect pieces. Many museums are finding this approach useful. Whether or not investment is the primary concern, every buyer wants to pay no more than necessary, and it is always important to be aware of the role condition plays in determining price.

The other major criteria determining the value of Chinese works of art are scarcity, quality, and fashion. Of the three, the most important in the long run certainly must be fashion, defined as the prevailing taste at any given time.

Fashion

Fashion is of concern not only to decorators and rich private collectors. There are also changes of fashion in art historical research, and a period or a category of works of art that may be regarded as aesthetically superior today can be ruthlessly demoted tomorrow by a change of the prevailing aesthetic theory. There need not be any real change in the dating, attribution, quality, or relative scarcity of the particular works of art. If the aesthetic criteria that are agreed among art historians and collectors to be the correct basis for judging the desirability and importance of a piece undergo significant change, then the desirability and the appraisal (in every sense of the word) of that piece will also change. This can occur without change in the piece itself and need not imply that the piece is "wrong" or fake; it has simply dropped out of fashion. When a work of art is no longer in vogue, fewer buyers will be chasing after it, and the relative scarcity and value of the piece must be affected. When one considers the role of fashion or taste in determining the value of a work of art, the conventional wisdom that most advisors give to buyers considering works of art for investment, "buy only the finest quality," begins to lose some of its validity. As the aesthetic criteria evolve over time and tastes change, so does the definition of what constitutes the "finest quality."

As an example of this process of changing taste at work in the market, consider the price history of Kangxi (K'ang Hsi) blue and white porcelain. In the late nineteenth century and during the early part of this century, Kangxi (K'ang Hsi) blue and white was among the most fashionable and most sought after of all Chinese porcelains. The praise of the art historians was echoed by the artists and aesthetes of the day. Whistler included Kangxi (K'ang Hsi) blue and white in his paintings, and leading collectors such as J. P. Morgan and Charles Langdon Freer constantly competed for the "best" pieces. These porcelains were not new to the West. A large supply had been exported to Amsterdam in the seventeenth century, and many early European collections, such as that formed by the Elector of Saxony in Dresden in the eighteenth century, included several examples of all the different shapes. The only difference was that these porcelains were suddenly in vogue, they were the height of fashion, and the prices paid for the "best" pieces soon began to reflect this state of affairs. Buyers became accustomed to paying relatively high prices for the best examples in perfect condition and with a "good" color of blue—the brighter blue the better, according to the aesthetic canons of the day.

In 1905, the famous A. C. Huth "blue hawthorne" vase was sold at auction for the then fantastic price of   5,900. The piece was a good example of a type of covered jar with white prunus blossoms on cobalt blue grounds, which is often referred to as a "ginger jar" and which is today regarded as one of the more common types of blue and white porcelain. The Huth blue hawthorne vase was resold in 1974; despite its famous history, the price in 1974 was £1,785. This is not an isolated case, nor was the craze for Kangxi (K'ang Hsi) blue and white short-lived. In 1914 or 1915, the famous art dealer Duveen sold to the American collector E. T. Stotesbury a fine large blue and white bottle approximately 17 inches high for a reputed $50,000. The vase was resold in 1958, properly identified as Kangxi (K'ang Hsi) with all its reputation, for $1,700.

There are similar stories to be told in other sections of the market. Tang pottery horses were very popular in the early part of this century, when they first appeared on the market in the West, but their popularity was not constant even though they are very much in fashion and expensive today. During the period 1927–48, it was almost impossible to find a Tang horse that sold for more than a few hundred dollars. The brightly glazed Song (Sung) Jun (Chun) wares, which were very expensive and very popular in the 1920s, gradually fell out of favor and were very low in public esteem, with prices to match, by end of the 1940s. Prices for Jun (Chun) Yao did not recover until the late 1960s, but there is now a well-established upward trend, and prices for the best Jun (Chun) ware are among the highest paid for any Song (Sung) ceramics today.

There have been many important sales of well-known Chinese art collections during the 1960s and 1970s. The heady success of these sales has been well recorded and widely publicized. As the prices paid for almost every lot far exceeded the original purchase prices, the sellers were declared to be wise and successful investors. But they were not in fact investors when they were buying. They were collectors. As collectors, they bought what they liked and not what they were told to buy. In many noteworthy cases, they bought exactly what they were told not to buy, and for some of the best pieces they may have paid much more than they were advised was the "right price" at the time. They also made some mistakes, and they had a great deal of fun.

The idea of buying Chinese works of art with investment values in mind is not new. In fact, it is possible to trace references to the investment potential of works of art to Chinese literature of the thirteenth century A.D. Nevertheless, the idea of setting out to purchase Chinese works of art solely for investment must be regarded as a new phenomenon. It remains to be seen whether pure investment buying will prove to be a successful strategy in the long run.

Acknowledgments

The author wishes to acknowledge the contribution of Jeremy Eckstein, Art Market Analyst for the Sotheby Group Ltd., in providing the accompanying analytical data, and the support and patient assistance provided by Robert Schonfeld, former director of Institutional Services, Sotheby Parke Bernet, New York.

A View from the Eighth Pole

George Peppard

Investing in a movie is like investing in oil—if you like wildcatting. The risks are high and the rewards uncertain. In 1974, I took a year off from acting and did nothing but explore independent financing for independent films. There were several tax shelters available at that time in film making, but I did not take advantage of them, feeling that potential problems with the IRS in the future could cancel any tax break I might promise an investor. I believed that one should invest in a

film only to make money, regardless of deductibility. Not all tax consultants agree that certain corporate write-offs in film investment are deductible.

During that year I talked and met with investors from California to Maine, from the State of Washington to Florida. I was amazed at the number of people who had invested in films in the past and had current capital to invest but would not touch film financing again with a very long stick. Most of these investors had been involved with what I have come to think of as "suede shoe" operators: real producers and supposed producers who started to shoot their pictures before their complete budgets were in the bank—a fatal error that raises the unappetizing possibility of having to *eat* rather than screen the film footage; would-be producers or promoters who swore that stars were committed to projects, but didn't have a script; actors who jumped into film making the same way you throw a baby into a pool to see if it can swim (incidentally, babies do better than actors); legitimate producers who produced a film, then could not get it distributed; fundraisers who might raise $300,000 in St. Louis and deliver $200,000 to the film's producer in Los Angeles. By keeping the real investors and producer separated, the fundraiser keeps the investors from finding out about the missing $100,000. The fundraiser has made a profit. The investors probably have no chance—partly because of the mythical, magical, illusive definition of "break-even."

Film investment falls into two main categories: investing with a major company, and investing with an independent. Financing a motion picture goes like this. All budgets are divided into two categories. One is above-the-line expenses, which include all of the creative talent: the actors, the director, the producer, the screen writer, and, if there is a purchase of a book involved, the amount of the purchase price. Below the line is everything else, from the sugared donuts you would normally find on the set, to the hard-to-find special brassiere for your buxom star, to the $480,000 you have to spend to create a diesel-powered futuristic tank that is amphibious.

In 1979, the average budget for an average film, if one can legitimately use the word "average" in this context, was $4.5 million. By the beginning of 1980, the "average" major studio productions were costing between 6.1 million and 8.4 million dollars. We'll stick with 1979 for our figures because the formula doesn't change, just the numbers. If extrapolation pleases you, go ahead. God knows what "average" will mean in 1981.

This total package figure may or may not include overhead, the cost the studio charges for the use of its facility. Studio overhead is usually 30 percent. Let's say our mythical friends in St. Louis have an honest fundraiser. Their original $300,000 investment would now have to return $390,000 before they get their money back. Film makers of all categories bitch unanimously and constantly about studio overhead, but it is partly this cushion of extra money that allows major film companies to produce numbers of films, knowing that some of them won't make money.

After the film is shot, additional expenses mount: the advertising and the prints you show in your local theater. The advertising budget, let's say, is $1,000,000—a topflight or "A" picture would be twice that. It can cost as much to advertise a $4.5 million picture as it does a $10 million picture, though major studios do spend more money to protect higher investments. Prints are not cheap. They run about $1,000 each. The number of prints could be 100 in a small release, 500 to 800 on a saturation release. So, the $4.5 million film is screened for the executives of the company. They have what they consider a chance to "break out" or *(Did they say their prayers today?)* "hit"! They order 300 prints of it, bringing its total cost to $5.8 million.

The distribution fee for a major distributing organization can range from 20 to 40 percent. This fee enables the major companies to maintain offices for distributing the film throughout the world. Of course, if they are good businesspeople, there is a considerable cushion in this distribution fee to tide them over the rough spots, and, make no mistake about it, they are very good businesspeople.

Where do the dollars come from and where do they go? This is the way it works. The theater owner makes a deal with the distributor in which the owner might agree to a 90–10 split on a blockbuster picture; that is, 90 percent of the box office dollars go to the distributor and 10 percent to the theater owner. The war between the distributors and the theater owners is legendary. The distributors claim the theater owners do not report proper box office receipts, that they keep the money from unscheduled screenings, and that they refuse to cut the distributors in on the take from the popcorn concession. Don't laugh about the popcorn concession. The theater owner can make more money on that with a full house of hungry patrons on a 90–10 deal than on a 50–50 deal in which the picture is a "dog." The theater owners claim that the distributors force them to play "flops," "dogs," or "turkeys" and lose money, or face the possibility of having the distributors deny them a chance to play a truly big budget picture with the biggest stars and an enormous publicity campaign. A $20 million picture gets about a $5 million campaign. At times, both the distributors and the theater owners are, no doubt, quite correct in their complaints.

For our imaginary picture, let us say the split is 60–40. That means for every dollar that comes in, the distributor will see 60 cents. That 60 cents and all the money that follows must first pay back the prints and advertising, in this case, $1.3 million. That same 60 cents is subjected to a distribution fee, of, let's say, 30 percent. So, 51 cents of every dollar received from the box office is applied toward repaying the cost of the film, which, in our example, has the 30 percent overhead built into the $4.5 million.

At the point that the picture has grossed box office $5 million, the distributor sees $3 million of that amount. Take away the $1.3 million for prints and advertising and $1.7 million is left. Accounting for the distribution fee now shown, the distributor reduces the production cost by $1.19 million. Now our average picture has grossed $5 million at the box office and is still $3.31 million in the red. *(Are you sure you don't like horse racing better?)* Insiders claim a break-even comes at 1.8 times cost of the film. Most studios do business on a 2.8 times the "in the can" cost of the film. So much for the majors.

The independent producer can take a property to a major studio for funding. If possible, the producer can presell to television as an encouragement to investors who want a better "take out." If the price from the network is high enough, then investors are not necessary. If the script is appealing and stars are well known, the producer can presell to foreign markets. If the script is sold to a network, the producer must cover the cost of editing any nudity or profanity for the television airing, and also subscribe to the network's complete casting approval. This is the same situation the producer faces by going to the major film company for financing.

Preselling foreign, a common practice, has the drawback of selling for less than the picture would get if it were completed, in order to induce the foreign investor to put up the front money to make the film. This can be an advantage. Reputedly, Joe Levine on the film *A Bridge too Far,* presold his multi-star epic for $11 million more than its cost, *before* the picture was released. It was great for Joe, but the exhibitors did not sell much popcorn on that one. The independent producer must keep open books for the investors, and it will cost $10,000 to $20,000 to audit a major. The overhead is not a flat percentage; the independent producer's expenses are as shown on the books. But, assuming the producer alone raises the money and completes the picture, a distributing organization is a must for prints and advertising. Because the picture has been completed at no risk to the distributing organization, the producer is in a better position to negotiate a distribution deal.

The one picture that I produced, *Five Days from Home,* was distributed by Universal Pictures. After prints and advertising had been deducted, my deal called for approximately a 50–50 split of all monies received, including the sale to television.

Will our friends in St. Louis have their original investment returned to them if the movie grosses $10,714,285.70 at the box office? No. A picture doesn't just have to break out. It has to break out *fast.* We haven't been counting the interest that the major levies annually on the full budget amount—*including overhead*—until the picture "breaks even." Normal release is considered complete after about three years with 80 to 90 percent of the gross in the first year. If you don't break out in those three years, that's $2,025,000 at 15 percent interest in carrying charges. So, even if the picture had grossed around $11 million on the last day of the third year, our friends would still be a couple of million in the red on the company books; the picture still has to gross another $5 million at the box office. Sixteen or seventeen million dollars would flow through the little opening in the glass beneath the sign "Matinee Today" before our investors in St. Louis got their money back.

Our major company executives are not *entirely* unhappy, however. After all, they put up only $3.15 million in cash. (Remember the 30 percent overhead? They do.) And, of the $16 million box office receipts, they have collected $4.8 million in distribution fees, $1.35 million in overhead, and $2.025 million in interest. They have collected around $8 million dollars (less expenses) and the investors are paid back—no profit for them, but what the hell, nobody's perfect. After all, the company charges the same fees for *all* the 20 pictures it makes and releases, doesn't it? *(How about Churchill Downs or Santa Anita?)*

Would the investors really be better off if they had invested with an independent? Neither the independent nor the major film company knows before shooting a picture if the public will like it. Indeed, sometimes the companies don't know until after a picture is released. The story goes that the box office smash, *Easy Rider,* an inexpensive film to make, was not recognized as a hit until a studio executive, enroute to a Broadway show, saw a line in front of a theater from his limousine window. Investors are better off in the sense that they have a substantial company spending a substantial amount of money. That company will tend to protect its own money, as well as that of its investors, and protect its reputation on Wall Street. In any given instance, then, is the investor investing money in a picture with a greater possibility of making money? No. Major companies have flops, just as do independents. Companies survive because they make a sufficient number of pictures. That gives them a chance at that magical hit, the *Star Wars,* the *Jaws,* the *Close Encounters of the Third Kind.*

So what does the investor look for? Company backing? Stars? Famous directors? No. The investor should look for a cinematic geologist. The investor can, of course, take a flyer because he or she thinks a movie would make money. Many of the disappointed investors that I contacted in 1974 were in this category. Their sad tales substantiated that, while not everybody wants to be in show business, everybody believes they understand movie making because they've seen so many movies. I don't blame them for falling into the exultant fantasy that *they absolutely knew* the picture would be a success. Everyone in the business has been transported by that dream of surety at least once. I do blame them for not soliciting expert advice. It is available. Primarily, advice on the quality and commercial possibilities of the script, the stars considered to be cast in specific roles, and, most importantly, the quality of the director. This does not guarantee a return on the investment, nor can it guarantee a hit, but it does prevent the investor from being carried away by his or her own uneducated fantasy.

The best way to invest in a film is *(Well, if you don't like Santa Anita, how about Saratoga, or Hialeah? It's your money.)* to form a syndicate of investors represented by one person who speaks for the group. Finding roperties to invest in is no problem. News gets around Los Angeles as fast as a 4.5 temblor. Scripts fall like rain, but which one to pick? What stars to cast? At what price? Which director? The syndicate representative can find good independent counseling in the business. There are several in Los Angeles. Charlie Powell of Powell and Young is an outstanding example.

The advantages of a syndicate start with the fact that there are no SEC regulations prohibiting investors from approaching a film producer; investors can talk to as many as they want. The reverse situation is necessarily subject to many strictures. During my fundraising period, an investor offered to invest $50,000 and wire it to me that day. At that point I couldn't even make a proposal to him without running the risk of breaking the SEC rule of public offerings. Assuming the members of the syndicate are not using money allocated for their car payments, their risk consists only of the portion of the investment that they put up. Their representative, whose time is paid for out of the money raised, delivers expert advice on where and how to place their money. Most importantly, a syndicate is in the position to invest not just in one film, but in several, thus attaining the posture of a miniature major film company by giving itself more than one chance to make money in an unpredictable market.

Can you make money investing in films? I can only say somewhat smugly that my investors did. I made *Five Days from Home* for $1 million, sold it to Universal for $1.25 million for domestic release only and retained all foreign rights as profit. Approximately ten months after I rolled a camera, my investors were repaid and are still receiving profits. While that may sound like bragging, I still don't know whether to laugh or cry. The picture had a well-publicized debut, but was disappointing at the box office. Universal expects to recoup its investment from pay TV and the network sale.

So, I can assure you, gentle reader, that *I absolutely know* my next picture will be a success, and I will welcome you with open arms when I produce my next film.

What was that you said? Me invest in someone else's picture?

You've gotta be kidding.

Hit or Wipeout

Gerald Schoenfeld

Gerald Schoenfeld, a practicing lawyer for most of his career, took on a new role in 1972 when he became Chairman of the Board of The Shubert Organization, a corporation that owns and operates 23 theaters (17 in New York, others in Boston, Philadelphia, Chicago, Washington, D.C., and Los Angeles), and both produces and invests in plays. As chairman, Mr. Schoenfeld has been connected with the production of such popular shows as The Sly Fox, Sherlock Holmes, Children of a Lesser God, Dancin', The Act, The Gin Game, *and* Ain't Misbehavin'. *The perfect person, we thought, to write a chapter on investing in the theater.*

Well, almost.

"I'd love to," was Gerry's response to our suggestion, "but I'd rather talk than write. Is there any reason we can't do it on a Q and A basis?"

None we could think of. Thus, tape recorder in tow, we appeared one morning at the Schoenfeld office in Shubert Alley. Here is the gist of what was said.

Q: Gerry, let's not beat around the bush. Does it make sense to invest in the theater?

A: It's like anything else. If you have a hit, it's a good investment. If you don't, it's not. But in the theater, a bad investment is usually a wipeout, and it usually happens quickly. Very few, if any, shows overcome unanimously negative reviews, particularly if we're talking about New York. Sometimes you may run a show awhile before you are totally wiped out, but it usually happens very close to opening night.

Q: Can you think of a promising-looking show that bombed out on night one?

A: We had high hopes for *Prince of Grand Street*, which never even made it to New York. It opened in Philadelphia to bad reviews. We moved it to Boston, where it got more bad reviews, and we closed it. Another one was *The Merchant*, starring Zero Mostel. Unfortunately, Zero died in Philadelphia. We continued with the Philadelphia production, then took it to Washington after laying off for a rehearsal with a new lead. When it opened in New York, we had to close because it didn't get good notices. *Ballroom* was another show that we had very high hopes for. It got marvelous notices in the wrong places and bad notices in the right places.

Q: What are the wrong places?

A: The weeklies, trade papers, and others that may be prestigious but don't have the readership mix or the following to make an impact. I never made an actual count, but I dare say that *Ballroom* received many more positive notices than negative ones. If numbers was the criterion, it would have been a hit. Occasionally, of course, a show will be popular even if it doesn't get a good notice in *The New York Times*. *Dancin'* and *Death Trap* are two examples of shows that were saved by good reviews in other media, namely television.

Q: What's an example of a big success?

A: We didn't produce it, but *Chorus Line* is a phenomenal success.

Q. Who produced it, and how do you define phenomenal?

A: The ownership of *Chorus Line* is split between Joe Papp and Michael Bennett, on a 75–25 percent basis. It was funded by the New York Shakespeare Festival, and it cost about $375,000 to move it from the public theater to Broadway. It had workshop costs and opening expenses at the public theater, so maybe it cost $700,000 in total. Profits on *Chorus Line* are probably approaching $40 million today. They're still gushing and will continue to do so for many years.

We were fortunate enough to have *Chorus Line* presented in our theaters so it's been a gusher for us. It has been a gusher for the whole American theater because it has provided weeks of playing time for theaters throughout the country, many of which are older theaters in downtown urban centers that are barely hanging on. When you have a *Chorus Line*, an *Annie*, a *Wiz*, an *Evita*, and other shows of that stripe, you are really sustaining the whole fabric of theater throughout the United States. Ultimately, of course, these shows will be in stock and in regional theaters throughout the country, so they move into the repertory of American theater.

Grease recently passed *Fiddler* as the longest running Broadway show, but *Fiddler* played in a much larger theater so I would assume that the number of people who saw *Fiddler* is greater than the number who saw *Grease*. But you can't simply judge by the New York audience. When you add in all the road companies, I couldn't say how many Americans have seen *Grease* as against *Fiddler*. Both are phenomenal income producers, not only in the area of the stage but also in that of movies and music.

Investor participation

Q: Do investors participate in the total financial fallout?

A: Yes and no. Investors share in subsidiary rights, which is income from motion pictures, radio, television, stock, amateur, foreign language, and the like, but they don't share in the music rights except for the original cast album. That doesn't mean that one day publishing rights to the individual musical compositions won't be acquired by a producer and shared by investors, but traditionally that is not the case. Today, all that the producer acquires in his or her own right is the right to present the play in the United States, Canada, and the British Isles. That includes, of course, the right to present bus and truck tours.

Q: Bus and truck being—?

A: A road company that travels by bus and truck, as distinguished from a first-class company that generally travels by air and plays for longer engagements. That does not mean that it's less professional, but the scenery and props are scaled down to meet the requirements of fitting on a truck, and the cast travels by bus. Rules are changing in this business, but bus and truck companies generally play where first-class companies don't, which are the smaller cities, and for shorter periods of time.

Q: Everybody has 20-20 hindsight in every business, but what's the difference between a *Chorus Line* or a *Fiddler* and a show that seems to have all sorts of promise but just doesn't make it?

A: A show is only as good as its creative people, so material is the most important criterion. If you don't like the material, obviously you are not going to go ahead. But the creative people also must be skilled in several important respects. They must be able to make changes under pressure. Understand one thing—you are dealing with authors, and authors have pride. They tend to be stubborn and don't like to see their material changed. The ground rules in this business are such that a producer or director cannot change the material without the author's consent, so intransigence on the part of an author is often the death knell.

The producer and director also have vital roles. The producer must be a strong general. He or she has to be coercive and manipulative, persuasive, endearing, and whatever. The producer is, or should be, in charge. Obviously you want your product as refined as possible before it starts rehearsals. That's why musicals will probably go through an evolutionary workshop phase in the future before going into rehearsal. With musical costs approaching the $1.5 to 2 million range, putting a show into rehearsal without going through a workshop period injects a big element of risk. You have to pay people during the workshop period, of course, but it gives you the chance to get your product as refined as possible.

The director is the one who welds the various creative elements of the show together. Today, many of the more successful directors function as both director and choreographer. In any case, you must make sure that you have a strong person at the helm in panic time when things do not go well. You really only see a musical for the first time when the rehearsal period is coming to an end. The various segments—the dancers, the chorus, and the principals—have been rehearsing their separate ways, and it's only when they are all put together as an ensemble that you get an idea of how the book and the score merge into a show and whether your appraisal of it from reading and listening to a tape of the music was correct. And then, of course, you have to have enough money in your budget to be able to pay for the changes that you need. If you have intransigence on the part of authors with respect to changes that you feel are necessary, you have a very difficult problem.

Chance for success

Q: How many shows make it and how many don't?

A: The majority don't make it, but making it is subject to definition. If you mean paying back the investment as determining whether or not a show makes it, maybe one or two out of five. But if you talk in terms of total profits, a show like a *Chorus Line*—which cost less than $1 million to produce and is now in its fifth year on Broadway—is still going strong and will offset the losses incurred by ten musicals. As an industry, I'd guess that the profits exceed the losses, but you have to be riding a winner. Just like the oil business. It's profitable in the overall sense, but if you invest in one well, the odds of coming up with a hole that is productive are against you.

Q: In the oil business, one out of nine wildcats is a success.

A: We have a much better record than that. But in addition to the economics, the lure of this business is the potential of being involved with show people and creative people, of going to auditions and to opening night and to the party that follows. And of telling your friends that you are an investor in *Fiddler On The Roof,* so everyone will say how smart you are and what taste you've got and how much you've made on your money.

Q: Sounds great. How do you go about investing in a Broadway show?

A: The financing of Broadway shows is done in an archaic manner. It goes back to a concept evolved in 1941 by John Wharton, probably the most respected and liked lawyer who was ever in this business. In essence, investors, who put up 100 percent of the money, participate in a limited partnership and share 50 percent of the profits after recoupment. Until recoupment, the investors take 100 percent of the profits to pay back their investment. After recoupment, the producer takes the other 50 percent of the profits. The producer also receives what is known as a cash office charge for running the production office. That used to be a couple hundred dollars a week, but it now goes to close to a thousand for a musical.

The producer also gets a percentage of the gross weekly box office receipts as a management fee, which generally goes to about 2 percent after recoupment of production costs. Some people have given the investors 60 percent of the profits and have taken 40 percent as the producer's share.

The production company also receives a percentage of subsidiary rights, such as motion picture and television sales, radio rights, foreign rights, stock and amateur rights, and so on, over a fixed period of time. Since the investors are the limited partners in the production company, they share this income with the producer, who is the general partner. Income from these rights belongs entirely to the investors until they recoup their capital contributions. A show that cost $300,000 might be a total loss but could be sold for a motion picture for, let's say, $400,000. The author must give the producer 40 percent of that, or $160,000, which will go entirely to the investors.

Unless it's an intrastate offering, you register the limited partnership interests with the SEC. Then you seek to sell the limited partnership interests to prospective investors. You are required, of course, to comply with the Blue Sky Laws of the states in which you are selling. There is often a provision for an overcall in the agreement. If you start out thinking you will need $500,000 of capital, you might have a 20 percent overcall provision. That means you can call on the investors to put in an extra $100,000. And every public offering contains a statement that says, in effect, that this is a highly speculative offering and that no one should invest in it unless he is prepared to run the risk of losing the total investment.

Q: Does the prospectus contain data on the producer's track record?

A: Yes, but you've got to remember that if I had had *Fiddler On The Roof,* I would have a good overall record even if all my other shows were failures. Investors may have lost $3 million on ten shows and made $15 million on *Fiddler,* and it may be that 500 people lost the $3 million while 100 made the $15 million.

A track record is significant, but each property is obviously different. The authors are usually different and there are various types of producers. There are producers like Hal Prince, who also function as directors. Hal Prince has demonstrated that he can do it, but you wouldn't want to touch some people who act as producer-director because the producer who functions as the director does not have a producer overlooking his or her work. You also have to look at the creative team that has been assembled—the director, the writers, and, to a somewhat lesser degree, although their contributions are invaluable, the costumer, scenic designer, and lighting designer. They are all important. A fellow who is going to design a bad set is going to hurt a production immeasurably, both in its operations and its production cost. The same is true of the costumer, because the critics judge each aspect of a show today.

Q: Are there big differences between musicals and straight dramas?

A: A straight drama is much less expensive to produce, but in a way it's also harder to figure out whether it will be a hit. The star is obviously important. So is the subject matter. You may be dealing with something that people regard as provocative or mind probing or intellectually stimulating. Those are marvelous terms but they're not necessarily audience grabbers. There has to be more to a play than the fact that it's intellectually stimulating. There has to be something in the subject matter that touches the common denominator of public opinion. Maybe a mystery like *Sleuth* or *Wait Until Dark* or *Death Trap.* Or a drama like *Equus.* That was the ideal case where you had subject matter that was intellectually stimulating and controversial, plus good performances, very imaginative staging, and even a little touch of nudity, coupled with the writing of a master and sets and staging that enhanced the production and added an extra dimension.

Q: What about a comedy?

A: Comedies are even more difficult because humor is a more subjective kind of writing. Something that is funny to one person is not funny necessarily to the next one. If you get somebody like Neil Simon, who is generally able to touch everyone's funny bone, you have a certain kind of success. There are other plays like *Luv,* which is exceedingly funny for a particular kind of humor. There's black comedy. There's slapstick. Then there's something like *Same Time Next Year,* which is very successful not only because it attracts the audience but also because its running costs are very low. Two people, one set. That doesn't mean, however, that every one-set, two-character show has more chance of success than other comedies. It's exceedingly difficult to write something for two characters and have their dialogue sustain an evening.

Q: Many Wall Street people seem to invest in the theater. Is there any particular reason?

A: It could be that Wall Streeters are known to more producers than non-Wall Streeters. A lot of producers are socialites who move in areas where parties are given in New York, Long Island, or other places where they run into people who have money. People in the theater or in the arts have entree to wealthy surroundings merely by virtue of their calling, whereas others who have different callings may not be as welcome.

In any case, I don't think that Wall Street people apply the same kind of investment evaluation to shows that they do to buying shares of stock. You can be very sophisticated in your own business, but if John Jones calls you on the telephone and says, "Hey, I have a hot tip, a stock that's going to double in two weeks," you'll call your broker and say, "Buy me a thousand shares," without even looking at it or evaluating it because John Jones called you, and John Jones was told by his good friend Henry Smith that this stock is hot, so you throw ordinary caution to the winds. That's the way many Wall Streeters approach investing in the theater.

Q: What are the actual mechanics of raising money for a show? Do you have underwriters?

A: Not usually. The issuer is generally the offerer. That does not mean that people don't act as underwriters, even though they shouldn't. John Jones is the producer, and has a friend Henry Smith, and Henry Smith knows a lot of people who are loaded. Henry says, "Look, John, I will go to my friends and I'll raise $200,000 for you, and in return you give me 5 percent of your 50 percent of the profits." John will say, "I'll give you 3 percent," and they'll strike a deal. Henry should not be offering, because he is not listed in the offering papers, but it's done.

Q: Let's assume there are no Henrys or rich friends. How does John find prospective investors once his offering is effective?

A: A great many people keep extensive card catalogues. Everybody who invests in limited partnership agreements is required to advertise in *The Law Journal* and other papers, and a lot of people clip the papers. They then make up lists of names, get other lists, and send out letters. The letter really is like a tombstone ad and says, if you are interested in investing in such-and-such a show, write for a copy of the offering papers. On a Wall Street offering, there is money in the budget to pay for the printing of a hundred thousand copies of the prospectus. In the theater, there is not that kind of money.

Q: Haven't I occasionally seen tombstone ads for shows in *The Wall Street Journal?*

A: That's a device some people are using, and I understand it brought a couple of hundred thousand dollars into *Sweeney Todd.* Another thing most people do is hold auditions or readings. You invite your friends and acquaintances and people who go to opening nights who you know have an interest in theater. If you've got the money, you may serve a little wine and hold the audition in a room at the St. Regis. You may get professionals to do the audition instead of the authors. Authors generally are not good singers or effective presenters, and you have to make sure your audition is carefully staged. You can't keep people there for two and one-half hours for a verbatim reading. So usually you capsulize the narrative and play a representative number of songs and try to convey in an hour what the musical is about. Straight plays generally do not have readings. The script is sent to prospective backers. But as I said earlier, in most instances, investors don't read the script or the prospectus, nor go to auditions. They rely on what John Jones, who's got his good friend Henry Smith, tells them.

Q: If financing is largely word of mouth, how does the guy who lives in Sheboygan, who might have an interest in investing in the theater, ever hear about it?

A: Sheboygan has different Blue Sky Laws than New York, so usually we wouldn't register the offering in Sheboygan. Unless, of course, I grew up in Sheboygan and have friends there. Then I might qualify the offering in Sheboygan. Somebody who wants to invest in the theater has to come to the offerer. That's why ads in *The Wall Street Journal* are effective. They alert the public to the idea that the theater is not a closed community for investment money.

The tax consideration

Q: If a show flops, is the tax situation the same as it is for a dry hole in the oil industry?

A: Yes. It's an ordinary business loss. But there are not that many people out there who are going to invest more than a token amount in the theater unless you know them or they have a personal involvement with the production or some special reason for investing. When you start getting investments in the $50,000 range or more, those people generally have some particular involvement. They may be the author's publisher or the brother or the uncle of the producer. They may be somebody who has merchandising rights or another interest in the show. They may be somebody from the oil business who is taking a flyer in order to have the glamor of being a dilettante in show business. But you don't usually get somebody to put $50,000 into a show simply because he or she thinks it's a good investment.

Q: How do things like ticket prices and theater size figure into the financial picture?

A: Many Broadway theaters are not capable of being used except for certain tailor-made shows, and certain houses are not capable of showing the larger musicals because they don't have enough seats. So investors must look at the operating costs of each show. They must ask themselves what's the likelihood, based on the scale of ticket prices, that the show will recoup in a certain period of time. Most shows rarely sell out, so you've got to try to figure out if the show can make it at a reasonable percentage of capacity.

Q: What's reasonable?

A: You would like to be able to break even at 60 percent, but that's a factor of ticket prices. If the ticket prices are not high, then you need 80 percent of capacity to break even. And you've got to remember that a Broadway show will run down even if it's a hit. It is never going to stay at 100 percent of capacity. It's not like a ten-week out-of-town engagement where you sell out for ten weeks, or when you bring in the opera or the ballet and you sell out for each performance. With a Broadway show you are dealing with open-ended bookings, so you really should try to see that the show is priced right. Obviously, the scale has to be realistic. You are not going to charge $50 a ticket and be able to make do with 35 percent of capacity.

The size of the theater must be related to the economics of the show, but in New York the size of the theater is a direct artistic judgment. I do not like to put shows in theaters where they won't have the proper quality of intimacy. When you go out of town with only one or two theaters in the town, you have no choice. Strangely enough, the out-of-town public doesn't know any better. But in New York, you would not put *The Elephant Man* in the Majestic Theater with 1,650 seats. By the same token, you would not put *Sweeney Todd,* with the production it has, in the 800-seat Booth Theater, even though the stage might accommodate it.

Each theater is not tailor-made for a particular show, and each show isn't tailor-made for a particular theater, but a show is certainly tailor-made for a certain kind of theater. *Annie* could be in a larger theater. It would make money in a larger theater. But then you get the argument, well, if it plays in a smaller theater, will the same number of people see it over a longer period of time?

In any event, you certainly don't want to play in a theater that's not going to provide a reasonable margin of profit. It's a combination of the artistic judgment versus the financial realities, and sometimes, if you don't have the right-size theater, you have to increase the price of the tickets. You are dealing with prevailing scales for both musicals and dramas, and those scales are not so rigid that every show in New York charges the same price.

It's a very risky business, both running the theater and producing the show. When you're gambling, you don't go to a crap table where the odds are against you. You look to get to a hot table and get on a run. By the same token, if you are investing in a Broadway show, you want to see that it is done as economically as possible so far as the production is concerned; that its running costs, both for salaries and royalties, are reasonable. And if they are high, that the price scale of the tickets and the theater in which the show is being presented will be adequate to enable you to return your capital in the shortest possible time.

Q: How do you feel about the future of Broadway?

A: Right now it feels good. With the ways we are now merchandising and selling theater, we are capturing a larger audience. During the 1974–75 season, approximately 6.6 million people saw Broadway shows. In the 1978–79 season, attendance came to roughly 9.8 million, and ticket sales during that span rose from $57.4 million to $136.6 million. Shows also are running longer, and as a consequence we are reducing the need for new product in quantity.

But you must have new product in quality, not only to sustain the theater but also to bring in people on a continuing basis. New shows and new ways of doing things are being developed. In the future, I have a feeling that straight plays and comedies will not be tried out in conventional ways any longer—in Philadelphia, Boston, and Washington—except in a few instances. Instead, the regional theater and off-Broadway will become the places where shows are tried out and refined before they are moved to the larger showplace of Broadway.

That will be good. It will eliminate a good deal of the risk, so that people will be investing in shows that they have had an opportunity to see and that will have had an opportunity to go through a period of refinement. I think that large musicals will go through a workshop situation and that they will probably try out in only one out-of-town stop. You can't try out in more than one city today because it's getting too expensive. I think the theaters outside of New York will, for the most part, be presenting material that has achieved prior success on Broadway.

There is also a vast network of theaters in America in which new plays are being done, of course, which means there's a tremendous system where new material can originate and find its way to Broadway. I see nothing wrong with that. Obviously, I would like Broadway to be the place where these things originate, but that's a chauvinist attitude on my part. The big musicals will necessarily continue to originate in first-class theaters because they're the only ones that have the equipment and know how to handle them. The big musicals will continue to have their origins in New York.

I also feel that we have come to the point where the public perceives the theater, not only in New York but elsewhere, as both a great economic resource and a cultural resource. The public is willing to support theater because of its economic contribution to the community, as an urban renewer, as a provider of jobs for low-income and minority people, and as a cultural resource. At the same time, the theater is growing up in a marketing sense. In a short period of time, a new computer that's already in operation in thirteen of our theaters will be in all Shubert theaters so that all ticket sales will be processed by computer. The use of credit cards and other devices for marketing and selling tickets have attracted a larger audience and resulted in a heightened awareness of the theater and the desire of people who have seen live theater to see more of it.

Q: What are the implications of the fact that record companies and entertainment complexes are investing in Broadway shows?

A: Companies in the entertainment business are looking more and more to Broadway as a source of software. This is not a new phenomenon because record companies in the past have invested in shows to get original-cast album rights, and motion picture companies have invested in shows to get motion picture rights. But I think we will be going into a period where more and more people will be investing in shows to acquire these rights. Broadway is a relatively inexpensive testing ground for material.

By the same token, however, we are in the business of presenting material for the stage. We are not presenting material with an eye to it becoming material for records or, say, cable TV. That to me is a prostitution of the art form and I don't believe that it is going to take place. Nobody with integrity in our business will go down that route. But that does not mean that we will be unaware of the value of these rights. We will seek to exploit them at the proper time and in the right way. Thanks to the coming of the video cassette and the disc, we will be able to preserve performances of plays that otherwise would be lost for the ages. Imagine how it would be now if we had had the means of seeing the great plays of the past.

As technology improves, I think there will be increasing demand for these rights and an increased desire on the part of corporate investors to participate in Broadway. Paramount, Twentieth Century Fox, Motown, and Columbia Pictures have already invested in Broadway. So have ABC and CBS, and I don't think they conditioned their investment upon the acquisition of subsidiary rights. I think there will be an increasing number of institutions investing, which is healthy for the business. The ability to attract creative talent will also be enhanced. A large number of creative people are returning to the theater. As a result of this and our marketing effort, more and more people are going to the theater, which is finally being regarded not as an elitist form of entertainment but as a popular form of entertainment.

Drink for Free

Frank J. Prial

Alfred Knopf, one of the grand old men of the publishing business, loves to show guests a hand-written book he keeps in his wine cellar. Flipping back through the decades, he will stop at a page and read off the name of a past dinner guest, usually a famous film star or a prominent novelist of the time.

"What," he will exclaim in mock surprise, "I served that idiot a 1934 Musigny? And to think it cost me three dollars a bottle." Mr. Knopf, who will probably serve wines almost as famous at that night's dinner, is having a little joke. He knows that a more recent Musigny will cost $40 to buy and will never be as good as that 1934.

Mr. Knopf is a serious collector of wines. You might also call him an investor, but there is a fine distinction. An investor in wines buys low and sells high; a collector buys low and drinks when the wine is ready. If it has become something rare and expensive, so be it, but the investment was in pleasure, and the return—well, it can't be shown on a balance sheet.

Cyril Ray, a well-known British wine writer and connoisseur, talked about his cellar. "I still have some memorable old Bordeaux," he said, "wines from the 1940s and 1950s, but they are far too valuable to drink. In fact some of them are going to buy me a new bathroom."

Mr. Ray sold a few of his old wines at auction and used the profits to pay for improvements to his London apartment. What he did was standard practice among knowledgeable wine enthusiasts in England. They buy good wines, planning to drink half and sell the other half when the price goes up. "It means that six bottles in each case that we do drink, we drink for free," Mr. Ray said.

As more and more Americans become familiar with wine, the idea of investing in it becomes more and more attractive. Even if it is never sold, people like to talk about their cellars. And, of course, everyone has heard someone say: "I could have bought this in 1965 at $3 a bottle and now, if you can find it, it goes for $150 or more."

It's no lie. Good wines have appreciated enormously in the years since World War II, particularly since the early 1960s. The 1945 vintage of Chateau Lafite-Rothschild sold in New York for between $2.00 and $2.50 at retail in 1948 when it was first released. A bottle is now worth anywhere from $350 to $450. Sherry-Lehmann, a prominent New York City retailer, purchased 800 cases of the 1959 Lafite-Rothschild at $29 a case. Almost all was sold in 1962 at $44 a case. At the time, it seemed like a reasonable return. Today a case of the 1959 Lafite is worth around $2,000.

Even a vintage such as 1975 has appreciated dramatically. Famous first-growth Bordeaux (a first-grown is one of the five chateaux graded tops in the wine trade) such as Chateau Haut-Brion and Chateau Latour were offered for around $160 to $185 a case when they first came on the market, which was about six months before they arrived in this country—this is called buying futures. Both now sell in the neighborhood of $550 a case, and the 1975 Chateau Lafite and Chateau Mouton-Rothschild are even higher.

The 1978 vintage in Bordeaux, hailed by many experts as a very great one, was offered at staggering prices even before the wine was bottled in the spring of 1980. Chateaux Haut-Brion, Mouton-Rothschild, and Lafite-Rothschild opened at $495 a case. Chateau Margaux was $475, and Chateau Petrus, the great Pomerol with very limited production, opened at $575 a case. That is almost $50 a bottle.

Abdallah Simon, president of Chateau and Estates Wine Co., a division of Joseph Seagram & Son, likes to recall the opening prices of the now legendary 1961 vintage:

"We were very nervous when we saw what the chateaux were asking," he said. "We realized we'd have to offer Lafite at around $10 a bottle to the public, and we seriously asked ourselves if Americans were ready to pay that kind of money for first-growth Bordeaux wines."

It would seem, then, that wine has been an excellent investment in recent years. Well, yes and no. Wine—and for that matter, vineyards, and wineries—can be deeply rewarding investments but, alas, not always in terms of money.

In 1972, Sherry-Lehmann in New York offered the 1970 Mouton-Rothschild (1970 was an excellent year) at $38.95 a bottle. The 1970 Lafite was $40.95—not all that different from prices for the 1978s, particularly when you factor in inflation. The Sherry-Lehmann catalog for 1972 said: "We have watched the 1961 and 1959 Lafite climb beyond $1,400 a case. Will this happen to the 1970s?"

The answer came soon enough. Three years later, Sherry-Lehmann was quoting the 1970 Mouton at $22.95 and the Lafite at $24.95, and they were much lower elsewhere. Only a very self-assured investor would have ridden out the wine slump of the mid-1970s and waited for prices to go up again.

In fact, most of the people who bought in the late 1960s and early 1970s were first-time buyers unfamiliar with the long-term swings of the wine market, and a lot of wine was dumped on the market at distress prices. Big London auctions of the time were rumored to have been packed with representatives of the chateaux in Bordeaux desperately trying to bid up their own prices.

The prospective investor should bear in mind that wine in the United States is not, if you will pardon the pun, a particularly liquid commodity. Thanks to holdover legislation from the repressive Prohibition days, it is illegal for a private citizen to sell wine in any state except Illinois.

Some years ago, an advertisement, offering "an extensive collection of old wines," appeared in a newspaper in one of the New Jersey suburbs of New York City. As the facts came out later, an official of the New Jersey Alcoholic Beverage Control Board, alerted to the ad, called the advertiser and told him such a sale was illegal.

When the ad continued to appear, state officials called on the would-be seller and pretended to be customers. When an offer was made, they revealed themselves and confiscated all the wines. The would-be seller was arrested, charged with violation of state liquor laws, convicted, and fined. He lost his wine and a lot of money, too. (A strange sidelight to that story: during the period before the trial, it was discovered that some of the confiscated wine had disappeared from the state warehouse. Several state employees were found to have stolen some of the better bottles and were dismissed).

The point is that selling wine is restricted to people with retail licenses. It is done extra-legally, of course, but the idea is not to get caught. Wine enthusiasts make deals among themselves and, occasionally, a knowledgeable retailer will buy up a cellar or make an advantageous exchange.

This is illegal because a retailer is not supposed to buy from anyone but a licensed distributor.

The most active market in wines outside of regular marketing channels is in England, more specifically London, where those old bottles provided Cyril Ray with a bathroom.

The big auction houses such as Christie's and Sotheby Parke Bernet conduct wine sales almost weekly, and a savvy buyer can often find superb bargains. "Savvy" is the operative word here because there can also be some dogs. The label "1869 Lafite" may be very romantic but it is no guarantee of what is in the bottle. Not that anyone ever drinks much of the stuff. Often it is merely held for a year or two and sold at another auction, like 100 shares of Xerox.

There is an old story in the trade that applies. It seems that a fellow buys 100 cases of sardines in Spain and sells them to an exporter. They are shipped to America where they are purchased by an importer who sells them to a jobber who sells them to a distributor who, temporarily pressed, sells them to another jobber and the whole process starts again.

At one point, one of the sellers opens a can. Appalled at what he finds, he telephones the original importer, who says to him: "What, you opened a can! Listen, sardines are for trading, not for eating."

So it is with many fine wines, particularly the very rare old bottles—magnums and jeroboams of nineteenth-century Bordeaux wines. Occasionally they are opened and drunk, and very often it is discovered that the wine has gone bad. Much better to keep it for a few years then sell it again. Experts in the wine trade claim that they recognize certain bottles every time they turn up at another auction.

"The auction catalogue will say, 'The last remaining double magnum of the 1870 Lafite,'" one wine specialist said, "but, sure enough, another one turns up the following year. It's the same handful of bottles being sold and resold."

The theory behind the London auctions is that there are still countless superb cellars in the stately homes of England and, sooner or later, death duties and other tax obligations ensure that they will turn up on the auctioneer's block. This is true, to some extent, but most of the wines sold at auction have come right out of commercial channels. They are inventory excess, wines that have not moved well or wines being sold by people who need cash first.

It is not at all uncommon for the wines offered at a London auction to be owned by someone in Los Angeles or Houston. They may well be wines that the owner has never seen and certainly had no intention of drinking. Most of the sophisticated wine merchants in England know that the purchaser of fine wines might not have any intention of drinking them. So they provide temperature-controlled warehouse space where the wines may be kept until the owner wants to put them up at another auction.

Like gold ingots in the Federal Reserve Bank, the wines may change ownership without moving. They may also be stored in bond, which means they have never legally arrived in Great Britain and can avoid many onerous import duties.

There's one auction that takes place in the United States annually, the Heublein Auction. It is held, amidst great fanfare, in a different city each year. To drum up interest there are preliminary tastings in other cities so that prospective buyers can get an idea of the treasures to be offered.

Good wines are to be found at the auction; also bottles that will be kept to appear at another auction a year or two hence; also a lot of wine that will go under the hammer at prices higher than the same wine brings in retail shops.

The Heublein Auction has introduced a lot of people to the excitement of wine trading; it probably has turned off just as many would-be enthusiasts by emphasizing the elitist side of wine drinking. It gives the impression that old bottles, high prices, and arcane wine language are important to the enjoyment of what is essentially a simple product—fermented grape juice.

Also, the Heublein Auction has no magic wand that enables it to avoid the realities of taxation. Any wine purchased at an auction in, say Denver, and destined for a cellar in St. Louis, must pass through the hands of a Missouri retailer, who is entitled by law to a cut.

Late in 1980, Christie's announced that it had received permission from the New York State Liquor Authority to hold one and possibly more auctions in New York City. Only wines "not available through normal channels" and at least 15 years old were to be offered.

You must have noticed by now that only Bordeaux wines have figured in this discussion. This is not by accident. Of all the millions of gallons of wine produced in the world each year, only a handful have even a prayer of lasting long enough to gain in value—some of the better Bordeaux, a few, very few, Burgundies, a few California reds, some great Sauternes (sweet white wines of Bordeaux), and couple of rare German Rieslings.

Most wines are meant to be consumed as soon as they are made, or shortly thereafter. An honest producer of Beaujolais will tell you that his or her wine probably should never be bottled at all, but simply drunk from the cask. Most bottled wines are good for a year or two, if properly cared for. After that, they are not even good as vinegar.

Champagne, contrary to the general conception, is not helped by aging. It is aged by the producers and is ready to drink when they release it.

Anyone who is keeping champagne to see it increase in value, or just to save for a daughter's wedding, is wasting money. There are old champagnes but they are usually kept in the cellars of the producers and not given their final treatment until a few months before they are released.

Fine Burgundies occasionally last 20 years but rarely beyond that. Most are finished after 10 or 12. California Cabernets, often billed as wines for the ages, may turn out to be somewhat overrated. Californians have a wonderful statement about their wines: they are good for drinking right now and they will last forever. Californians are forgiven their inconsistencies, of course, but that doesn't mean the wines are going to last.

Quite a few California Cabernets, billed as long-lasting when they were bottled a decade ago, fell apart after seven or eight years. Laying down these wines with an eye to appreciation could be risky.

Well-made Bordeaux red wines will last for very long periods of time—maybe. If they are stored properly, which means in a constant temperature cellar, in the dark, with no vibration and proper moisture control, they may go on forever. Even then, it is a question of vintages.

Take this past decade. The 1970s were magnificent. Will they last? Perhaps. The 1971s were good, too. Will they last? Some say longer than the 1970s, some say not. The 1972s, the 1973s, and the 1974s are not expected to last. The 1975s will last for years; the 1976s and the 1977s will not. The 1978s and 1979s probably will. But no one can be sure. A lot of highly heralded vintages have collapsed long before their predicted time.

And, even with great years, quality will vary from bottle to bottle. Even at the great chateaux of the Medoc, it is often necessary to open two or three bottles of an ancient vintage to find a good one. If you don't own a chateau, you will have to invest in a cellar or pay storage charges which, for wine, can be quite high.

Most wine lovers who invest in good bottles do so without any thought of ever selling. They take pleasure just from knowing that their wines are getting better-tasting all the time and that one day they will open them and enjoy them regardless of what their monetary value may then be.

Prices of fine French wines—and good California wines, too—may go higher at any time or they may collapse. In fact, they probably will do both. But whatever the prices, the wines will probably continue to improve. To a true wine lover, that is what is really important.

But suppose you want to go beyond the bottle, so to speak, right to the source. Vineyards are even riskier investments than the wines they produce. This is true in spite of the fact that wine consumption continues to increase every year in this country and that there are regular shortages of good grapes.

During the 1960s, when the wine boom was beginning to gather mo-

mentum, thousands of people invested in vineyards, both for long-term
income and for tax shelters. The failure rate of those investments, particularly during the wine slump of the mid-1970s, was very high.

Bedazzled by the dramatic upward curve of wine consumption, investors failed to realize that most of that increase was in very cheap wine,
much of it made from cheap grapes. The vineyards in which they had invested were in shy-bearing, expensive vines, subject to disease and frost
and slow to come into economical production.

Also, they invested in red-grape vineyards, mostly, at a time when the
great switch to white wine was just getting under way. By the time their
new vineyards were ready to produce, there was simply no market for the
fruit.

Louis Gomberg is probably the dean of America's wine consultants.
He also has owned a vineyard or two of his own over the years, so he
knows the subject professionally and personally. "I get calls every day
from banks and financial consultants asking about vineyard investments," he says. "I tell them what I tell clients who come here to San
Francisco to see me: do you really know what you're doing and thinking?
Because, like any agricultural investment, wine and vineyards can be an
invitation to economic disaster. Indeed, they have been disastrous for
many."

Mr. Gomberg's advice to anyone interested in investing in vineyards
is, first, to get to know the wine business—to understand the relationship
between grape growers and wineries. In good years, there is a market for
grapes; in poor years, the market can wither like a vine in the Central
Valley sun. When there are plenty of grapes, prices go down, often to the
point where there is no profit for the grape grower. There have been years
recently when growers shrugged and turned their back on handsome
crops, leaving them to rot on the vine, simply because they knew there
was no market for the fruit.

"Establish a relationship with a winery," Mr. Gomberg says, "even to
the extent of investing in a winery along with the vineyards. You've got to
have a home for your grapes. Without that insurance, your chances of
survival solely as a vineyard owner are much less than fifty–fifty."

And often it is the type of arrangement that counts. Gomberg continued, "A new vineyard investor will say to me, 'Oh, we've taken care of
that. We already have a ten-year contract with United Vintners or Fran-
ciscan or Gallo.' Then I ask if he or she realizes that five years from now
the cost of grape production might be 50 percent higher than the current
cost of grapes. Usually, the investor hasn't thought of that."

There is also the question of management. If you are not going to live
on your property, you will have to hire a management company. Mr.

Gomberg points out that management fees are just the same in bad years as in good years—and they add considerably to your costs in any year.

On the other hand, Mr. Gomberg believes that most of the small wineries that have been popping up all over California like mushrooms after a summer rain will probably make it. "That's because they are mostly mom-and-pop operations," he says. "They usually have backers and the up-front investment can be considerable for young people. But their biggest investment is their time and dedication and that makes the difference."

Not a large number, but a few Americans have invested in the wine business abroad. Some, like Thomas Heater in Bordeaux, actually own a wine property and work it. Mr. Heater is the owner of Chateau Nairac in Sauterne, the capital of sweet white wines in France. Others, like businessman Charles Wohlstetter, put together groups and buy major properties. Mr. Wohlstetter's group purchased Chateau Bouscaut in Bordeaux, a big, handsome property in the Graves region. They recently sold it to the Lurton family, old-line Bordeaux wine growers and shippers.

In the 1960s, Alexis Lichine put together a group of wealthy New Yorkers and bought Chateau Lascombes in Margaux. It was sold in the early 1970s to a British group. Mr. Lichine himself is the owner of Chateau Prieure-Lichine, like Lascombes in the commune of Margaux.

The most famous American-owned Chateau in Bordeaux is first-growth Chateau Haut-Brion, also in the Graves, which is owned by former U.S. Ambassador to France Douglas Dillon. It was purchased in 1935 by his father, financier Clarence Dillon. There are vineyards in Burgundy and the Rhone Valley fully or partially owned by Americans, and a number of estates in the Chianti region of Italy, south of Florence.

Needless to say, the legal and economic problems of investing abroad are enormous. The profits, if any, are illusory and the thrill of ownership usually fades away after a year or two unless the shareholders and passionately interested in wine—and they usually are not.

Nowadays there is no need to limit one's horizons to California. Recent changes in wine laws in many states have permitted the construction of small wineries without heavy tax burdens. At present, there are working commercial wineries or wineries under construction in New York, Connecticut, Rhode Island, Massachusetts, Virginia, and the Carolinas.

Most of them depend on the special French-American hybrid grapes because of the harsh eastern climates. Several have become quite successful, particularly in New York's Hudson Valley. What the long-term prospects for Eastern wineries may be is still unknown. But Eastern investors who prefer to be near their money might prefer one of these operations. They make excellent wines, by the way.

In any case, Mr. Gomberg returns to the small California winery as the best investment these days for anyone interested in the production side of the wine business. The thing to look for, he says, is the so-called boutique winery that wants to produce around 15,000 to 20,000 cases of wine a year. "There is a strange and quixotic dichotomy in the business," he says. "The giant wineries are booming, but so are the tiny ones. It's the mid-size operations with big overheads and marketing problems that are in trouble."

Indeed, there seems to be no end to the number of small wineries the market can absorb. As they open, their production is snapped up, first by eager California wine enthusiasts, always looking for a new place, and then by out-of-staters, jealous of the Californians' access to so much good wine. Many of the smaller wineries in the North Coast Counties—and now some of the new ones in the new regions north of Santa Barbara—have put all their customers on allocation. Some, in recent years have limited sales to mail order and to buyers who actually show up at the winery.

Eventually, there will be a shaking out in the boutique winery business, too, but that seems rather far off right now. "If you are willing to work 16 to 18 hours a day and have a good outside income," Louis Gomberg says, "your chances of survival with a small winery are extraordinarily good. Of the 176 boutique wineries that opened in California between 1970 and 1978, only one has failed. But you have to be able to live off a pension or dividends during the start-up years."

It follows that outside investors who can find a small winery interested in partners, usually limited partners, stand a better chance of one day seeing a return on their money. And, if it does not pan out, at least there will be some good wine to drink.

If all of this has not deterred you, and you still insist on getting into wine, there are a few things to keep in mind. Local retailers may be your friends, but they have problems, too. For example, if one claims to have some fantastic Bordeaux in off-years, watch out. If another has a wonderful price on Beaujolais Nouveau and it's now August, watch out. And if one has some unbelievable red Burgundy that is actually declassified Nuits-St. Georges, pull your hat down around your ears and march out. They are trying to move inventory. The off-year Bordeaux could be 1969, 1972, or even 1977; the first two were not much to begin with and are definitely over the hill now, and the third was a mediocre year with not much future that's being offered at rather outlandish prices.

The Beaujolais Nouveau, which is only partially fermented so as to get it to market within six or seven weeks of harvest, is good for six or seven months. By the following summer it is finished and should be passed up whatever the price. As for the declassified wine, it is in the same league as the so-called Brooks Brothers suit with the label removed. Sad to say, there is enough monkey business in Burgundy even when the labels are left on.

Declassified wine is created when there is overproduction in a prominent vineyard. French law allows a vintner to make just so much wine from any particular piece of ground. Anything over that must be classified as cheap table wine. This is to get the growers to stop pushing the vines to double the quantity. For the most part, it works. There really isn't much declassified wine around because it is not profitable to the growers to make it.

If you can afford them, buy and lay down 1976 and 1978 Burgundies; 1975, 1976, 1978, and 1979 Bordeaux, and California Cabernets of 1976, 1977, 1978, and 1979. If you are partial to sweet white wines, you might think of the 1975 and 1978 Sauternes and the 1975 and 1976 top-of-the-line Rhines and Moselles—but only the Beerenauslesen and Trockenbeerenauslesen, and if you want explanations of those jawbreakers, you are going to have go elsewhere.

With proper care, all of the above will last 20 years or more. The Bordeaux will keep improving all the while; the Burgundies will get better for 10 years at least. So will the Sauternes and the German wines. The Californians—well, no one knows yet. It is still a new world. But they will last 10 years, most of them, with little problem.

All this presupposes several things, most particularly a fat pocketbook and a good storage area which is dark and even-temperatured. About 55 degrees is best, but 50, 60, or even 65 would do provided there are no quick changes up and down. Elegant wine racks are impressive but hardly mandatory. So long as the bottles are on their sides, keeping the corks moist, many wine enthusiasts never open the cases.

One of the toughest parts of laying down wines is determining when they are ready to drink. In the good old days, one opened a bottle each year until it was evident that the wine had reached its peak. But now, at $20 a bottle or more, who can afford to sample? By the time the wine is ready, you may be down to the last of the 12 bottles you were able to afford.

The only thing to do is buy, lay it away, and hope that the geniuses in the computer industry come up with something like a brain scanner for wine in the next few years. They could work on worse things.

Not for the Faint of Heart

Alan Joel Patricof

You are standing at a cocktail party in Palo Alto, California, sipping your Perrier, when a small fellow with long hair and glasses, looking rather serious, sidles up to you and starts a pleasant conversation about a variety of things, one being the fact that he has heard that you like to invest in promising new ventures. Somewhere along the way, he mentions a new microprocessor that he has developed. The product, described as having a multiplicity of potential applications, was used, your new friend tells you, to control the lighting in the Broadway version of Hair. *Having seen the show and vaguely remembering that you liked the lights, you decide that this could be an interesting product, particularly when you then hear that the Playboy Club Discotheque and a newly renovated TV studio on New York City's West Side that is being turned into a discotheque to be known as Studio 54 will also be using this microprocessor. You become even more interested when he tells you that the real prospects for the company he has formed to produce his microprocessor are not in discotheque lighting but in the application of the technology to control energy use in high-rise office buildings. When you ask what discotheques have to do with energy savings, he proceeds to tell you about his M.I.T. degrees and the broad applications of microprocessor technology that are too confusing to follow. You offer him your card, never expecting to see him again. But when you arrive at your office at 9:00 a.m. Monday morning, the first call you receive is from your*

new friend who wants to drop by to show you his business plan. In spite of the fact that his company has only three employees, is behind on its payroll taxes, and its books are a mess, a $75,000 investment in the business would solve all his problems because it would trigger a $350,000 Small Business Administration guaranteed loan from a bank. For that investment, he is willing to give you one-third of the company. . . .

You are running counterclockwise around the reservoir in Central Park in New York City when an old acquaintance, running in the opposite direction, sees you and reverses field to run alongside. After a few minutes of chitchat, he tells you, between breaths, that he had heard you are looking for investments in interesting companies and it just so happens that there is a little piece left of a new cookie company which has been started by a literary agent whose wife developed a formula for making shortbread and whose brother-in-law had been the marketing vice-president of Sara Lee, or was it Stouffer's. In any event, they produced 5,000 pounds of cookies at Christmas, which were packaged and sold through Macy's, Bloomingdale's, and a few other outlets at $10 a pound. The product has been favorably marketed in the Best Bets section of New York Magazine, and at least six other department stores have indicated an interest in selling it in their gourmet food departments. Your old acquaintance is buying two shares in the deal which is all sold except for the last unit. . . .

Most of us are intrigued by a new idea and, from time to time, are offered the opportunity to make an investment in a friend's, or a friend of a friend's, or a neighbor's new company or plan to buy out an existing company. While one should not resist the temptation entirely, it is important to recognize that this type of investment is usually very risky, highly illiquid, and should never be undertaken without a great deal of prior investigation and analysis. Once the investment has been made, you are, to one degree or another, a partner in the business. Moreover, even when sufficiently satisfied as to the validity of the project, one should restrict this type of investment to a limited portion of available funds. While it is fun to take a fling every now and then, it is also important to realize that venture capitalism is a demanding business that is best left to the professionals.

History

As an industry, venture capital took shape shortly after World War II, spearheaded to a large degree by General George Doriot and his American Research and Development Co. AR&D was fortunate to have made an early commitment in Digital Equipment Corporation, commonly known as DEC, thereby parlaying $200,000 or so into several hundred million dollars (no discotheques for them!). While that story is hard to top, the list of successful venture capital investments that have returned 50 to 100 times on the original investment grows each year.

Most such stories are focused in the electronics industry and involve names like Cray Research, Storage Technology, Qume, Tandem Computer, Four Phase Systems, Rolm, and, most recently, Apple Computer, which has risen from a mere startup in late 1977 to what will be a $150 million business in 1980. According to Steve Job, the 26-year-old co-founder and chairman of Apple, who quit his job at Atari, sold his Volkswagen, and joined forces with a friend who had just traded in his HP-55 calculator and left Hewlett-Packard, it was merely a question of "painting the bulls-eye correctly on a defined target of opportunity."

Perhaps an even greater venture capital success story is Federal Express, which was started in 1974. It has since totally revolutionized the concept of small-package delivery systems within the United States. Its fleet of red, white, and purple aircraft, which fly nightly across the country out of Memphis, Tennessee, will produce revenues of over $500 million in 1981 and make more than $40 million after taxes. This company, too, was started by a young man in his late 20s. In this case, it took a substantial amount of his family's capital, together with outside investors, four rounds of financing at decreasing prices, several public offerings, and lots of senior bank financing to reach the current level of profit.

While American Research and Development is considered the first bona fide company to engage in venture capital, the business was conducted in the 1950s and 1960s on a professional basis by recognized family names, mostly from the East Coast. The roster included William Burden, J. H. Whitney, Venrock (the investment vehicle for the Rockefeller family), Bessemer Securities (the vehicle for the Phipps family), Payson & Trask, and many leading investment banking firms that devoted a certain portion of their partnership capital to imaginative risk-oriented investments outside of their general stock market activities. Such names as Armand Erpf of Loeb, Rhodes and the Loeb family; Jacob Klingenstein of Wertheim & Co.; Lazard Freres; and Lehman Brothers all participated in one way or another in investments which could be characterized as venture capital in that they involved significant equity positions in young or restructured companies.

But it was not until the booming new-issue market in over-the-counter stocks in the late 1960s, which resulted in overnight fortunes being made by original investors in early stage companies, that the industry as such actually began to take shape. For the first time, pension funds, insurance companies, and hundreds of wealthy individuals fostered the creation of investment partnerships focused entirely on venture capital. These partnerships have today become the essential means of participation by individuals and institutions into small and, for the most part, private companies that have the ultimate objective of obtaining, over a minimum ten-year period, gains substantially in excess of what the stock market and most forms of investment can be expected to produce. Warburg Pincus & Co., New Court Securities, Brentwood Associates, Sutter Hill, Heizer Group, Kleiner Perkins, and more than 200 other partnerships have sprung up in the past ten years, located from West to East coasts, developing geographical and area specializations. While single participations in these partnerships range from as little as $100,000 to as much as $10 million, and while the pools themselves range in overall size from $3 million to $100 million, a typical partnership will have no more than 14 participants with positions ranging from $500,000 to $3 million.

The venture industry today is generally described as having $3-4 billion in capital. While individuals still account for a portion of these funds, institutional investors are the predominant factor. Because of the capital available in these groups, the size of an average investment position tends to range from $250,000 to $5 million. In other words, this is not the group that is financing your average neighborhood business.

In most investors' minds, venture capital will always refer to high technology, high-risk startups. (In addition to the names already mentioned, venture capitalists have had a major hand in the development of Evans & Sutherland, Coherent Radiation, Data General, Thermo Electron, Floating Point Systems, Measurex, Prime Computer, and a host of others.) Many of these companies took shape during the exuberant days of the late 1960s and early 1970s when a great entrepreneurial surge throughout the country resulted in the formation of companies with names that began or ended in *electronics, data, computer, onics*, or *technology*. Entrepreneurism was at its height in those days, and the tax structure was such that capital gains were taxed at 25 percent, stock options for management—as well as outright issuance of founder's stock—made it very attractive to form a new company, and there was a vibrant public market that provided a profitable exit from these investments in a very short period of time.

This environment came to an abrupt halt in the mid-1970s as a result of a dramatic decline in the public's appetite for young companies, a reflection of the collapse that had taken place in the overall public securities market. This development, coupled with the enactment of a less-favorable tax code, created a period of hibernation, both on the part of entrepreneurs and venture capitalists, that resulted in a reshaping of the venture industry and the development of a longer-term perspective to the role of venture capital.

There also emerged a more sobering awareness of the need to balance and diversify a venture portfolio, carefully mixing startups with more mature investments and the development of techniques for eventual exit other than the public market. Venture capitalists also created the so-called leveraged buyout, a new area of investment that lately has absorbed large amounts of capital. This type of investment refers to the purchase of companies or subsidiaries of companies by managements who have financed a substantial portion of the purchase price through a layer of senior bank or insurance financing, supported by a layer of subordinated debt or preferred stock provided by venture investors, plus some financing from the selling company itself.

The venture industry today

Nevertheless, the inherent instinct of the venture capitalist is to seek out the next DEC, the next Intel, or the next Federal Express. Among the areas receiving the most attention today and creating some degree of excitement are such esoteric fields as gene splitting and recombinant DNA, which have resulted in the formation of companies with valuations that stagger the imagination and which have attracted substantial corporate and institutional venture funds. Other areas of current interest include the future applications of television as a two-way vehicle for the dissemination of information. In addition, two-way TV via cable, with shopping and banking from the home, as well as accessing data bases, are bound to be a major area of interest in the 1980s. New materials for space and water, as well as everyday living, fish farming, word processing and the office of the future, micro-electronics, fiber optics, new medical electronic devices (both implanted and external) for diagnosis as well as anything to do with computers or peripherals are some of the other areas that venture capitalists will be focusing on in the next decade.

In addition to the office of the future, there is much talk about the car of the future which, by 1985, will include a single micro-computer chip that will control and diagnose almost every aspect of the car's operation. But venture capital is not just high technology, and many in industry are financing new consumer products, basic industrial activities, and the restructuring of many fundamental existing enterprises.

In the past decade, most venture capitalists have achieved an impressive rate of return, ranging from 10 to 20 percent compounded annually and for shorter, more recent periods, as much as 30 percent. This is more than two to three times the gains racked up by such standard market indicators as the Dow Jones Industrials and the S & P index.

However, in a world where inflation is raging at a rate in excess of 15 percent per annum and interest rates for prime borrowers hover near 20 percent, venture investments will have to achieve even greater results to appear attractive in light of the perceived risk of illiquidity which is a meaningful barrier to overcome.

The unique aspect of venture capital is that it operates in an inefficient market where there are not an equal number of buyers and sellers. Since purchases are made privately and, to some degree, as a matter of chance based on a matching of interests and geographic location, valuations are often determined on a subjective basis. And since many of the companies are too young to determine scientifically a value at the outset, there is the opportunity for spectacular gain. A good example is Qume Corporation, which was founded in 1973 with slightly more than $1 million in equity capital. Qume is credited for broadly commercializing the "daisy wheel" printer, which has become the nucleus of most of the modern generation of typewriters and word processing machines. When ITT acquired the company in 1978 for over $17 million, investors received shares of ITT with an annual dividend of more than twice their original investment and realized 30 times their investment.

This is a perfect example of venture capital at its best. On the other hand, investors who financed the 1975 concept of splitting *Saturday Review Magazine* into four separate magazines lost $20 million before it was repurchased by its original owners and put back into its original configuration. Who could have objectively determined an appropriate valuation for investment purposes in 1973 for Qume. And for every Qume there are probably three or four complete failures and a few adequate performers where the return is good but not great. Nevertheless, the underlying elements of venture capital investing—namely, that when you lose, all you can lose is what you invested, and when you are successful, the reward can be unlimited—create a set of conditions such that, if you invest wisely and often enough and pay careful attention to details, over a period of time you should achieve impressive results.

Diversification

Venture investing, which typically involves young companies with new products and often untried management, has built-in features that create greater problems than investing in marketable companies that are more mature and where, when difficulties crop up, one can readily get out. The only way to hedge against venture disasters is to diversify as to the kind of portfolio companies, and to include among your investments startups, expansion financings, and turnarounds. For example, unless one were prepared to develop a high-risk profile, it would not be a good idea to invest in ten computer startups but rather to spread the risk over different industries and to limit the number of startups to no more than three or four.

While a large source of venture capital today comes from institutions, individuals have, to a certain extent, an extra benefit in that they can sometimes structure an investment in such a form as to obtain an immediate writeoff of early-stage losses through a limited partnership or a sub-chapter S Corporation. These structures reduce the down-side risk and, on the up-side, allow investors to obtain capital gains treatment, thereby improving the risk/reward ratio.

Regardless, for an individual to even consider participating in venture capital, it is desirable to be in the 50 percent or higher marginal tax bracket. Moreover, other than an occasional "fling," one should probably not consider venture investing unless one has sufficient capital to participate in a professionally managed pool or a willingness to assume the responsibility of preliminary analysis and subsequent supervision and to make enough individual investments to spread the risk. While anyone can make an isolated investment of modest size to assist a friend or acquaintance or to back an idea that sounds particularly romantic, whether it be in microprocessors or cookies, serious venture investment should only be done by those who can allocate a meaningful amount of funds to achieve adequate diversification. Even with sufficient capital available, this segment of a portfolio, because of its higher risk profile and its lack of reliable current income, should probably not represent more than 5 or 10 percent of one's investments.

One of the appealing elements of venture investments is the psychic income that one obtains. There is a much higher degree of identification with the investment than in the stock market, and the satisfaction obtained is much greater than just seeing a stock go up. How many times have you heard someone say, "I own 10 percent of that dress company or a piece of that magazine or a share of that new restaurant?" As a matter of fact, most of the individual type of investing occurs in products or projects that are close to home and that have some consumer aspect or some degree of visibility. One of the sure ways you know you are approaching the area with a greater professional objectivity is when you can make an investment in a situation that has no identification factor associated with it.

Case history

The following, a typical venture capital story, highlights some of the highs and lows that a venture capitalist will run into. In 1970, we were approached by an enterprising team of three Ph.D.'s who had developed advanced techniques for the design of computer communications networks under the auspices of the government. They perceived that the next decade would usher in an era of computers that would talk to each other as people had become accustomed to doing. This would require both corporations and government agencies to develop new communication networks for the more efficient routing of messages at the greatest speed and the least cost.

The company operated out of a leased mansion in Long Island, located on nine acres in a pastoral setting intended to re-create the atmosphere of a university; most of the 12 initial employees held advanced mathematical or physics degrees and had come from a college or think-tank environment.

The company was founded with $150,000 of outside capital for which the investors received 15 percent of the company. One Friday evening, about six months after our investment was closed, we received a phone call from the company's president indicating that the company had only enough funds to last out the month and that he was voluntarily turning over the reins to another of the founders, since he had failed as the marketing element of the team and was a drain on the survival of the business. It was readily apparent that all of the initial capital had been expended through the payment of salaries and day-to-day operating expenses. It was not that anyone had done anything wrong. It was just that the hoped-for contracts had not developed.

Rather than close down, which would have been a shattering event for both the principals and investors, it was decided to regroup, terminate six of the employees and place three others in part-time teaching positions in the area with the two remaining founders and an assistant deferring their salaries to await the award of a particular contract on which they had placed a great deal of emphasis and which was still a few months away. That summer in Long Island, three people sat in a 30-room mansion with three desks and a telephone. It must have been a strange sight to anyone who took the time to peer behind the solemn walls of ivy.

In October the company obtained the contract it had been waiting for, rehired their brethren who had been farmed out, and, like the Phoenix, rose from its ashes and grew over the next several years into a profitable enterprise. It looked as though there would be no need for additional capital. That is, until the recession of 1975, which resulted in government cutbacks and a severe drop in commercial business. At that point, the investors came up with an additional $150,000 in capital. The world was different in 1975, however, and a lot of the effervescence of valuation in 1970 had fizzled. As a result, despite the fact that the company was now an operating business with five years of history and 50 employees, this time the investors got 20 percent of the company for their $150,000, half of which was purchased by the employees.

The company pulled out of that downturn, tightened its belt, redirected its marketing efforts, and improved its pricing structure. Before long, business was booming again and space had become a problem. There was no choice but to move to a real office building with sufficient additional space for expansion. This created a temporary period of underutilized facilities and extra overhead which, as you might expect, coincided with another downturn in business. But this time, the company was agile and had diversified its business and improved its management skills sufficiently so that the downturn was hardly noticeable.

At this point in its history, the company is headed by seasoned businesspeople who have developed the necessary marketing, finance, and budgeting skills. It has an established reputation in its field and has become a leader in communications network design. It has almost 100 employees and a second office in Washington and is being noted and quoted throughout the trade press. To make things even better, it has received an offer from a major New York Stock Exchange company, which is anxious to acquire the firm at a significant multiple of the investor's cost.

The company truly has gone through all of the stages from venture capital startup, reformation, turnaround, and, finally, rapid growth. The founders have achieved a high degree of success in both a professional and business sense, and the venture investors, who have been good partners, will end up with a compound rate of return on their investment approaching 30 percent. It was not without some heartaches and some worrisome moments, but it also provided the kind of excitement and satisfaction that is possible with venture investments. At one time, we could have lost everything. At others, there was euphoric high. It did not produce a return of 50 times our investment but, on the other hand, it produced a return far in excess of what comparable market opportunities had been during the same period of time. It's a classic story—the kind that happens often enough to make venture capital a stimulating and profitable area in which to be involved.

It demonstrates, however, that the venture capital business is not for the faint of heart. And while we are all tempted as individuals to dabble in small-business investments from time to time, as an ongoing activity it is better left in the hands of professionals where risks can be minimized. The degree of attention required is such that full-time involvement is needed to improve the odds of success. Nevertheless, the next time someone calls you on the phone and asks for 30 minutes to tell you about a new concept he or she has developed for a computer, a book publishing venture, or a new type of furniture, listen. If it is a worthy idea, offer encour-agement—maybe even a little money. And if you take this entrepreneur out for lunch, don't forget to pick up the check. Who knows? It may be the next Apple Computer.

Dos and don'ts

If, in spite of all my admonitions, you decide that venture capital is for you—and that you can afford to take the risk and cannot afford not to ac-cept the challenge—here are a dozen rules that should be kept in mind.

1. Try to invest in companies, not products or ideas.
2. It is better to back a team of people who have had some prior experience together, preferably in the same area that they are going into with their new project.
3. Avoid projects designed to change the world. Educating a market that it needs a product takes twice as long and costs three times as much money as expected.
4. Avoid projects that have a high critical mass for success or require approval of industry associations or political bodies. These types of deals also take more time and money than you could ever anticipate. Example: selling a material-handling system to the airline industry requires that all of the airlines agree to one similar approach. They might, but it could be costly to count on it.
5. Always invest first and foremost in people, people, people. It is as significant as location, location, location is in real estate. Talented, capable management can always improvise and redirect their strategy as to markets and products. A product without good management cannot do likewise.
6. Always make sure that a business plan has sufficient provision for a margin of error. Remember Murphy's Law: Whatever can go wrong, will go wrong.
7. Take the trouble to check the entrepreneur's references.
8. Plan the financing so that a "second round" capability is available; chances are more money will be required than originally envisioned.
9. Try to structure the financing so that your capital is returned at the earliest possible date while retaining a residual equity interest. This improves your return on investment and reduces risk.
10. Structure the financing so that after the closing the entrepreneur has both positive and negative incentives to meet and, indeed, exceed projections.
11. Ask for a cogent business plan. Generally speaking, if one can't write it down, one can't execute it.
12. Before the financing, agree upon a procedure that will provide an on-going flow of reports between the entrepreneur and the investors.